CHILDREN AND THEIR EDUCATION IN SECURE ACCOMMODATION

This highly topical book integrates theory and practice about children and their education provision in secure accommodation. Bridging the fields of education, health, and youth justice, it provides a unique interdisciplinary perspective outlining the importance of taking a holistic approach to the education and rehabilitating of children who are 'locked up'.

The book has brought together contributors from across the UK and beyond to share their academic research, practical knowledge, and experiences working with children and young people. Shedding light on the intricacies and realities of working in the context of secure settings, the book is divided into the following five parts:

- Contextualising the field
- Practice insights
- Case examples and models of practice
- Inclusion and voice
- Recommendations from research

Children and Their Education in Secure Accommodation unravels the complexity of the topic and offers 'whole-system' perspectives, as well as a child-centred view, on the issue of educating and rehabilitating children and the needs and rights of children in such settings. With unique and valuable insights from those involved in policy or provision, this book will be an essential text for researchers, practitioners, and students in this interdisciplinary field.

Diahann Gallard is a Senior Lecturer and researcher in the Liverpool John Moores University School of Education and a Fellow of the Higher Education Academy. She is a Chartered Member of the British Psychological Society (BPS) and a committee member of the BPS Psychology of Education Section. Her current research interests are the innovative approaches to education in the secure setting context and compassionate-focussed practices.

Katharine Evans has over 20 years' experience of working with children and young people across a range of practice contexts, including youth and community work, alternative education, early intervention, and youth crime prevention. She has worked in academia as a Senior Lecturer in Education (Liverpool John Moores University) and as Director of Safeguarding Programmes (University of Chester). Katharine is a Board Member for the Domestic Abuse Safety Unit, North Wales and the National Association for Youth Justice.

James Millington is a HCPC registered Consultant Clinical and Forensic Psychologist and Lead Psychologist for Specialist CAMHS at Greater Manchester Mental Health NHS Foundation Trust. He is an Associate Fellow of the British Psychological Society (BPS) and the Child and Adolescent Representative on the BPS Division of Clinical Psychology, Faculty of Forensic Clinical Psychology Committee.

CHILDREN AND THEIR EDUCATION IN SECURE ACCOMMODATION

Interdisciplinary Perspectives of Education, Health and Youth Justice

Edited by Diahann Gallard, Katharine Evans and James Millington

Routledge
Taylor & Francis Group
LONDON AND NEW YORK

First published 2019
by Routledge
2 Park Square, Milton Park, Abingdon, Oxon OX14 4RN

and by Routledge
711 Third Avenue, New York, NY 10017

Routledge is an imprint of the Taylor & Francis Group, an informa business

© 2019 selection and editorial matter, Diahann Gallard, Katharine Evans and James Millington; individual chapters, the contributors

The right of Diahann Gallard, Katharine Evans and James Millington to be identified as the authors of the editorial material, and of the authors for their individual chapters, has been asserted in accordance with sections 77 and 78 of the Copyright, Designs and Patents Act 1988.

All rights reserved. No part of this book may be reprinted or reproduced or utilised in any form or by any electronic, mechanical, or other means, now known or hereafter invented, including photocopying and recording, or in any information storage or retrieval system, without permission in writing from the publishers.

Trademark notice: Product or corporate names may be trademarks or registered trademarks, and are used only for identification and explanation without intent to infringe.

British Library Cataloguing in Publication Data
A catalogue record for this book is available from the British Library

Library of Congress Cataloging in Publication Data
Names: Gallard, Diahann, editor. | Evans, Katharine, 1976 October 10- editor. | Millington, James, 1973- editor.
Title: Children and their education in secure accommodation : interdisciplinary perspectives of education, health and youth justice / edited by Diahann Gallard, Katharine Evans, and James Millington.
Description: Abingdon, Oxon ; New York, NY : Routledge, 2019. | Includes bibliographical references.
Identifiers: LCCN 2018019305 (print) | LCCN 2018035098 (ebook) | ISBN 9781315528212 (ebook) | ISBN 9781138694392 (hbk) | ISBN 9781138694408 (pbk) | ISBN 9781315528212 (ebk)
Subjects: LCSH: Juvenile delinquents--Education--England. | Juvenile delinquents--Education--Wales. | Juvenile delinquents--Rehabilitation--England. | Juvenile delinquents--Rehabilitation--Wales. | Reformatories--England. | Reformatories--Wales.
Classification: LCC HV9146.A5 (ebook) | LCC HV9146.A5 C55 2019 (print) | DDC 371.930942--dc23
LC record available at https://lccn.loc.gov/2018019305

ISBN: 978-1-138-69439-2 (hbk)
ISBN: 978-1-138-69440-8 (pbk)
ISBN: 978-1-315-52821-2 (ebk)

Typeset in Bembo
by Taylor & Francis Books

Printed in the United Kingdom
by Henry Ling Limited

CONTENTS

List of illustrations viii
Preface x
List of contributors xiii

PART I
Contextualising the field 1

1 Troubled and troublesome children: Education, participation, and restoration 3
  Ben Byrne

2 An historical perspective on education in secure accommodation in England and Wales from 1850 to the present 21
  Caroline Lanskey

PART II
Practice insights 43

3 Specialist education provision within secure CAMHS units 45
  Faiza Ahmed

4 Roles and relationships of care and education staff inside a secure children's home 61
  Caroline Andow

vi Contents

5 How psychological services and education link up in secure children's homes 75
Alex Smith and Sarah Mack

6 Children's lives, education, and secure care in Scotland 96
Alison Gough and Claire Lightowler

7 Education for U.S. youth in secure care: The sum of the parts is not whole 117
Deborah K. Reed

PART III
Case examples and models of practice 129

8 'Behind the headlines, inside the walls – teaching Britain's hidden children': Perspectives and practices within the secure children's homes network 131
Melanie Prince, Aileen Conlon, Marc Herbert, Phillippa Brooks and Sarah Douglas

9 A secure children's home in Wales: Care and educational provision from clinical, management, and educational perspectives 146
Richard Pates, Alison Davies and David Tiddy

10 Aligning with the chaos and navigating through the trauma 162
Deirdre McConnell, Kate Brown, Yanela Garcia and James Stephens

11 The nature-based residential treatment centre as an alternative model for meeting the needs of children and young people 178
Steven Klee, Joanna L. Becker and Miyako Kinoshita

PART IV
Inclusion and voice 191

12 Youth voice and participation in secure settings for young people 193
Caroline Lanskey

13 Children's views of education in a young offenders institution 205
Ross Little

14 Safeguarding children in the youth justice secure estate 219
Katharine Evans

15 Identifying barriers and facilitators for educational inclusion for young people who offend: Practitioner and youth perspectives 248
Jenny Twells

PART V
Recommendations from research **275**

16 Re-engaging young offenders with education in the secure custodial setting 277
Adeela ahmed Shafi

17 'The banter levels are good': Developing social and human capital through education 299
Anita Mehay and Nina Champion

18 'Where are we going?': Context and directions for policy and practice in children's education and learning in secure accommodation 314
Ross Little

Index *335*

ILLUSTRATIONS

Figures

2.1.	Custodial institutions for children in the criminal justice system (England and Wales 1850s – present)	23
7.1.	Potential secure care placements and movement among the settings for court-involved youth	118
10.1	Supervision and managerial model for the therapy	174
15.1	Barriers and facilitators: professional perspectives	250
15.2	Barriers and facilitators: young people's perspectives	251
15.3	Systemic factors: professional perspectives	252
15.4	Systemic factors: young people's perspectives	254
15.5	Parenting and care related factors: professional perspectives	255
15.6	Care and parenting related factors: young people's perspectives	259
15.7	School related factors: professional perspectives	260
15.8	School related factors: young people's perspectives	263
15.9	Individual factors: professional perspectives	266
15.10	Individual factors: young people's perspectives	268
16.1	Facilitators and barriers to re-engagement with education in a secure custodial setting	289
17.1	The three objectives.	300
17.2	Theory of change for prison education (Champion and Noble, 2016)	302
17.3	Human capital (Champion and Noble, 2016)	303
17.4	Social capital (Champion and Noble, 2016)	304

Tables

5.1	What does SECURE STAIRS stand for?	93
8.1	The ARC framework	142
9.1	Adverse childhood experience rates at Hillside compared to the Welsh population	149
9.2	Trauma history of children in SCHs compared to children on the Child Protection Register in Wales	149
10.1	An overview of the interventions provided in one year	175

PREFACE

This book is the outcome of a consultation with leading authors, researchers, and practitioners in the field of secure accommodation for children and young people. It is a compilation of chapters that provide a 'whole-system' overview of issues and practice relating to the education of children and young people who have lost their liberty due to acute welfare concerns, necessary secure mental health care, or as an outcome of offending behaviour. Sometimes an author writes specifically about custodial provision for young offenders, at other times the focus is welfare or care provision, sometimes it is both. We encourage you to read all chapters as they offer different lenses which will help extend your understanding of the issues from a range of perspectives, and allow consideration of the similarities, differences, tensions, and barriers that exist for interdisciplinary thinking and practice.

An important theme in this book is how the authors frame children and childhood. You will see that there is clear focus on the 'care' and 'protection' of the individual, as well as 'rehabilitation'. We hope that, through learning more about the underpinning and contextual factors of the lives and lived experiences of these children, there will be greater appreciation for how children in secure accommodation often have complex and diverse needs, vulnerabilities, and difficulties associated with troubled childhoods and deprivation, are troubled, are from unstable backgrounds; their behaviour is often a consequence of impoverished early life chances and disadvantage, which is why in this book there is a consistent promotion of the value of therapeutic approaches.

Modern approaches to work with this group of children are trauma informed and compassionate and not wholly about punishment and creating isolation from society. Readers new to the field might find this concept challenging, especially if their own lives have been touched in a negative way by incidents involving children who appear to be 'out of control' and engaged in problematic or troublesome behaviour. Progressive thinking in this area is focussed on how most children in secure settings have experienced trauma and find it difficult to form relationships or feel a connection and belonging to society; thus, the growth and maintenance of trust and compassion within these settings is vital to positive outcomes and educational achievement with children and young people. Also, how we understand their experiences, how they see themselves, others and their world, will shape how effective we are at keeping them safe.

What we know is that education for any young person is important and that these educational experiences must be child-centred. It is the vehicle for enabling meaningful change and improving lives. The book provides a view of education in its broadest sense; not just as instruction and schooling, but as including social and emotional pedagogies of working with this unique group of learners to enhance both thinking and feeling and to enable a sense of belonging and connection to others and society.

> There can be no keener revelation of a society's soul than the way in which it treats its children
>
> *(Nelson Mandela)*

The different chapters of this book give insight into the perspectives of practitioners, academic scholars, and, importantly, the young people who are, or have been, resident in secure accommodation. At the start of the process we knew we wanted to bring together experts from academia and the specialised workforce in the secure estate to look at multi-agency and interprofessional aspects of practice and provide a space for reflection and critical perspectives of education provision; a 'think tank' looking specifically at education in a multi-disciplinary way, and we have posed questions, such as; 'How do you define education in a secure settings?' and 'What does education look like in the context of your work?' However, we did not want to be prescriptive and we saw this book as a space for the invited contributors to explore those issues they deemed significant within their context: to enlighten the audience and as empowerment. Previously, few books on this topic existed and with hindsight we know that this was likely to have been because there is much complexity in bringing together thinking spanning the disciplinary boundaries. In truth, we have found that full transfer of knowledge between disciplinary roles and perspectives does not yet exist, however there are individuals and collective groups of people who think in a multi-disciplinary way, but they face challenges: philosophically, politically, economically and practically, as articulated throughout different chapters in this book. What is clear is that there is no 'obvious solution' for how to encourage silos groups into thinking and working beyond disciplinary boundaries; however, we do assert that the provision of high quality interdisciplinary education and training for staff is imperative for continued improvement in the sector. Also, the mental health and wellbeing of those that provide care, education, guidance, and security is equally important if the desired outcomes for the children are to be realised; and it is no less important to support the adults tasked with the 'corporate parenting' of these children, so that they have the skills, support, and reflective capacity to provide consistency and predictability. Further, organisations must invest in systems and infrastructures that nurture a resilient and trauma-informed culture.

You will notice that the chapters provide a 'voice' for multiple stakeholders within the sector, allowing the reader an opportunity to build their own understanding of the different contexts, as well as the issues faced by children who have entered secure accommodation and by the professionals who work with them. The book has brought together contributors to share their academic research evidence, practical knowledge, or experiences as strong leaders working with children and young people, and their insight is invaluable. Included are findings from research, practitioner perspectives, models of practice including case studies and alternative models, all of which will be of interest for readers wanting to learn more about what happens 'behind the curtain' in secure settings. We are grateful for each contributor's willingness to collaborate on this project and to share reflections, experiences, and insider information about systems and processes in secure environments, views of the current issues and challenges, explain their work in championing, representing, or promoting the rights of children; we value each contributor's authenticity in this respect. We are also appreciative that every contributor is passionate about what they write about, their research or their practice.

As an editorial team, we see this book as a space for showcasing research and practice. It is the diversity of voices and perspectives that represents a strength of the collection of works bringing together a community of practice. You will notice that the voices and ways of explaining sheds light on existing tensions and barriers that will need to be addressed before multi-disciplinary working can be fully realised. We believe that, currently, in the field, there is positive change occurring and we hope that this book plays an active part in reshaping thinking going forward; as a facilitator for sharing to improve outcomes for children and for informing others about the challenges that practitioners face in their education, health, care, or youth justice work. This book rightly draws from multiple perspectives.

Diahann Gallard
Katharine Evans
James Millington

CONTRIBUTORS

Adeela ahmed Shafi has a background in psychology and education and has been teaching in higher education for over 15 years. Her doctoral research drew on psychological theories to explore how to re-engage young offenders with formal education and learning in a secure custodial setting. Adeela's other research includes how to develop academic resilience and buoyancy in higher education students. She has also worked on international projects in Rwanda, Pakistan, and currently a European Erasmus+ project on emotional education and early school leaving. Adeela is an active community worker in her home town of Bristol where she also stood for MP in 2010.

Faiza Ahmed is an assistant psychologist within a number of inpatients CAMHS units in Greater Manchester. She has previously worked in various mental health services from community to inpatient services across Manchester and has extensive experience of working as a clinical studies officer within mental health research. She has previously published articles with the British Psychological Society. She is currently working on her own research project investigating creativity in Parkinson's disease and aspires to work as a Clinical Psychologist within neurodevelopmental disorders.

Caroline Andow is a lecturer in criminology at the University of Winchester. Caroline's undergraduate degree in Sociology was at the University of Exeter, and she completed her Masters degree in Social Policy at the University of Southampton. Caroline's research interests centre on young people and deviance, as well as experiences of institutionalisation and incarceration. Her doctoral research, funded by the Economic and Social Research Council, gained rare insight into everyday life inside a secure children's home. Caroline is currently involved in collaborative research which explores pathways into, and experiences of, different types of secure setting for young people. Caroline is passionate about applying research findings to inform policy and practice and is currently a Trustee of the National Association of Youth Justice, which works to promote the rights of, and justice for, children in trouble.

Joanna L. Becker is a research associate at the Sam and Myra Ross Institute at Green Chimneys and a psychologist in the Green Chimneys Residential Treatment Center. Dr Becker recently published a grant-funded study which measured the impact of including dogs in social skills training for children with autism. In clinical practice, she uses Animal-Assisted Interventions (AAIs) with horses and dogs to increase behavioural control, self-regulation, and communication in children with emotional disorders. She also holds a Masters in teaching and she works with school personnel to improve the academic and behavioural functioning of children with special needs in the classroom.

Phillippa Brooks has been Head of Education at Lansdowne Secure Children's Home since the School opened in 2013. Over the last five years the education provision has received three Outstanding judgements. Phillippa works closely with leaders of the Care and Health teams – the Home is currently judged to be Good and showing Improved Effectiveness. Phillippa plays an active role within SAN Ed, the national Secure Accommodation Network's Education Body. In previous roles Phillippa has worked in the UK and overseas, in mainstream, MLD (moderate learning difficulties), and SEMH (social, emotional, and mental health) settings, most recently with the SABDEN Multi Academy Trust, which has oversight of the provision of education at Lansdowne.

Kate Brown qualified as a dramatherapist in 2012 from the University of Derby. Currently she is an associate with the Emotional Trauma Support team at One Education. Her practice focuses on the psychological responses to trauma. Her caseload of therapeutic clients have varying needs and levels of trauma, mostly children, adolescents, and young adults. Her work includes crisis intervention for children in transition who have experienced neglect, physical and sexual abuse, and domestic violence. Kate has also worked with refugee children. She has developed and delivered innovative resilience and whole school wellbeing programmes, supported and trained staff as part of their Social, Emotional and Mental Health – SEMH provision. Kate is a qualified EMDR therapist for both adults and children.

Ben Byrne is Head of Early Help and Family Services at Surrey County Council. He is a qualified social worker who has previously been Head of the Youth Justice and Youth Support Services in Surrey. These services have been recognised nationally for their pioneering work to develop integrated and restorative approaches for children and young people. Ben's primary research interest is in complex and vulnerable young people and includes work published by the Howard League, Safer Communities, and Research in Practice. He is a trustee of the National Association for Youth Justice and a member of the Youth Justice Board for England and Wales.

Nina Champion worked at the Prisoners' Education Trust (PET) from 2011 to 2018. She has co-authored numerous reports and publications on learning in custody and was a driving force behind the formation and running of the Prisoner Learning Alliance. Nina began her career as a criminal defence solicitor, before working for various charities managing prevention, rehabilitation, and resettlement projects. She then worked in parliament whilst completing an MSc in Government, Policy, and Politics. Nina represented Western Europe at the European Prison Education Association and sat on the steering group of sports and arts criminal justice alliances. In 2017, she was awarded a Winston Churchill research grant that took her to Denmark, Poland, Belgium, and the USA researching prison/university partnerships. In July 2018 Nina became the Director of the Criminal Justice Alliance.

Aileen Conlon has been Head Teacher at Aycliffe since September 2016. Aileen started her career as a mainstream secondary teacher, followed by twelve years at Silverdale School in North Tyneside, a special school for young people with social, emotional, and mental health needs, beginning as a classroom teacher before becoming first assistant and then deputy head. During this time Aileen completed a further certificate in education with a focus on the historical context and current educational approaches to adolescent emotional and behavioural difficulties. She has worked with a number of schools in different local authorities on whole-school improvement planning and preparation for the Ofsted process. She is committed to the belief that every child, no matter how challenging their behaviour or circumstances, has the right to access to the very best education, and using an analytical, evidence-based approach to any school development work. Aileen is currently working on a programme of learning and development for teachers, alongside a project to bring greater access to digital learning resources for young people within the secure setting.

Alison Davies has been a qualified social worker for 30 years and is a qualified teacher. Currently, she is Head of Hillside Secure Children's Home for young people, the only secure unit for children and young people in South Wales. Previously, she was safeguarding principal of a local authority, having previously led on safeguarding in education, was a children's guardian in the family courts, and area director for CAFCASS Cymru for Caerphilly and Blaenau Gwent. Alison is currently undertaking a professional doctorate at Cardiff University; her thesis is about the voice of the child versus professionals in cases of child sexual exploitation. Last year she was part of the team that won the Police and Crime Commissioners force award for multi-agency partnership working and this year won the

Police and Crime Commissioners award for outstanding contribution to partnership working.

Sarah Douglas has been Head of Learning at Aldine House Secure Children's Home since 2013. She began her teaching career as a primary practitioner and English specialist but has worked in many settings, including the hospital education service and in secondary special school with young people with social and emotional difficulties. Sarah has worked in leadership roles since 2005 and completed her NPQH in 2011. Sarah has been a therapeutic foster carer and is passionate about the Quality Circle Time Model. Sarah is part of the Operational Management Team at Aldine House.

Katharine Evans has over 20 years' experience of working with children and young people across a range of practice contexts, including youth and community work, alternative education, early intervention, and youth crime prevention. She has held strategic leadership positions across multiple sectors spanning children's services, community safety, policing, and as voluntary and community sector lead for a children's trust. In more recent years, Katharine has worked in academia as a senior lecturer in education (Liverpool John Moores University) and as Director of safeguarding programmes (University of Chester). She has a particular interest in participative research that gives voice to children and young people experiencing disadvantage and social exclusion. Katharine is a board member for the Domestic Abuse Support Unit, North Wales.

Yanela Garcia is a qualified counsellor and has worked in schools and other settings with young people and families for over 18 years. She is assistant team leader and designated safeguarding lead for the One Education Emotional and Trauma Support team. She delivers brief and long term interventions for looked after children; young carers; refugee and asylum seeking children and families who have experienced trauma. Her work also uses non-verbal mediums. Yanela takes the lead and is passionate about delivering the internationally accredited Pharos intervention, for refugee children. She has trained staff in delivering the intervention in primary and secondary schools. Actively liaising in multi-agency contexts and managing cases of victims of child trafficking and sexual exploitation is another of her passions.

Alison Gough is the Secure Care National Adviser at the Centre for Youth and Criminal Justice (CYCJ). She qualified as a social worker in 1991 and worked for 20 years in social worker, specialist practitioner, and social work leadership roles in Scottish local authorities and the third sector, including as head of service leading a complex residential school care resource for children with emotional, social, and behavioural difficulties. She joined Children's Hearings Scotland (CHS) in 2011, when CHS was a new body, and as the operational director she was instrumental in the development, design, delivery, and implementation of National Standards for Scotland's unique Children's Panel. She is passionate about making sure lived experience informs practice and policy development.

Marc Herbert has been Head of Education at the Atkinson Secure Children's Home since January 2017. Marc's background is physical education/outdoor instructor and has worked in a number of different settings. He was a head of year in a mainstream school for a number of years and has also taught in HMP, ASD, and EBD establishments. Marc is very passionate about the education of pupils with additional needs and securing the best outcomes for them.

Miyako Kinoshita has a Masters in Educational Studies and is the Farm Education Program Manager at the Green Chimneys Farm and Wildlife Center and Sam and Myra Ross Institute at Green Chimneys. She serves as the key facilitator for over 200 children with psychosocial disabilities currently in residence and day school and facilitates and supervises a wide range of animal and plant-based nature assisted programs. She manages and supervises human-animal interactions and horticulture activities as well as co-treating clients directly with clinicians on campus. As a noted speaker, Miyako has lectured extensively in the United States and internationally at regional, national, and international conferences on topics of various nature based programs in educational, vocational, and therapeutic settings, as well as animal welfare and ethics in human animal interaction programs.

Steven Klee received his MA and PhD in Clinical Psychology from the University of Louisville in Kentucky. He received a diplomate degree in clinical psychology from the American Board of Professional Psychology (ABPP) in 2002. Dr Klee joined Green Chimneys in September 2005 and serves as the Associate Executive Director for Clinical and Medical Services. Dr Klee's clinical and research interests include cognitive therapy, childhood depression, ADHD in children and adults, legal/ethical issues, and human-animal interaction. He has presented at both national and international conferences on these issues. Dr Klee's publications include articles on child custody, animal assisted therapy, and psychotherapy.

Caroline Lanskey is a lecturer in Criminology and Criminal Justice and Deputy Director of the Centre for Community, Gender, and Social Justice at the University of Cambridge Institute of Criminology. She joined the Institute in 2006, after an earlier career in teaching and educational research. She has a specialist interest in the education of young people in the youth justice system, with a particular focus on issues of social inclusion and citizenship and voice. She has worked on several projects with young people in custody and under youth justice supervision in the community including a case study of the education pathways of young people in the youth justice system in England and Wales and an evaluation of an alternative residential educational programme in Germany for young people sentenced to custody.

Claire Lightowler is the Director of the Centre for Youth and Criminal Justice (CYCJ) which works to improve policy, practice, and knowledge about youth and criminal justice in Scotland (www.cycj.org.uk). Her career has focused on supporting the use of evidence (of all types) to improve policy and practice across the social services, working across a range of government, public sector, and academic based organisations. Claire is involved in strategic decision making across youth justice, the Children's Hearing system, and the social services in Scotland. She conducts research about evidence use in the social services, and on coproduction, participation, and inclusion in a youth and adult justice context.

Ross Little works as a senior lecturer in criminology and criminal justice at De Montfort University in Leicester. He has previously worked in a range of roles developing skills in research, youth work, and education, with a particular interest in criminal justice. He is Chair of the National Association for Youth Justice, a membership organisation that promotes the rights of, and justice for, children in trouble with the law (http://thenayj.org.uk).

Sarah Mack is a clinical psychologist working for Greater Manchester Mental Health NHS Foundation Trust in a secure children's home and women's prison. Sarah has a range of clinical experience, particularly in criminal justice settings. She has worked in a young offender institution (YOI), a medium secure forensic adolescent unit, a male prison, an inpatient adolescent unit, and community settings. Sarah's work has involved offering specialist assessments, formulations, interventions, and staff training. The key models that underpin Sarah's clinical work are attachment and trauma. Sarah has special interests in engaging young people and adults with complex histories, and non-epileptic attack disorder (NEAD) in forensic settings. Sarah has published several journal articles on psychosis.

Deirdre McConnell is a teacher, art psychotherapist, and experienced clinical supervisor. She leads One Education's Emotional and Trauma Support team of over 20 therapists who deliver both early intervention and complex casework, primarily in education settings, in close partnership with social care, voluntary sector, and CAMHS. Deirdre's areas of interest include: children's rights and human rights; creativity and neuroscience; psycho-spiritual and self-care models; and the interface between the arts therapies modalities. She is honorary lecturer at Manchester University and guest lecturer at the Sheffield-based Northern Art Psychotherapy Programme, Leeds Beckett University. She has spoken at national and international conferences. Her Research Masters focused on sustainability of arts therapy interventions, across economic crises. She has started doctoral studies at Sheffield University.

Anita Mehay is a health psychologist and research fellow at the University of East London where she works in various capacities with socially disadvantaged and ethnically diverse communities and groups who experience some of the worst outcomes. She has a particular expertise in prison(er) health and education having completed her PhD at Royal Holloway University of London which explored understanding and strengthening health literacy through participatory and peer-based approaches in a young offender institution. She also undertakes consultancy roles for various third sector organisations such as Prisoners' Education Trust as well as NHS England, Public Health England, and the Mayor's Office for Policing and Crime.

Richard Pates is a consultant clinical psychologist at Hillside Secure Children's Home in Neath, South Wales. He has spent his career working with children and in addiction. He is a Visiting Professor of Psychology at the University of Worcester, the editor-in-chief of the *Journal of Substance Use* for the past 17 years, and the author of many papers on addiction, and edited a number of books on addiction and writing for publication. He has run workshops around the world on publishing for junior researchers. He has been a member of the Advisory Council on the Misuse of Drugs (advising the Home Office) and chaired the Welsh advisory panel on Substance Misuse. He is also a consultant for UNODC developing community treatment in Nigeria.

Melanie Prince has been Head Teacher at Clare Lodge Secure Children's Home since 2010. She began her teaching career in a mainstream comprehensive, teaching English. Following that she worked in residential EBD schools, as an education liaison officer for an independent fostering agency, and worked part time at another secure unit for seven years whilst her children were younger. Melanie has been in leadership roles since 1997 and completed her NPQH. She is Chair of the Secure Accommodation Network, and has been the chair of a local primary school governing body.

Deborah K. Reed earned her PhD in special education from the University of Texas at Austin. She currently serves as the Director of the Iowa Reading Research Center and as Associate Professor at the University of Iowa College of Education. In addition, Dr Reed is a member of the Board of Directors of the International Dyslexia Association's Iowa Branch, an editorial board member of *Learning Disabilities Research* and *Practice and Learning Disability Quarterly*, and a past president of the Council for Learning Disabilities. Her current research interests include appropriate uses of reading data in instructional decision making and identifying evidence-based reading practices for teaching vulnerable youth.

Alex Smith is currently in post as an assistant psychologist at FCAMHS NW, a new forensic CAMHS outpatient team commissioned by NHS England, working across the North West of England with young people presenting with mental health difficulties and complex risk behaviours. This includes working in the community and in secure settings. Other experience includes CAMHS acute inpatient ward and on a forensic mental health learning disability adult ward, with good understanding of risk management. Alex's education includes BSc (Hons) in Forensic Psychology and Criminal Justice, and MSc in Forensic Psychology, aspiring to eventually to work in clinical psychology.

James Stephens is a registered dramatherapist. After qualifying from the University of Derby in 2012 he joined the Emotional and Trauma Support team at One Education. He has delivered individual and group work in primary, secondary, and special schools, also providing consultations and staff trainings. Referrals range from preventative early intervention at the universal level, to systemic multi-agency work with complex needs at the targeted level. His current clinical caseload includes: children and young people in the Youth Justice Service; families requiring co-facilitated therapeutic interventions where children are not in education; and young people with learning disabilities and co-morbid diagnoses. James has a special interest in the powerful impact of dramatherapy for young people on the autistic spectrum

David Tiddy left school in 1986 and started working as an engineer, before retraining as a design technology teacher at Caerleon College. David's first post was as a technology teacher in Duffryn High School, Newport. In 1997 David moved to Mynyddbach Girls School in Swansea as head of department. In 2000 he became Head of the Technology Faculty at Daniel James community school in Swansea. In 2003, David also managed the alternative curriculum for older pupils struggling to engage with a standard school curriculum, and pastorally responsible for 80 pupils. In 2011, David left mainstream education taking the post of Head of 6th Form at Ysgol Pen Y Bryn Special School in Swansea. He became Education Manager at Hillside Secure Unit in March 2015.

Jenny Twells is an educational psychologist working at Wandsworth Schools and Community Psychology Service. She gained her Doctorate in educational, child and adolescent psychology at IoE/UCL in 2016. Her career started as a primary school teacher in North London, which helped her to decide on focusing her future work on supporting vulnerable groups of young people to access education and achieve. She worked with young carers in central London which then led to working as an education caseworker for children looked after (CLA) for ten years in an inner London local authority. Her doctorate training led to focusing on youth offenders engaging with education and she delivered her research at the International School Psychology Association Conference in 2017.

PART I
Contextualising the field

1
TROUBLED AND TROUBLESOME CHILDREN
Education, participation, and restoration

Ben Byrne

In this chapter there is a consideration of the importance of education and participation as a central platform for efforts to reform secure care and in supporting children in the community so that they do not need to be deprived of their liberty. Nobody wants to lock children up. Yet that is what we do to thousands of children each year. It results from either acute welfare concerns because they meet the threshold for secure mental health care, or as a response to offending.

There are two underpinning arguments in this chapter: that we unhelpfully differentiate between children by too rigidly separating them along these distinct pathways and that a more holistic and integrated approach to our most troubled and troublesome children is likely to be more effective. It is proposed that such alternative approaches can lead to less reliance upon a secure response and in doing so support improved experiences and outcomes for our society's most vulnerable children. Firstly, there is an overview of the 'three pathways' into secure environments for children, the degree to which adverse childhood experiences and acute disadvantage are common to the children who enter secure care and custody, before then considering the divergent environments they can expect to encounter dependent upon the pathway which is chosen for them. Then, there is a consideration of the policy developments which increasingly identify a set of approaches which are relevant to children in all three pathways. Here we capture the principles for systems and service transformation which are common to policy developments, although they are typically pursued separately in each of the three pathways. When drawn together these principles have the potential to reduce the need to use secure options and can improve the experience and outcomes for children at risk of entering (or re-entering) secure settings. Finally, there is a look at Surrey's attempt to develop a whole system approach which provides more integrated and holistic responses to children entering the mental health, social care, and justice pathways. From this example we draw on evidence of improving outcomes but also recognise the distance still to be travelled to provide the services which troubled children require.

Which children do we place in secure settings?

> Children whose needs have not been adequately met see the world as comfortless and unpredictable and they respond by either shrinking from it or doing battle with it
>
> *(Bowlby, 1973: 208)*

There are in the region of 1800 beds (when at 100% capacity; note that there is currently significant unused capacity within the youth justice secure estate) for children in secure settings in England and Wales (Hales, 2017), approximately 70% of which are in the youth justice secure estate. The number of children placed in secure settings on criminal grounds has reduced markedly in recent years from an average of a little under 3000 children (at any one time) for the period 2000–2008 to below 1000 since 2016. This significant reduction points to the importance of system changes which have facilitated a move away from reliance upon custody towards greater use of community responses, underpinned by a range of informal disposals that have reduced the total number of children entering the formal justice system (Bateman, 2016). The potential for similar systems management approaches to be used in relation to the mental health and welfare secure routes is something to which we return later in the chapter.

Research into the characteristics of children who reach the apex of the youth justice system has consistently identified that these children have overwhelmingly experienced acutely difficult and damaging childhoods (Jacobson et al., 2008; Department of Health, 2009). These environmental factors co-exist with a high level of special educational needs and disabilities (Harrington et al., 2005) and contribute to high levels of mental health problems (Chitsabesan et al., 2006; Youth Justice Board, 2005; Bateman, 2015). These characteristics mean that these children will typically have had contact (of varying types and intensity) with children's social care and mental health services but that it is specifically as a response to their offending behaviour that they are detained rather than as a response to their underlying health and welfare needs. Black and minority ethnic children and young people are significantly over-represented in the youth justice secure estate (Bateman, 2016) reflecting systemic and institutional discrimination within and beyond the criminal justice system (Lammy, 2017).

In England there are approximately 100 welfare beds in Secure Children's Homes (SCH). Children entering SCH provision under welfare grounds do so as a result of an order under s.25 Children Act 1989 which requires a family court to determine that the child must be secured in order to ensure their safety. As with the juvenile justice estate, demand for welfare beds fluctuates significantly but does so over shorter cycles (Abrams, 2015). With a smaller number of beds in welfare settings than in justice and with less headroom when demand increases, the SCH provision frequently experiences acute bed pressures (Timpson, 2016). There is limited available research describing the characteristics of children entering secure environments through the welfare route but what is available indicates that these are typically children who frequently have attachment disorders and have suffered significant childhood trauma and abuse, as well presenting with additional learning needs including autistic spectrum disorders (Bailey, 2004; Hart and La Valle, 2016). Evidence of the characteristics of this cohort of children also comes from the description of conditions catered for by SCH (Secure Accommodation Network, 2016).

Secure mental health care is currently provided for up to 396 children in England (21 high dependency, 147 psychiatric intensive care, 138 low secure, and 90 medium secure) (Hales, 2017). Available evidence suggests that many of the children entering mental health secure facilities will have similar backgrounds to those in welfare secure and the youth justice secure estate. This is particularly the case for children who have reached the secure forensic tier of provision (also described as medium secure facilities) which is reserved for those whose risk to themselves and to others is greatest (Bailey, 2004; O'Herlihy, 2007; NHS England, 2018). Children in secure mental health settings will typically differ from peers in the community who suffer the more common adolescent emotional and mental health disorders with their conditions more often being identified earlier, more acute and enduring, and more frequently linked to childhood environmental adversity (Dolan and Smith, 2001; DoH, 2014).

It should be acknowledged that not all children requiring secure mental health treatment will have experienced specific environmental childhood adversity. Adolescent mental health conditions reflect an interplay between genetics, neurobiological development, and environment, which is complex, yet to be fully understood, and will differ from person to person (Rutter, 2004). That said, attachment disorders, experience of abuse and neglect, and other childhood trauma and adversities are prevalent and are particularly clustered in those children who require treatment in a forensic setting:

> their social backgrounds are often characterised by socio-economic deprivation, multiple losses and traumas, adverse life events, family discord, poor scholastic achievements, learning difficulties, substance misuse and criminality. In addition, some young people are involved with multiple agencies in complex legislative frameworks
>
> *(NHS England, 2013)*

In this respect, children who enter medium secure mental health facilities (recognising that those who experience forensic settings will also often step up from or step down to lower security mental health provision) have more in common with those children who enter secure settings through welfare and justice routes than they do with the other, significantly larger number of children and young people who experience less severe emotional and mental health problems.

It is not within the scope of this chapter to provide a detailed taxonomy of the characteristics of the population of children who enter the three types of secure care but, even in this brief review, it is evident that there are significant overlaps in the life histories of these children. What is concerning, considering these common adverse childhood experiences, is the contrasting responses a child can expect depending on which of the secure pathways they find themselves on and this is what we will turn to next.

Secure responses

Custodial detention for children

Custodial detention for children is heavily shaped by the punishment paradigm. Although English and Welsh legislation does not include punishment as a principle in sentencing children, the regimes to which they are subject are typically imbued with the same philosophy of containment and control which dominates the adult custodial system (Bateman, 2016). Predominantly run by the Prison Service, staffed by prison officers, and with high child to adult ratios (1:10), young offender institutions cater for over 70% of children in custody (607 under-18s at the end of January 2018: Youth Justice Board, 2018) and are routinely described by inspectors as dangerous and damaging environments where violence, self-harm, and pain-inflicting physical restraint are common and increasing (HMCIP, 2016; Ministry of Justice, 2016). Younger and/or more vulnerable children are placed in secure training centres (165 children as of January 2018: Youth Justice Board, 2018). These are privately run establishments (although Medway has been taken 'in-house' and is currently run by the National Offender Management Service) which have a lower staff to child ratio (3:8) but suffer from many of the same problems as young offender institutions. STCs have failed to demonstrate good levels of care in any recent inspections and the Medway Secure Training Centre Improvement Board Report variously described conditions as 'over-controlling and degrading' and 'dehumanising'. In the same report, one young person summed up his feelings about his care by saying 'they treat you like an animal and it's when you need real help' (HMI Prisons, 2016). Again, it should be noted that it is Black and Minority Ethnic (BME) children and young people who are recognised to disproportionately experience the most punitive of the secure environments.

Secure children's homes

The other form of custody experienced by children in the youth justice system is the secure children's homes (SCH). SCH provision tends to be reserved for the youngest children (especially those serving long sentences) or those who are assessed as the most vulnerable. Youth justice reformers have typically seen SCH provision as the preferred option (where there is no realistic alternative to custody) because of their role as an extension of the care system and an explicitly care orientated philosophical base (NAYJ, 2015). With only two children to each adult, SCHs should be better equipped to meet the needs of children detained in the youth justice system than the rest of the juvenile custodial estate. There are currently in the region of 100 youth justice beds in SCHs, about half of the total SCH bed provision.

The SCH is unique in English and Welsh secure provision in that a number of establishments provide for both children who have been placed as a result of welfare orders and those requiring a secure environment because of offending. This conjunction of 'welfare' and 'justice' placements does present its own problems, particularly as a result of the high rates of self-harm, which it has been argued leads to distinctive identities (often reinforcing and exacerbating the welfare and justice labels a child has when placed in secure care) and also significant problems with managing children presenting with diverse needs and behaviours (Andow 2018). Notwithstanding this challenge, when only a secure setting is appropriate, the SCH model is still widely extolled as currently the best method of responding to the acute welfare needs common to many children in the justice system and for those who come through the family court (Children's Commissioner, 2015).

Secure mental health facilities

Secure mental health facilities for children are sub-divided into those which provide for high dependency needs and intensive care, medium and low secure environments, and in total offer beds to up to 400 children at any one time. These children will (almost without exception) have been sectioned under the Mental Health Act and therefore are involuntarily detained. The mix of secure children's mental health provision includes a further sub-division of settings including those which specialise in the care of children with eating disorders, learning disabilities and those for younger children (under the age of thirteen). The intake of forensic settings, for children who pose the greatest risk to others and often themselves, is in many respects similar to SCH and young offender institutions (DOH, 2014).

The range of secure mental health facilities contrasts with the limited diversity across provision for those presenting with justice and welfare needs who require a secure setting. To a degree this reflects the heterogeneity of children requiring mental health treatment, but also indicates the limited nature of the offer to children in the welfare and justice systems where there is little difference in levels of security and limited access to different types of care. The defining philosophy of the mental health secure system is one of treatment (detention is only possible for assessment or treatment) within hospital settings predominantly staffed by medical practitioners.

This brief review of the child population in secure settings suggests there is a high degree of commonality of life experiences frequently reflecting acute attachment and trauma issues, which underpin the behaviours that typically lead to children meeting the criteria for a form of secure detention. These shared adverse childhood experiences contrast with the diverse responses within and between the justice, welfare and mental health settings in how (and if) they respond to the therapeutic needs of children, shaped as each setting is by differing justice, welfare and treatment philosophies. This suggests there is a need for a more coherent and integrated response from justice, health and welfare systems to the needs of children who have experienced the most damaging childhood experiences.

This is particularly likely to be the case for those children who inhabit the boundaries of each of these systems, moving between the pathways and experiencing any one or all of these forms of secure care/custody (although empirical evidence on the movement between the three secure pathways is limited; see Hales, 2017). Evidence from young people who have experienced these systems demonstrates their ineffectiveness in supporting the most disadvantaged:

> Those with multiple needs struggle to navigate systems designed for education, mental health, social care or youth justice. A proportion rapidly drop out of view without receiving any assessment. Many fall between the cracks of the multiple referral pathways. Other bounce between systems for many years before support rapidly evaporates at the boundary of adulthood
>
> *(Little et al., 2015).*

Depending on the assigned pathway, and sometimes depending on the presentation and behaviour on a given day, a child with acute emotional and behavioural difficulties may find themselves subject to grossly different responses and levels of care between the differing settings. This response is arbitrary for many children and young people (Little et al., 2015; Khan, 2016) and many professionals (Children's Commissioner, 2015) and reflects organisational and system needs rather than those of individuals.

New pathways and integrated models of care

Policy developments in relation to children in secure care/custody increasingly recognise that the current health, welfare, and justice pathways are too siloed and only identify the common formative experiences of many children in secure settings as a basis for rethinking both secure care and the pathways into it from the community.

Charlie Taylor's youth justice review has identified the reduction in children entering the formal justice system has meant that 'the children who remain in the system are those that display the most challenging and ingrained behaviour and have the most complex needs' (Ministry of Justice, 2016). The Taylor review therefore proposes greater integration of community services for vulnerable young people and a 're-imagining' of youth custody to one where the focus is primarily educational. Similarly, the report of the Children and Young People's Mental Health Taskforce 'Future in Mind' (Department of Health/NHS England, 2015) recommends integration of care pathways and a transformed (less medicalised) practice, spearheaded through the children and young people's Improving Access to Psychological Therapies programme (CYP IAPT). In addition, there are now, for the first time, common health care standards for children across all types of secure settings (RCPC, 2013).

Whole system reform is further encouraged through Child and Adolescent Mental Health Services (CAMHS) Transformation programmes in each local authority, through a number of integrated pathway pilots sponsored by Department for Education's Social Care Innovation funding (see below) and from an increasing understanding of 'polyvulnerability' (Radford et al., 2011; Beckett and Firmin, 2014) where the needs of children exposed to a number of overlapping risks are best met through integrated service responses organised around the child (Hanson and Holmes, 2014).

The Social Research Unit's report into young people facing multiple and severe disadvantage captured the challenge of supporting children and young people in the face of multi-faceted adversity: 'Risks rarely arrive alone. They come in pairs and clumps and basketfuls, tangled like yarn' (Little et al., 2015). To meet this challenge, services, and importantly the families and communities outside the normal reach of specialist interventions, need new ways to be supported and support each other, and for there to be a break from traditional siloed systems responses.

Leading the work to better understand the trajectories of children who end up in the various forms of secure setting is the Central and North West London Health Trust's 'Pathways to Secure Care for Young People Project'. This project has, for the first time, mapped the range of provision across the three pathways and is exploring the experience of children within the various settings.

The policy and practice developments outlined above suggest an appetite to reform the responses to children who enter secure care and custody. This both means re-imagining the secure settings themselves and ensuring that the pathways into them are better understood and better integrated, meaning that children can access the help they need when they need it. With this endeavour in mind, there will now be a consideration of the principles and practice that research suggests should underpin a reformed approach to children in secure settings and those who are at greatest risk of ending up there.

Shared principles in responding to troubled children

With increased interest in integration of services to children who come to the attention of CAMHS, youth justice, and social care, and recognising the importance of high quality educational provision for these children, it is appropriate to ask whether there are principles that can be applied across these systems that reflect common concerns, a shared evidence base, and a framework for greater integration. Several sources can be drawn upon to develop such a template. Hanson and Holmes's (2014) review of the literature about working with adolescent risk offers a broad and authoritative perspective on what is most likely to work, particularly in relation to adolescents identified as in need of protection. A distinctive approach set out in the youth justice literature, which shares many of the principles established by Hanson and Holmes, is the work of Haines and Case pursuing what they describe as 'Positive Youth Justice' (Case and Haines, 2015). In advocating for reform of the children's mental health system, and building on the recommendations of Future in Mind, the Centre for Mental Health's work shares much with the approaches promoted to reform the pathways into the welfare and justice secure systems.

Drawing on the work outlined above and supported by an increasingly coherent and consistent evidence base, a core set of principles and approaches emerge which should inform the development of a reformed response to troubled children: one which is built around the common experiences and needs of children who are at risk of reaching the pinnacle of the justice, welfare, and health systems. Firstly, we look at the principles common to these approaches as they pertain to whole systems (both local and national) and then how these are manifested in service development. For explanatory purposes it serves to separate out these two domains but in practice these are not two discrete realms as services are core to systems, and many of these principles are applicable at both the system and service level.

Systems principles

Children's rights and adult responsibilities

The UK has not fared well in respect of its compliance with the United Nations Convention on the Rights of the Child (UNCRC) especially in regard to how it treats children within vulnerable and disadvantaged groups; this is most obvious in relation to the functioning of the youth justice system and youth incarceration (Goldson, 2005; Children's Commissioner, 2015). The principle that adults should be held responsible for the welfare and development of children is often at odds with how we 'responsibilise' (Muncie, 2004) children who have had the most damaging and disadvantaged childhoods. Nor should the responsibility and intervention be purely individualised but should consider the wider milieu in which children grow up:

> We should not solely target psychosocial individual, familial and educational issues, but also the prevalent macro-level, socio-structural factors which leave children vulnerable to social exclusion arising from childhood poverty and associated structural inequalities such as high levels of crime, victimisation, deprived neighbours and reduced employment opportunities.
>
> *(Case and Haines, 2015)*

Any reform will need to re-balance the rights of children and the responsibilities of adults to properly attend to obligations in accordance with the UNCRC and to reflect the needs of children whose life chances are constrained by their formative experience and environment.

Early intervention

Adverse childhood experiences that are common to children who reach the pinnacle of the justice, welfare, and mental health systems can often be prevented, and where they are not prevented (or preventable) children have a right to timely and high quality support to address their needs. Working Together to Safeguard Children describes early help as 'providing support as soon as a problem emerges, at any point in a child's life, from foundation years through to the teenage years' (DfE, 2015). Any system which wants to reduce the numbers of children it locks up needs to ensure this help is available to all children to ensure problems do not become entrenched and acute. This requirement goes to the heart of the ability of national and local systems to safeguard children and support their healthy development, thereby recognising that a whole system response is required to address the pathways into secure accommodation for those children who have the most acute safeguarding needs.

Diversion and systems management

As described above, the demand for secure provision fluctuates both over time and between the three types of provision at any one time. Research suggests this demand is largely the result of economic and political changes as reflected in social policy, legislation, and official attitudes to various social concerns rather than changes in children and young people's behaviour (Phoenix, 2009; Bateman, 2015). This suggests that if it is understood that our reliance upon secure care/custody is socially constructed and socially determined, we can, if we choose to so do, through policy and practice, reduce this use.

Systems management approaches encourage a view of the whole system, recognising the interdependencies of a system's component parts. This suggests that understanding the demand for secure care/custody requires a view of the whole system(s), how systems inter-relate, and how forces act to 'heat up' or 'cool down' these systems. The reduction in the use of youth custody demonstrates how, through local and national policy and practice change, different systems outcomes can be achieved. Similar techniques for systematically addressing the use of welfare and mental health provision is equally possible, particularly when allied to better community pathways which intervene earlier and more effectively and do so while consciously avoiding the dangers of net-widening and labelling (Becker, 1963; National Association of Youth Justice, 2015). Evidence for the iatrogenic nature of the criminal justice system is well established (McAra and McVie, 2010) and similarly damaging impacts from systems contact are evident in the care and mental health system, thereby indicating alternative pathways designed to appropriately divert children from formal justice, welfare, and mental health systems should be pursued.

Universal, informal, and normalising approaches

The importance of universal educational settings (included here are early years and informal youth settings), identifying children's safeguarding and developmental needs and continuing to include those whose behaviour and experiences might set them apart from their peers, is critical to future outcomes (The Prince's Trust, 2007). This contrasts with common practice of excluding and marginalising these children. It also suggests that specialist services, such as youth offending, CAMHS, and social work, would do well to blend as far as possible with universal provision to support children in mainstream settings and avoid the stigma and labelling which commonly comes with receiving discrete specialist services in what are typically overly formal environments. Normalising and making informal the way in which support is provided to children makes it more likely this support will be accepted and be effective (Ward and Maruna, 2007; McNeill et al., 2012).

Children in secure care/custody have almost all been in mainstream educational provision but have typically moved into specialist or alternative education prior to being detained in a secure setting. The importance of providing high quality education within secure settings is identified elsewhere in this book as a springboard to rehabilitation and resettlement. Having settings in the community which can accelerate (rather than retard) this rehabilitation and promote opportunities to reintegrate is identified as key to effective resettlement and care planning in the community.

Participation

There are two different but related meanings of participation both of which are relevant to developing systems which are more or less likely to mitigate or exacerbate the circumstances of children who have experienced disadvantage and adversity. Firstly, participation refers to agency, empowerment, and user voice: putting children's views, wishes, and aspirations at the heart of the systems which are seeking to support them (DfE, 2015; YJB, 2016). Secondly participation refers to active involvement in education and employment with a view to acquiring the skills and abilities needed to move successfully into adulthood. Maintaining children who have additional needs or challenging behaviour in education, ideally mainstream education, is increasingly recognised as a key protective factor in supporting emotional wellbeing, promoting safeguarding, and reducing the likelihood of offending (The Prince's Trust, 2007; Wikeley et al., 2007). Non-formal education, participation in activities, and skills development with peers are also recognised as promoting positive outcomes. Both forms of participation need to underpin any system seeking to engage and include children who are commonly excluded, marginalised, and whose voices often go unheard. As will be described below participation for the children about whom we are most concerned will also involve restoration.

Service principles

Think systemically

Systems approaches, which consider the totality of influences and pathways for children and families, hold out the best prospect of harnessing opportunities to promote positive outcomes for children who have had significant adverse experiences and face disadvantage. Appreciating how systems impact on children and how their various systems interact is crucial to shaping services and can provide positive pathways for those who have had adverse childhood experiences. Work using the whole family approaches to influence family systems, the social pedagogic approaches which shape care environments, working with peer groups to promote positive, supportive relationships, and working through educational institutions to include, connect, and nurture children are all examples of systems approaches. When allied to the principles below, these approaches provide the best opportunity to support troubled children and reduce the likelihood of entering or re-entering secure environments. Although they are equally applicable to secure and non-secure environments, the 'totalising' nature of closed institutions needs attention in considering the particular processes at work within secure environments (Goffman, 1961; Andow 2018).

Integrated/one-stop shop

Children and young people say they want services where they can get a range of their needs met, they do not want to have to go to different places and different providers, and they do not want to have to keep re-telling their stories (Cohen et al., 2009; Adamson and Poultney, 2010; DoH, 2004). Bringing a range of multidisciplinary staff together and equipping practitioners with the skills and confidence to deal with a diverse range of needs means that children and young people are more likely to take up the services on offer. We talk about 'hard to reach' young people when all too often it is the services that are hard to reach because they are not accessible or well advertised and not designed around the needs of their target users (Hanson and Holmes, 2014).

Developmentally attuned

Research increasingly recognises the importance of developing services which are bespoke to the stage of child/adolescent development (Blakemore and Choudhury, 2006; Coleman, 2011). A specific criticism is that the systems designed to protect and support children do not distinguish between the different stages of a child's life course and typically fail to recognise the needs of adolescents and the context in which they are at risk. Applying our knowledge from an increasing understanding of the physical, psychological, and neurological stages of child development requires services to develop bespoke approaches for the needs and stage of development of the children or young people with whom we are working; what Hanson and Holmes (2014) call 'going with the grain'.

As well as recognising the need to adapt to normal child/adolescent developmental needs services should also be attuned to the particular needs of children whose adverse life experiences have shaped their development, making them more vulnerable and in need of greater understanding of how these experiences will impact upon their learning and behaviour. The experience of multiple exclusions on the way to a secure setting is a familiar one for many children facing severe disadvantage and suggests that services are not currently shaped around the particular needs of these children. In re-designing services, we need to get ahead of behaviour which is predictable in children who have had experienced various forms of adversity and are often traumatised.

Relational

Literature dealing with children in care (The Care Inquiry, 2013), children who offend (Haines and Case, 2013), and children who have experienced significant emotional and mental health problems (Khan, 2016) emphasise the critical importance of establishing and maintaining relationships with adults who consistently demonstrate they care to support healthy development. These successful helping relationships are predicated upon adults demonstrating that they care (Brandon, 1982; Graef, 1997; Smyth and Eaton-Erickson, 2009; Hanson and Holmes, 2014). As well as the child–practitioner relationships, effective approaches need to promote supportive relationships between young people and their family and their peers (Fergus and Zimmerman, 2005; McNeil and Weaver, 2010). Typically, services do not place continuity of relationships at the heart of service design or care pathways and, therefore, lose out on the powerful potential of relationships to enable change. For children who have experienced trauma and insecure attachment, continuity and consistency are of utmost importance, but it is these children who will often experience the greatest instability and discontinuity in caring and professional relationships (Ibbetson, 2013).

Holistic

Children whose behaviour is risky, challenging, and sometimes frightening will often be defined in terms of that behaviour with labels such as young offender, self-harmer, absconder, or some such term which reflects their 'otherness'. Children and young people are of course much more than these labels but, so defined, these can be self-fulfilling and constraining. Services which are similarly defined by a behaviour or presenting need can pathologise their users and fail to respond to the whole child and to realise the opportunities to build upon strengths, skills, and protective factors which may lie well beyond the purview of any one specialism. A holistic service will therefore draw on multi-professional skills and knowledge basis, considering the wellbeing of body and mind, providing rich and diverse opportunities for children and young people with a variety of needs and experiences.

Restorative

While restorative practice can describe a wide array of approaches and has diverse applications, a common thread is a focus on preventing and addressing harm; it has significance for children who have experienced harm and who may have caused harm to themselves or others. Restorative practice seeks to give expression to the voices of participants, to provide opportunities to promote understanding and connectedness, and to identify how people can get their needs met. Restorative practice offers the prospect of restoring children to communities, to families, and, most importantly, to themselves, and to promote empathy and inclusion with those working with them (Braithwaite, 2002).

Case study: Surrey's integrated care and support pathway

In Surrey, in recent years, new and more integrated approaches have been developed which bring the services for children at greatest risk of escalating to the top of the care, mental health, and justice systems much more closely together. There are two manifestations of this approach; the Hope shared education, social care, and mental health pathway and the integrated Youth Support Service.

Having recognised the often overlapping provision of services (yet traditionally separate pathways) between children's social care and CAHMS, with the limiting educational provision that children with emotional and mental health problems often experience, the Hope service was established to provide therapeutic and educational responses to children known to CAMHS. Many of these children are also known to children's social care or are in care. In recognition of the success of Hope's integrated and holistic approach, the service was awarded Social Care Innovation Fund investment to further enhance the model. In 2016, the Extended Hope Service was established to provide intensive outreach and respite residential care for children at the top of CAMHS tier 3 services who were at risk of requiring tier 4 in-patient provision.

Hope and Extended Hope have incorporated the service design principles outlined above to bring together professional responses to educational, mental health, and welfare needs to provide a holistic response to children whose primary presenting needs are in relation to their emotional and mental health. The multi-disciplinary approach, holistic and integrated care packages, flexible hours, and assertive outreach all reflect a service designed around its users in line with the evidence base on what is most likely to be effective. The initial evaluation of the Extended Hope service (DfE, 2017) indicates that the model has reduced the number of A&E and paediatric hospital admissions and reduced the number of children and young people in Surrey requiring tier 4 in-patient admission.

Surrey's integrated Family Services (SFS) provides services to a variety of vulnerable children and young people. Building upon the Youth Support Service, and continuing to provide specialist adolescent support, the SFS undertakes a range of services including those previously provided by the Youth Offending Team, Connexions, the youth service, as well as delivering aspects of CAMHS, children's social care services, and housing departments' responsibilities. While statutory requirements are fulfilled, young people receive essentially the same services and opportunities from the same professionals regardless of whether their entry route to the service is through offending, homelessness, mental health, unemployment, or other factors which lead them to be identified as in need (Byrne and Brooks, 2015).

Critical to the development and delivery of the SFS is the service's mission to ensure all Surrey children and young people are supported within the family system and participating in the wider system of education and their communities. This integrated approach, focusing upon participation, was extolled in the Taylor review of the youth justice system:

> In Surrey ... the youth offending service has been successfully integrated into the local authority's wider youth services, meaning that a child or young person in the criminal justice system can access the same broad spectrum of provision as a child who is homeless, not in education, employment or training (NEET), or has other welfare needs. This promotes a more comprehensive response to young people who offend and increases the opportunity to divert young people from the youth justice system and into effective services, while allowing greater flexibility in the length and intensity of support provided.
>
> *(Taylor, 2016)*

The SFS has developed a model of relationship-based practice, centring on one key practitioner in a working partnership with a child or young person and their family; it seeks to address concerns about the overly bureaucratic processing of children (Phoenix and Kelly, 2013), the multiple referrals within multi-disciplinary teams (Ibbetson, 2013), and the criticism that human interactions and the voice and experience of the child have been subordinated to routinised operations (Munro, 2011). The active and meaningful engagement of children in their assessment and interventions is a key ambition for the service, as part of its goal to promote the full participation of its service users as active members of their communities. Critical to the development of integrated youth support in Surrey has been the wide-ranging application of restorative practice and the gate-keeping of the formal youth justice system (Mackie et al., 2014) resulting in Surrey having the lowest level of first-time entrants to the YJS and being one of the lowest per capita users of custody in England and Wales (Ministry of Justice/Youth Justice Board, 2015). Surrey has a largely transformed approach to youth justice which has reduced the use of youth custody by 80%.

Children identified as offending are not labelled or dealt with separately from other young people who require help. They will often be alongside children and young people who have come through the CAMHS and social care pathways. In addition, those who require specialist CAMHS intervention can access services through HOPE which are well integrated with social care and provide bespoke educational responses. As a result, entry to secure welfare and mental health provision is now much better gatekept.

The further aspiration in Surrey is that, through application of early intervention and systems management approaches to the formal social care and mental health pathways (as applied successfully in youth justice), improved outcomes for a greater number of children can be achieved. Key components of this newer approach to whole-system reform will include further integration of the care, health, and justice pathways predicated upon access to the right 'early help' and, where required, more integrated and holistic help later. This whole-system reform offers the potential for fewer children to reach the 'top end' (greater need) of the health, social care, and justice systems and ultimately will mean fewer children require secure placements. The next stage of development in Surrey is to now ensure that the HOPE services is more fully aligned with the integrated youth support provision and that both are supported by a more mature early help system, to reduce adverse childhood experiences and better identify and support children who have had these experiences. While Surrey's attempt to reform the pathways that lead children into secure care offers encouragement, it also offers a sobering reminder as to how much further we need to go to effectively change the trajectories of children who experience the greatest disadvantage. It is also a reminder that current innovative attempts to develop holistic and integrated approaches, in Surrey and elsewhere, will butt-up against entrenched justice, welfare, and mental health systems responses which will be resistant to reform described by Little et al. (2015) as 'the 'natural state' of complex multi-agency and multi-professional networks is really one of 'dis-integration'.

Conclusion

It is evident that too frequently we fail to recognise or respond appropriately to the adverse childhood experiences and multiple disadvantages common to many of the children who we detain in our secure care and custodial settings. We also unhelpfully differentiate between these children based upon their presenting behaviour, thereby obscuring common underlying needs. As a result, children enter justice, welfare, and mental health secure settings that offer very different levels of care and contrasting approaches to rehabilitation, which is difficult to justify in light of the shared adverse formative experiences of these children.

Drawing upon an increasingly established evidence base, it is possible to define the design principles for systems which can lead to less reliance on secure detention and improve experiences and outcomes for children. This work is underway in many parts of the UK, and Surrey is offered as an example where integration and innovation is taking root. The challenge will be both to make integrated, holistic, and restorative approaches the norm in the community and, simultaneously. reform secure settings in line with the same principles.

References

Abrams, F. (2015) BBC Radio 4's File on 4 [online]. Retrieved from: www.bbc.co.uk/news/education-31659495

Adamson, J., and Poultney, J. (2010) *Increasing the engagement of young people in positive activities*. London: Centre for Excellence and Outcomes in Children and Young People's Services.

Andow, C. (2018) Roles and relationships of care and education staff inside a secure children's home. In D. Gallard, K. Evans, and J. Millington (Eds), *Children and their education in secure accommodation: interdisciplinary perspectives of education, health and youth justice*. Oxon: Routledge.
Bateman, T. (2015) *The state of youth justice – 2015*. London: National Association for Youth Justice.
Bateman, T. (2016) *The state of youth custody*. NAYJ Briefing. Retrieved from: www.thenayj.org.uk
Bailey, S., and Hales, H. (2004) Children and adolescents. *Journal of Criminal Behaviour and Mental Health*, 14, Suppl. 1, 51–52.
Becker, H. (1963) *Outsiders. Studies in the sociology of deviance*. New York: Free Press.
Beckett, H., and Firmin, C. (2014) *Tackling child sexual exploitation: a study of current practice in London* (Summary Report). London Councils and the London Safeguarding Children Board/University of Bedfordshire.
Blakemore, S.J., and Choudhury, S. (2006) Brain development during puberty: state of the science. *Developmental Science*, 9, 1, 11–14.
Bowlby, J. (1973) *Attachment and loss: Vol. 2*. New York: Basic Books.
Braithwaite, J. (2002) Setting standards for restorative justice. *British Journal of Criminology*, 42, 3, 563–577.
Brandon, D. (1982) *The trick of being ordinary*. London: Mind Publications.
Byrne, B., and Brooks, K. (2015) *Post-YOT youth justice*. Howard League for Penal Reform. Retrieved from: http://socialwelfare.bl.uk/subject-areas/services-client-groups/young-offenders/howardleagueforpenalreform/174662HLWP_19_2015.pdf
Case, S., and Haines, K. (2015) Children first, offenders second: The centrality of engagement in positive youth justice. *The Howard Journal of Crime and Justice*, 54, 2, 157–175.
Children's Commissioner for England (2015) *Unlocking potential*. London: Office of the Children's Commissioner for England.
Chitsabesan, P., Kroll, L., Bailey, S., Kenning, C., Macdonald, W., and Theodosiou, L. (2006) Mental health needs of offenders in custody and in the community. *The British Journal of Psychiatry*, 188, 534–540.
Cohen, A., Medlow, S., Kelk, N., and Hickie, I. (2009) Young people's experiences of mental health care. *Youth Studies Australia*, 28, 13–20.
Coleman, J. (2011) *Nature of Adolescence* (4th edn). Oxon: Routledge.
Department for Education (2015) *Working together to safeguard children (statutory guidance)*. London: DfE.
Department for Education (2017) *Extended Hope (service evaluation)*. London: DfE.
Department of Health (2004) *The National Service Framework for Children, Young People and Maternity Services: the mental health and emotional well-being of children and young people*. London: DoH.
Department of Health (2009) *The Bradley Report: Lord Bradley's review of people with mental health difficulties and learning disabilities in the criminal justice system*. London: DoH.
Department of Health (2014) *2013/14 NHS standard contract for secure forensic mental health service for young people*. London: DoH.
Department of Health/NHS England (2015) *Future in mind: promoting, protecting and improving our children and young people's mental health and wellbeing*. London: DoH. Retrieved from: https://assets.publishing.service.gov.uk/government/uploads/system/uploads/attachment_data/file/414024/Childrens_Mental_Health.pdf
Dolan, M., and Smith, C. (2001) Juvenile homicide offenders: 10 years' experience of an adolescent forensic psychiatry service. *The Journal of Forensic Psychiatry*, 12, 2.

Fergus, S., and Zimmerman, M.A. (2005) Adolescent resilience: A framework for understanding healthy development in the face of risk. *Annu. Rev. Public Health*, 26, 399–419.

Goffman, E. (1961) *Asylums: essays on the social situation of mental patients and other inmates.* New York: Anchor Books.

Goldson, B. (2005) Child imprisonment: a case for abolition. *Youth Justice*, 5, 2, 77–90.

Graef, R. (1997) Fostering success. *Community Care*, May, 17. Retrieved from: https://www.scie-socialcareonline.org.uk/fosteringsuccess/r/a1CG0000000GXKTMA4

Haines, K.R., and Case, S.P. (2013) The Swansea bureau: a partnership model of diversion from the youth justice system. In *Howard League for Penal Reform: papers by the winners of the Research Medal 2013*, 15–34. Retrieved from: https://howardleague.org/wp-content/uploads/2016/04/Justice_for_young_people_web.pdf

Haines, K.R., and Case, S.P. (2015) *Positive youth justice: children first, offenders second.* Bristol: Policy Press.

Hales, H. (2017) *Pathways to secure care for young people.* NAYJ Seminar, 10 May.

Hanson, E., and Holmes, D. (2014) *That difficult age: developing a more effective response to risks in adolescence.* Dartington: Research in Practice.

Harrington, R., Kroll, L., Rothwell, J., McCarthy, K., Bradley, D., and Bailey, S. (2005) *Psycho-social needs of boys in secure care for serious or persistent offending.* Journal of Child Psychology and Psychiatry, 46, 8, 859–866.

Hart, D., and La Valle, I. (2016) *Local authority use of secure placements.* London: DfE.

HM Chief Inspector of Prisons (2016) *Annual report 2015/16.* London: HM Inspectorate of Prisons.

HM Inspectorate of Prisons (2016) Inspection of Medway Secure Training Centre report. Retrieved from: www.justiceinspectorates.gov.uk/hmiprisons/inspections/?post_type=inspectionandsandprison-inspection-type=secure-training-centre-inspections

Ibbetson, K. (2013) *Child F – serious case review.* London: Tower Hamlets Safeguarding Children Board.

Jacobson, J., Bhardwa, B., Gyateng, T., Hunter, G., and Hough, M. (2008) *Punishing disadvantage: a profile of children in custody.* London: Prison Reform Trust.

Khan, L. (2016) *Missed opportunities: a review of recent evidence into children and young people's mental health.* London: Centre for Mental Health.

Lammy, D. (2017) *Lammy review* (final report). London: HMSO.

Little, M., Sandu, R., and Truedale, B. (2015) *Bringing everything I am into one place.* London: Dartington Social Research Unit.

McAra, L., and McVie, S. (2010) Youth crime and justice: Key messages from the Edinburgh study of youth transitions and crime. *Criminology and Criminal Justice*, 10, 2, 179–209.

Mackie, A., Cattell, J., Reeder, N., and Webb, S. (2014) *Youth restorative intervention evaluation* (Final Report). Retrieved from: www.surreycc.gov.uk/people-and-community/young-surrey/help-and-advice-for-youngpeople/youth-restorative-intervention-independent-evaluation

McNeill, F., and Weaver, B. (2010) *Changing lives. Desistance research and offender management.* SCCJR Project Report; No.03/2010. Glasgow: Scottish Centre for Crime & Justice Research (SCCJR), University of Glasgow.

McNeill, F., Raynor, P., and Trotter, C. (2012) *Offender supervision.* Devon: Willan.

Ministry of Justice (2016) *Medway Improvement Board: final report of the Board's advice to Secretary of State for Justice.* London: MoJ.

Ministry of Justice/Youth Justice Board (2015) *Youth justice statistics 2014/15.* London: MoJ.

Muncie, J. (2004) *Youth justice: responsibilisation and rights.* In J. Roche, S. Tucker, R. Flynn, and R. Thomson (Eds), *Youth in society: contemporary theory, policy and practice* (2nd edn). London: Sage Publications in association with The Open University Press.

Munro, E. (2011) *The Munro review of child protection: final report. A child-centred system*. London: DfE.

National Association of Youth Justice (NAYJ) (2015) *National Association of Youth Justice manifesto*. Retrieved from: http://thenayj.org.uk/wp-content/uploads/2015/06/2015-Youth-Justice-Manfesto.pdf

NHS England (2013) *Standard contract for forensic mental health services for young people*. London: NHS England.

NHS England (2018) Child and Adolescent Mental Health Services. Retrieved from: www.england.nhs.uk/commissioning/spec-services/npc-crg/group-c/c03/

O'Herlihy, A. (2007) Provision of child and adolescent mental health in-patient services in England between 1999 and 2006. *Psychiatric Bulletin*, 31, 12, 454–456.

Phoenix, J. (2009) Beyond risk assessment: the return of repressive welfarism. In F. McNeil and M. Barry. *Youth Offending and Youth Justice* (Research Highlights in Social Work). London: Jessica Kingsley.

Phoenix, J., and Kelly, L. (2013) 'You have to do it for yourself': responsibilization in youth justice and young people's situated knowledge of youth justice practice. *British Journal of Criminology*, 53, 3, 419–437.

Radford, L., Corral, S., Bradley, C., Fisher, H., Bassett, C., Howat, N., and Collishaw, S. (2011) *Child abuse and neglect in the UK today*. London: NSPCC. Retrieved from: www.nspcc.org.uk/globalassets/documents/research-reports/child-abuse-neglect-uk-today-research-report.pdf

RCPC (2013) *The Royal College of Paediatric Children's Health: health care standards for young people in secure settings 2013*. London: RCPC.

Rutter, M. (2004) How the environment affects mental health. *The British Journal of Psychiatry*, 186, 1, 4–6.

Secure Accommodation Network (2016) Home page. Retrieved from:http://www.securechildrenshomes.org.uk/secure-accommodation-network/

Smyth, P., and Eaton-Erickson, A. (2009) Making the connection: strategies for working with high-risk youth. In S. McKay, D. Fuchs, and I. Brown (Eds), *Passion for action in child and family services: voices from the prairies*. Regina, SK: Canadian Plains Research Center. Retrieved from: http://cwrp.ca/sites/default/files/publications/prairiebook2009/Passion_for_Action_in_Child_and_Family_Services.pdf

Taylor, C. (2016) *Review of the youth justice system on England and Wales*. London: MoJ.

Timpson, E. (2016) *Secure children's home reform*. Retrieved from: www.gov.uk/government/publications/secure-childrens-homes-reform-edward-timpson-letter

The Care Inquiry (2013) *The Care Inquiry report: making not breaking: building relationships for our most vulnerable children* (Findings and recommendations of the Care Inquiry Launched in the House of Commons on 30 April 2013). Retrieved from: www.adoptionuk.org/sites/default/files/articles/care-inquiry-full-report-april-2013.pdf

The Prince's Trust (2007) *The cost of exclusion: counting the cost of youth disadvantage in the UK*. London: The Prince's Trust.

Ward, T., and Maruna, S. (2007) *Rehabilitation*. Oxon: Routledge.

Wikeley, F., Bullock, K., Muschamp, Y., and Ridge, T. (2007) *Educational relationships outside school: why access is important*. York: Joseph Rowntree Foundation. Retrieved from: www.jrf.org.uk/publications/educational-relationships-outside-school

Youth Justice Board (YJB) (2005) *Mental health needs and effectiveness of provision for young offenders in custody and in the community*. London: YJB.

Youth Justice Board (YJB) (2016) *YJB participation strategy*. London: YJB.

Youth Justice Board (YJB) (2018) *Monthly custody report October 2018*. London: YJB.

2

AN HISTORICAL PERSPECTIVE ON EDUCATION IN SECURE ACCOMMODATION IN ENGLAND AND WALES FROM 1850 TO THE PRESENT

Caroline Lanskey

> Upon one subject the whole of the evidence and all the opinions are quite unanimous, – the good that may be hoped from education ... There seems in the general opinion to be no other means that affords even a chance of lessening the number of offenders.
>
> *(Report of the Committee of the Lords in Carpenter, 1851: 351)*

> Education is important for all children, but for those involved in offending it is vital. We need a resolute focus on giving children in trouble with the law the skills, qualifications and aptitudes to lead successful, law-abiding lives. We must have as high expectations for these children as we do for any others.
>
> *(Taylor, 2016: 2)*

The Government report cited by Mary Carpenter in 1851 and the review of youth justice led by Charlie Taylor in 2016 express a remarkably similar view of the value of education for children who break the law. Both argue its importance for addressing offending and bemoan the inadequacy of existing provision for children in custody. At the time Mary Carpenter was writing, children who broke the law were sent to prison and spent long periods locked up in their cells receiving very little, if any, education. Today, despite significant changes to custodial contexts for young people, the quantity, quality, and range of educational provision is again up for scrutiny. It is an opportune time therefore to reflect on the history of education in secure settings and to consider why, after 165 years, the provision of education for young offenders in secure accommodation is once more a matter of concern.[1]

A challenge to any historical account of this type is that definitions of 'education' and 'secure accommodation' have changed over time and across context. In today's young offender institutions (YOIs), education and vocational training are treated as separate components of the regime (see for example, Ministry of Justice, 2017) whereas the 'training' in secure *training* centres (STCs) combines both academic and vocational education (see Rule 28 of The Secure Training Centre Rules 1998). Historically, some residential settings for young offenders have been defined as educational establishments, e.g. reformatory schools and approved schools, whereas others have emphasised the secure function, e.g. youth custody centres. The discussion here will refer to all formal learning activities (academic and vocational) planned as part of the regime within the secure setting. Similarly, the term 'secure' has meant in practice different degrees of confinement within and across settings. In the reformatory schools and the later approved schools, for example, children would be expected to stay on the premises, but it was not envisaged that they would be locked up in the way that they would be in prison or in a secure unit. However, there are reports of reformatory schools having cells and locking children up in practice (Hagell and Hazel, 2001) and some approved schools began to operate 'closed blocks' onsite in response to young people absconding from the premises (Hood and Sparks, 1969). This review will include all residential institutions to which young people charged with or convicted of a criminal offence have been sent.

The scope of this historical overview extends from the 1850s to the present (see Figure 2.1). Although there were earlier independent educational initiatives for children in prison,[2] it was in the mid-nineteenth century that the issue became a matter of national debate. This chapter draws on secondary historical sources, research studies, government reports, and parliamentary records to review the main themes that have characterised this debate over time. These sources address the aims of education for children who have been sentenced to custody, its perceived importance relative to other youth justice agendas, and views of the success or otherwise of particular models. The discussion is loosely structured chronologically and identifies five main narratives: late-nineteenth century perceptions of the reformative value of education through religious instruction, industrial training and discipline; post first-world war beliefs in education as a means to instil the values of liberal citizenship; a reductionist narrative in the latter half of the twentieth century when education is subsumed within larger reformative programmes of psycho-therapeutic treatment; punishment and deterrence; and the return of a broader but as yet unrealised vision for education in the twenty-first century bolstered by children's rights discourses, a revived belief in its therapeutic contribution and its perceived cost-effectiveness as a youth justice policy. These narratives are gendered and shaped by social class. They are also blurred, disrupted, and complicated by counter-narratives which lie in the gaps between ideology and practice and in the social distinctions between childhood and adulthood, offending and non-offending populations.

1850s–1910s schooling in religion, industry, and discipline

Reformatory and industrial schools

Prior to the 1850s, there were very few prisons for young people. Some were housed in two prison hulks ships and others in a site at Parkhurst Prison (Hagell and Hazel, 2001) but frequently children who broke the law were imprisoned

FIGURE 2.1. Custodial institutions for children in the criminal justice system (England and Wales 1850s – present)

1850s Youthful Offenders Act 1854	1908 Prevention of Crime Act Children Act	1920s–40s 1933 Children and Young Person's Act	1952 1948 Criminal Justice Act	1969 Children and Young Person's Act	1971	1982 Criminal Justice Act	1988 Criminal Justice Act	1994 Criminal Justice and Public Order Act	2007 – 2016 Apprenticeships Learning and Skills Act 2009 Proposal for secure colleges – 2014 Charlie Taylor Review 2016
	Probation Homes/Hostels				Local Authority Community Homes With Education			Local Authority/private (Secure) Children's Homes	
Reformatory and Industrial Schools		Home Office Approved Schools (1933)							
						Local Authority Youth Treatment Centres	Secure psychiatric units		
			Remand Centres						
				HMP Youth Detention Centres				Private Secure Training Centres	
						HMP Youth Custody Centres	HMP/Private Young Offender Institutions		
	Borstal	'Modified Borstal'/Young Prisoner Centres							
Prison									

Key:
▓ Welfare–orientation: managed by local authority/health/private welfare and education providers
▓ Penal–orientation – managed by prisons/police/private criminal justice providers

alongside adults, sometimes before transportation to the colonies. They would be placed in 'dark cells' or 'solitary cells' within prisons and spend long periods of the day in isolation from others (May, 1973). Oscar Wilde, during his stay in prison between 1895–1897, reported that children were hungry and devoid of affection and could be locked in their cells for up to 23 hours. Evidence of kindness towards them from staff resulted in dismissal (Wilde, 1897).

Such practices were subject to increasing criticism by a group of social reformers, politicians, and prison governors who argued that prison was physically and mentally damaging to children, expensive, and ineffective at reform. In her publication *Reformatory Schools for the Children of the Perishing and Dangerous Classes and for Juvenile Offenders,* published in 1851, Mary Carpenter proposed the establishment of independently run reformatory schools for children convicted of a criminal offence and industrial schools for those who were homeless or engaging in petty crime. The primary aim was to prepare children for 'an honest livelihood in society'. She believed that they committed crime out of ignorance and this was as a result of 'a lack of moral, industrial and religious training' (Carpenter, 1851: 27). She argued that without such training the mechanical teaching of reading and writing (which she suggested children experienced in prison) could lead to greater 'audacity in crime'. She envisaged similar regimes in both reformatories and industrial schools, but the former would have a firmer approach because children in these schools would have to be 'encouraged' out of bad habits. The views of Mary Carpenter and others found favour amongst prison governors and chaplains frustrated by statistical evidence of their prisons' inefficiency at deterring or reforming young people (May, 1973) and amongst politicians who viewed state imprisonment of children to be a highly costly policy and who were concerned about the potential for 'contamination' by adult offenders (Hurt, 1984). In 1854 the Act for the Better Care and Reformation of Youthful Offenders in Great Britain formally recognised reformatory schools as places to which young people between the ages of 10 and 16 years could be sent for between two to five years. In 1857, legislation was passed to send children convicted of vagrancy to industrial schools.

Political support for reformatory and later industrial schools can be understood as part of a wider state interest in education as a means of social reform (Johnson, 1970). However, the exclusively educational approach to the reform of children who broke the law did not receive unanimous political support initially. There was a view that young offenders should receive some form of punishment for their misdeeds and until 1899 children were required to have two weeks' imprisonment prior to being sent to a reformatory school. One of the arguments for the imprisonment condition was that otherwise parents might encourage their children to commit crime to receive a free education (Stack, 1994).[3] A related argument was based on the principle of 'lesser eligibility' – that young offenders should not gain educational advantages over law-abiding children as that would lead to jealousy (Carlebach, 1970). To address these concerns, managers of reformatory schools reportedly aimed to make educational provision an unpleasant experience for the children who were sent to them (Hyland, 1993).

The reformatory and industrial schools were run by a range of independent charities and religious organisations which led to inconsistencies and failings in provision despite being subjected to inspections by the state (Hyland, 1993). By 1866 there were 50 reformatories including training ships and farm schools, as well more traditional schools for girls and boys. A daily timetable might comprise three hours of English, arithmetic, and religion with the remaining hours devoted to producing 'the ideal labourers'. Boys would be prepared for work in agriculture, the army or the merchant navy and girls for domestic service (Clarke, 2002). Several of the boys' reformatories had their own brass bands and some who played in them joined military bands after leaving (Parker, 2016). Often, much of the industrial training was chosen in order to generate profit for the reformatory owners. Boys would make bricks, chop wood, and salvage paper. Girls would do laundry and cleaning jobs (Carlebach, 1970). Regimes in the schools were frequently harsh and punishment was severe. In response to children's resistance, some reformatories became more like penal institutions with window bars and locked cells (Hagell and Hazel, 2001).

Educational classes were frequently accorded a low priority by reformatory managers in favour of financial interests. Sometimes classroom learning would be scheduled for the evenings so that the children could complete a full day's work (Radzinowicz and Turner, 1952). Classrooms were frequently cramped and with little decoration on the walls. There was often only one teaching room in which all classes would be taught at the same time (Hurt, 1984). Teachers were untrained and uninformed of innovations in pedagogy: 'I feel sure that (teachers) would be able to do more … were they acquainted with the method of presenting truth to the mind of a child; this is especially the case with the elements of Reading and Number' (Report of the Reformatory and Refuge School Union, 1906). In response to criticisms from government education inspectors who were dissatisfied with the standards of education, reformatory school teachers argued that their focus was 'to correct rather than instruct' (see Carlebach, 1970: 98).

Borstals

The other major component of the youth justice reform movement at the end of the nineteenth century was the borstal. At this time, children over the age of 16 years were classified and imprisoned as adults. Following criticisms of this policy in the Gladstone Report of 1895, an experimental regime was set up for young offenders aged 16 years and over who were too old for school. Originally in Bedford prison in 1901, the scheme subsequently transferred to the village of Borstal in Rochester, Kent, in 1902. The perceived success of the experiment led to the establishment in the 1908 Prevention of Crime Act of a sentence to detention in a borstal institution of between one and three years. The vision of the prison commissioners was for a regime of 'firm and exact' discipline and 'hard work' which included physical, educational, and religious training (see Warder and Wilson, 1973).

Daniel Buckley, an American visitor to Borstal in 1912, described the daily regime:

> At 5:30 the prisoner arises and begins the day with a biscuit and milk after which he cleans and tidies up his cell. At 7 o'clock he breakfasts on bread, porridge, margarine and with tea and coffee, if he is in the special grade. At 7:30 he is in the workshop or in the open; and carpentering, blacksmithing, boot-making, building, gardening, cooking, cleaning, or laundry work, occupy him until noon, when dinner, consisting of bread, meat, potatoes and pudding await him. After an hour and ten minutes for dinner and rest he resumes work which continues until 5:30 when work ceases and there is a general parade reviewed by the Governor after which he gets his last food for the day, generally consisting of bread and cheese and a mug of cocoa. At 6:15 there is a general meeting in the Chapel when short addresses are given by the Chaplain and others and encouraging letters from discharged boys who are doing well are read. Then they go to the evening classes after which there is recreation for a few moments until 8:30 when they go to their cells and shortly after lights are out.
>
> *(Buckley, 1912: 26)*

A boy would receive on average five hours' tuition during the week and would remain in those classes until he had passed the examinations. There was an incentive scheme and boys whose behaviour was deemed good enough also had access to lectures in a large hall. Buckley writes that the use of 'magic lanterns' (early slide projectors) added to the popularity of these lectures (Buckley, 1912). Despite the few evening classes, the principal focus was on vocational training and remedial education during the day led to the criticism that the Prison Department of the Home Office regarded the main function of a borstal education to be that 'borstal inmates are brought up to a minimum level for effective functioning at work in society, rather than seeing education as a means whereby a real attempt could be made to develop latent ability' (Stratta, 1970: 121).

The first borstal for girls opened in a wing of Aylesbury Convict Prison in Buckinghamshire in 1909. As in the reformatory and industrial schools, girls in borstals during this period were trained in skills considered appropriate to their gender and class. They were taught domestic and housekeeping skills: cooking, sewing, laundry, cleaning; basic farming skills, flower arranging, and nursing. There was also a programme of physical exercise: netball, exercise classes, dancing, and table tennis. Although physically separate, the regime for the girls shared the same disciplinary regime as the adjoining prison (Gelsthorpe and Worrall, 2009). The harshness of the discipline which included frequent use of solitary confinement and handcuffs was criticised by the state Children's Association. In their defence, prison commissioners argued that such a regime was necessary because these girls presented extraordinary difficulties as a consequence of having led 'wild and dissolute lives' under war conditions (The Children's Association, 1922).

Remand and probation homes

Alongside the reformatory schools and borstals, there was provision in the 1908 Children Act for residential placements in remand homes for children given short custodial sentences (up to three months) or those awaiting trial. In these homes, which were run by the police, children of compulsory education age (up to 11 years) received a typical provision of reading, writing, and arithmetic. At one remand home, Forhill House in Birmingham, boys were divided into year groups and had lessons from 9.30 am to 4.30 pm. The difference in approach to other schools was related to educational ability: 'owing to the large proportion of backward boys', there was a focus on craft and practical activities some of which were seen as having a therapeutic role:

> Much attention is … devoted to the puppet theatre in which one or two boys at a time are allowed to act a scene which they themselves devise. Their acting often brings to light certain features of their mentality, the knowledge of which helps to determine the best method of dealing with them.
> *(Radzinowicz and Turner, 1952: 74)*

The older boys were given work related to site maintenance, gardening, construction. Recreation time was carefully managed and involved reading, writing letters, playing draughts, making model aeroplanes, sport (billiards, table tennis, boxing). Quiet talking and one cigarette were allowed. There were also occasional trips to the cinema or sports matches with local youth clubs or schools (Radzinowicz and Turner, 1952).

Following the introduction of a supervisory probation service with the Probation of Offenders Act, 1907, children could also be sent to probation hostels. These homes were seen as a less extreme alternative to committal to a reformatory school or borstal. They might offer education on site or children might reside in the probation homes and attend a local school. Probation homes became more frequently used as a residential option for children as the harsh disciplinary regimes of reformatories and borstals lost popularity (Wills, 2005).

Although varied in form, these early residential institutions established a common set of perceptions and approaches towards education in secure accommodation which have persisted over time. Firstly, they introduced the principle of residential education as a means of reform and social control of delinquent children. Adherence to this idea remained strong despite variation of the custodial model according to the age and gender of the young offender, and the perceived severity or persistency of their offending. Secondly, education was tailored to existing class and gender expectations. Its focus on industrial training, physical fitness, and self-discipline aimed to produce compliant and productive young men and women of the working classes, (Clarke, 2002; May, 1973). Thirdly, despite the rhetoric, the provision of education was shaped and at times curtailed by financial interests and was in frequent tension with punitive agendas. Fourthly, their independent status and diverse approaches revealed the administrative challenge of regulating education provision and the related welfare of children in secure settings under different forms of ownership (Hurt, 1984; Carlebach, 1970).

1920s–1940s: liberal vision of education and citizenship

The extent to which early penal establishments were educational or a source of child labour became a matter of political debate and inspection reports in the second decade of the twentieth century indicated a growing dissatisfaction with the regimes of harsh discipline and training in the reformatory schools and borstals (Hagell and Hazel, 2001). However, despite criticisms of institutions, greater social dangers were envisaged if they were released: 'boys and girls who are admittedly mentally deficient, and have proved criminal tendencies, ... set completely at liberty will, we fear, result in the birth of more illegitimate and defective children and in further offences against society' (The Children's Association, 1922).

Residential interventions remained the preferred response to persistent offending by children, but a new approach was called for. Liberal ideals of citizenship and education gained popularity as the new means to 'gentle' the population of juvenile offenders. The reading of 'good' literature was one example. In 1921, the Newbolt Report cited CEB Russell, a Reformatory School Inspector:

> The taste for good reading ... acquired at school ... may provide them with an interest which, when games and athletics and youthful hobbies are faded dreams, will be as strong as ever, which will compensate them for the loss of other good influences and last their lives ... if they have learnt to love books they will seldom lack friends. The drab uniformity of their lives will be illumined by imagination; they will have taken up something of their heritage of civilisation; their interests and sympathies will be wider, their sense of citizenship more keen ...
>
> *(Board of Education, 1921: 148–149)*

An example of the progressive shift in educational thinking had been Homer Lane's 'The Little Commonwealth', established for young neglected children and older children (from 13 to 19 years) who had been convicted of crime. Over its six years of operation from 1913–1918 it grew from a small community of 15 to 42. Formally classified as a reformatory school, The Little Commonwealth was a self-governing community. Everyone from the age of 14 was classed as a citizen of the community. Education at the Little Commonwealth was not envisaged as hours in the classroom passively learning traditional academic subjects, instead children would learn through their participation in community governance and community activities such as constructing buildings and looking after the animals on the farm. Lane's approach to education through self-governance was characteristic of an emerging body of theorising by an international group of educationalists who formed the 'New Education Foundation' and who established independent progressive schools based on democratic principles (Brehony, 2006). However, the Little Commonwealth community itself was short-lived as the Home Office withdrew its licence following complaints by two children at the school of being sexually abused by Lane (see Delap, 2018). This case illustrates clearly the limitations in the regulatory oversight of reformatory schools and the gap between the rhetoric and practice in their treatment of children.

The Little Commonwealth was representative of a growing practice of combining in one residential setting so-called neglected children with children who had committed criminal offences as the popular view became that 'there is little or no difference in character and needs between the neglected and the delinquent child' (Home Office, 1927: 71). In the Children and Young Persons Act of 1933 reformatory and industrial schools were formally merged and renamed Home Office approved schools.

Home Office approved schools

Children up to the age of 15 years could be sent to the new approved schools for between one to three years' training. Children who received shorter sentences (of up to 12 months) continued to be sent instead to a smaller number of probation hostels. Allocation to an approved school was decided after an initial period of assessment in one of four classifying centres. Rather than on distinctions between 'neglect' and 'delinquency', classification was now based on age, religion, and distance from home. However statistical data indicated that there were gendered differences in the decision-making processes: the majority of boys (95%) sent to approved schools had been convicted of an offence in contrast to only 36% of girls who were sent mainly for reasons of 'care and control' (Hyland, 1993: 31).

The 1933 Act established the requirement for 'proper provision' for the education and training of children in custody. The teaching provided in these settings was often described as 'remedial' as levels of reading and arithmetic of the children were assessed as lower than average (Rose, 1967). Girls would frequently visit local schools for their classroom lessons whereas boys would usually be taught in the school. The provision of trade training continued to reflect social assumptions about the children's future roles in society, for example, gardening, carpentry, cookery, painting, and decorating.

In line with the broader welfare philosophy of the 1933 Act approved schools aimed to create a positive environment in which children would learn how to become 'good citizens':

> It is better by far to send a boy away to be brought up a good citizen than to leave him indelibly impressed with the mark of a sordid home environment, probably to add to such conditions himself when he reaches manhood.
>
> *(Borgat, 1941, cited in Gill, 1974)*

Citizenship was presented not only as a right but as a duty – to vote, to behave responsibly and to contribute economically. In contrast to the unquestioning obedience expected in the reformatory and industrial schools, citizenship was presented as 'active' and 'critical' (Wills, 2005). In High Beech probation hostel, for example, young people were encouraged to reflect critically on newspaper articles and the *Approved Schools Gazette* suggested holding mock elections prior to the 1950 general election as part of civic education (Wills, 2005). However, the 'critical' approach citizenship did not include the questioning of class divisions and social hierarchies. There were therefore tacit limits to the remit of citizenship assumed for these children.

Borstal reforms

Significant changes were also made to borstal regimes under the new leadership of Alexander Paterson in the 1930s. Paterson wanted to disassociate borstal from its penal roots and base it on a public school model. He abolished prison uniform, established a house-based community, and recruited teachers from public schools and universities (Hood, 1965). The focus of the regime was on 'character building', which included games playing and inter-house competitions. There were outward bound trips: canoeing expeditions, mountain climbing, and camping treks designed to provide tests of courage and leadership and to make the boy 'fit, strong and mentally alert' and able to respond quickly to instructions (Hood, 1965: 152). Religious education continued to play a prominent role in the revised borstal regime. It was still seen as 'the first line of defence against crime – which after all is sin in another form' (Home Secretary of the time in Hood, 1965) and the first housemasters in the borstal were chaplains. There was also encouragement of the development of middle-class hobbies and cultural activities: stamp collecting, music, and, again, 'good English literature' so that the boy would not 'easily return to the drivel that once enslaved him' (Paterson in Hood, 1965: 112).

In Paterson's view, the length of stay in a borstal was to be determined by the young person's progress within the regime rather than by a fixed length sentence. He envisaged young people remaining until they had acquired 'the sense of honour which is the proud possession of our public school boys' (Paterson in Hood, 1965: 112). Paterson spoke of a 'Borstal Blue' being similar to an 'Etonian or Harrow Blue' – a recognition of pride in one's existing social status (Humphries, 1981); boys were encouraged to work to the best of their ability rather than to aspire to social mobility:

> Whatever work or game you take up can be performed to the best of your ability ... It's no use asking a carthorse to win the Derby, but he can win a ploughing match with equal credit. So, realise your own limitations and don't set out to equal those whose lives lead to higher spheres than those of your own ...
> *(Governor of Rochester Borstal, in Hood, 1965: 111)*

Despite the radical shifts in the approach towards education for children in borstals, provision continued to be curtailed by class assumptions about the role and place for such children in society.

1950s–1980s: treatment vs punishment and the minimalisation of education in secure regimes

In the 1940s and 1950s approved schools were subject to growing criticism. As they were overseen by the Home Office rather than the Department of Education, questions were raised as to whether teaching and training approaches 'were up to date' (Simmons, 1946). However, it was the treatment of the children and their frequent absconding rather than their educational contribution that became the primary focus of public scrutiny and criticism (Hayden, 2007). Three government inquiries following disturbances at Standon Farm in 1947, Carlton House in 1959 and Court Lees in 1969 revealed harsh and abusive disciplinary practices and the imposition of longer than usual periods of detention in school in order to improve success rates (Hyland, 1993). Public concern about these incidents alongside falling success rates led to more general questioning of the continuing relevance of the approved school system and its values.

The vision of a public school model of borstal education for the older young offenders faltered too. As with the approved schools, there was a powerful undercurrent of resistance amongst the young people sent to borstal (Humphries, 1981: 218), including complaints about the use of corporal punishment and staff treatment. Problems with absconding and discipline, and an increasing rate of reconviction fuelled an official discourse of 'children who could not be trusted'. Paterson's educational model lost popularity; it came to be viewed as too soft and irrelevant 'to the actual lives which people are going to live and the actual temptations which they are going to experience' (Lady Wootton in Hansard, 1 May 1961: c. 1155). It was suggested that authority based on social prestige and religious principles was less meaningful to a generation brought up in an era of greater social awareness antagonistic to the traditional class system and the appeal to 'hobbies' and decent standards of leisure could not compete against the more 'sophisticated entertainment' of the day (Hood, 1965). Concerns were also expressed about the high cost of running the institutions as well as the effectiveness of the indeterminate borstal sentence (for example Morris et al., 1960). The borstals were no longer considered to be offering a distinctive approach as the central idea of training had spread across the secure estate. The similarity of problems faced by the approved schools and borstals did not however generate a single policy response. Penal custodial policies divided along the lines of welfare and treatment for younger children who were 'troubled' and 'disturbed' and punishment-oriented approaches for the older, wilful, and persistent young offender. Education played a subsidiary role in both models.

Community homes with education

The government paper 'Children in Trouble' (Home Office, 1968) represented a shift to a more community-based approach towards young offenders with a stronger focus on intervention and treatment. Building on a policy orientation towards care and protection, which had instigated the raising of the age of criminal responsibility from eight to ten years in 1963, the distinction between young neglected child and young child offender in this paper all but disappeared. There was a strong lobby against the use of custody for young offenders. Proposals were for preventative work, social support, and treatment for very young offenders in their home settings rather than in an institution. Wills (2005) argues that the shift to local solutions was indicative of a broader shift within society – a decline of the ideal of the nation state and a more fragmented, localised approach to community. In the ensuing 1969 Children and Young Person's Act, approved schools and probation homes were amalgamated into community homes including some with dedicated educational units called community homes with education (CHE) to which children would be sent on residential care orders. Responsibility for the homes was transferred to the Department of Health and Social Security and to local authority children's departments. It was at the discretion of local authority social service departments whether or not a young offender receiving a care order from the courts would receive treatment in their own community or be placed in a home. In the CHEs, education was provided on the premises for those who were not able to attend mainstream schools. In contrast to the structured regime of formal education, vocational training, and 'character building' in approved schools, the CHEs were to have a more flexible approach to education which included guidance and social education in preparation for responsibilities in adult life.

This period also witnessed an expansion of secure accommodation within the care system (see Milham et al., 1978). New secure units were established in regional observation and assessment centres and some CHEs (Jones, 2012) and, in 1971, the first of two secure treatment centres was opened. The prevailing rationale was that more children were 'suffering from serious personality and behaviour disorder than in the past and those with histories of disruptive behaviour required some form of perimeter security until they had stabilized' (Hoghughi, 1973: 14).

Research and inspections of educational provision of CHEs and the secure units identified problems in the quality of education amid the challenges of providing education in an environment where children had significant social and emotional needs, varying levels of ability, and were resident for different lengths of time (e.g. Department of Education and Science, 1980). A Social Services working party report on CHEs (Social Services Liaison Group, 1976) noted that the process of entering and leaving the homes led to inconsistency and breaks in children's education and access to teachers and to educational resources in comparison to mainstream schools was limited due to the small numbers of children in the homes. The working party felt that one of the difficulties related to where the accountability and loyalty of teachers working for the Department of Education in settings run by local authorities lay. While basic skills teaching was considered to be good and therefore the needs of the less able were being met, the breadth of the curriculum, in particular the provision of art, music, drama, sport, and science, was limited (Bullock et al., 1990) and 'educational inspiration' was, as in most community homes, 'poor' (Milham et al., 1978). Despite the benefits to some children of experiencing the routine of 'sitting in the classroom', it was felt that education was too 'isolated from general practice' (Milham et al., 1978). Questions were raised too about the relevance of sending girls to CHEs and the assumption that they had 'distinctive psychological and behavioural problems which needed a treatment intervention model rather than an educational model' (Gelsthorpe and Worrall, 2009).

The preference amongst local authorities and social services for community alternatives to custody for young offenders precipitated an overall decline in the use of CHEs. There was a national shortage of places for girls in CHEs and those who were recommended to a CHE often had long waits for treatment (Social Services Liaison Group, 1976). Research studies questioning the links between deprivation and delinquency were said to have directed policy interest away from treatment and rehabilitative programmes and towards youth custody (Tutt, 1981). It was argued too that, following the 1969 Children and Young Person's Act, magistrates who wanted to guarantee a custodial sentence were directing young people to penal custody rather than issuing them with a care order (Bottoms, 1974).

In contrast to the welfare-oriented response towards the young neglected offender, government policy towards the older and persistent offender in the youth justice system had been developing a more punitive tone since the late 1940s (Warder and Wilson, 1973). There was a revival of interest in disciplinary regimes which would instil 'a right attitude in the individual and in the community to society, to work, to authority, to decency, and order, to life' (Home Office, 1953: 138) and a new form of custody, the detention centre, was introduced in 1952 for young people under the age of 21 years sentenced to six months or less. Rather than an educational and reformative experience the detention centre was designed to give young offenders a 'short, sharp, shock' which would deter them from future offending (Hagell and Hazel, 2001). The punitive rhetoric surrounding detention centres did not always filter into practice as a result of the commitment of some practitioners to the provision of education; there remained, in some of these centres, a significant educational programme and offenders of school age were expected to attend classes during the day (Muncie, 1990). A detention centre was opened in 1962 for girls but closed after seven years as the 'practice of military drill and physical education was not considered "appropriate training" for young women' (Muncie, 1990: 56).

Despite controversy over the effectiveness of harsh disciplinary regimes for young offenders, political belief in the value of reform through deterrence resulted in a later revival of the 'short sharp shock' custodial experience. In the Criminal Justice Act 1982, military style regimes were set up at two centres: Send (for 17–21-year-olds) and New Hall (for 14–16-year-olds) (Newburn, 1996). Strenuous physical education was a major part of these regimes but other forms of education were minimal; a construction training course run by NACRO was closed at New Hall because it did not fit with the new tough regime (Muncie, 1990). However, these regimes were abandoned following a Home Office evaluation which reported negative effects (Thornton et al., 1984).

The division between welfare and penal responses to youth crime and between departments responsible for custodial placements had generated by default rather than design a disjointed and inconsistent approach to the provision of custody for young offenders. Children could be sent to community homes, secure treatment centres, detention centres, borstals, young prisoners' centres, or sections of adult prisons. Wide regional differences were found in the provision and use of secure accommodation for young offenders (Stewart and Tutt, 1987), and it was argued that:

> young people with similar problems are drifting around different welfare and control systems ... where problematic people end up seems largely a matter of local as well as national policies and of the resolve and ability of some settings and agencies to hang onto difficult clients rather than transfer them.
>
> *(Bullock et al., 1990: 208)*

The need for rationalisation prompted a review of provision. Borstals and young prisoner centres were amalgamated into one custodial option – the youth custody centre. No outward semblance of an educational establishment remained; these were to be prison-like regimes run by staff in prison uniform. Although it was envisaged that they would provide a 'constructive training regime', which would link prison work and education in one overall training programme, little thought had been given to educational provision in the early planning stages. In the final version, instead of the minimum of six hours' education designated in borstals, each youth custody trainee had to attend a minimum of two hours' education and two one-hour sessions of physical education per week (Genders and Player, 1986). Although training opportunities were similar to those offered in the borstal regimes, they had to accommodate the introduction of short determinate sentences, and the resulting higher turnover of the youth custody population (Genders and Player, 1986).

The absence of dedicated provision for the small minority of girls sentenced to youth custody training resulted in girls being housed in adult prisons. The gendered assumption (perhaps out of convenience) was that they would benefit from care rather than contamination from the adult women they resided with. Educational resources in these prisons were limited and shared with adults and because of the legal requirement for age appropriate education, girls received educational classes ahead of the adult population. Training for girls in these institutions continued to be shaped by stereotypical assumptions about female roles in society: instruction in domestic and household skills and in beauty and hairdressing (Genders and Player, 1986).

1990s–2000s: education and punitive control

The focus on penal custodial options continued in the Children Act 1989 which ended the use of care orders as a disposal for young offenders. Consequently, a large number of young people who had previously been placed in CHEs because of their offending came out of the care system. There was piecemeal closure of CHEs and most had closed by 1993. Nevertheless, there remained a small minority of places for very young children who had committed offences and were still housed in what were named in 1989 *local authority secure children's homes*. These continue today to provide education as part of the residential experience. The successor to the secure treatment centre was the secure psychiatric unit to which 'mentally disordered juveniles' could be sent under the Mental Health Act of 1983.

With declining numbers of young people in custody in the 1980s (see Newburn, 1996) and ostensibly little difference in approach between them, youth custody centres and youth detention centres were merged into young offender institutions (YOIs) in 1988. The programme of activities in the YOIs, comprising education, training, and work activities, was designed 'to foster self-control and to develop young people's interests and skills for employment after release' (The Young Offender Institution Rules, 1988). Educational provision was contracted out to adult education providers and differences in the range, quality and character of education in these institutions from mainstream educational curricular persisted. These were partly due to the limitations imposed by safety agenda, partly also to limited perspectives about the future employment options and social status of young offenders, which, although not explicitly stated, resided in the tacit messages of citizenship curricula and political discussions about citizenship education for young offenders (see Lanskey, 2010; 2011).

Amid concerns about growing youth crime rates and 'misspent youth', a more punitive tone, 'no more excuses', and a focus on personal responsibility characterised youth justice policy making in the 1990s which included a belief in the effectiveness of prison. In 1993, a new custodial model for young persistent offenders from the ages of 12–15, the 'secure training centre' (STC), was established. In these privately run centres education was subsumed within the concept of 'training' and instrumentally aligned to the goal of 'tackling' offending behaviour. Critics argued there was little detail about education in the draft specifications apart from references to offending behaviour courses and HIV/AIDs awareness raising. Educational issues were however overshadowed by controversies surrounding staff treatment of children in the centres (Hagell, Hazel and Shaw, 2010; Taylor, 2016) in particular the use of physical restraint which resulted in the deaths of two children, Gareth Myatt and Adam Rickwood, in STCs in 2004.

2007–2016: rights and rhetoric: a renewed focus on education

Over the first decade of the twenty-first century, education inspection reports across the secure estate – the secure children's homes, secure training centres, and young offender institutions – identified overall a picture of inconsistent practice. At best, education was considered to be engaging young people and successfully addressing the gaps in their knowledge resulting from earlier disrupted educational careers (e.g. Ofsted, 2014); at worst it was found to be unchallenging, fragmented and insufficiently tailored to young people's needs (e.g. Ofsted, 2010). A control agenda dominated the regimes. Education inspection frameworks in secure institutions were themselves altered from the mainstream to provide a stronger focus on containing behaviour rather than on academic achievement (Lanskey, 2011).

The UK government had been criticised for several years by the United Nations Committee for the Rights of the Child, for not providing young people in custody with a statutory right to education and for delegating responsibility for education to the Home Office rather than the Department of Education (see House of Lords and House of Commons Joint Committee Report, 2005). As part of a growing political pre-occupation with children's rights which included the Every Child Matters agenda and the establishment of the Children's Commissioner, the Apprenticeships, Children and Learning Act was passed in 2009 which brought the education of children under the legislative umbrella of mainstream education including the responsibility for the delivery of the school 'National Curriculum'. A new department was established – the Joint Justice and Education Unit – which was intended to ensure recognition in mainstream educational policy of the educational needs of young people in custody. However, under the cost-cutting 'austerity' agenda of the 2010 coalition government, the joint education youth justice unit was disbanded and responsibility for education in the secure estate returned to the Ministry of Justice. The return was presented as a means to 'increase clarity and accountability'; however, subsequent changes to mainstream educational policy, such as to the timing of national examinations, were found to have adversely affected the educational options of young people in custody (Lanskey, 2014) and raised questions again about the political interest in these young people's education.

In the second decade of the twenty-first century, political interests in cost-effectiveness and dissatisfaction with the high number of young people re-offending after release from custody prompted a renewed focus on education in secure institutions. The government proposed the creation of secure colleges as 'a new generation of secure educational establishments where learning, vocational training and life skills will be the central pillar of a regime focused on educating and rehabilitating young offenders' (Ministry of Justice, 2014: 3). These plans, although legislated for in the Criminal Justice and Courts Act of 2015, were later abandoned. It was argued that the 'nature of the challenge' had changed because of a decline in the population of young people in custody and a concern about the cost of building the new college. Rising levels of violence and self-harm amongst the population of young people in custody also raised concerns about placing such a large proportion of the youth custody population in the same institution (Hansard, 6 July 2015 c. 5710)

Education, however, remained a key political focus in youth justice policy intentions. A review of the youth justice system in 2016 restated the political interest in prioritising education: 'Rather than seeking to import education into youth prisons, we should create schools for young offenders in which we overlay the necessary security arrangements' (Taylor, 2016); however the parameters for the discussion were redrawn. The recommendations were for smaller custodial establishments, presented as a secure version of the 'free school' model with closer links to local education providers as, once again, the separation of management of education from mainstream provision was identified as problematic. In addition to the persistent remedial focus on 'basic skills' of literacy and numeracy, these new secure schools were envisaged as having a therapeutic dimension – an echo of earlier welfare-oriented interests.

Concluding reflections

The profile of education in secure accommodation has waxed and waned over the 170 years since the introduction of reformatory schools for juvenile offenders. Initially seen as the route to reform, firstly through religious instruction, hard work, and training, secondly through the instilling of liberal citizenship ideals, it was the operating principle of secure institutions for young offenders until the middle of the twentieth century. The emphasis on education lessened over the following 50 years as other approaches were given greater emphasis: treatment and welfare for the neglected and troubled child and punishment and control for the persistent or serious offender. There was a revival of interest in the first decade of the twenty-first century as children's rights entered the political arena and education became a statutory right for children in custody. A broader educational curriculum was envisaged which extended beyond basic literacy and numeracy skills to include emotional and social wellbeing and which was equivalent in breadth and quality to any within the education sector in the community. However, economic restraints and more immediate concerns about safety and safeguarding in secure institutions continue to challenge the positioning of education 'at the heart of detention'.

It is possible to identify a mix of ideological, economic, social, and administrative interests and assumptions which have played a role in shaping the changing function and profile of education in secure institutions over this period and which may well continue to challenge and shape future provision. A key ideological driver has been the extent to which education is perceived to contribute to the reduction of re-offending by young people and in particular its perceived effectiveness as a strategy in comparison to more punitive or treatment-oriented approaches. Political decision-making on these issues has been influenced by personal beliefs, by the activities of social reformers and by the perceived support of the public. Economic considerations have also played a role.

Whether by design or default educational provision has also been shaped by the organisation and administration of the penal, the educational, and the welfare functions of the state. The distinction between offender and neglected child has arguably had less impact than the distance between educational practice in the secure estate and in the community which has continued to challenge the coherence, quality, and the contemporariness of educational provision in the secure estate.

The activity of teaching and learning in secure institutions has generated its own set of dynamics which has altered the profile of education in these settings too. With few exceptions since the 1850s, residential educational interventions have been overtly put to the purpose of individual reform and social control based on the premise that young people would become socially compliant through the disciplined experience of learning itself as well as through the acquisition of basic literacy, numeracy, and vocational skills for working class occupations. Young people's resistance to this social project has challenged and disrupted educational provision. Political and popular allegiances to educational approaches have shifted either when such resistance by young people has threatened the operation of the institution or when institutional controlling mechanisms become overly oppressive.

Two further social ideas about young offenders have arguably shaped the profile of education in secure accommodation. One is the assumption of the 'lesser eligibility' of young people in custody. Although no longer supported legislatively it has appeared tacitly in practice, in the gaps between educational and criminal justice policies, and in divisions in the management and administration of education within the secure estate. While the political rhetoric has changed to one of equal rights and entitlement, action to address these gaps in practice has been slow. The second is the contrastingly optimistic belief in the transformative potential of education. Whether through bible study, puppet shows, magic lantern talks, outward bound expeditions, or democratic practices the efforts and aspirations of pioneering practitioners have continued to receive popular and political support because they align with a core principle of the youth justice project in England and Wales: that there is potential for changing the young person and that the state can intervene to effect that change.

Notes

1 Editor's note: This chapter looks specifically at the history of secure custodial provision for young offenders. Please also refer to the previous chapter and subsequent chapters for more information about the different forms of provision, including secure mental health secure facilities and welfare secure accommodation.
2 In 1817 for example, Elizabeth Fry set up education classes for children imprisoned with their mothers in Newgate Gaol (see Cooper, 1981).
3 Reformatory schools preceded the introduction of universal education in 1870.

References

Board of Education (1921) *The teaching of English in England* [The Newbolt Report]. London: HM Stationery Office.
Bottoms, A.E. (1974) On the decriminalisation of the English juvenile courts. In R. Hood (Ed.) *Crime, criminology and public policy: Essays in Honour of Sir Leon Radzinowicz*. London: Heinemann.
Brehony, K.J. (2006) A new education for a new era: the contribution of the conferences of the New Education Fellowship to the disciplinary field of education 1921–1938. *Paedagogica Historica*, 40, 5–6, 733–755.
Buckley, D. (1912) Borstal – England. *Journal of Prison Discipline and Philanthropy*, 51, 24–28.
Bullock, R., Hosie, K., Little, M., and Millham, S. (1990) Secure accommodation for very difficult adolescents: some recent research findings. *Journal of Adolescence*, 13, 3, 205–216.

Carpenter, M. (1851) *Reformatory schools, for the children of the perishing and dangerous classes, and for juvenile offenders*. London: C. Gilpin.
Carlebach, J. (1970) *Caring for children in trouble*. Abingdon: Routledge.
Clarke, J. (2002) The three Rs – repression, rescue and rehabilitation: ideologies of control for working class youth. In J. Muncie, G. Hughes, and E. McLaughlin (Eds), *Youth justice: critical readings*. London: Sage. pp123–138.
Cooper, R.A. (1981) Jeremy Bentham, Elizabeth Fry, and English prison reform. *Journal of the History of Ideas*, 42, 4, 675–690.
Delap, L. (2018) 'Disgusting details which are best forgotten': disclosures of child sexual abuse in twentieth-century Britain. *Journal of British Studies*, 57, 1, 79–107.
Department of Education and Science. (1980) *Community homes with education: a survey of educational provision in 21 community homes with education on the premises (CHEs) in England and Wales 1978*. London: HMSO.
Genders, E., and Player, E. (1986) Women's imprisonment: the effects of youth custody. *British Journal of Criminology*, 26, 4, 357–371.
Gelsthorpe, L., and Worrall, A. (2009) Looking for trouble: a recent history of girls, young women and youth justice. *Youth Justice*, 9, 3, 209–223.
Gill, O. (1974) Residential treatment for young offenders: the boys' perspectives. *British Journal of Criminology*, 14, 4, 318–335.
Hagell, A., and Hazel, N. (2001) Macro and micro patterns in the development of secure custodial institutions for serious and persistent young offenders in England and Wales. *Youth Justice*, 1, 1, 3–16.
Hagell, A., Hazel, N., and Shaw, C. (2000) *Evaluation of Medway secure training centre*. London: Home Office.
Hansard, HL. Deb 01 May 1961 vol 230 c1155.
Hansard HC *Secure Colleges – Written Question*. c5710 (06 July 2015 WQ). Retrieved from: www.parliament.uk/business/publications/written-questions-answers-statements/written-question/Commons/2015-07-06/5710/.
Hayden, C. (2007). *Children in trouble: the role of families, schools and communities*. Basingstoke: Palgrave Macmillan.
Hoghughi, M.S. (1973) To the Editor. *International Journal of Offender Therapy and Comparative Criminology*, 17, 2, 173–177.
Home Office (1927) *Report of the Departmental Commission on the Treatment of Young Offenders* [The Moloney Report]. London: HMSO.
Home Office (1953) *Report of the Prison Commissioners for 1952* (Cmnd 8948). London: HMSO.
Home Office (1968). *Children in Trouble* (Cmnd. 3601). London: HMSO.
Hood, R.G. (1965). *Borstal re-assessed* (Vol. 20). London: Heinemann.
Hood, R.G., and Sparks, R.F. (1969) *Community homes and the approved school system*. Cambridge: University of Cambridge, Institute of Criminology.
House of Lords and House of Commons Joint Committee Report (2005) Human rights. Retrieved from: https://publications.parliament.uk/pa/jt200405/jtselect/jtrights/jtrights.htm
Humphries, S. (1981) *Hooligans or rebels?* Oxford: Blackwell.
Hurt, J. (1984) Reformatory and industrial schools before 1933. *History of Education*, 13, 1, 45–58.
Hyland, J. (1993) *Yesterday's answers: development and decline of schools for young offenders*. London: Whiting and Birch.
Jones, D. W. (2012) *Conditions for sustainable decarceration strategies for young offenders*. Doctoral dissertation, The London School of Economics and Political Science (LSE).

Johnson, R. (1970) Educational policy and social control in early Victorian England. *Past and Present*, 49, 96–119.

Lanskey, C. (2010) Citizenship education for young people in secure institutions in England and Wales. *Educação, Sociedade and Culturas*, 30, 41–56.

Lanskey, C. (2011) Promise or compromise? Education for young people in secure institutions in England. *Youth Justice Journal*, 11, 1, 47–60.

Lanskey, C. (2014) Up or down and out? A systemic analysis of young people's educational pathways in the youth justice system in England and Wales. *International Journal of Inclusive Education*, 19, 6, 568–582.

May, M. (1973) Innocence and experience: the evolution of the concept of juvenile delinquency in the mid nineteenth century. *Victorian Studies*, 17, 1, 7–29.

Milham, S., Bullock, T., and Hosie, K. (1978) *Locking up children: secure provision within the child care system.* Farnborough: Saxon House.

Ministry of Justice (2014) Transforming youth custody: government response to the consultation. London: Ministry of Justice. Retrieved from: www.gov.uk/government/uploads/system/uploads/attachment_data/file/273402/transforming-youth-custody-consultation-response.pdf.

Ministry of Justice (2017) *Young people (juvenile offenders)*. [Online]. Retrieved from: www.justice.gov.uk/offenders/types-of-offender/juveniles

Morris, T., Martin, J., Little, A. and H. M. (1960) The treatment of young offenders. *The British Journal of Delinquency*, 10, 3, 216–220.

Muncie, J. (1990) Failure never matters: detention centres and the politics of deterrence. *Critical Social Policy*, 10, 28, 53–66.

Newburn, T. (1996) Back to the future? Youth crime, youth justice and the rediscovery of authoritarian populism. In J. Pilcher and S. Wagg (Eds), *Thatcher's children? Politics, childhood and society in the 1980s and 1990s*. London: Falmer Press.

Office for Standards in Education, Children's Services and Skills (2010) *Transition through detention and custody: arrangements for learning and skills for young people in custodial or secure settings*. London: Ofsted.

Office for Standards in Education, Children's Services and Skills (2014) *Improving skills for vulnerable, disengaged young people*. London: Ofsted. Retrieved from: www.gov.uk/government/publications/improving-skills-for-vulnerabledisengaged-young-people.

Parker, R. (2016) Boys' bands in children's homes: a fragment of history. *Journal of Children's Services*, 11, 1, 73–84.

Radzinowicz, S. L., and Turner, J.C. (Eds). (1952) *Detention in remand homes: a report of the Cambridge Department of Criminal Science on the use of Section 54 of the Children and Young Persons Act 1933*. London: Macmillan.

Reformatory and Refuge School Union (1906) *Fifty years record of child saving and reformation work, 1856–1906*. Jubilee Report. London Reformatory and Refuge School Union.

Rose, G. (1967) *Schools for young offenders*. London: Tavistock.

Secure Training Centre (1998) Rules. Retrieved from: www.legislation.gov.uk/uksi/1998/472/contents/made

Simmons, M.M. (1946) *Making citizens: a review of the aims, methods and achievements of the approved schools in England and Wales*. London: HMSO.

Social Services Liaison Group. (1976) *Community homes with education: report of a working party*, Exeter: Association of Directors of Social Services.

Stack, J.A. (1994) Reformatory and industrial schools and the decline of child imprisonment in mid-Victorian England and Wales. *History of Education*, 23, 1, 59–73.

Stewart, G., and Tutt, N. (1987) *Children in custody*. Aldershot: Avebury.

Stratta, E. (1970) *The education of borstal boys*. Abingdon: Routledge.

Taylor, C. (2016) *Review of the youth justice system: an interim report of emerging findings*. London: MoJ.
The Children's Association (1922) *Boys and girls in borstal institutions. Letter to the editor. The Spectator*, 8 April. Retrieved from: http://archive.spectator.co.uk/article/8th-april-1922/10/boys-and-girls-in-borstal-institutions-to-the-edit
The Young Offender Institution Rules (1988) Young Offender Institutions, England and Wales (SI: 1988/1422). Retrieved from: www.legislation.gov.uk/uksi/1988/1422/made
Thornton, D., Curran, L., Grayson, D., and Holloway, V. (1984) *Tougher regimes in detention centres: report of an evaluation by the Young Offender Psychology Unit*. London: HMSO.
Tutt, N. (1981) A decade of policy. *The British Journal of Criminology*, 21, 3, 246–256.
Warder, J., and Wilson, R. (1973) The British borstal training system. *The Journal of Criminal Law and Criminology*, 64, 1, 118–127.
Wilde, O. (1897) 'The case of Warder Martin: some cruelties of prison life', letter to the editor. *The Daily Chronicle*, 28 May. Retrieved from: www.nationalarchives.gov.uk/education/prisoner4099/historical-background/transcript-letter.htm#part7
Wills, A. (2005) Delinquency, masculinity and citizenship in England 1950–1970. *Past and Present*, 187, 157–185.

PART II
Practice insights

3

SPECIALIST EDUCATION PROVISION WITHIN SECURE CAMHS UNITS

Faiza Ahmed

Education is an important part of self-development. Education helps to develop academic knowledge but also to develop personal skills, such as social skills or organisation skills that shape us as individuals. Access to education is a requirement for young people and children in alternative provision if education cannot be provided in partnership with mainstream schools, for example, in the case of a young person admitted to hospital for physical or mental health problems (Department of Education and Department of Health, 2015). This chapter will discuss how education is implemented in two inpatients CAMHS units in England (an acute unit and a medium secure unit). There is a discussion of the benefits of providing education whilst a young person is on an inpatient ward and the challenges of a specialist education provision.

All local education authorities have a statutory requirement to provide education provision for young people of compulsory school age who may not receive suitable education within a mainstream school. This may be in the form of a pupil referral unit or education on site within a secure provision, such as a children's home or secure hospital unit (Education Act, 1996). The Department for Education states that it is a compulsory requirement for all children to receive full time education from the ages of 5 to 16 years and they are required to receive up to 30 lessons a week. Post-16 learners are required to attend up to 15 lessons a week to be considered a full time learner in further education. If the learner has not achieved GCSEs in English and Maths they are required to complete these qualifications in post-16 education as an addition to 15 lessons a week.

The young people described in this chapter are from the two inpatient CAMHS units who attend one college with responsibility for the education of the young people in both units. The provision of a full time education is an essential aspect of care, treatment and recovery. Young people on both units have access to education that is on par with education they would receive within a mainstream school, for both pre- and post-16 learners.

Learners on the units

Each young person is different and unique. Most young people in the secure CAMHS settings have usually fallen out of education and are considered dis-effective learners who haven't necessarily had a positive experience of learning. Currently, the average age of learners across both units is 16 years. The longest a young person has missed education is six years (all of their secondary school education). The majority of the young people in both units have fallen out of education and are termed as NEAT (Not in Employment, Education, or Training). They may not have had the opportunity to undertake any GCSE course. That young people have not made educational progress or have deviated from usual educational pathways towards academic qualifications is unsurprising considering the length of missed education.

Nearly all young people on the unit have seen a significant family history of abuse, crime, violence, and substance misuse which has impacted on their engagement in education. The units can also have a mix of high flying engaged students who are meeting or exceeding national attainment levels at school but are suffering from mental health problems impacting on their education. Both units have had young people with ASD that have struggled in mainstream school with all the issues that ASD brings along with their mental health needs.

The education offer on the unit is secondary education focusing on core subjects of mathematics, English, and science. On the medium secure unit, young people are offered more practical subjects including catering and horticulture accredited by an awarding body in addition to core subjects. Post-16 learners who are in college are offered the opportunity to continue learning their chosen subject and teachers can be bought in to provide these specialist subjects or further training for teachers can be provided.

The stage the young person is at in their education will influence their education needs and the type of education timetable that can be offered. For young people who have fallen out of education, mathematics and English competencies are usually missing. Much of their missed education comes from embarrassment or underlying learning difficulties or learning preferences that haven't been picked up on. Also, a young person can be incredibly school phobic so, to meet their educational needs, the college might consider starting them on subjects they really enjoy and then build in other subjects.

The college aims to 'treat each learner as a young person who just has some additional needs rather than wrapping them in cotton wool' (college educator). To experience success, the young people have the opportunity to fail and challenging them is part of the college's philosophy. By doing so it supports the young person to complete their assessment or qualification and stretches them as individuals too.

Consideration of restricted patients and risk

Most young people admitted to an inpatient CAMHS unit are perceived to have a high risk to themselves (e.g. suicide risk) or to others where they are not able to be kept safe within the community. Some young people may be admitted informally (with a consideration of capacity) or under a section of the Mental Health Act (1983). The type of section depends on their reason for admission and route of admission. For example, a young person may be admitted on a section 2 for an assessment of mental state or a young person may be admitted on a section 37/41 where a hospital order is given by the Crown Court. Regardless of section, education will be provided to the young person but, due to differences in risk and restrictions, the type of educational package offered can differ and will relate to the individual needs, educational history, and specific interests of the young person.

All activities within a classroom have been assessed for risk. The teaching team at the college will compile a risk assessment in which they will list the types of activities they do, assess the potential risks and explain how they can mitigate the risk. The approach of the assessment is based on the viewpoint that 'this is the activity we are going to do, so how can we do this safely?' as opposed to 'can we do this activity or not?' The college uses a system called Team-Teach (see: www.teamteach.co.uk) which is about respect for each other and knowing your young person and their differences and the use of this approach to develop dynamic risk assessments. A multi-disciplinary team (MDT) approach is also implemented within the college to ensure educational activities are provided with the young person's risk and safety in mind.

Similarly, as well as considering restrictions and risk within the classroom environment, the college must consider implications in relation to educational visits. Having young people on certain sections does make educational visits much more challenging and does limit the types of visits that can be facilitated. The college uses an educational risk assessment completed online through the local authority for any visit outside of a two-mile radius from the unit. Educational visits are discussed with the hospital occupational therapists and organised to develop the young person's communication, personal, and behavioural skills. Examples of visits that the college have completed are: Yorkshire Sculpture Park, fishing, Affleck's Palace in Liverpool, and career fairs. Using an MDT approach has been successful in providing education packages that include the individual's mental health needs and taking account of the needs of being a young person.

How is information gathered when a young person is admitted?

Education

Education timetables within the units are matched to the individuals' mainstream school wherever possible. The education liaison officer would contact the young person's home school to obtain information about their current academic level, reports, and attendance. If the individual has not been in mainstream education, the college will try to contact the individual's parents, where possible, or the local authority if there is a current Education and Health Care Plan – EHCP (Department of Education and Department of Health, 2015), and also speak to the individual to find out when they last went to school, what went wrong, why they were excluded, and where did they go. Educational information about young people can also be collected through a system called the Fischer Family Trust – FFT (2001). The FFT stores data from previous key stages and provides information that would help to set targets or get an idea of the learner's academic ability. However, the majority of young people who are admitted to an inpatient ward are more than likely to be from a dysfunctional and chaotic family, so some learners may not be in the FFT database as they may have never been in one school long enough for a cycle of data collection to take place. Based on the information that is available, the foundation of the individual's education package is built looking at the individual capabilities and using individual assessments on mathematics and English (specifically reading and writing) to judge age appropriate levels.

Mental health

The education team utilises relevant information about a young person's mental health needs. Information on any index offences, risk of violence to themselves or others, and family history is required to ensure safeguarding during education activities. The information also gives insight into how they are likely to progress daily in college and their previous response to educational approaches which supports planning of future lessons. One member of the education team will attend the admission meeting and will be able to gather information that is relevant in relation to meeting the young person's education needs. In addition to this, the college may have already gathered information about capability, barriers to learning and social interactions which can be shared with the MDT and form part of the formulation (psychological assessment). The college also has one dedicated member of staff who has access to the Trust's patient record system and obtains information from clinical team meetings, psychology reports, risk formulations, and nursing notes to build an educational picture of the young person.

The following case study gives further insight into the process.

Case study

Patient 1 (age 14) and Patient 2 (age 16) were admitted to the medium secure unit. Both were of secondary school age and both patients had completed Key Stage 2 (primary school); however they had not been in the education system long enough for data to be collected. Typically, when a young person reaches secondary school they are set targets from the primary school data, but there was no data from even a first year in high school for these two patients, so the targets had to be based around them as 10-year-old children. To set the targets in a similar way to mainstream and in line with their peer group was very difficult because certain reports were below P-scales for patient 1 and entry level 2 for patient 2 and those levels would be expected for someone in primary school so there was a big void. Timetables were personalised to match what they would do in mainstream according to their age but delivered in a format for a 10-year-old child with the aim to build this up to match their peer group age so that their pathway out would be to get back into education. Both patients showed significant improvements in their attendance to the college, attending more vocational subjects and tying this in with leave out of the hospital.

A multi-disciplinary approach

The college use an effective multi-disciplinary approach to the young person's mental health as well as their education. The college staff will regularly attend ward reviews, care programme approach (CPA) meetings, and other professional meetings to give information about a young person as well as receive updated information that might indicate a change in the young person's education needs. The MDT provides information about any barriers to learning and a forum to ask questions around how the young person's clinical presentation will impact on their learning at the college and how to plan the individual's timetable to incorporate education. The MDT is also important in relation to risk as the college can effectively manage risk assessments with a broader viewpoint when deciding on new activities and educational visits. The MDT is also able to liaise with the college team for input into the young person's mental health. The college can provide information on attendance, academic ability, interactions with staff and peers, and progress which incorporate a holistic approach of looking at the young person.

The college environment

The vision is that education is parallel, and similar, to local authority education; however, this is not always possible due to resource availability. Within the college, and across both units, there is a small group of teaching staff who, like in mainstream schools, all are of qualified teacher status and can teach a wide range of subject areas up to A-level. However, the number of resources available and dedicated subject rooms are limited to those considered to be a low risk and easy to monitor.

The college has been set up to mirror the type of classroom or educational environment that an individual would experience within a mainstream school. There are noticeboards across the college units showcasing the work students have achieved and classrooms are set up with the typical arrangement of tables, books, and resources.

Due to factors, such as risk, there are certain security needs that must be met. The number of resources accessible within a classroom is limited and locked away and this can make lessons more challenging as resources are not readily available and to hand. To keep the college environment safe, advice is provided by the clinical staff, for example, not having pencil sharpeners readily available which is different to a mainstream school where something like a pencil sharpener might be considered relatively 'safe'. Other item restrictions include spiral bound books, blu-tac, or any other items contraband on the ward. Defining what a 'safe classroom' looks like on the unit can be challenging but using the expertise of the nursing team, and involving them in looking at the classroom environment and providing advice on safety, can ensure that the classroom is continually monitored and assessed in light of changing risk and needs of the individual and particular cohorts of young people.

All young people benefit from a vibrant educational atmosphere which is gentle yet purposeful, for example, you might go into classrooms where there might be a little bit of music on in the background and people might be chatting, but the work is being done. One young person mentioned that the college is 'hitting the spot' for them whereas at their previous college, which was in a similar setting, they said, 'all the staff were too nice and everything was really quiet and everyone talked really quietly to each other but it was like being in a library'.

There are good educational reasons for assessing the classroom environment specifically for young people with ASD. Having ASD-friendly rooms that are less cluttered will help with security and help those young people settle in too.

The importance of routine

Routines are a high priority for young people on the unit as, often, there has not been any routine or structure for the young person. The timetable is set up in similar form to mainstream school or college. In the *medium secure unit*, the day starts with activity time in the morning. The nursing team are involved in assisted daily living activities which is about developing a routine in the morning of getting up, having a shower and getting ready for the day. The college day starts at 10am, running until 3pm, with a break and lunch. In the *acute unit,* the college routine begins at 9am with a 15 minute 'plan your day' meeting, which is intended to be a multi-disciplinary meeting and involves setting out the expectations for the young person and considering any clinical appointment, leave, or visits that day so that both the education team and MDT are mutually aware and informed to support the young person fully with their personal routine. Young people will then have lessons from 9:15 to 3pm, including breaks and lunch.

Lessons are structured and timed using the SIMS structure (see: Capita-Sims, 2017). Using this software, personalised educational packages are then built and developed into a timetable to suit the young person's needs. Breaks are arranged within college as, previously, when young people went back onto the ward, they would be less likely to go back to college and continue with lessons. Young people are provided with lunch on the ward.

Keeping young people safe when using the internet

With advances in technology and the increased reliance on the internet and developments of social media, young people are more vulnerable to the dangers of the internet, for example, exploitation or grooming (Campbell, 2017). As with any school, it has become extremely important to ensure that young people have access to the internet but are kept safe. To maintain internet security, the college staff receive regular internet security training. In addition, the college uses a secure system called E-safe which tracks every key stroke that every user makes on the system whether this is on a webpage or a Word document. If there is anything that the system identifies as a concern, the SLT (senior leadership team) will get an email from E-safe with information about what was inputted, which day, which computer, and by which person. This information is then followed up with an intervention with the young person to gain further information. The E-safe system also has a category filter so anything that has been identified by E-safe as being pornography, violent, gambling, or shopping is automatically blocked. As the internet is constantly changing and new webpages are being added daily, the college can create their own black list, and individual URLs can be added by the college.

Acknowledging learning preferences

Learning preferences are important in supporting individual to learn, whether this is in mainstream education or in a specialist education provision. The learning and teaching preference information ('learning styles') for young people on the unit is identified via an information gathering process for the EHCP. Typically, on the units, most young people have a similar profile of not liking activities involving writing, reading, or mathematics; often, this is an avoidance rather than a specific learning difficulty. The EHCP can also be useful for gathering information about already diagnosed difficulties, for example dyslexia.

Teacher judgement is involved in identifying learning styles. Although the application of the theory of learning preferences can be a valuable tool, well-planned and differentiated lessons with interesting and engaging resources will meet different learning preferences. A report by the Sutton Trust (2014) identified the key factors that are important in teaching practices to be successful. The idea of identifying learning preferences was not considered as important as other aspects. In the Sutton Trust report, having a good reward system, teacher credibility in relation to subject knowledge, clear boundaries and instructions, effective behaviour management strategies, and good teacher–pupil relationships were considered more important than teaching to learner preferences. As the young people on both units are not typically from mainstream education, teachers need to be prepared to change their lesson plan constantly because the young person might have fluctuating or depressed mental state/mood, or certain medications may be affecting their performance on the day, and so knowing what needs be achieved in the lesson and using the Team-Teach (2016) approach is seen as more important than focusing on pre-defined learning preferences.

Accessing the curriculum

The National Curriculum (Department for Education, 2014) sets out the framework for study and targets for children and young people up to Key Stage 4 and must be followed by all local authority run schools nationally. The college, as a specialist education provision, is not legally required to follow the national curriculum. However, to maintain continuity for the young people, by aligning with the way they are used to thinking about education and considering their destinations outside of the unit, the college does follow the national curriculum to maintain this consistency. Right from the start, from their admission to the unit, the young person and the team around them will be thinking about the next steps for when they leave the college, and goal setting for educational attainment leading to employment is key to forward planning.

In the past, the primary focus at the college, as with other secure provisions, was health and wellbeing rather than education. Often, young people were given work that didn't match their abilities and there was a strong focus on entry level certificates. Some young people who regularly attended an education programme may have already, for example, been doing their A-levels in Mathematics and were targeted an A* Mathematics by their schools but when they were admitted would have an automatic target of entry level mathematics which will not have matched their current education level and attainment. There was also a stronger focus on activities to help young people get into routines rather than focusing on precise education outcomes. The college has upgraded the education programme to make sure that the national curriculum is accessed to support the young person reach *their* potential with parity to if they were learning in mainstream education. Unfortunately, accessing the national curriculum is not appropriate in all cases as the main educational package for some inpatients, particularly for young people identified as NEAT. Through identifying knowledge and skills deficits (usually in English and mathematics), the college often works first on functional skills, such as offering vocational courses or work experience opportunities (for example, the college have successfully provided young people with work experience opportunities within the hospital trust). The education 'package' the college now provides is individualised to include the national curriculum, where possible, and non-curriculum activities with the aspiration of aligning the experiences with an educational offer they would receive in mainstream education.

Personal, social, health, and economic (PSHE) education is an aspect of the national curriculum that is implemented within the college, following the AQA guidelines and providing young people with a GCSE in PSHE. Sessions are delivered by teachers or external professionals. PSHE is taught through a topic-based approach. PSHE topics include British values, radicalisation, child sex exploitation (CSE), charity, careers, and mindfulness. However, as this teaching takes place in an inpatient setting, the education team need to work closely with the MDT and be broadly aware of the triggers and challenges beforehand and will be sensitive to how an individual may respond to the topics and will tailor the teaching accordingly.

Case study

The college were going to deliver a PSHE lesson on child sex exploitation (CSE), specifically for a young person who was on the ward that was at risk of CSE. Using an MDT approach, the college liaised with the inpatient clinical psychologist and nurse in charge and a support worker was made available to sit in the session with the young person. The young person engaged well until the last ten minutes when they left quietly as they couldn't manage and were then provided with emotional support by the MDT.

Inspection and regulation

The Office for Standards in Education, Children's Services, and Skills (Ofsted) role is to inspect and regulate services that care for children and young people, and services providing education and skills for learners of all ages (Ofsted, 2014). Specialist education provisions are also inspected by Ofsted. There is no difference in the criteria Ofsted will use to assess a mainstream school and the special education provision within a secure unit, and with no obligation to recognise that the college is working with young people with mental health difficulties.

The Ofsted inspection process has limitations in the secure context. Firstly, Ofsted inspections in a mainstream school are very different to a specialist provision. Mainstream schools are more aware when an inspection is going to happen as they occur regularly, whereas Ofsted inspections are more unpredictable in an inpatient education provision, and length of the inspections can vary. Furthermore, within a mainstream school the cohort of young people starting in Year 7 is usually the same up until Year 11 and so it is much easier to track progress and put things in place. On the units, however, the cohort of young people constantly changes. The average stay on the acute unit is around eight weeks and the college need to be able to demonstrate progress across at least eight weeks to Ofsted. The majority of young people on the unit have missed a considerable amount of education and are therefore not part of the national statistics but are judged based on national expectations. Attendance and progress are judged the same as in mainstream. In reality, attendance and progress for young people on the unit is inextricably linked to their current mental health state, stability, and medication. For the college to be able to show progress in attendance to Ofsted, bespoke timetables and expectational attendance targets set by the consultant are used instead.

Use of a set timetable and expecting the young person to turn up to college as they would in mainstream is not practical for inpatients. The disruption that happens or the amount of intensive nursing or medication changes the individual has means that attendance changes daily. A young person might attend 25 lessons one week and only ten lessons the following week. The college share this information alongside a pupil survey about their wellbeing with Ofsted.

The college uses a process of tracking at four points per year. Targets are set at these points, informed by assessments made, to see if the young person is on target, below target, or above target. In the acute unit the young people also have weekly assessments using TAPS (Primary Science Teaching Trust, 2017) which tracks a pupil's attitude to task, adult, peer, and self. Every week all teachers make a short note about how the young person has performed in their lessons and they give TAPS figures, which are aggregated into an average and used to track progress for the week. If a young person's progress is consistently low then the college is able to undertake interventions or, if they have been performing well and there is a sudden drop, then this would be a cause of concern, which can be shared with the MDT. The college also uses data available from the FFT to set 'aspirational' targets but given the fact that some young people on the ward have had quite chaotic lives or they have been really poorly, using the expected target from the FFT data may or may not be useful or appropriate. The information from tracking can be used to report on progress to Ofsted.

The college uses a process of self-evaluation to outline the college perspective on their education service provision. Ofsted now use self-evaluation forms and inspect the college to see whether they agree with the self-evaluations or not. The college makes assumptions that Ofsted teams are consistent and hope that whoever does the inspection has expertise in their special education context, but unfortunately this isn't always the case.

Engaging learners

Engagement is an ongoing challenge for the college team on the unit. Many young people come from very dysfunctional backgrounds where education was probably not on the list of priorities for them or their parents, or they may have really struggled in education and so they disengage to avoid feeling embarrassment. The view is that each young person is capable but, due to their earlier life experiences, it is likely that they will think they are not.

The college use an integrated approach to encourage engagement. The teaching team will visit the ward daily to encourage young people in their education, for example, singing outside a young person's room to wake them up and get them moving! The college will regularly meet with young people who are not engaging in education to try to identify the reasons for this and, consequently, tailor the young person's timetable to make it more appealing. Persistence is key. Talking to the young people and saying 'are you coming to college today?' but not forcing them to turn up prompts responsibility for attending rather than feeding the 'refusal thrill'. If young people see others taking part, they are more likely to attend (especially if this person is viewed by others as the 'group leader').

As part of the MDT process, specifically on the medium secure unit, young people's educational progress can impact on their therapeutic rewards, for example, if a young person engages in education then they will be provided with more therapeutic leave. It is important to break any 'negative' view of engagement that some young people have derived from their mainstream education.

Managing challenging behaviour

The college uses the Team-Teach principles to manage challenging behaviour. The Team-Teach principles state that knowing your young people, noticing little changes in their behaviour, and being able to recognise triggers can allow for short, quick interventions to take place. Relational 'security training' is also provided by the Trust about the process of de-escalation to be able to maintain physical safety for everyone in the college environment. The college staff can communicate with the ward team via radio if they feel a young person's behaviour is becoming too challenging to manage by themselves. All teachers will wear an alarm that is connected to a central hub to enable instant response by staff colleagues if needed.

The college have a restorative discussion policy, so if young people are disrespectful or abusive towards staff, they will require the young person to go away and think about their actions and they will be expected to then enter a mediation process which includes the staff member and young person and selected support staff to talk through things.

Case study

Patient 3 started education on the unit, really enjoyed it, and had good relationships with staff; however over time he became very difficult to manage and became disruptive in class, abusive towards staff and very hostile. Working with the psychology team, the student and the college team developed a safety plan support him to manage his behaviour. The safety plan was effective and worked well in being able to manage his behaviour because, for example, if he was starting to 'bubble up', instead of sending him back to the ward or making him continue, he would be given five minutes away from the situation and then brought back.

Use of rewards

Young people on the unit are always praised for attending lessons and engaging in their education. Phone calls and postcards home about progress, certificates, end of term events, or takeaways or shower gels are provided as rewards. Young people are rewarded with 'student of the week' if they have met or exceeded their expected attendance target for the week. The rewards also form part of an incentive that is linked with the unit, so if a young person gets 85% attendance or more every week, money is provided towards a weekend treat for the young person.

Partnership with parent/carer

Being able to communicate information to parents/carers is not as straightforward as it would be within a mainstream school. In a mainstream school parents/carer would be invited to attend parent teacher meetings, school events, and fairs and would usually attend. The challenge for some young people within the unit is that they often come from very dysfunctional families, are looked after children, or on child protection plans so parents/carers are probably very 'out of touch' with their child's education and so would be less likely to have interest with their child's education when they are on the unit. Furthermore, specifically in the medium secure unit, many of the young people are from various parts of the country, so parents being able to attend every meeting or be fully involved can prove to be quite challenging.

The college makes every effort to ensure that parent/carers are involved in their child's education, if appropriate. Parents/carers would be contacted during their child's admission by the education team to explain the education offered on the unit and to 'touch base'. The college regularly send out progress reports, praise post cards, and invitations to parent/carer events so they can feel involved in their child's care and education whilst away from the home environment. The college hosts up to three celebration events at the end of each term where parents can come in to celebrate the young person's success. Parents of young people in the acute unit are often familiar with working in partnership with education staff and they are used to attending parents evening or speaking to school. In this case, in so far as is possible, the usual partnership is replicated. With young people on the medium secure unit, in most cases, there is typically family dysfunction and so, if parental involvement was not already occurring in the community, it is not expected whilst the young person is on the unit; however, partnerships with parents may still occur on an ad hoc and individual basis.

Governance

School governance is an important part of any education provision. A governing body allows collaborative working, ensures that the educational needs are met for each child and holds the head teacher to account for the school's performance and ensuring the school budget is properly managed (Department for Education, 2017). Governance is incredibly important to the college. The college regularly works with the governing body to ensure that the college is meeting the Ofsted criteria and regularly providing feedback to the senior leadership team (SLT), for example, the head teacher will be open to 'on the spot' grilling about leadership, current issues, and where the college see themselves in the future.

The governance panel consists of the head, the chair of governors, a student governor, a link governor for parents, health governor, school governor, and voluntary governors who are normally individuals from the community. Each governor has a specific role, including; managing finance, reviews, setting appraisal targets, post-16 learners, learner outcomes, leadership and management, personal development, welfare, and behaviour, which par with the Ofsted criteria. The governing body set targets for the SLT and appraisal targets linked to the school improvement plan and self-evaluation forms. The governance panel link with the MDT by ensuring that health governors on the panel include ward managers and operation and strategic managers so that the education system combines both the young person's education and mental health needs effectively.

The college is funded via the local authority for each bed per year, not each learner. This can make it challenging to stretch funding when the unit may have up to 130 admissions in a year, but the college is only funded for 30 beds. The local authority will obtain funds from young people's 'home' local authority. As with any school, the vast majority of funds go on staff salary. For the college, the funding is also used for leasing the building, maintenance costs, staff CPD, training, staff cover, and resources.

The college conduct many fundraising events. In a mainstream school fundraising events would be organised by the parent-teacher associations; however, due to the challenges around some of the young people, being able to run a similar system would be difficult. Therefore, fundraising events are planned by young people and ward staff together in the similar way to a parent-teacher association. The college aim to organise six events each year, three to raise money for charity and three for the student fund. Young people are heavily involved in deciding which charities to raise money for and the ideas for events to run which will depend on which ones they most identify with. Charities that the young people have been involved in raising funds for in the past include Macmillan, Red Nose Day, and a local hospice. Fundraising events across the wards have included a summer BBQ, afternoon tea, and Christmas fairs. The student funds are used to buy things for young people, such as a reward meal or Christmas presents. The fundraising events are developed to support young people develop their personal and social skills, such as communicating with other people, organisation, team working, manners, and handling money which are viewed as equally important to academic skills.

Case study

Italian night on the medium secure unit

This was an event hosted by the unit, to raise money for the student fund. Each young person on the unit was responsible for their own dish, including the preparation, presentation, and service. Each young person was responsible for setting up tables, handling money, receiving orders, and overall running of the event. The event involved some risk items, such as metal cutlery which some of the young people had not seen for a long time due to their own risk, and being responsible for handling money. The event received positive feedback from everyone who attended, and the young people are keen to run similar events in the future.

The college head teacher is the Designated Safeguarding Lead, and there is a Designated Deputy Safeguarding Lead for both units (the deputy head teachers). All staff are fully trained up to Level Three for safeguarding children which is updated regularly.

The Local Authority Designated Officer (LADO) is contacted for any safeguarding concerns, and the appropriate hospital safeguarding leads are informed too. The procedure for reporting safeguarding issues involves writing a 'notice of concern' which is placed in a lockable safe and completed electronically on a tracking system provided by the local authority to ensure safeguarding concerns are followed up.

The college follows the same guidelines and principles set out for any mainstream school as indicated by the Department for Education. This also includes the

SEND code of practice which set outs the minimum requirements for delivering education within a hospital setting (Department for Education, 2015).

Managing discharge transitions for young people

For young people, the college aims to provide education that matches their attainment and education to ensure smoother transitions for the young person to be able to pick up their education in their usual school when they return to home ('home school'). However, in some cases, specifically for young people with no educational background or due to their mental health and wellbeing, bespoke timetables can be offered that include more vocational subjects instead. The ability to deviate from mainstream curriculum guidelines is important and can help to be able to capitalise on individual interests and focus on where progress is happening for the young person, even if they are just turning up to college.

Throughout the young person's stay in the unit, the college will have regular contact with the home school (the education setting the young person has come from and is likely to return to), to update on progress but also to start putting together an educational package that can be used by a young person's home school when they are discharged. Educational information that is provided at discharge will very much depend on where the young person is being discharged to, if they are pre-16 or post-16 learners and how much information is available and the extent to which the young person engaged with education. For young people who have reached 18 years, the situation is slightly different. Adult courses are not funded. However, if the young person has an EHCP this will provide financial support through to the age of 25 for continuing into education.

The college provides information on completed work and assessments or qualifications obtained, progress reports and a case study about each young person, including the barriers they had to education and the interventions the college has put in place to manage these. Information about any successes in accreditation and academia, their wellbeing, attendance, and evaluation reports will be provided for the new setting.

Young people on the medium secure unit who are transitioning back into the community with a limited education background are supported via the Ministry of Justice who allow the young person to develop links with colleges, career fairs, obtain work experience, do site visit taster days to be able to make some links for when they have been discharged, which is helpful if the young person has not been used to a mainstream college environment before. The college aims for a seamless transition into mainstream, linking with social workers and YOT services (if applicable).

Some young people may not have any education provision in place near discharge and this could be for such reasons as: the home school may not be able to support their needs, they are post-16, or have not secured a college placement. The college will work with the young person's local authority and education liaison officers, as the compulsory responsibility is to ensure that the young person has an offer of education provision. The college is time limited in what they can provide when the young person is discharged as their education with the college will cease and so making sure that plans are in place before discharge (and being aware if home schools have concerns about a young person's return) sooner is crucial to ensuring that the young person's continued education is enabled.

Conclusion

Education is considered an important part of a young person's therapeutic package on both units. The education that young people receive on the units is provided in parallel to the education they would receive in the community with a focus on ensuring that the young person has a streamlined transition back into mainstream education when and where possible.

Engagement is considered the biggest challenge for the college, specifically for young people who haven't had the best experience of mainstream education. The college benefits from being able to offer smaller classrooms and 1:1 support for young people which allows them to overcome obstacles which made them previously 'fall out' of the system and supports them to build their confidence and enable a positive healthy future.

Being a specialist provision, the college can deviate from the guidelines set by the Department for Education and so are able to provide bespoke educational packages to young people. However, even though the college is providing education to young people with mental health needs, they continue to be assessed using the same Ofsted framework for a mainstream school. Due to constantly changing cohorts on the unit and changes to mental health, this adds complexity and presents a significant barrier to effective reporting to Ofsted, and this remains a core discrepancy between the college and mainstream settings. Thus, for the future, there needs to be greater recognition of the value, purpose and practice of education in secure units for young people and more consideration of the essential differences and challenges (detailed in this chapter) of specialist education provision within secure CAMHS units compared to mainstream settings.

Acknowledgements

Acknowledgement for contributions to this chapter: David King and Paul O'Reilly.

References

Campbell, D. (2017) Facebook and Twitter 'harm young people's mental health'. *The Guardian* [online], 19 May. Retrieved from: www.theguardian.com/society/2017/may/19/popular-social-media-sites-harm-young-peoples-mental-health

Capita-Sims Website (2017) *SIMS management information systems from Capita SIMS*. Retrieved from: www.capita-sims.co.uk/

Department for Education (2014) *The national curriculum for England*. London: DfE. Retrieved from: www.gov.uk/government/collections/national-curriculum

Department for Education (2017) *The constitution of governing bodies of maintained schools. Statuary guidance for governing bodies of maintained schools and local authorities in England*. London: DfE. Retrieved from: www.gov.uk/government/uploads/system/uploads/attachment_data/file/640562/The_constitution_of_governing_bodies_of_maintained_schools_2017.pdf

Department for EducationandDepartment of Health (2015) *Special educational needs and disability code of practice: 0 to 25 years* (Statutory Guidance). London: DfE/DoH. Retrieved from: www.gov.uk/government/uploads/system/uploads/attachment_data/file/398815/SEND_Code_of_Practice_January_2015.pdf

Education Act 1996, c.56. Available at www.legislation.gov.uk/ukpga/1996/56/section/19

Fischer Family Trust (2001) *Education Analysis and Research-FFT*. Retrieved from: https://fft.org.uk/

Mental Health Act 1983. Available at www.legislation.gov.uk/ukpga/1983/20/section/2

Office for Standards in Education, Children's Services and Skills (2014) *Raising standards, improving lives: the Office for Standards in Education, Children's Services and Skills. Strategic plan 2014 to 2016*. London: Ofsted. Retrieved from: www.gov.uk/government/uploads/system/uploads/attachment_data/file/379920/OfSted_20Strategic_20Plan_202014-16.pdf

Primary Science Teaching Trust (2017) Teaching assessment in primary science. Retrieved from: https://pstt.org.uk/resources/curriculum-materials/assessment

The Sutton Trust (2014) Many popular teaching practices are ineffective, warns new Sutton report. Retrieved from: www.suttontrust.com/newsarchive/many-popular-teaching-practices-are-ineffective-warns-new-sutton-trust-report/

Team-Teach (2016) *About Team-Teach*. Retrieved from: www.teamteach.co.uk/

4

ROLES AND RELATIONSHIPS OF CARE AND EDUCATION STAFF INSIDE A SECURE CHILDREN'S HOME

Caroline Andow

> just the same as you know, you would want the ideal parent to be ringing up saying, 'just to make you aware that so and so might be a bit of a problem today because of this, that and the other'... the more that we can actually cause that triangular, putting the young person at the centre with education and care working hand in hand, the best chance the young person has got at succeeding. I know it's a bit more difficult because obviously with the care being in shifts and there is going to be sometimes a little bit of breakdown in communication, but if we're all singing from the same song sheet ...
>
> *(Malcolm, Head of Education)*

This chapter looks at the roles and relationships of education and care staff in a secure children's home (SCH) in England. The focus is on how the staff in these groups are organised, what they do, how they present themselves, and how they interact. Analysis of interactions and experiences has revealed tensions and a lack of communication between the education and care staff following the introduction of 'teaching assistants'. The main contention is about who is responsible for delivering education when young people are excluded from lessons. The insights provided in this chapter go some way towards filling the gaps identified in the literature, and should be of interest to students, academics, policy-makers, and practitioners working in, or with an interest in, secure settings.

Education inside secure children's homes

SCHs are locked institutions, catering for young people aged between 10[1] and 17[2] who have been deprived of their liberty. They are registered children's homes that form one part of the secure estate[3] in England and Wales. SCHs are unique in this estate in that they can accommodate young people perceived to pose a risk to themselves – under Section 25 of the Children Act 1989 ('welfare' placements) – alongside young people who have been charged with, or convicted of, an offence ('justice' placements). SCHs have therefore been described as 'both incarceration and an alternative to incarceration, a form of control imposed in order that care can be provided' (Harris and Timms, 1993: 4). Over time, SCHs have reduced in number and some have chosen to specialise by providing only welfare or justice placements. As of 31 March 2016, there were 15 SCHs in England and Wales; six accommodating both types of placements, seven accommodating welfare placements only, and two providing justice placements only.

SCHs are not standardised institutions, but rather they vary according to local authority practices (Rose, 2014). This chapter draws on data generated through 396 hours of in-depth participant observation and 38 semi-structured interviews with staff (24) and young people (14) inside one SCH in England between January and July 2014.[4] I visited the SCH at different times of day and on different days of the week, in order to build a comprehensive understanding of the setting. Details of the SCH that acted as the case in the study are withheld to protect the anonymity of the institution.

In the SCH, a part of the main building was colloquially referred to, by the staff and young people, as 'education'. This area was separate from the residential 'units'. There were many similarities between education inside the SCH and what one might expect to find in mainstream school. There were several classrooms,[5] an art room, a woodwork room, a large sports hall, and a central staff room. The school day ran from 9am to 3.15pm, Monday to Friday, and term dates were in line with those of the schools within the same local authority. Finally, following a change just prior to my arrival, the young people all wore school uniforms, albeit in various modified ways. However, there were also many contrasts between education inside the SCH and mainstream school practices. Significantly, all the doors within 'education' – and the secure area of the SCH – were kept locked. Staff carried keys, and the young people's movements required staff accompaniment at all times. Further, the windows did not open – to prevent absconding – and there were no toilet seats, because 'anything that is removable can be used as a weapon' (Patrick, Junior Care Staff).

Moreover, classes were very small, with a maximum of four young people, with one 'teacher' and one 'teaching assistant'. Young people were allocated into 'sets' depending on their ability and maturity, rather than age. Further, the young people were allowed to request 'time outs' during the lessons, which meant leaving the classroom with a teaching assistant to go for a walk if they were feeling frustrated. The maximum number of 'time outs' was normally three per day but could be increased according to a young person's needs. Further, a rewards system was in place, with points and raffle tickets awarded for good behaviour. The raffle was drawn during assembly, in the last lesson on a Friday afternoon, and the title of 'Student of the Week' was given to the young person who had achieved the highest number of points. Points were converted into cash rewards, which worked as a good incentive for the young people. Aaron, a young man on a justice placement, described this system by saying 'you're getting paid for technically going to school'. In contrast, young people that misbehaved were excluded from education for a period of time. Unlike in mainstream school, in this circumstance the young person was returned to the residential unit, not home.

Developing knowledge about staff inside secure children's homes

Little is known about the staff who work inside SCHs in England because the literature has focused primarily on the experiences of young people (O'Neill, 2001; Goldson, 2002; Ofsted, 2009; Ellis, 2012). Indeed, gaining a sense of how education and care staff present themselves and interact in this type of setting is much like trying to complete a jigsaw using pieces drawn from other puzzles. Ellis' (2012) research provides the most pieces, even though her study – also a case study of a SCH in England undertaken as doctoral research – focused on the experiences of girls. Within this, Ellis revealed that the staff did not wear a uniform, but she did not elaborate as to how the staff dressed, or whether style of dress differed according to role. Further, Ellis said that the staff appeared to the young people only in 'work mode' (2012: 155), with a 'professional demeanour' (2012: 157), but without defining her use of these terms.

In a discussion of the character of interactions between the staff and young people, Ellis suggested that while staff maintained professional boundaries with the young people in their interactions, relationships were closer than might normally be associated between a professional and a young person, because of the amount of time spent in close confinement. Ellis (2012) drew on Hochschild's (2012) notion of 'emotional labour' to describe how staff in SCHs are required – paid even – to display caring emotions. Ellis found that staff differed as to how far they engaged in such 'surface acting' (Hochschild, 2012: 33), identifying themselves either as carers or prison guards.

Knowledge about interactions between staff members in SCHs can only be drawn from two studies, both of which also focused primarily young people's experiences (O'Neill, 2001; Barry and Moodie, 2008). These studies described inconsistencies, especially around the enforcement of sanctions and rules, leading to confusion and uncertainty for the young people. What is missing from all of these studies however is an exploration of differences between staff. Instead, the staff are constructed as a homogenous group.

In this chapter, concepts from Goffman's dramaturgical perspective as outlined in *Presentation of Self* (1959) are used to conceive of the staff as 'actors' playing different 'parts' in a 'performance' that takes place for the 'audience' of young people. Attention is drawn to how the staff signalled the part they played through their 'front'. Goffman (1959) described two aspects of 'front'. The first he called the 'setting', which he defined as 'involving furniture, decor, physical layout, and other background items which supply the scenery and stage props for the spate of human action played out before, within or upon it' (1959: 32–33). This draws attention to the construction of the stage upon which the actor performs.

The second, 'personal front', Goffman defined as 'items that we most intimately identify with the performer himself and that we naturally expect will follow the performer wherever he goes' (1959: 32–35). Goffman referred to different 'sign vehicles', such as clothing, that convey information about 'personal front' (1959: 34). Goffman further distinguished between two aspects of the personal front; 'appearance' and 'manner' (1959: 34–35). The former includes information intended to convey social status, while the latter 'may be taken to refer to those stimuli which function at the time to warn us of the interaction role the performer will expect to play in the oncoming situation' (1959: 35).

According to Goffman:

> a given social front tends to become institutionalized in terms of the abstract stereotyped expectations to which it gives rise, and tends to take on a meaning and stability apart from the specific tasks which happen at the time to be performed in its name. The front becomes a 'collective representation' and a fact in its own right.
>
> *(Goffman, 1959: 37)*

Goffman's concept of 'collective representation' encourages an analysis of how the staff in different roles inside the SCH presented themselves.

Family staff and education staff

The staff in the SCH studied can be thought of as representing key institutional spheres in young people's lives – family (care staff), education (teaching staff), health (nurse and psychology team), and authority (managers). This conceptualisation fits with the aspiration for SCHs to provide 'wrap-around support' in an environment concerned with the holistic wellbeing of the young person (Secure Accommodation Network 2014: 4). This chapter focuses on the family and education staff; those who spent the most time working directly with the young people.

Family staff

The family staff include 'parents' (junior care staff) and 'grandparents' (senior care staff). The Head of Care is a management position, and therefore within the authority sphere in this analogy.

'Parents'

The role played by the junior care staff closely resembles the role typically associated with parents in the domestic sphere. The junior care staff looked after the young people day-to-day: from doing domestic chores, to spending time talking with them, and participating in activities. Members of this staff group woke the young people in the mornings and were responsible for enforcing bedtimes. The junior care staff were also tasked with managing the behaviour of the group of young people, resolving tensions and encouraging pro-social behaviours, like parents of siblings.

The junior care staff can be conceived of as performing their roles on the 'residential set' (Goffman, 1959). This setting provides the 'scenery and stage props' which supports this notion of the care staff as performing parenting roles (Goffman 1959: 32). For example, the junior care staff relaxed with the young people on sofas in the lounge in front of the television, they served meals in the fully equipped kitchen, and they ate with the young people at tables in the dining room.

In terms of 'personal front', the appearance of the junior care staff also resembled that of parents in a domestic setting. These staff dressed casually, with some distinction in terms of gender; the men wore jeans or tracksuit bottoms with t-shirts and sweatshirts; the women wore jeans or leggings, with blouses and/or cardigans. All wore casual shoes; generally, trainers for the men, and trainers or flat boots for the women. There was some prescription; hooded tops and scarves were prohibited, in case a young person attempted to restrict a member of staff's vision, strangle them, or remove the scarf to later use as a ligature. Also, skirts and dresses – which could cause embarrassment in the case of the restraint of a young person – and long earrings and necklaces – which could be pulled at – were not allowed.

Finally, in terms of 'manner', the junior care staff were very informal in their interactions. Like all the staff at the SCH, they addressed each other using first names. The junior care staff generally presented themselves as friendly and approachable and were typically very tactile in their interactions with the young people.

Several of the junior care staff themselves used the analogy of a 'parent' to describe how they experienced their roles. For example, Trev said in his interview 'you like to think that you can fill a parenting role'. Similarly, Theo, again in the context of an interview, said 'a lot of these young people see us in a parenting role'. Cyrus described in his interview how his interaction with the young people was framed by his perspective that his role was to be like a parent:

> These kids sometimes they look at you and ... because you've challenged them, and then you might have challenged them again, and then challenged them again, then it's a 'You don't like me, you don't like me'. It's not, it's not about that. It's about 'You're doing something wrong and I'm challenging it. I have to be like your parent in here.'

At the same time, Phil recognised constraints on enacting a parenting role fully within this type of institutional environment. In his interview Phil said, 'I mean we're meant to be in parenting roles but if I used to misbehave at home I'd get grounded and you can't really use grounded as a thing here because obviously they can't go anywhere anyway.'

The junior care staff were also perceived by others as fulfilling a parenting role. Rhianna – a very slight young woman soon to be leaving Woodside having served a three-month justice placement – said in her interview, 'I've got parents here that I call 'Mum' and 'Dad''. Similarly, Reika, another justice placement, was really upset with herself after she punched Fred, a member of the junior care staff, in the stomach, because she thought of him as her 'second dad' (20.02.15).[6] For Sean, the Head of Care, the role of the care staff was 'to parent and role model to individual young people and the rest of the group in order to maintain control', as expressed in his interview. As another example, in one team meeting, several of the care staff expressed concerns about not being able to meet the needs of two young people who were self-injuring. In attempting to reassure them, Catrina, the psychologist, disagreed, saying instead that by 'acting as parents and enforcing boundaries', they were meeting the young women's needs (12.02.15). However, although the junior care staff perceived themselves, and were perceived by others, as acting as 'parents', they found it difficult to offer a definition of what this meant in practice. All of the care staff interviewed struggled to define the nature of their role, which is in line with the finding that 'care work defies easy definition' (Standing, 2001: 17). For example, when asked to describe his role, Phil, said: 'I don't know? Just, support worker I guess, just there to support and help them, enforce boundaries, try, don't know really.'

There was also a noticeable gender divide across the junior care staff in terms of how they spoke about their roles. The women generally emphasised the caring nature of their role, describing themselves as 'carers' (Mel) or 'care officers' (Natalie), or working in a 'care environment where we do what we can to try and help them' (Connie). In contrast, the men tended to focus on what they did with the young people. For example, Phil spoke about enforcing boundaries, while Patrick said his role was to: 'just sort of chill out with the lads, play football'. This may be influenced by the traditional gendering of care work as something women do (Abel, 2000). It also reflects traditional gender differences in task allocation within families, where mothers spend more time on the physical care of children, while fathers are mostly involved 'in the interactive care activities of talking to, playing with, reading to, teaching, or reprimanding children' (Craig, 2006: 270).

'Grandparents'

The Senior Residential Care Workers and Unit Leaders ('senior care staff') were ranked above the 'parents' in the organisation hierarchy and, in line with the 'parent' analogy, hereafter are referred to as 'grandparents'. Most of the 'grandparents' had been 'parents' themselves, although two new 'grandparents' had gained their position through academic training and were younger than many of the 'parents'. In comparison to the 'parents', the 'grandparents' worked directly with the young people less often. The 'Senior Residential Workers' can be conceived of as 'close grandparents'; each individual in this role worked one out of approximately every seven of their shifts alongside the 'parents'. The 'Unit Leaders' were more like 'distant grandparents'. They visited only when there was an issue to be resolved with one of the young people and did not participate in the domestic life of the units.

Like the 'parents', when the 'grandparents' ('close' or 'distant') worked directly with the young people, they acted on the 'residential sets'. The domesticity of the setting supported their 'performances' as senior kin (Goffman, 1959). In terms of appearance, there was a similarity between the 'parents' and the 'grandparents'. Like the 'parents', the 'grandparents' dressed casually, with only one, Nasa, a 'close grandparent', opting to always wear a shirt, but still tucked into jeans, and with trainers. It was a difference in 'manner' that marked a crucial distinction between the 'parents' and the 'grandparents' (Goffman, 1959). In contrast to the 'parents', the 'grandparents' presented as more detached. They were generally less playful in their interactions with the young people, and less tactile.

The 'grandparents' themselves describe their roles both in terms of their direct work with the young people and their seniority in relation to the 'parents'. For example, in his interview, Matt, a 'close grandparent', said:

> I still view myself and I still consider myself to be a residential social worker. But I'm slightly different from the majority of staff in so far as I'm a senior as well so I'm a duty officer/senior practitioner, so I work on the floor as a member of the staff team for some of the time, and then the other part of the time I'm the duty officer which means I'm not working directly, but in the absence of the management I'm the decision maker.

Emphasising his seniority even further, Roger, also a 'close grandparent', said in his interview:

> I'd describe my role as middle management, I'm looking after the staff ... and they in turn look after the young people, so I don't describe myself as having a role where I'm looking after the kids, I'm more and more looking after the building, and the staff than I'm looking after kids, more and more of my duties at the moment are supervisory.

The 'grandparents' had a clear sense of their seniority in relation to the 'parents'.

Education

Within the 'education staff' there was also a split, between the 'teachers' and the 'teaching assistants'. The Head of Education, much like a head-teacher of a school, was in position alongside the Head of Care in the 'authority' sphere.

Teachers

The teachers 'performed' their roles on the 'education set'; they were very rarely seen on either of the 'residential sets'. Moreover, they only performed at certain times; between 9am and 3.15pm Monday to Friday, and only during what was designated as term time. Each teacher had their own classroom, where the walls were adorned with the young people's work and information related to the subject being taught – Maths, Science, English, Woodwork, Art, or Food Technology.

The classrooms for the more practical sessions were equipped appropriately; the art room had a sink, the woodwork room a workbench and food technology had a fully functional kitchen. These settings provided the props needed for the teachers to play their subject-specific performances, and the audience of young people could predict what type of performance would take place on the basis of the set of each classroom. In addition, in each classroom, there was a space for the teacher – a large desk, or a particular area of the workbench – and smaller desks and chairs for the young people. This symbolised a power difference between the teacher and the young people.

There was a very clear distinction in terms of the 'personal fronts' of the teachers as compared to the 'parents' and 'grandparents'. First, their appearance was much different. The teachers dressed formally; smart trousers and shirts, for the men, and blouses, for the women. There were no jeans, tracksuit bottoms, or leggings. Further, all wore smart shoes; no trainers were seen on the 'education set.' Their manner was different too. The teachers were authoritative in their interactions with the young people. They were not tactile, like the 'parents', and they were even more detached than the 'grandparents.' Hugo, a teacher, acknowledged in his interview how his presentation differed from that of staff in other roles: 'I mean I'm probably compared to some of the staff, not distant to the young people, but I quite often come across as more of a teacher'.

Unlike the 'parents', the teachers had a very defined sense of remit, not only as teachers, but as subject-specific teachers. According to Valerie, her role was more important to her than the setting: 'I don't think I particularly did apply to work in a secure setting, I applied because I wanted to do the art teacher job'. Moreover, the teachers interpreted that their role was to teach, rather than to manage behaviour. For example, in his interview Hugo said:

> Certainly, when I first got here there were rules such as if someone was to swear at a member of staff [a teacher], so aggressively swear, not just sort of run of the mill, that would be automatically they'd be taken away from that situation, they'd be taken back [to the residential units].

In this instance, a teacher could ask a teaching assistant to remove the young person from the class and walk them back to the residential area.

Teaching assistants

The teaching assistants occupied a newly created position, taking over a role previously performed by the 'parents'. The teaching assistants were introduced in the SCH to give 'parents' time during the day to complete paperwork, in line with new requirements about evidencing work with young people (Carol, a 'distant grandparent', 28.01.14). The teaching assistants performed on the 'residential set' when they collected the young people for education in the morning, returned them at the end of the day, or when a young person had been excluded from school. The remainder of the time – again specifically between the hours of 9am and 3.15pm – the teaching assistants performed on the 'education set', helping the teachers in lessons, working with the young people on their activities. During school holidays, when the teachers were on leave, the teaching assistants took more of a leadership role, arranging and facilitating activities for the young people.

The 'personal front' of the teaching assistants depended on where they were acting. They dressed less casually than the 'parents' and 'grandparents', but not as formally as the teachers. When they were on the 'education set', the classroom setting supported their roles as facilitating the young people in their learning. At these times, the teaching assistants took on a more authoritative manner with the young people. However, during their interactions with the young people on the 'residential set', and when walking between the two sets, they were more informal and relaxed: more akin to the 'parents', but still not as tactile. Interaction at these times developed closer relationships between the young people and the teaching assistants, than between the teachers and the young people. Hugo, a teacher, viewed this positively, as captured in his interview: 'certainly, the LSA's [teaching assistants], one of the good things about their role is they bond more with the children, they're more sort of building relationships in that way and I think that's something we have that's very good.'

Relationships were not as positive between the education staff and the 'family' staff however.

Tensions between education staff and 'family' staff

This research found that in practice there was a palpable 'split between education and care' (Matt, 'grandparent') inside the SCH. This was attributed to the introduction of the teaching assistants described above. Theo, a 'parent' described in his interview what used to happen, prior to this change:

> so in the morning, as a parent, you would wake your child up, they'd have breakfast, you'd walk across to school with them, you'd spend the day in lessons, you'd come back because there's an expectancy of behaviour in education, if they needed to be returned they were returned and they were sanctioned and the education would carry on at home, that's what a normal parent would do. And then in the evening, the young person's at home and you'd get on with the rest of your time. Now, the young person is picked up and taken to education, the level of expectation of behaviour has gone, so the young person raises the game in education … Before the young person knew that 'Shit, I can't misbehave throughout and eff and jeff and walk in and out of lessons because that person's going to be with me for the rest of the shift and my, that's going to incur on what I do this evening.' Now, they go to school, they come back and it's like two different things, there's no level of

expectation of behaviour over there. They're all in and out of lessons and doing what they want to do. Then when they come, it takes an hour when they come back to the unit to just bring them back down again. Whereas before, we didn't, we didn't have any problems.

Theo also believed the previous arrangement worked better because the 'parents' knew the young people very well and could be proactive in preventing incidents:

We used to be able to pre-empt an incident before it happened because you know that young person inside out and you could see, you'd say the teacher 'I'm just going to take X out for a walk' because you could see them simmering or bubbling and it defused it, you know. And it worked, it absolutely worked.

Expressing a similar perspective in a separate interview, Matt (a 'grandparent') described the change as 'very detrimental'. He reflected that previously:

it was almost like a seamless service because people were in education, they knew what had gone on with the kids in education, so when you came back to the unit, there was that continuity, and it went both ways.

Stuart, a 'parent' bemoaned that since the teaching assistants had started, 'everything has fallen apart'.

The displacement of the 'parents' by the teaching assistants led to increasing animosities between the 'family' and 'education' teams. For example, the 'parents' often complained about the punctuality of the teaching assistants. To illustrate, in his interview, Matt, a 'grandparent' said: 'if you can get the LSAs ['teaching assistants'] over to pick the kids up at 9 o'clock you're a miracle worker ... Or they come back ten minutes early – well hold on a minute, we're not ready yet.'

The 'family' staff also felt that teachers did not deal with poor behaviour appropriately and were too quick to exclude the young people from school. For example, Rich, a 'parent', said in his interview, 'They've only got to swear three times and they're excluded. But they can come back on the unit and swear as much as they want at the care staff.' Similarly, Phil, also a 'parent', thought the education staff should be doing more in terms of behaviour management in the classroom. Phil said:

I know obviously this is a different environment but at the end of the day, a lot smaller classes, outside they've got 30 kids in a class, here they've got one or two, and yet they can send them back just because they swore a couple of times ... so I think making it harder to come back to the unit from school would help because obviously they can just get out of school and come back and chill and do nothing on the unit all day.

In such situations, the 'parents' were left to try and complete their paperwork as well as supervise the – often multiple – young people who had been excluded from school.

However, far from appreciating this, the teachers criticised the 'parents' for being too lax when the young people were returned to the unit. Valerie, a teacher, explained in her interview her frustration that instead of making the young people complete school work, the care staff would allow them to 'play video games or watch the telly'. Hugo, also a teacher, spoke about this issue at length, suggesting that the 'parents' were not aware of the sanctions they should have been imposing:

> it's very easy to blame the other side ... but certainly with regards to care I would think there's been problems ... if a young person was being sent back from education they generally weren't given any sanction on the unit. Now not draconian but they were going back and watching TV and that very quickly sort of instilled a situation where you don't care about being sent back if you get sort of, a mild reward at the end of it. And that's why I think we had a lot of problems.

The issue appeared to stem from some confusion as to who was responsible for a young person that had been excluded from school. Matt (a 'grandparent') said, 'You know, you are a teacher ... you want to have a kid out of school on the unit that's fine but put somebody in there to play education with them.' However, Malcolm, the Head of Care, suggested that it was the 'parents' responsibility to make sure those that had been sent back from education did schoolwork. Malcolm perceived that the 'parents' own experiences of school, and therefore their attitudes to education, affected how far they encouraged the young people to engage with schooling inside the SCH. Malcolm said,

> And you know, you do get a variety, some care staff are, you know, really pushing them and when they go back on the unit for whatever reason they would be encouraging them to do that, some are really forceful, some are what you would hope and others are less ...

At the same time, the 'family' staff questioned as to why a young person who had been excluded was returned to the unit, as opposed to being kept in 'education'. Phil, a parent, suggested 'having rooms where they just have to sit and go and do school work on their own in a classroom over there'.

This disconnect between the staff in the 'education' and 'family' spheres impacted on the young people. Scott, a 15-year-old young man who been accommodated for two years, expressed his frustrations with his experience of education inside the SCH. Scott had been resident prior to the introduction of the 'teaching assistants' and he appeared to side with the perspective of the 'family' sphere when he said:

> Some of them are cool, like, but they just … they're just, quick, so quick to send people back to the unit and once you're sent back to the unit they say 'Alright you're not in education for the rest of the day'. It's like, why do you want to take my education away from me? You're begging me to go over there, otherwise I get a sanction, and then when I get over there I do one thing wrong and I've got to come back. It's stupid. It's proper stupid.

Like Phil quoted above, Scott thought that young people should be kept in 'education' when they misbehaved, as expressed in his second interview:

> Because if you go to education yeah, like say you get, you start like being an idiot. Say you have a funny five minutes yeah and you're like 'Oh fuck off I'm not doing nothing' … like having a funny five minutes and cussing everyone, they'll be like 'right that's your third warning, that's your warning' like 'go back to unit, you're not allowed in school until like period two tomorrow'. When they should be like, it's education, they should be like, they're so quick to send people back to the unit, it should be like … If they're going to cause trouble, then they should cause it in there not on the unit because its education time. So like they should try and manage it instead of sending them back to the unit quickly. Do you get what I mean?

The problem stemmed from a lack of communication between these two groups of staff, despite their proximity within this small closed institution. Recognising this, Hugo, a teacher, said:

> I think if we could get better communication between the two of us then that would be much, that would solve a lot of problems. I don't know all the members of staff names over there, I try and go over when I can but I don't think that's particularly good. I think we've got an excellent opportunity and we don't really use it.

Returning to the epigraph at the beginning of this chapter, the education and care staff inside the SCH were far from 'singing from the same hymn sheet.'

Conclusion

This chapter has provided a rare insight into staff roles and relations inside a SCH. The staff were conceived of as representing key institutional spheres in young people's lives. I demonstrated how the 'education' and 'family' staff signified the different parts they played through their appearance, manner, and the props provided by the institutional setting. This recognition of the heterogeneity of staff inside this type of institution contributes to a gap in the literature which has thus far focused primarily on the experiences of young people.

Analysis of relations between staff in the 'education' and 'family' spheres revealed tensions that had developed since the introduction of the teaching assistants. The 'parents' felt displaced and perceived that the young people behaved less well in class because of the disconnect created between 'home' and 'school'. Disagreement centred around which staff team should be responsible for a young person that had been excluded from lessons. The lack of communication led to frustrations: for the education staff, the care staff, and the young people.

The findings of this research can be used to make two recommendations for practice inside SCHs, which may be of relevance to other institutions responsible for both the education and day-to-day care of young people. First, there needs to be effective means of communication between staff groups to ensure the seamless provision of education to young people. Second, clear policies must establish what happens when a young person is excluded from lessons. These should detail where a young person should go when excluded from the classroom, and who is responsible for their education at these times. These policies should go some way towards achieving the child-centred approach that the Head of Education described as essential for helping a young person to succeed.

Notes

1 Approval from the Secretary of State is needed to place a child younger than 13 in a SCH.
2 Young women can be accommodated in SCHs up to age 17, but for young men the maximum age is 16. This is linked to provision for young men and young women in the secure estate.
3 The secure estate in England and Wales is comprised of three different types of locked institutions for young people: secure children's homes (SCHs), secure training centres (STCs), and young offender institutions (YOIs).
4 The study was funded by the Economic and Social Research Council and undertaken as doctoral research. Due to ethical concerns, supporting data cannot be made openly available.
5 Exact details are omitted to protect the anonymity of the institution.
6 Where a date is given, this indicates the date that the data was generated through informal conversation. All other quotes from participants were generated in interviews.

References

Abel, E.K. (2000) A historical perspective on care. In M.H. Meyer (Ed.), *Care work: gender, labor and the welfare state*. Oxon: Routledge, pp. 8–14.
Barry, M., and Moodie, K. (2008) *'This isn't the road I want to go down': young people's perceptions and experiences of secure care, who cares?* Strathclyde: University of Strathclyde.
Children Act1989, s.25. Available at www.legislation.gov.uk/ukpga/1989/41/section/25
Craig, L. (2006) Does father care mean fathers share? A comparison of how mothers and fathers in intact families spend time with children. *Gender and Society*, 20, 2, 259–281.
Ellis, K. (2012) 'There are no good kids here': girls' experiences of secure accommodation. (unpublished PhD thesis). University of Sheffield.
Goffman, E. (1959) *The presentation of self in everyday life*. London: Penguin Books.
Goldson, B. (2002) *Vulnerable inside: children in secure and penal settings*. London: The Children's Society.

Harris, R., and Timms, N. (1993) *Secure accommodation in child care: between hospital and prison or thereabouts?* London: Routledge.

Hochschild, A.R. (2012) *The managed heart: commercialization of human feeling*. Berkeley: University of California Press.

O'Neill, T. (2001) *Children in secure accommodation: a gendered exploration of locked institutional care for children in trouble*. London: Jessica Kingsley Publishers.

Office for Standards in Education, Children's Services and Skills (2009) *Life in secure care: a report by the Children's Rights Director for England*. London: Ofsted.

Rose, J. (2014) *Working with young people in secure accommodation: from chaos to culture* (2nd edn). New York: Routledge.

Secure Accommodation Network (2014) *'They helped me, they supported me.' Achieving outcomes and value for money in secure children's homes*. London: Justice Studio.

Standing, G. (2001) Care work: overcoming insecurity and neglect. In M. Daly, *Care work: the quest for security*. London: International Labour Office, pp. 15–31.

5

HOW PSYCHOLOGICAL SERVICES AND EDUCATION LINK UP IN SECURE CHILDREN'S HOMES

Alex Smith and Sarah Mack

The focus of this chapter is to explore how psychological services link with education in two secure children's homes (SCHs). To enable this, the chapter will include the reflections of psychologists who work in these settings. The chapter will present an overview of the different roles these professionals have, including elements of their work, and the environment that this creates together. The chapter will also explore the challenges faced in the SCHs. A case example will provide a practical insight of how multi-disciplinary working has enabled positive change for one young person. The chapter will conclude by considering how new services, such as Secure Stairs, aim to extend multi-disciplinary thinking and ensure a holistic approach is embedded within secure settings.

Basic assumptions underpinning joint working in the secure children's homes

Most young people who end up in secure settings have basic needs relating to their mental health. Many of the young people in SCHs will have emotional, behavioural, and educational needs due to a lack of support and consistency throughout their lives, which could lead to a limited-future perspective and low expectations (Smeets, 2014). Alongside this, these young people are also at a crucial point in their education trajectory. Therefore, they are strongly encouraged to access education provision in these settings even though they may not have been able to do so previously in the community.

Inreach mental health teams are in place to assist young people with their mental health needs and prevent such issues becoming a barrier to accessing all the opportunities that the SCHs afford, including education. Inreach teams aim to support young people and help them address their mental health needs in a variety of ways. For instance, they will work collaboratively with young people to develop care and safety plans that detail how to best support them with their needs. These teams may also provide training for staff, therapies for young people, liaise with internal teams, and work closely with education staff to ensure shared thinking. Working in an integrative way with young people at the centre means balancing their needs for a safe, secure, inviting environment alongside them understanding the expectations regarding their behaviour (as provided by the rewards and sections schemes in SCHs). Having these foundations in place reduces uncertainty and ambiguity, which in turn creates an environment where a young person mostly engages in education provision as opposed to not.

Providing an inviting environment

It is mostly recognised that the environment a young person resides in, accesses education in, and/or receives therapeutic support in is important to their engagement. How comfortable they feel in the room (e.g. light, warmth, safety, and so forth), can have an impact. In the SCHs the environment young people are taught in is visually inviting. There is lots of artwork displayed on walls and some settings have positive statements (written by the young people) on the walls for other pupils to see. It is anticipated that the environment creates an engaging atmosphere that promotes a healthy mind-set for young people to work in.

The quotes below are from a psychologist. The psychologist describes some of the environments in the SCHs and how this can affect a young person.

> School have good expectations everywhere. It looks nice and it is really well presented. Good displays and well cared for.
> *(SCH Psychologist 1)*

> Lovely room, with a beautiful big mural on one wall, nicely lit and well painted, big comfy sofas in and a table. There was a special place they could go with positive statements on the wall. Could go and do some get involved with some music, talk about feeling and focus on breathing.
> *(SCH Psychologist 1)*

> Most of the young people struggle due to lack of educational opportunity and missing school. So, on their levels they are very poor, but if a cognitive assessment is done, they are usually around average. The issue is that it is very much about the environment.
> *(SCH Psychologist 1)*

Young people connecting with their external world

In the SCHs the educational staff try to integrate ideas, such as mindfulness, into the education curriculum. They do this to try to equip young people with some coping mechanisms for regulating their emotions, cognitions, and behaviours. For instance, in lessons the educational staff may talk about and provide psychoeducation on emotions. They also model mindfulness by undertaking practical exercises with young people. Education staff recognise that a young person's emotional and behavioural needs are equally as important as their educational needs, and that whilst in the SCH, all young people's needs should be addressed where appropriate and possible.

Behaviour management

Behavioural management plans are written for students that display problematic behaviours in the classroom. This is usually due to them struggling with their mental health and can be helpful for teachers to know how to best manage the young person when they are becoming distressed. These plans are usually written by a team of educational staff and psychologist to create a more thorough plan. They are often used in SCHs as many of the young people can struggle to manage their behaviour due to experiencing heightened emotions. The quote below illustrates how education staff in these settings have a good understanding of where the young person's behaviour has derived from and how they can work with this.

> They usually have the inability to concentrate and sit still. The staff team have a good psychological understanding of that and that it is not a cognitive deficit, but as part of how they have been educated and their parenting. They have never had the opportunities to learn those skills. There is no push from education provider to medicate them, they want to do more classroom-based approaches and help them to learn skills. They have a good understanding of this.
>
> *(SCH Psychologist 1)*

In secure units, management plans are created which can be quite lengthy and not always useful.

Attendance

Attaining 100% attendance in education may initially be unrealistic for some young people in SCHs for a variety of reasons. For instance, education may not be the priority for them due to them awaiting court proceedings. The young person may also have external worries and/or mental health needs that need addressing (e.g. restlessness, agitation, difficulties regulating emotions, apathy, low mood) and/or may be detoxing from substances, which would all impact on their ability to concentrate. In addition, some young people may find it difficult to focus on and learn new information at first due to never previously being encouraged to engage with education. They may also have come from chaotic unstable backgrounds meaning the consistency of attending education could be unfamiliar and strange to them. Lastly, the young people may also struggle to understand the work presented and so could become quiet and/or avoidant, or behave disruptively to mask their difficulties due to the potential fear of shame/embarrassment. For all these reasons, it is imperative that education staff balance encouraging consistent attendance and engagement in educational activities alongside understanding that for some young people this could be difficult and so be a gradual process. Therefore, endorsing an encouraging and caring, rather than punitive attitude may eventually help a young person feel safe and secure in education and the SCH environment as a whole. Likewise, the SCH residential staff understand that a young person's attendance in education is key to their engagement and they encourage this.

The quote below demonstrates how quickly attendance can decrease if consistent encouragement is not endorsed.

> Massive push around attendance ... Had it in the past where attendance was good, however only takes one or two to stop attending and then it crumbles. It needs to be implemented all the time.
>
> *(SCH Psychologist 1)*

Usually in education it is important for the attainment of targets or for young people to achieve highly in standard achievement tests (SATs), however in a SCH the educational need is not seen as synonymous to the targets. A more flexible approach in the educational system in a SCH means that these units are more able to accommodate learning that extends beyond the classroom. This is done by incorporating timetables that are that are not too rigid or academically focused.

Psychological training for staff

In general, education staff do not receive very much psychological training as described in the quote below.

> A lot of the teaching staff have come from various educational establishments with special interests in kids with various levels of needs including EBD (emotional and behavioural difficulties). Some of them have had training in other settings, as they do not get a lot as part of the secure estate. They are included in training that the care staff get, however this is not much.
>
> *(SCH Psychologist 1)*

'Psychology' (staff and services) in SCHs has a remit for joint working with and supporting 'education' (staff and services) where possible. One way they do so is by providing training. The principal training provided to educational staff in these settings is the Playfulness, Acceptance, Curiosity, and Empathy (PACE) model (Hughes and Golding, 2012). This approach is a stance rather than a strategy and means that the educational staff can remain engaged with the young person and are emotionally available. This active interaction helps to respond to and reflect upon the child's affective experience, meaning they feel understood and validated, and in turn builds trust and security in the educational setting. Psychology anticipated that training educational staff would help them feel more equipped to support young people who may have experienced difficulties in their life and consequently struggle forming attachments. It was also thought that the training would help staff understand the attachment needs of young people and that these needs exist always, thus in educational settings as well as on the units in the SCHs.

Educational staff in the SCHs have engaged well in the PACE training and shared positive feedback to psychology. For example, they described having increased confidence in their understanding of psychological ideas and also reported having observed intrapersonal changes in how they regard difference in pupils, think about young people's behaviour as arising from developmental trauma, and think about how their pupils' learning difficulties could relate to their early experiences of abuse and neglect. The quote below reflects the impact training can have on teaching practices.

> Teaching staff will reference developmental trauma and how their learning difficulties could relate to their early experiences, to their early development and experiences of abuse and neglect ... Teachers respond to the attachment-based training really well.
>
> *(SCH Psychologist 1)*

It is encouraging that despite educational staff not having a qualification in psychology, they have reported being able to utilise psychological theory whilst teaching and having discussions with and about the young people in their classes. Preferably all education provision in SCHs would receive standardised training in the same model. The new 'Secure Stairs' framework may address this issue (as discussed later in the chapter).

The role of the psychologist

Young people in secure settings often have a history of disrupted early attachments, trauma, and loss (Smeets, 2014). As such, young people may need psychological intervention to address a range of difficulties including early life trauma. In SCHs, a young person could be referred to psychology directly by a member of the Inreach team. Alternatively, a member of staff in the SCH could raise concerns about a young person or submit a referral to the Inreach team. The Inreach team would subsequently discuss the referral at a multi-disciplinary team (MDT) meeting. The MDT would then agree on what level of input to offer first by considering the referral information (e.g. young person's presenting problems, presentation, risk issues, offending behaviour, history) and NICE guidelines. For instance, they could have sessions with the registered mental health nurse (RMHN) if this was deemed appropriate. In contrast, the psychologist may work indirectly on a young person's case by providing consultation at review meetings and/or offering psychological advice and formulations to staff (where possible due to limited capacity).

The psychologist in the MDT contributes specific knowledge of psychological theory and processes. Due to the psychological and therapeutic knowledge the psychologist possesses, they can make evidence-based judgements. Likewise, they are also able to develop formulations that can be applied in practice to either enable the young person's health, care, and education needs to be met, and/or identify risk issues so that these are known, shared, and appropriate measures put in place.

Formulation

A safety plan is a proactive plan which is created to try and keep the young person safe, which can include the young person's thoughts and what can trigger their unwanted behaviour. The aim of the plan is to try and manage this before it escalates and to minimise any outcomes along with highlighting how the young person can seek help if they need to. The safety plan will be reviewed after a period to see how effective it is and to see if any amendments need to be made.

A formulation is a hypothesis to summarise the young person's core problems, and what are the maintaining influences of these. This includes problems at the current time and in certain situations, and can indicate a plan of intervention (Eells, 2011).

Safety plans and formulations are very important not just in psychology but also education. This is because the young people spend a lot of their time in education, meaning the experience they have in education can directly influence how safe they feel internally and externally, as explained by the quote below.

> The head teacher recognised that the school needs copies of the young person's safety plan which includes all of their triggers … and that the staff may be triggering the young people all the time.
>
> *(SCH Psychologist 1)*

It is important to note that compared to a mainstream school many of the pupils in education in a secure setting will have experienced some sort of trauma. This factor may be contributing to them having a reduced motivation to engage in education. Therefore, it is relevant for teachers to be aware of the young person's formulation, so they can encourage them in education in a manner that is appropriate for them.

The formulation created for each young person in the SCHs will refer to different triggers, ways of approaching the young person, protective factors, and/or their coping strategies. It will also contain historical information that might be useful for education staff to be aware of such as specific sensitive issues and trauma. For example, if it is known that a young person has been a victim of child sexual exploitation (CSE), it is important for the educational staff to be aware of this and their triggers. This is because the personal, social, health, and economic education (PSHE) lesson covers the topic of sexual health, which includes CSE. It is imperative that education staff approach the topic in a sensitive manner otherwise a trauma reaction could be inadvertently triggered in the young person. Similarly, a young person who has heard and/or witnessed domestic violence growing up may struggle to tolerate raised voices, shouting, or conflict. If the perpetrator of domestic violence was male, the young person may also struggle to tolerate male authority figures. This situation in education (and on their unit) could trigger a trauma reaction (i.e. fight/flight/freeze) causing the young person to feel angry and see 'red' very quickly, which would mostly likely be exhibited as disruptive/destructive behaviours. However, the formulation would help the young person and staff know how to respond if such situations arose since it would have identified and planned for this in advance.

Adopting a rescuer role

Balancing the delivery of education provision whilst holding in mind a young person's diverse needs is a difficult challenge for education staff in SCHs. Fortunately, education staff generally possess a good understanding of young people's mental health from working with children in various educational establishments and/or having a special interest in this area. Furthermore, some may also have had significant training in this field. Nevertheless, working in an environment with young people who present with highly complex needs and histories increases the risk of educational staff taking on a 'rescuing' role. A 'rescuer' role/adopting a 'rescuer' role means that staff are quick to jump into situations and take control for reasons related to their own self-esteem, rather than focussing on the needs and self-efficacy of the young person. It is not an unusual phenomenon in caring professions

The quote below demonstrates how assuming this role can quite easily happen in SCHs.

> Staff can be pulled into a more caring role and this can blur the boundaries … it is hard for the teaching staff due to the young people having been through awful abuse … staff's needs may be put into the kids as they feel they need to rescue and to care.
>
> *(SCH Psychologist 1)*

For example, taking on a rescuer role could arise when educational staff are aware of the significant trauma and abuse a young person has experienced. They may assume a caring rather than a teaching role because understandably they want to care for, support, rescue, and protect the young person from any further harm. Unfortunately, this could lead to boundaries between education staff and other provisions (e.g. keyworkers, unit staff, mental health, and/or psychology) becoming blurred. This can cause problems as a young person may then solely rely on that one individual member of staff (i.e. the 'rescuer') as in their view that individual may have shown them a greater level of care. Subsequently, they may not form attachments and obtain support from other individuals. They may also struggle if that identified individual member of staff is not available and/or able to respond to them and their needs. This could lead to the young person feeling rejected. As a result, the young person may then become avoidant and cautious in building relationships with other people in the SCH. Alternatively, it could trigger an extreme emotional response in them, which may not match the situation but might represent underlying feelings about their previous adverse experiences.

Although taking a 'rescuer' role is often unintentional and well meaning, it can be emotionally harmful to a young person to become excessively dependent on one person (for some of the reasons described above). Likewise, the person who adopts the 'rescuer' role can also be emotionally harmed in that they can suffer from burn out, struggle to focus on their own needs, and often assume this role to achieve self-esteem. This brief example illustrates why it is extremely important that professionals' roles and boundaries are clear, and that psychology and education work in an integrated coordinated way. These roles are similar to the description of the 'persecutor, rescuer and victim' roles which are described in Karpman's Drama Triangle (Karpman, 2011), in which unhelpful dynamics can be played out between staff that are in conflicted, and in this circumstance by educational staff in the SCH.

Emotional support of staff

Educational staff do not receive supervision (i.e. a regular opportunity to reflect on their work with a knowledgeable other when operating in 'high stress' relational roles) in the same way that psychologists/therapists do. Psychologists in the MDT will, however, often provide feedback and reassurance. This is a valuable support service as similar to psychologists; education staff will be directly involved with young people that present with challenging needs and behaviours. As a result, they are also highly likely to be exposed to an emotionally charged environment.

Silo working

The potential risk with different provisions working in the same setting is that they do not communicate well and can work in isolation. This can lead to resources being wasted and risk young people being over-assessed. For example, education staff might deem an assessment from an educational psychologist necessary for a young person. However, problems could arise when education request this without consulting the Inreach psychologist. In such cases, education would make the request and the local authority would fund this assessment. Yet, whether undertaking the assessment would be beneficial to the young person would depend on their view regarding the assessment and the potential impact of it, and the outcome of the assessment. The outcome might change nothing regarding the young person's care, or it could change a lot if for instance the young person received a diagnosis. Even though liaising with external professionals could be deemed multi-disciplinary, it could be argued that it is not the most efficient way of working in SCHs and does not necessarily endorse a holistic approach to young people's care, as stated below.

> An outsider may come in, but it is not a holistic approach.
> *(SCH Psychologist 2)*

Alternatively, if the Inreach psychologist was consulted prior to any external referrals being made, then what education perceived the young person's needs as, and their rationale for requesting an assessment, could be clearly identified. The Inreach psychologist could then consult with them regarding the appropriateness of the assessment, which is particularly important if the young person were someone they were working directly with. This is because they may have already completed or be in the process of completing the assessment education are requesting meaning that resources would not be duplicated, time and money wasted, and importantly a young person would not have to experience an unnecessary assessment. On the other hand, the timing of the assessment might need negotiating due to their on-going work, or the psychologist may want to link with the educational psychologist to share information, or the psychologist may deem the assessment unnecessary and provide their reasons why.

At present, a key barrier that can prevent a holistic approach to a young person's care (as detailed above) is the hours that members of staff in the Inreach mental health team have allocated to the SCHs. This means that they may not be able to facilitate all the workload requested including assessments and formulations, as they do not have the capacity to complete these. For instance, the psychologist may develop a high-quality formulation with a young person or for the purposes of aiding the educational staff's understanding. However, unfortunately, the psychologist may not be able to attend specific meetings and be able to share, discuss, review, and amend the formulation with staff due to their limited capacity. As such, information may not be fully understood, which could reduce the utility of the formulation being applied in all settings in the SCH (i.e. on the unit, in education and in other activities), as depicted below,

> Formulations are shared with education; however, this may not be used in the educational setting ... ideally it is the psychologist who would explain the formulation to the education staff, however with only working one day a week this may not be possible to share it at the staff meeting which is one day a week.
> *(SCH Psychologist 2)*

Earlier in the chapter it was noted that educational staff responded well to training, however, because of their limited capacity and other responsibilities (i.e. managing caseloads and other queries) psychologists are not able to facilitate this training as much as is needed. Furthermore, education staff may struggle to access a psychologist in the SCH if they are only present one day a week; equally it is difficult for the psychologist to be regularly available for them because of this. As such, reflective practice can also not be facilitated, as demonstrated below,

> There is no supervision or communication time.
> *(SCH Psychologist 2)*

Although supervision and reflective practices are not occurring regularly at present, this does not mean they are not considered important. Time for staff to reflect, give, and receive feedback is important. Similarly, having the opportunity to receive advice and share updates on what may be working well or not so well for a young person is also valuable. It could be anticipated that as the 'Secure Stairs' framework (discussed later in the chapter) highlights the importance of 'emotionally resilient staff', this framework will implement such practices to support staff.

As discussed above, lack of capacity seems to be a key barrier preventing provisions working more effectively together. Another reason why provisions may work separately may be because professionals are possibly focused on their own role and responsibilities. Therefore, they do not automatically consider how other provisions could assist a young person to address their needs and achieve their full potential.

The risk of working in isolation is that rich information and feedback regarding the progress of young people is not shared. There is also the potential risk that some young people struggling with their mental health could be missed because they perhaps function well (e.g. attend education without concern or difficulty) no one notices that they could be masking their emotions and putting on 'a front'.

> Educational staff never approach psychology as they feel that they already know what they are doing in their role and are confident enough in themselves. This can be worrying as they could be missing something important.
> *(SCH Psychologist 2)*

Nonetheless, education and mental health feedback is provided at risk and review meetings in the SCH. Therefore, if there were concerns about a young person's mental health then it could be anticipated that they would be raised in this forum and where appropriate the Inreach RMHN would share them with the psychologist.

Diverse provisions working in an integrated coordinated way is the ideal for SCHs. However, as identified above, there are challenges that need overcoming before this can transpire. The new national strategy entitled 'Secure Stairs' (discussed later in the chapter) will most likely address and overcome these identified issues so that young people can rightfully receive integrated, consistent, coordinated care (Bush, 2018).

Diagnosis

Many young people in the SCHs have a diagnosis of, or suspected diagnosis of, ADHD (attention deficit hyperactive disorder). This is sometimes queried as autistic spectrum disorder (ASD). Both diagnoses may be incorrectly identified when the young person presents with a developmental trauma or adverse childhood experiences (ACEs). The problems with such diagnoses are that educationalists may see the diagnosis rather than take a holistic approach to consider all the needs of the young person. For instance, instead of adopting a trauma informed approach that recognises that anyone can suffer from the effects of trauma irrespective of their diagnosis (Bush, 2018), the diagnosis may be the main focus for the planning and delivery of education. Additionally, if a young person with such a diagnosis is not engaging in education then it may be attributed to their diagnosis rather than other factors such as trauma.

> The teaching staff themselves have various levels of understanding of things like ASC (autistic spectrum condition) … they start diagnosing and state they know how to manage kids with autism, however they are very complex, and this is not helpful.
>
> *(SCH Psychologist 1)*

Encouragingly, psychologists can work alongside education staff to ensure that the connection with trauma is made and appropriate strategies are put in place. Furthermore, with the new national strategy of 'Secure Stairs' (discussed later in the chapter) stressing the importance of a joined-up approach to care utilising all provisions, young people's needs in SCHs should be correctly identified and addressed (Bush, 2018).

A psychologist at one of the SCHs has provided the following case example. It shows how, with the right environment in a SCH, along with the motivation and commitment from a young person, significant change can be achieved in their education to enable them to reach their full potential. This case also highlights the valuableness of formulation at all stages and its links with education.

Frank[1]

Frank is 14 years old and the eldest of five children. His parents are together but have experienced their own difficulties through substance misuse, mental health problems, and criminality. Growing up, Frank witnessed extensive domestic violence between his parents. Frank has always had difficulties sleeping and experienced a number of losses at a young age. Frank was referred to Child and Adolescent Mental Health Services (CAMHS) when aged 8 years old by his school due to concerns about a change in his behaviour. In mainstream school he would regularly run out of class. When aged 9 years old, he moved schools due to 'emotional and behavioural problems' and shortly after was suspended for fighting and threatening a teacher. Frank attended four sessions in CAMHS before disengaging. Frank's mother wondered whether he might have attention deficit hyperactivity disorder (ADHD), however, this was never assessed. At aged 13 years old, Frank was remanded into custody for a violent offence. This was Frank's first time in custody.

Initial formulation

Frank came to the attention of psychological services via recommendations from a court report. This indicated that he might need support to aid his emotional and intellectual development. Prior to meeting with Frank, the clinical psychologist (CP) reviewed the information available to complete an initial formulation using the five Ps model, i.e. Presenting problem(s), Predisposing, Precipitating, Perpetuating and Protective factors (Johnstone and Dallos, 2013). The formulation also included 'future risks and recommendations'. At this stage, the formulation was shared internally with the relevant agencies in the SCH (i.e. Frank's keyworker, his interventions worker, and education) to aid their understanding of Frank's background, risk, and protective factors. The formulation also guided the CP's approach for how to engage and work with Frank in a way that would be beneficial for him and his education. The CP hypothesised that Frank would not be one to seek support and ask for help, and would have limited emotional awareness, regulation, and coping strategies. The formulation was not shared with Frank at this stage because he had only been in custody a short time and was still adjusting to the environment, was in the process of receiving a criminal conviction, and adapting to being away from his family for the first time. Furthermore, at this point Frank had not established any therapeutic relationships with anyone so sharing it could have been damaging. For instance, he may not have been ready to talk about or confront his background. Additionally, he could have found this intrusive; both reasons could have hindered his engagement.

Assessment

When the CP first tried to talk to Frank he would turn around and go the opposite way. As such, the CP went in to the unit every week for two months so that Frank could become familiar and comfortable with them before they broached the idea of undertaking direct work.

Frank was seen in the lounge on the unit during time allocated for his education. At first, Frank presented as anxious, fearful, and hesitant to talk. He also seemed to have difficulty concentrating, therefore initial sessions were kept short. To begin with, Frank would direct the format of sessions, such as agreeing what to work on and then requesting to end with an activity (e.g. a game of pool, kicking a football together, and other activities). Initial sessions comprised a comprehensive assessment including psychometrics (see below for details).

Experience of education

With regard to education, Frank described himself as 'a naughty boy'. He attributed his disruptive behaviour as the reason for him moving schools and subsequently being excluded. Frank reported that he went to a school for young people with behavioural problems. Frank was not enthusiastic about education, and he reported that he would 'lose concentration' and 'switch off' due to being disinterested. Whilst in the SCH, Frank had attended education without a problem. The only concern raised by the education team was about Frank's level of understanding, as they were unsure how much information he was taking on board and whether it was suitable for his level of ability.

Experience of custody

Frank described feeling 'shocked' about coming into custody for the first time and that it took several months to sink in. He experienced significant loss and disruption and talked about how long he had been away from his mum and family.

Formulation

Although Frank had not yet been formally assessed, the CP hypothesised that he had an anxious-avoidant attachment style in that he would try to care for and protect his mum (i.e. not worry her) rather than seek care himself (most likely due his earlier experience of witnessing domestic violence). The CP considered how this attachment style might present in a custodial setting, which in later sessions was explained to Frank using the metaphor of a swan; that externally, Frank would be composed like a swan is graceful and elegant. This would present as him adjusting well and adhering to the rules and boundaries (i.e. 'nothing to see here'). However, it was highly likely that his external presentation did not match his internal experience (i.e. that internally he was highly anxious like a swan who underneath the water is rapidly paddling their legs). The CP had concerns that if Frank did not receive support then he might draw on maladaptive coping strategies to manage (i.e. aggressive behaviour, violence, hyperactivity, and/or internalise his distress), as he had not yet developed adaptive ones, which could be displayed in his educational setting.

Sharing the initial formulation

Once a trusting therapeutic relationship had been established and work had progressed, the CP informed Frank of the initial formulation they had completed. This was subsequently shared with him. Frank was always keen to know what information the CP knew about him before he would be willing to reciprocate. The CP attributed this to his attachment style in that Frank did not tolerate uncertainty well so preferred to know what to expect, such as what information you knew. Given this, and that the CP had always tried to be transparent when working with Frank (as far as is possible in criminal justice settings), they wondered how Frank would receive the formulation. Frank responded well and together with the CP revised the formulation to correct inaccuracies and reflect his progress to date.

Intervention and evaluation

Prior to being remanded into custody, psychometric assessments had been completed with Frank. Three months into Frank receiving support and following an observable change in presentation and demeanour, Frank and the CP deemed it a good time to repeat the psychometric assessment. These comprised; the Beck Youth Inventories (BYI-ii; Beck, Beck, Jolly & Steer, 2005), the Resiliency Scales for Children and Adolescents (Prince-Embury, 2006), and the Trauma Symptom Checklist for Children (TSCC; Briere, 1996). These different psychometric assessments are important when linked with education, as they can help give a better understanding of where the young person is at with their mental health and how to help them. For example, if the BYI indicates that the young person is struggling with their anxiety, the education team may be able to adapt their education plan to assist with this such as scheduling 1:1 lessons and encouraging the young person to engage in smaller groups. The Resiliency Scale may indicate how resilient (i.e. strengths and vulnerabilities) the young person is if they become withdrawn from education, and whether they are likely to engage again or if they need more support from staff. Overall, with regards to Frank, there were clinically significant improvements on all the psychometric assessments. This corresponded with staff members' observations of Frank becoming more confident, responsive, and forthcoming.

For the same reasons described above, at a later date, the Weschler Intelligence Scale for Children – Fourth UK Edition (WISC-IV UK; Weschler, 2004) was also repeated. The results indicated that there had been significant improvements in Frank's cognitive functioning. It is likely that a number of factors contributed to Frank's improvement, such as: him being sentenced, residing at the SCH for 18 months (thus feeling safe and secure), being encouraged to pursue academia (this was the longest period he had remained in education), being more equipped to manage his emotions, being familiar with the administrator, Frank's attitude to education and his own development, his increased maturity, and his own hard work. With Frank's consent, he was referred to the speech and language therapist at the SCH for further assessment and intervention to support him with his verbal comprehension.

It is valuable to share the results of these assessments with education as a young person may function similarly on their unit, in education, with interventions and psychology. The more information that is known about this, the more opportunity there is whilst the young person resides at the SCH to assist them to enhance their cognitive functioning. It is imperative that such opportunities are utilised since a young person may never have successfully engaged or achieved in education before. For example, the results of such assessments could assist education to 'pitch' work at the right level for a young person so that, ultimately, they are able to reach their full potential.

Coping strategy work

Frank was resistant to undertaking any coping strategy work, possibly because he did not believe the strategies would be helpful. Nevertheless, over time he became more open to discussions around the importance of equipping himself with coping strategies, particularly ones he could use if he were to transition to a different environment. Frank identified the following as his strategies: watching television, talking to his mum most days, going to the gym, playing football, playing computer games, listening to music, reading football material, keeping up to date with his football club, and playing pool. Some mindfulness and imagery techniques were also attempted, although Frank was sceptical about the utility of these because he was more practically minded.

ADHD assessment

Whilst working with Frank he requested an assessment for ADHD. He said that he had always been told he had ADHD, but this had never been formally assessed. A combination of the Conners-3rd Edition (Conners, 2008) completed by the young person, their keyworker, and a teacher along with other information were used to assess Frank. Frank did not meet criteria for ADHD. However, due to reporting longstanding sleep difficulties, he was prescribed melatonin, which he reported as having a good effect.

Index offence work

Initially Frank did not talk about his offence. However, once the CP and Frank had developed a trusting therapeutic relationship and he was equipped with coping strategies, he wanted to explore this further. Although the CP's work was not index offence focused, it was anticipated that obtaining Frank's narrative would aid his processing of this event and help inform risk and further interventions. Using elements of West and Greenall's (2011) framework, Frank talked through an account of his index offence, which he said he was extremely remorseful for.

Potential concerns

Although Frank had discussions in sessions about diverse criminal justice settings and his sentence length and future (e.g. relapse prevention work and scenario planning), an on-going concern was that he could transition to another establishment at any time. Professionals were concerned that if this were to happen, Frank's threat response (i.e. fight/flight/freeze), his core beliefs, and rules for living (e.g. if I am threatened then I will stand up for myself) would be activated. Furthermore, based on the formulations, it could be hypothesised that Frank would internalise any distress. This could lead to him being overlooked in a larger establishment, which might have had a detrimental impact on his mental health and wellbeing. Fortunately, with the support of professionals, Frank remained at the SCH. Following an appeal, his tariff got reduced. He also had a parole hearing and, due to his extraordinary progress, he was successful in obtaining open conditions.

The challenges

Engaging young people in criminal justice settings is no easy feat, however, it is widely recognised that a large proportion of young people who end up in such settings have suffered trauma (Paton et al., 2009). As highlighted by the Youth Justice Board (2017), the effects of trauma impede engagement with activities, education, interventions, and obtaining support from others (including professionals). Without taking the time to build a trusting relationship, young people will not feel safe enough to engage. In addition, young people do not come into criminal justice settings with a tabula rasa; they arrive with a whole host of experiences, including previous encounters with professionals and services.

In Frank's case, engaging him took time for various reasons. Unfortunately, his previous experience of CAMHS seemed to have had a significant impact on his perception of mental health services, as evidenced by his initial reluctance to engage with the CP. Frank described this input in a negative light. He reported that as a young child he did not understand why he was attending CAMHS. He described being given options to draw or write yet found neither option desirable. He reported finding this boring and unhelpful, which ultimately resulted in him walking out and refusing to return.

On reflection, Frank described himself as a very energetic child and that he probably would have engaged with CAMHS had they suggested an outside activity that he enjoyed. He thinks he would have gradually built a therapeutic relationship with the professional and talked to them whilst engaging in the activity. Frank stated that professionals should not just 'jump straight in' and expect a young person to talk because it takes time to trust someone. He believed that engaging in 'ice-breakers' with the CP such as games of pool, football, and other activities helped him engage.

Interestingly, although Frank had also encountered challenges in education in the community, at the SCH he was able to engage in education relatively quickly without much difficulty.

Another challenge for professionals in SCHs and other criminal justice settings is the sentence length a young person receives. This can often influence whether Inreach mental health teams and specialist provision are able to work effectively and in a timely manner with a young person. As Frank was given a long sentence this was not an issue. On reflection, when the CP asked Frank about his view on young people's sentence lengths in custody, Frank reported that he had found stability in his length of sentence because he had not had to move placements. He thought that if he had had to move (e.g. to a youth offenders institution), then all the hard work he had started would have been undone very quickly due to the change of setting and him having to protect himself. In contrast, Frank also thought that when a young person's sentence is extremely long they must become quite hopeless and feel like it is never going to end.

It could be expected that placing young people in criminal justice settings can be challenging. However, the positive effect a SCH environment can have on young people should not be underestimated. For instance, in Frank's case, the difficult earlier experiences he encountered and his initial presenting problems seem to have been partially offset and ameliorated by this environment. Frank has thrived from the relational security, structure, and consistency of the SCH including the routines, education, reward system, and expectations. Furthermore, the relationships he formed with staff have been very important in helping him develop healthy patterns of relating to others. Various staff members have also served as models for how to behave and regulate emotions. Importantly, in this environment Frank has been able to ask for help when needed.

Frank's reflections and thoughts

Frank reflected that he was four months into his sentence before he started to engage in any therapeutic work. He emphasised the importance of him having time to settle in the SCH. He also found the time and approach professionals took to engage him as beneficial. Additionally, Frank reflected that he had found it beneficial to have the same two therapeutic professionals involved in his case from the beginning to present day (i.e. a CP and interventions manager, who would help in managing and tracking interventions).

Frank believed that if he had been in a different secure setting he would not have been granted a reduction in his tariff. He thought that even though he would have tried his best in a different setting, people would not have got to know him or understood him, like they have on his unit, in education, psychology, and interventions staff at the SCH. Frank stated that people have a perception of what he is like by what they see written down on paper (i.e. his index offence); however, his experience at the SCH is one where people have got to know him as a person first.

Transition from the secure children's home

When a young person first comes into the SCH, they will usually have a lot of involvement from different services such as social services, youth offending teams (YOT), youth justice, domestic violence units, YOI and CSE teams. Some young people find this level of involvement overwhelming whereas others do not. Given that most young people in SCHs have experienced social deprivation resulting in some of them engaging in criminality, it is unsurprising that they may not have deemed education a priority or attended school for a long time. They may also have had long and frequent school exclusions resulting in them being placed in specialist education provision such as pupil referral units (PRUs) because of their behaviour. Considering this, from a psychological perspective, it can be hard to get a coherent narrative regarding these experiences.

The young person may have an idea of what they want to do when they leave education, however, limits, curfews, and/or convictions with specific licence conditions and restrictions will affect where they go and what they can do. These restrictions can change the young person's outlook and have an impact on their progress. If their educational next steps are not in place ready for when they leave the SCH, they may not continue with their education. Furthermore, if educational aspirations are not given sensitive attention, they may be overlooked and more basic and pressing needs focussed on, as illustrated in the quote below.

> Transition from the SCH is also not very smooth, especially regarding education, as many of the young people may not know where they are going to live, and therefore education is not a main priority.
>
> *(SCH Psychologist 2)*

Restricted provision

Despite some young people in the education provision doing well, some young people in the SCH do not reach their full potential. With staff being aware of young people's histories, namely the lack of education consistency, this can create a 'low achiever identity'. If an academically able young person comes onto the unit, they are likely to disengage if the activities are targeted to a group who are less academically able.

> Can get some very intelligent kids ... they are encouraged, however overall the provision is not for them.
>
> *(SCH Psychologist 1).*

This arises when only a certain number of resources (physical and financial) are available. Those young people between 16 to 18 years of age who had previously been doing a practical qualification often cannot carry on whilst in the SCH, and consequently do not continue when they leave the unit. Some SCHs help the young people do a half transition and return to their usual education environment half a day per week; however most secure units cannot do this due to staffing restrictions. This is unfortunate as having this type of continuation could benefit them for the rest of their lives.

Extending multi-disciplinary thinking with new services such as Secure Stairs

Over the period of 2016 to 2020, a national strategy will be rolled out starting in 2018. The objective of the strategy is to implement a framework for integrated care in the Children and Young People's Secure Estate (CYPSE; Bush, 2018). The name of the framework is 'Secure Stairs' and its aim is to ensure that all children and young people in the secure estate receive the same evidence-informed care regardless of where they are located (Bush, 2018). The framework will have an 'interpersonal/attachment focus' whilst 'supporting trauma-informed care' using 'a whole-system approach' (NHS England, 2017). The purpose of 'Secure Stairs' is to improve the outcomes and future for young people in secure settings. The name SECURE STAIRS is an acronym, which is explained in Table 5.1.

'SECURE'

The SECURE part of the model recognises that it is the frontline staff that spend the most time with young people. Therefore, protecting the staff and promoting a therapeutic environment will in itself be beneficial for the young people. Investing resources in creating a more holistic approach would mean the SCH would benefit whilst also facilitating a consistency in the day-to-day care of the young people by frontline staff who understand the needs from an attachment/trauma perspective. The approach includes regular supervision, training, and formulation meetings. The recognition of the wider staff team and acknowledging their emotional needs helps with staff recruitment, retention, and in turn creates a more stable environment in the SCH and acknowledgement of the statement that 'Every Interaction Matters'. It was noted earlier in the chapter that educational staff do not get much contact time with psychologists to discuss formulations and the best way to manage a young person. However, with this new framework implementing more supervision, support, and reflective practice, this should enhance communication and meeting the needs of the young people.

TABLE 5.1 What does SECURE STAIRS stand for?

S	staff with skill sets appropriate to the interventions needed
E	emotionally resilient staff able to remain child-centred in the face of challenging behaviour
C	cared for staff: supervision and support
U	understanding across the establishment of child development, attachment, trauma, and other key theories
R	reflective system, able to consider impact of trauma at all levels
E	'Every Interaction Matters' – a whole system approach
S	scoping covering what the presenting problems are, who the key players are in the young person's 'home' life, and what change is wanted by whom
T	targets agreed by the establishment, the young people, and their 'home' environment for their time on the estate – 'your time here matters'
A	activators of the young person's difficulties with reaching their targets identified
I	interventions developed at multiple levels (from those delivered by frontline carers to those provided by specialist departments) that address those activators
R	review of movement towards targets regularly undertaken and used to evaluate and revise plans as necessary
S	sustainability planning considered from the outset

'STAIRS'

The STAIRS section of the framework aims to actively plan within the team and create clear destination targets for young people. As highlighted in Frank's case study, it is important that each young person in SCHs has a formulation. This new model will enable this to be undertaken whist also ensuring that the multi-disciplinary team (i.e. education, health, and care staff) work in a joined-up holistic manner. The formulations that are developed will be incorporated into care plans and then implemented in their educational management. It is envisaged that this will provide a greater understanding of why the young person is not engaging and how educational staff can respond, thus meeting the young person's needs. It also recognises that the education programmes currently available in SCHs may be too task focused, and that for young people in these settings this may not be the best approach.

Through identifying issues such as these, it may highlight that for some of these young people, their learner development is to be able to sit in a room with other people and to be able to engage. By working in a more flexible approach, it helps the young person's emotional development, which they would not have the opportunity in a mainstream school. These individual formulations that are created are regularly reviewed, with targets for attainment which are not necessarily academic and can help provide a clearer focus on the highest expectations for young children to meet their potential despite being in the secure settings.

Conclusion

This chapter has discussed how psychology and education provisions operate in SCHs, the importance of having a trauma-informed environment in the SCHs, the role of a psychologist and formulation, and the current challenges these provisions face when attempting to work in a more integrated way. The case example illustrated how much can be achieved by one young person in a SCH when they are committed and motivated and receive the right level of support at the right time. Lastly, the chapter ended with discussing the new 'Secure Stairs' framework. It is anticipated that a lot of the challenges highlighted in this chapter will be addressed once this framework is embedded in the SCH.

To conclude, it is important that young people know they matter. This is especially important in SCHs where the young people in these settings may have encountered appalling adverse experiences and trauma. Nurturing young people in these settings and enabling them to reach their full potential is a big challenge. However, all provisions need to work together to rise to this challenge and enable these young people to achieve all that they aspire to, so they can lead happy healthy lives.

Note

1 The young person consented for their case to be described in this chapter and was involved in the write up. All identifying details have been changed to protect the young person's identity.

Acknowledgements

Acknowledgement for contributions to this chapter: Dr Bridie Gallagher and Dr Grace Crawford

References

Beck, J.S., Beck, A.T., Jolly, J.B., and Steer, R.A. (2005) *Beck youth inventories – second edition manual*. San Antonio, TX: Pearson.
Briere, J. (1996) *The trauma symptom checklist for children professional manual*. Lutz, FL: Psychological Assessment Resources.
Bush, M. (2018) Addressing adversity: prioritising adversity and trauma-informed care for children and young people in England. *Addressing Adversity*, 1, 1–187.
Conners, C.K. (2008) *Conners manual (3rd edition)*. North Tonawanda, NY: Pearson.
Eells, T.D. (2011) *Handbook of psychotherapy case formulation*. New York: Guilford Press.
Hughes, D., and Golding, K. (2012) *Creating loving attachments: parenting with PACE to nurture confidence and security in the troubled child*. London: Jessica Kingsley Publishers.
Johnstone, L., and Dallos, R. (2013) *Formulation in psychology and psychotherapy: making sense of people's problems*. Oxon: Routledge.
Karpman, S.B. (2011) Fairy tales and script drama analysis. *Group Facilitation*, 11, 49.
NHS England (2017) *Briefing paper: end of scoping, mobilisation and next steps*, August.
Paton, J., Crouch, W., and Camic, P. (2009) Young offenders' experiences of traumatic life events: a qualitative investigation. *Clinical Child Psychology and Psychiatry*, 14, 1, 43–62.
Prince-Embury, S. (2006) *Resiliency scales for adolescents a profile of personal strengths manual*. San Antonio, TX: Pearson.
Smeets, E. (2014) Education in young offender institutions and secure youth care institutions. *Educational Research and Evaluation*, 20, 1, 67–80.
Wechsler, D. (2004) *Weschler intelligence scale for children (UK 4th edition) (WISC-IV UK)*. London: Pearson.
West, A.G., and Greenall, P.V. (2011) Incorporating index offence analysis into forensic clinical assessment. *Legal and Criminal Psychology*, 16, 144–159.
Youth Justice Board (2017) *In-brief: trauma-informed youth justice. Effective practice in youth justice*, September [Online]. London: YJB. Retrieved from: https://yjresourcehub.uk/our-community/resources-for-sharing/item/495-trauma-informed-youth-justice-briefing.html

6

CHILDREN'S LIVES, EDUCATION, AND SECURE CARE IN SCOTLAND

Alison Gough and Claire Lightowler

> Secure care is still seen as being for young people who are in trouble. I haven't done anything wrong but I was in with someone who had set fire to another person. But then I guess that young person might have had bad things happen to them
> *(Young adult reflecting back on their experiences, in 2016)*

In this chapter we think about the lives of children and young people who experience secure care in Scotland. We briefly explore the history of the Scottish secure care sector, in the context of prevailing narratives and assumptions about children in difficulty and their education. We outline how the past continues to influence secure care today and how things have changed, particularly in relation to education provision. We reflect on strengths and shortfalls informed by what we have learned about and from children and young people who are in and on the edges of secure care.

We have undertaken an intensive stakeholder engagement programme during the Secure Care National Project, an *'independent, strategic, analytical and practice focused review'* of secure care commissioned by the Scottish Government. This included focused conversations with sixty children and young people with experience of secure care, the majority of whom were in secure care at the time that they spoke with us. We were humbled and inspired by the young people we met and often shocked and saddened by what they told us about the challenges they had faced.

We have been struck by the many accounts of fragmented childhoods, shared with us during this project, and in our wider work at the Centre for Youth and Criminal Justice (CYCJ). People's stories tell us there is often a gap between stated policy and the reality of children's lives. In this chapter we are writing as individuals and the views we express are our own, but we are privileged to draw on learning from the Secure Care National Project, and to be able to share the voices of young people and the practitioners caring for them. Our reflections are also informed by CYCJ's work across Scotland with practitioners, policy makers, researchers and people directly affected by the care and justice systems in Scotland.

The history of secure care in Scotland

> the vertue and godlie upbringing of the youth of this Realm
> *(John Knox, 1560, First Book of Discipline)*

> You've got to use your time in here wisely, take the opportunities and that, and dinnae bother about anyone else. You have to be selfish for yourself. It's your life
> *(Young Person in secure care talking in 2016)*

Scotland was the first country in the world to offer universal school education to children when it began more than 450 years ago. The national education system designed by Knox back then, including parish primary schools, burgh grammar schools, high schools, and the so-called 'ancient' universities, helped to encourage the 'democratic myth' of self-improvement: that a poor child could 'make it' via the medium of education. This conceptualisation of public education as democratising, which 'became, and remained, a central part both of the Scottish sense of nationhood and of the image which others have formed of the Scots' (Anderson, 1983: 1), still endures. In the lead up to the independence referendum in 2014, when Scotland asked whether it wanted to be an independent nation or not, the then First Minister, Alex Salmond, even opened the introduction to Scotland's Future (the Scottish Government's guide to an independent Scotland) with 'Our national story has been shaped down the generations by values of compassion, equality, an unrivalled commitment to the empowerment of education' (Scottish Government, 2013: viii).

There are five secure care centres now operating in Scotland, between them offering places for 84 children. The origins of all four of the nationally contracted, (Scotland Excel) independent charitable secure care centres (the fifth which provides six places to children in one area is the only one delivered directly by a Scottish local authority) can be traced back to the Victorian era. This saw an explosion in educational 'corrective' institutions including industrial and reform schools, set up by State, Church, and charitable organisations (Shaw, 2007). From there, what were known as approved schools were established in 1937; and later List D schools, due to being listed under the letter d, in an administrative list associated with the Social Work (Scotland) Act, 1968 (the 1968 Act).

The 1968 Act led to radical changes in Scottish child welfare and justice approaches and paved the way for the Children's Hearings System which has continued to operate since 1971. In Scotland we champion this System and its founding 'Kilbrandon principles', so called as Lord Kilbrandon chaired the Committee whose report, published in 1964, set out the basis for the 1968 Act and all that flowed from it. They still underpin our welfare-based approach to children and young people in trouble including those who are in conflict with the law and are held now at the heart of the Scottish Government Getting it Right for Every Child (GIRFEC) strategic approach and implementation programmes.

The authorities had identified a need for 'closed blocks' within the approved school regime to keep safe and contain children whose behaviours were especially worrying and/or who were persistently running away and at risk before Kilbrandon (Millham, Bullock, and Hosie, 1978). Although the concept and their design drew on the prison system and the legacy of the 'Reform' school era, the secure care centres which developed were always part of the child care system. They were underpinned by a rehabilitative and therapeutic rather than punitive intent. From the outset they aimed to meet the needs of young people as well as address their behaviours when these were troubling or harmful to others. Kilbrandon (1964) famously noted that these children's family, home, and life circumstances meant they

> may be said at present to be, more than most, in a real and special sense 'hostages to fortune'. The time has come we believe … to extend to this minority of children, within a sustained and continuing discipline of social education, the measures which their needs dictate, and of which they have hitherto been too often deprived.
>
> *(Kilbrandon, 1964: 76)*

However, more than half a century on, the accounts of children and young people in secure care including those shared with us during the Secure Care National Project indicate that Scotland remains at best ambivalent about responses to the minority of children who continue to find themselves 'hostages to fortune'. Many children and young people across the UK in and on the edges of secure care consistently report being misunderstood, blamed, judged, and stigmatised by the care and justice systems, and in particular by social workers and the people and tribunals which decide to contain them in secure care (Moodie and Barrie, 2008; Ellis, 2016; Gough, 2016; Gough 2017).

Although the numbers of children and young people detained in prison or secure care here have continued to fall, in early 2018, there were eight times as many Scottish children (aged 16 to 18) on sentence or remand in a prison setting (Polmont YOI) than there were on sentence or remand in our secure care sector, and we have continued to deal with many children through our adult justice system (Dyer, 2016). Those who are in secure care often identify themselves as being in a custodial rather than care setting (Gough, 2016; Gough, 2017) and less restrictive legal orders to keep young people safe, such as intensive support and monitoring (with a movement restriction condition) as an alternative to secure care, are used infrequently (Simpson and Dyer, 2016).

Throughout the history of Scottish secure care and education, there has been an ever-present thread of tension pulling between care and control, and between protection and punishment, in terms of perceptions of secure care and the young people who are placed there. We suggest that if a poll was conducted now to test Scottish public awareness and understanding, few people would know that it is a form of residential school care and fewer still would be aware of the extreme harm and adversity present in the backgrounds of children and young people in secure care. Negative assumptions about these children and those who care for them are still common, as we heard when we took part in conversations with a group of secure care practitioners for a podcast about secure care in Scotland (Iriss fm, 2017).

Continuing progress in the range and quality of educational and learning opportunities across the sector has nevertheless been made. For many years, all the centres here have been registered with, and inspected by, the statutory regulators in Scotland both as children's homes and as schools (Care Inspectorate and Education Scotland). They are not young offender institutions and they are subject to the same expectations and inspected against the same national standards as all schools. The introduction of the Curriculum for Excellence in Scotland with its 'four capacities' (successful learners, confident individuals, responsible citizens, and effective contributors) has seen interest in the small sector here from across the UK and as far away as New Zealand (McIntosh, 2016) in part because of the integrated, multi-professional, and innovative approaches in most of the centres to delivering what is described as the '24 hour curriculum'.

However, whilst expectations, scrutiny, and recognition of the education provision in secure care have increased, the use of secure care for Scottish children has reduced as outlined and the average length of stay for a Scottish child in secure care during 2015 to 2016 was around four months (Scottish Government, 2018). So, whilst the secure care centres operate as schools (and we will discuss evidence that shows that the majority of children who are secured engage with education whilst there) no longitudinal studies have been undertaken in Scotland to specifically examine the whole education journeys of these children, or their attainment and life outcomes in the longer term.

Children's lives: adversity, inequality, and education policy

Policy rhetoric in Scotland increasingly regards education as key to tackling social inequality. In 2015, the Scottish Government launched the Scottish Attainment Challenge, aimed at achieving equity 'by ensuring every child has the same opportunity to succeed, with a particular focus on closing the poverty-related attainment gap'. Official statistics published for 2015 to 2016 show some children have better opportunities than others, and that children from more privileged backgrounds continue to far outperform their less privileged counterparts, with 15% of those from the poorest backgrounds not reaching a so-called positive destination, compared with less than 4% of those from the wealthiest backgrounds.

Attainment levels and positive post school destinations for looked after children (and particularly those looked after at home and in residential care) also continue to lag well behind when compared to children who are not in care. Whilst 86% of all school leavers were awarded one or more qualification at SCQF level 5 (SQA) and 91% moved on to education, training, or employment, only 40% of looked after children attained one or more such qualification and 71% reached a positive destination (Scottish Government, 2018). In the same year, looked after school leavers who had experienced more care placements in the year also tended to have lower levels of qualifications. The same report shows that 80% of looked after leavers who had just one placement all year achieved one or more qualification at Level 4 or better but, of those who had four or more placements during the year, only 64% achieved this. The higher the level of qualification, the starker the contrast, so that less than a quarter of looked after school leavers who had experienced multiple placements reached Level 5 or more, whereas 45% of looked after young people who didn't move during the year achieved Level 5 awards or higher.

The political context and position of the government of the day on education will always have significant impact for some of the least privileged children, where their behaviours trouble others. This is because there is an inextricable link between governments' policy position on universal and 'specialist' education and their position on children in difficulty where children's behaviours pose a challenge to others including educators and/or conflict with the law. We saw this when the post devolution Labour led Scottish Government was in office, and education policy focused on 'inclusion' and 'mainstreaming', beginning an exponential shift away from the use of residential and so called 'out of authority' education placements for children and young people who have additional learning support needs, which continues now. Yet, simultaneously, their tough stance on 'youth offending' and children in conflict with the law saw the introduction of youth court pilots, anti-social behaviour legislation, and millions of pounds invested in increasing the size and capacity of the secure care 'estate' (Smith and Milligan, 2005).

In contrast, a dramatic reduction in the use of secure care by the Scottish authorities has occurred during the Scottish Nationalist led administration, so that in January 2018 we saw the average number of Scottish young people in secure care (40) halved in comparison to that in January 2013 (78). This may be partly due to the Scottish Government's GIRFEC strategic approach which has seen in a raft of legislative and policy initiatives aimed at prevention and promoting positive wellbeing outcomes, from the early years through to early adulthood.

There are four core principles to the GIRFEC approach. Firstly, that it is child-focused to ensure that the child or young person, and their family, is at the centre of decision-making and the support available to them. Secondly, it is based on an understanding of the wellbeing of the child, looking at their overall wellbeing across what have become known as the SHANARRI indicators (an acronym for how safe, healthy, achieving, nurtured, active, respected, responsible, and included they are) so that the right support can be offered at the right time. Thirdly, identifying needs as early as possible to avoid bigger concerns or problems developing, and fourthly, joined up working with children, young people, parents, and the services they need working together in a coordinated way to meet the specific needs and improve their wellbeing (Scottish Government, 2018).

The GIRFEC principles extend to youth justice policy and, since 2011, this has included the whole system approach which was introduced across the local authority areas to promote best practice in responding to children who may come into conflict with the law and has been evaluated as having had an overall positive impact (Murray et al., 2015).

Yet under both administrations, education policy has continued to stress the 'behaviour modification' and 'rehabilitative' aspects for those children who are categorised and labelled as experiencing emotional and behavioural difficulties. In 2018, the Scottish Government website describes the secure care centres as working with and educating young people to improve their outcomes '*by encouraging behavioural changes*'.

The available evidence suggests that where children in conflict with the law are concerned, there is some way to go before GIRFEC can be said to have been successful across the whole system for every child. We like to think that GIRFEC has enhanced our integrated and welfare-based system for responding to *all* children in Scotland, priding ourselves on our child centred Children's Hearings System as noted, and we still celebrate Kilbrandon's vision through a national Kilbrandon Lecture. In 2017, this was delivered by the First Minister Nicola Sturgeon, who suggested that were he alive today, Kilbrandon would recognise the guiding principles behind GIRFEC because:

> He [Lord Kilbrandon] sought to reduce what he called 'the arbitrary effects of what is still too often a haphazard detection process' for identifying children who experienced what we now know as adverse childhood experiences – whether they involve abuse, neglect, violence or poverty. So, we are working to prevent those experiences, to help children to heal from trauma, and to improve the wellbeing and resilience of children who encounter them.
> *(Extract from transcript of the 15th Kilbrandon Lecture; Sturgeon, 2017)*

In reality, however, the legal system and legislation here allows children aged under 18 years, including those who are in care if they have been accused of a very serious offence, to enter the adult justice system and courts and to be imprisoned, albeit at Polmont Young Offender Institution (Dyer, 2016).

Some educationalists also characterise Scottish education policy in the 21st century as failing to uphold rights [UNESCO adopted the Convention against Discrimination in Education way back in 1960, which qualifies it as 'any distinction, exclusion, limitation or preference based on race, colour, sex, language, religion or political or other opinion, national or social origin, economic condition or birth'] by further marginalising and discriminating against the most vulnerable and least privileged children (Riddell, 2009).

The Edinburgh Study of Youth Transitions and Crime was a longitudinal programme of research on pathways into and out of offending, following a cohort of around 4300 young people starting secondary school and until they turned 25 years old (McAra and McVie, 2010). This study has produced robust evidence which indicates that at every age through the teenage years and into adulthood, the decision-making practices of institutions (including the police, children's hearings, and the criminal courts) disproportionately focus on young people from impoverished backgrounds (McAra and McVie, 2010, 2013, 2017).

As part of the Scottish Government's investigation into the minimum age of criminal responsibility here (which is likely to be raised from 8 to 12 years), the Scottish Children's Reporter Administration (SCRA) explored the backgrounds of 100 younger children (aged between 8 and 11 years) who had been referred on offence grounds during 2013 and 2014 (Henderson, Kurlus, and McNiven, 2016). The levels of adversity and multiple risks experienced by these children is startling. Most had previously been referred to the Children's Reporter due to concerns about their own safety and wellbeing as a result of lack of parental care or as victims of abuse, and 26% were already subject to compulsory measures through the children's hearings system. For the 37 children where the offence was part of a pattern of behaviour, 70% were experiencing educational concerns, 43% mental health problems, and 81% had parents or carers presenting risks to their wellbeing.

So, we know that children whose behaviours are in conflict with the law and/or are troubling for others are very clearly in need of protection, yet the evidence shows us that they are often criminalised by the system. They are too often deprived of and excluded from the opportunities that a rounded education and a good, stable school experience can provide.

Children who experience secure care

> Mental and emotional health and wellbeing should be taught in primary and secondary schools, learning about self-esteem and how to look after yourself and get help should be in the classroom.
> *(Secure care experienced young adult reflecting back on their education)*

The vast majority of young people in secure care in Scotland placed by Scottish authorities are subject to an order made by a children's hearing. The Children's Hearings (Scotland) Act 2011 provides the legal framework, including specific conditions which are referred to as the 'secure care criteria', which must be satisfied before a children's hearing issues an order with authorisation for placement in secure care. Then there is a second stage of decision making, involving the local authority chief social work officer and the head of the secure care centre who have certain powers and duties in relation to whether to implement the authorisation. Where the courts are imposing a sentence or remanding a young person, there are national standards which state that secure care and detention should be used only when it is the most appropriate disposal, and alternatives have been considered.

We know that children who arrive in secure care by either route are likely to have faced multiple adverse childhood experiences (Smith, Dyer, and Connelly, 2014; Gough, 2016; Moodie and Gough, 2017). These include: abuse (sexual, physical, and emotional); neglect (physical, emotional), and household dysfunction (familial substance abuse, familial mental illness, domestic violence in the home, incarceration of a household member). A study undertaken by one of the secure care centres found very high levels of adverse childhood experiences amongst those entering their safe centre (secure care centre). Over a third of boys and half of girls at Kibble had experienced six or more of these adverse childhood experiences and over half of all the children had symptoms of post-traumatic stress (Kibble, 2015). A paper comparing data across several countries including Sweden, Scotland, and the USA further highlighted the prevalence of trauma impact among Scottish children in secure care (Johnson, 2017). Unpublished analysis of mental and emotional health and wellbeing needs was undertaken by another of the secure care centres, Rossie, in 2014. This revealed that 72% of the young people placed there had a current or prior mental health diagnosis. For those children who pose a serious risk of harm to others, evidence from an analysis of referrals to the IVY service (Interventions for Vulnerable Youth) shows over 60% of children were known to have experienced domestic violence (Vaswani, 2018).

In addition, a significant proportion of children who experience secure care are likely to have specific speech, language, and communication needs. Around 50 to 60% of children in the youth justice system probably have some speech, language, or communication need, rising to between 75 to 90% for children in custody (Vaswani, 2014: 3). We know that some behaviours we find challenging have an association with people having difficulties expressing self or being understood.

We also know that education is particularly important as a protective factor to help mitigate against further adversity, as a mechanism to help children cope; and as a route to improve life chances after facing trauma and adversity. The Edinburgh Study we have referred to (McAra and McVie, 2010) found that there are critical moments in the early teenage years which are pathways out of offending, and that exclusion from school was the second most significant factor for determining whether a child would continue offending (the first being previous contact with the children's hearing or justice systems) (McAra and McVie, 2010). This finding has been supported by research with young people in Scotland's young offender's institution, Polmont, where at least 80% of the young men there reported they had experienced school exclusion, for many including from primary school (Smith et al., 2014).

Our conversations with young people and young adults with experience of secure care during the Secure Care National Project indicate that most had poor and/or disrupted opportunities to benefit from the school system. They had often had negative experiences of mainstream school (Gough, 2017: 24).

During research about local authorities and into use of secure care in Scotland, we interviewed the majority of chief social work officers in Scotland, and many acknowledged a lack of 'join up' in relation to universal services and planning for those services which takes account of risk and childhood adversity from the outset. Several highlighted the need for better integrated preventative approaches, and the role of schools and early years' education in supporting vulnerable children and families and ensuring that young people presenting distressed behaviours are responded to at the earliest stage. One chief social work officer put it that:

> We need to change our thinking and move away from building based services to relationship based services, better support and outreach and best use of staff skills ... and avoid the finality and labelling that secure care and residential childcare can mean for young people.
>
> *(Moodie and Gough 2017: 50)*

Some advocated high intensity relationship-based care, treatment, and education support, with multi-skilled teams including specialist practitioners and clinically qualified staff to deliver effective wrap around services. In some areas, these forms of intensive community support, including small group living residential care settings for children, were already in place or were being considered or commissioned. In others, however, whilst chief social work officers acknowledged the need and the gaps in service, the capacity to shift investment and resources towards a true GIRFEC early support and intervention approach was lacking.

As a consequence, children were still being 'escalated' through the care system, often moving from foster care, to residential care, to 'specialist' out of authority placements before eventually being placed as a 'last resort' in secure care, having each time experienced disrupted relationships, potential school moves, and broken contact with family and friends and the fracturing psychological and emotional impact that this can cause.

The young adults (aged between 18 and 24) who reflected back on their care experience and talked to us about their histories vividly outlined similar journeys. They had all experienced early traumas or losses. They urged a 'whole system approach', and more done to 'join up' services and to recognise the needs of children who experience abuse, neglect, and separation from family. They were particularly keen to stress the importance of the school and education system, describing how a lack of recognition of needs, alongside an absence of help to articulate and understand abusive and hurtful experiences, can lead to young people being judged for their behaviour rather than being supported to grow, learn, and develop as individual people. They gave examples of punitive responses from carers and from teachers and schools and said adults too often respond to young people's behaviour rather than developmental stage and needs, and that they label them as 'problematic', 'aggressive', and 'difficult', so the developmental harm caused by bullying, exploitation, and abuse is then exacerbated by school exclusion, risking further layered stigma, and the young person beginning to self-identify with these negative labels.

The approach of early years education staff and the role of primary and secondary education is critical, they suggested, and nurseries and schools have a crucial part to play in supporting children and families through difficult times. Teachers and social workers should find ways to talk to children about mental and emotional wellbeing and managing feelings. This shouldn't wait until there is an evident 'problem'. It should be integral to the curriculum and the school environment. Yet children are often being placed on an emergency basis, and at a point of acute crisis, having experienced multiple home and school placements.

Our research indicated that despite their ambivalence about the benefits (if any) of secure care, chief social work officers and referring authorities continue to expect that secure care will achieve behavioural correction, prevent re-offending, and result in risk containment as well as educational attainment for these young people (Moodie and Gough, 2017).

Practitioners, including teachers and learning support staff across the secure care centres, expressed frustration at the confused demands and expectations of placing authorities in this context. They described undue pressure on young people and on the educators and said that authorities' actions often demonstrated a lack of understanding of young people's histories and conditions. 'Sometimes it feels like we're providing a service that nobody really wants, for young people who nobody knows what to do with and who feel like nobody cares about them' (senior manager, secure care centre talking in 2016).

The 'empowerment of education': children's achievements in a challenging context

> It's really been the best thing for me. I came in here a dafty, but I've changed in here. I'll think twice and do things differently out there.
>
> I wasn't in school for 3 years before coming here – I didn't have a clue what to do – came into education and thought what can I do? But they've (education staff) been good – I'm managing to learn.
>
> *(Young people in secure care)*

So, the secure care centres are attempting to deliver a holistic, rounded, and motivational education experience to children and young people who are very likely to have faced multiple adversities, trauma, and disrupted home and school lives and the accompanying developmental impact. In addition, children may often be placed with them for less than two school 'terms'. Where they are aged over 16, children and young people are not obliged to attend school and if on remand and aged over 16, they are under no compulsion to engage in any form of education or programmes. The expectations for all of the centres is that despite this, they will be able to deliver education, life skills, and evidence based programmes and interventions aimed at supporting these young people to address underlying issues.

This all has implications for 'readiness to learn' and raises questions as to whether the responsible authorities and commissioners fully consider the developmental perspectives and educational needs of the 'whole child' when considering these children. Thinking about the needs of the whole person, this challenging context also begs questions about the demands and expectations that are placed on children arriving in secure care, which some of the young people who spoke to us described as confusing and frustrating, and others disempowering:

> They tell you [in reviews and hearings] that you're going to be here for months and months but don't tell you the steps to get out.
>
> Having a plan really helps, but they need to involve us; half the time you don't know what's in your plan or you're seeing it at the last minute.
>
> *(Young people in secure care talking about expectations of social workers and decision makers)*

However, Education Scotland inspection reports consistently show that the vast majority of children in secure care *do* engage with learning and do achieve and grow. In this next section we focus on children's experiences of the approach taken by the secure care centres which have been identified as 'outstanding' by the inspection bodies. What are the elements that come together to 'get it right'? It is our view that it is a combination of relational based, holistic, and hopeful education practice that enables this, and that relationships built on foundations of respect and understanding are the real key.

The challenges and adversities faced by individual young people who arrive in secure care are, as outlined, considerable. But, as for all of us, these difficulties are only part of human stories. Our conversations with young people who had experienced, or were experiencing secure care, highlighted they are creative, caring, talented, fun, and have incredible insight, knowledge, and understanding. They impressed us time after time as did the consistent warmth, humour, kindness, and respect with which the young people and the adults caring for them communicated with each other. Observing some class groups and sharing a meal with groups of staff and children, the enjoyment in each other's company was evident.

> They're a laugh but they can be strict as well. Like you don't take any crap. That helps us.
>
> I'm 16 so I don't have to go to school but I am expected to here and that's good. I'd missed out on a lot of school and it's small classes so you get a lot of help here.
>
> *(Young people in secure care)*

Although many children who spoke to us said they had initially been frustrated at being expected to attend formal education, overall, they were engaging and described having found confidence in their abilities and hidden talents for art, writing, music, or specific subjects, whilst in secure care. They explained that having structure, purpose, and focus to your day can also really help to combat the potential for boredom, loneliness, and related stress and depression which can accompany life in a restricted environment. They were aware they had missed out and they had an appetite to 'catch up': 'It's actually really good here in education and in the unit. Where else would you get 4 or 5 people in a class group? There's lots of choices in subjects and you can get 1 to 1 support.'

The whole child and the 'whole school' approach

The secure care centres in Scotland consist of between one and five locked children's houses, each having four, five, or six individual ensuite bedrooms and each with its own communal living, dining, and relaxation spaces. These individual secure children's houses are connected to a school or education base and recreational spaces which are in the same building or campus and linked by secure corridors.

All of the centres have invested in, and have ongoing plans to further improve, the fabric of their buildings and the range and quality of facilities on site. To promote wellbeing and '24-hour curriculum' opportunities, they have variously built and enhanced leisure, social, and recreational facilities including sports halls, gyms, swimming pools, therapy and relaxation spaces, IT, art, technology, music, and multi-media suites; and all have ongoing refurbishment programmes in place for children's own rooms, and shared living and learning spaces.

Usually there is a maximum of four or five young people in each class or learning group with a qualified teacher and/or instructor depending on the subject/qualification being studied, and at least one classroom/teaching assistant supporting learning. Where young people need intensive support, they are often tutored individually for part of the school week. Some of the centres have well-developed peer and student mentoring schemes and young people described this as positive, appreciating each other as sources of advice and support, particularly in the early stages of a placement when getting to know staff and young people and feeling 'part of the group': 'Other young people; they explained how things work in here'.

The secure care centres also employ a range of people including psychologists and therapists to offer individual and group support and help to young people whilst they are in secure care. Most have effective arrangements in place with speech and language and other specialists to ensure every child has access to the support that they need and that their individual learning plan is tailored with and for them.

We were struck during the Secure Care National Project at the evident 'whole school' approach adopted in most of the centres. That is, the strong sense of 'school community', cohesion and shared understanding about the impact of one part of the day-to-day living and learning experience in secure care on another, and how important it is for everyone, whatever their professional background or job role, to understand their potential impact on and contribution to children's wellbeing, learning, and development.

> The majority of young people who are secured here haven't been looking after themselves, and many have been hurt by others ... most will have a range of difficulties with day to day functioning and relationships ... whether you work here as a teacher, a cook or a psychologist, our job is to respond to that all day every day in a way that helps that individual young person to move forward.
> *(Secure care specialist interventions manager)*

What also stands out from joint inspection reports (Education Scotland and the Care Inspectorate undertake an 'integrated inspection' of each secure centre at least every few years in addition to frequent Care Inspectorate inspections) is the significance of the relational and cultural climate at the most highly rated centres in ensuring a child centred (whole child) and integrated (whole school) approach.

Two of the centres (Kibble and The Good Shepherd Centre) received Excellent and Very Good grades across all the areas of their schools when evaluated during joint inspections. They were each praised overall for 'outstanding' (sector leading) aspects, whilst a third (Rossie) was praised for aspects of teaching which were 'outstanding' and has separately won recognition from Scotland Excel for innovation and its whole school/learning organisation approach. Whilst the physical environment, school facilities, and quality of teaching and leadership all contributed to the inspection outcomes, importantly inspectors noted:

> As a result of the very good relationships in care and education, young people trust and respect staff. They know that staff are committed to keeping them safe and caring for them. All young people are aware of their rights as individuals and know the rules and boundaries established by the service. As a consequence, the atmosphere in care and education is calm and settled and young people's behaviour is generally good.
> *(Good Shepherd Centre Inspection Report, 2015)*

> The impact of strong nurturing relationships between education and care staff and young people.
> *(Rossie Inspection Report, 2014)*

> Strong, trusting relationships between all staff and young people.
> *(Kibble Inspection Report, 2016)*

The secure care centres commended by inspection bodies evidenced highly effective arrangements for identifying children's needs within integrated assessment and staff training and professional development frameworks. Their teachers and education staff were reported to have a sound understanding of children's lives and the impact of trauma and attachment issues. They were observed practising with significant skill in responding to young people with compassion and respect, managing their anxieties and engaging them in learning. The integration of psychology, education, and child care methodologies was also apparent at each of the focused conversations we undertook with groups of staff across the centres.

This is all the more noteworthy given the challenges teaching and education staff teams face due to the level of emergency and short-term placements. They also told us about significant variance in the level and quality of information shared with teaching staff by education authorities/educational psychology services and young people's previous schools. Several teachers at different centres stated that young people had moved through and on from the secure care placement and they had still not received full background information.

Many also expressed concern that young people coming into secure care have previously unrecognised or/and unmet speech and language difficulties. They described situations where young people had been in part-time minimum hours 'alternative' education for considerable periods of time and had missed out on basic core language and number skills.

Most young people who spoke to us during the Secure Care National Project described feeling cared for and respected. Many were keen to name individual teachers and classroom support staff who they described as being particularly inspirational, caring, supportive, and helpful. The majority were very positive about the school experience in secure care, often comparing and contrasting it with their previous school experiences. They felt accepted and not judged from the start. 'You know where you stand from the minute you're in here'. 'Staff don't judge you in here. They've seen it all before'.

All of the young people spoke positively about group activities and opportunities for example team sports and most talked about 'whole school' events such as celebration days and drama productions. They described what this gave them in terms of building confidence, team working and other skills, friendships, physical fitness, and a sense of contribution and achievement. In the majority of centres there was a wide choice of class subjects, skills-based opportunities, and space for self-expression and in particular creative arts and craft subjects, music, IT/multi-media studies, and vocational courses, such as barbering and hairdressing, and young people were particularly enthusiastic. Importantly, they described having been motivated, challenged, and supported by teachers and others whose company they enjoyed. 'I came in here with nothing. Now I've got Nat 4 Maths, English. I've done a barbering course'.

Hope and expectation

Children and young people told us that having a sense of hope for the future and for those around you to have hope for you, and believe you can 'make it', is very important. Hope is powerful, so much so that one of the secure care centres (Good Shepherd Centre) has added another letter to SHANARRI for Hope.

> Look at what we've all achieved despite everything we've been through.
> *(Secure care experienced young adult)*

> My social worker, I think she hated me before cos I used to kick off. I didn't like her either but she's on my side now, she thinks I'm brilliant.
> *(Young person in secure care talking about adults who help)*

This sense of hope and self-belief is encouraged not just through access to academic subjects but the 'interventions' and 'programmes' offered to young people to support mental and emotional wellbeing and help them make sense of their experiences in order to move forward. The sense of being cared for and being cared about by all of the staff underpins the school curriculum, the clinical care if needed, and the formal engagement in personal development programmes:

> I had loads of opportunities like the [theatre group] drama therapy, creative therapies and stress massage and relaxation classes.
> *(Secure care experienced young adult)*

> [Programmes] have helped. Like you do get to think about things that happened before and how you'd do things different. Like consequential thinking and reflecting on stuff, I'll use that my whole life.
>
> *(Young person in secure care)*

The breadth, range, and ambition of the school curriculum itself is very important and reflects how hopeful and ambitious schools are for their children's futures. Historically, secure care was regarded as limited and limiting in its 'academic' offer because, in common with most forms of residential school 'alternative care', the centres did not offer a full curriculum and subject range, perhaps reflecting limited expectations of and for children in care. It was not until the introduction of the Children (Scotland) Act 1995 that children's right to equal educational opportunities in care and secure care were fully recognised (SIRCC, 2005).

Inspection reports now comment on the broad and often innovative range of SQA accredited (Scottish Qualifications Authority) courses and other awards ranging from Duke of Edinburgh's Award, John Muir Trust and ASDAN, work experience, college placements, and apprenticeships. The majority of secure centres are offering, and children placed there are achieving, 'an impressive range' even though they are often placed in secure care for short and indeterminate periods (Education Scotland and Care Inspectorate reports). Ken McIntosh, Principal of New Zealand's Central Regional Health School, who visited Scotland in 2016, was so impressed with the breadth of offer from one secure care centre that he blogged about it on the CYCJ website. He commented on:

> The structure, the resources, the services and most of all the people were fantastic. Looking at Kibble and asking, 'what one aspect/service would I like to take away the most?' It would have to be the Young Workforce Development. The breadth and depth of the programmes, the support for young people and endless possibilities took my breath away. The young people I met were engaged in purposeful learning that was clearly goal focused and part of meeting their wider social, health and education needs.
>
> *(McIntosh, 2016)*

Moving on: transition support and readiness

Few studies have looked at longer term outcomes for young people who have experienced secure care in Scotland but those that have highlight the importance of education in determining young people's opportunities in adulthood. Kendrick et al. (2008) found that, alongside placement and community support, school, further, higher education, or work based or vocational training all provided hope, structure, purpose, routine, and real opportunities to develop as an individual, including new knowledge and skills, friendships, and a sense of direction as young people made the transition into adulthood.

Overall, the majority of young people described to us having had very good support, help, and opportunities to reflect on the situations that had brought them into secure care and to think about what they wanted for the future. This is important they said because moving on is about being emotionally ready to move forward. Those who felt ready to move forward talked positively about what they had achieved. They were clear about the next steps and stated that they had gained skills, confidence, qualifications, and hopes for the future whilst in the secure care setting, including plans for their working lives and careers and/or for further education. They talked about the help and guidance they had received from care staff, interventions and wellbeing staff, education and careers, their social workers, their children's rights workers, and their families. Again, emotional readiness was also identified as key by young people still in secure care who were looking towards the end of their placements:

> I don't know, it's sometimes like a switch in your head, like you might be wild but then you're just ready to change.
> As you get more freedom and independence, I get to go out and do stuff in the community, work experience, cadets; loads of opportunities.
> At the end of the day some of these staff have genuinely changed my life and changed me for good in different ways, they really have.
> *(Young people talking about readiness and moving on from secure care)*

Education Scotland also recognises in inspection reports the importance of a holistic approach to preparation and support for the future; that this is not just about attainment of qualifications, though that is important:

> The wellbeing team provide a wide range of specialist programmes and therapies which are carefully selected to meet individual young people's needs. Wellbeing staff also offer parents and young people family support to strengthen relationships and help young people to return to their home and local community. Occupational therapists, clinical and forensic psychologists and speech and language therapists also provide additional support as required.
> (Education Scotland and Care Inspectorate report of inspection, Good Shepherd Centre, 2015).

However, there are practical challenges for most of the centres in relation to providing good transition support to young people moving on from secure care into other education and learning settings. At the local authority run centre in Edinburgh, teaching staff are able to undertake visits and transition meetings to receiving schools and colleges and some similar effective transition support is provided at the other centres on occasion. But the practicalities of distance and the need to ensure teaching cover make this unusual where young people are moving back to their home locality. Local authority funding for meaningful transition support was also often missing. Staff in all of the four independent centres described situations where the effort invested by children and the secure care team risked being undone because of factors including lack of careful planning or appropriate transition support provided by the placing authority, or unplanned and sudden 'endings' to placements:

> It's heart-breaking when you see what a young person has achieved in here and how they've changed and then they're terrified about what's going to happen cos they're telling everyone that they're not ready to move on yet ... we've had situations where the system has just set them up to fail.
> *(Secure care centre service manager)*

We found significant variation in how local authorities and partner agencies including health, CAMHS, and education services interface with the secure care sector and how involved and engaged corporate parents are in sharing information about young people, contributing to transition planning, and ensuring continuity of care and relationships when young people move on from secure care. Looking forward positively, and preparing for moving on, can be difficult if you are going to be moving a long way away to your next placement or back to your home area. Young people said it had been frustrating for them to begin work experience or 'mobility' whilst in secure care, and then face having to move and 'start again'. 'How can that be right? You start work experience or something but then you're going all the way to the other side of the country, so you can't carry on with that.'

The impact of separation and disconnection from home and community and the challenges faced by young people and those caring for them when young people are in, and then moving on from, secure care are thus significant. This is particularly so for the increasing numbers of children and young people who are being placed from England in Scottish secure care. Since 2016, there has been a rise in these numbers which to some extent has happened 'under the radar', perhaps reflecting the limited public awareness, attention to, or understanding of, children and young people in and on the edges of secure care generally. But this is a real issue with serious implications for children and their families in terms of fundamental children's and human rights; for the realisation of GIRFEC principles and policy; and for the future commissioning, governance, and sustainability of intensive support and secure care services.

Figures show that at one point in early 2018, there were no vacancies in secure care here and half of all children placed were from England (Gov.uk, 2018). The individual impact for children is perhaps highlighted most when thinking about transitions; how might it feel to travel in 'secure' transport for possibly hundreds of miles to be admitted by strangers into a secure care centre in a different country? To try to understand and be understood when voices and words and idioms are so different to your own? How can you experience effective transition support if you are, say, a young person who is returning to the south of England and hoping to attend college after a year living in Scotland in secure care?

How did Scotland reach this point? The answer lies in the challenges facing both Scotland and England for different reasons. In Scotland, one of the drivers for the

Secure Care National Project was the unpredictability and ambivalence about use of secure care here (numbers had been falling since 2011) whilst in England there was a 21% reduction in secure accommodation places available in England between 2010 and 2016 (National Statistic, DfE, 2016) and demand outstripping availability. These UK government figures show that there were 254 places commissioned at secure units in England and Wales in 2016, down 34% on the 390 places available for use ten years earlier. This led to increasing use of Scottish secure care centres by English authorities, until Sir James Munby issued a High Court Ruling in 2016, in which he concluded orders made by the English courts placing a child in a secure unit north of the border could not be enforced or recognised in Scotland.

The ruling was made after Munby had considered the cases of two children who had been placed in secure units in Scotland due to no places being available in England. He recommended an urgent review of the law in this area. However, in December 2016, the UK (England and Wales) Children's Minister Edward Timpson tabled amendments to the Children and Social Work Bill that would amend Section 25 of the Children Act 1989 to enable such cross-border placements. The Scottish Government gave 'legislative consent' to these aspects of the Children and Social Work Bill and in the Legislative Consent Memorandum (which Deputy First Minister John Swinney lodged with the Scottish Parliament in 2016) justified this as necessary to 'deal with a gap in the law'. The Memorandum states that allowing local authorities in England and Wales to continue to place children in Scottish secure accommodation 'provides valuable flexibility in the secure accommodation estate across the UK and is in the best interests of the children involved'.

It is not clear on what basis the best interests of children has been determined, but this change in law has had significant impact and means many more vulnerable children are being placed in secure care in a different UK country to their usual residence. Yet in the Memorandum these changes are described as 'limited and technical in nature' and there are evident financial and service drivers for the Legislative Consent:

> There will be no costs to the Scottish Government or public authorities as a result of the amendments. There would only be financial/resource implications if cross-border placements were to cease. The withdrawal of English placements would lead to a loss of income to one or more of the Scottish units, with the possibility it would force at least one provider into an early and unplanned closure.

The provisions to which the Scottish Government gave Legislative Consent were introduced in April 2017 and figures to be published in 2018 will show that children placed from England have made up between a fifth and as many as half of all children in secure care in Scotland since.

Where next?

There is something of a crisis of confidence (as well as the serious lack of availability) in secured settings in England; ironically the Scottish secure care centres are regularly receiving approbation for the quality of care and education they offer to English children despite the questionable rights and ethical challenges of cross-border placements, as outlined. Were it not for the English placements, the facts do suggest the Scottish secure care sector here would not continue to be viable in its current form and capacity.

The issue is currently vexing many of the members of the Secure Care Strategic Board which the Scottish Government established in 2017 to take forward the recommendations arising from the Secure Care National Project (see Scottish Government website). The report, setting out the key messages and recommendations (including a strategic board to act as a vehicle for change) arising from the project (Secure Care in Scotland: Looking Ahead, Gough, 2016) was published before the changes to law which led to the increase in cross-border placements.

Simultaneously, as we have described, we found through our work that the authorities' appetite for, and understanding of, the 'outstanding' care and education offer that the majority of the centres here can deliver for the most vulnerable children, is weak.

Perhaps we are all asking the wrong question. Rather than focusing the debate and the arguments around policy, structures, and funding on whether 'to secure or not to secure?' might we instead better expend energy on asking 'what works'?

We suggest that now really is the time to revisit Kilbrandon's concept of 'social education' in Scotland, and to ask ourselves how do we regard and respond to the most troubled children, and particularly those who harm others, and what does this mean for their wellbeing and treatment? The answer will require radical re-thinking and will take considerable courage. But we can equip ourselves, if we choose to, with the robust evidence we already have from children and young people's lived experience as well as from practice and research, about what works, including across the UK.

The highly skilled workforce, specialist knowledge base, and evidence informed, outcomes focused, integrated approach hailed by Education Scotland in our best regarded secure care centres have developed through strong leadership and investment choices. The question is, how can we replicate that and empower nursery workers, teachers, social workers, whole schools, and the whole system to recognise and understand the needs of these children and work towards 'getting it right' for all children who need intensive support to help them grow and achieve?

References

Anderson, R.D. (1983) *Education and opportunity in Victorian Scotland*. Oxford: Clarendon Press.
Department for Education (2016) *Children accommodated in secure children's homes: England and Wales (National Statistics report)*. London: DfE. Retrieved from: www.gov.uk/government/uploads/system/uploads/attachment_data/file/541766/SFR09-2016_Text.pdf
Dyer, F. (2016) *Young people at court in Scotland*. Glasgow: Centre for Youth and Criminal Justice. Retrieved from: www.cycj.org.uk/wp-content/uploads/2016/02/YoungPeopleAtCourtFINAL.pdf

Education Scotland and Care Inspectorate (2014) *Inspection report for Rossie.* Retrieved from: https://education.gov.scot/assets/inspectionreports/rossieyoungpeoplestrustins220714.pdf

Education Scotland and Care Inspectorate (2015) *Inspection report for Good Shepherd Centre secure/close support unit.* Retrieved from: https://education.gov.scot/assets/inspectionreports/goodshepherdfinal100315.pdf

Education Scotland and Care Inspectorate (2016) *Inspection report for Kibble.* Retrieved from: https://education.gov.scot/assets/inspectionreports/kibbleeccins060916.pdf

Ellis, K.H. (2016) 'He's got some nasty impression of me he has': listening to children in the secure estate. *The British Journal of Social Work,* 46, 6, 1553–1567.

Gough, A. (2016) *Secure care in Scotland: looking ahead.* Glasgow: Centre for Youth and Criminal Justice. Retrieved from: www.cycj.org.uk/wp-content/uploads/2016/10/Secure-Care-in-Scotland-Looking-Ahead.pdf

Gough, A. (2017) *Secure care in Scotland: young people's voices.* Glasgow: Centre for Youth and Criminal Justice. Retrieved from: www.cycj.org.uk/wp-content/uploads/2017/10/Secure-Care-Young-Peoples-Voices.pdf

Gov.uk (2018) *Statistics: secure children's homes.* Retrieved from: www.gov.uk/government/collections/statistics-secure-children-s-homes

Henderson, G., Kurlus, I., and McNiven, G. (2016) *Backgrounds and outcomes for children aged 8 to 11 years old who have been referred to the Children's Reporter for offending.* Stirling: SCRA. Retrieved from: www.scra.gov.uk/wp-content/uploads/2016/03/Backgrounds-and-outcomes-for-children-aged-8-11-years-old-who-have-been-referred-for-offending.pdf

Irissfm (2017) Podcast episode – 183: secure care in Scotland (31 May). Retrieved from: www.iriss.org.uk/resources/irissfm/secure-care-scotland

Johnson, D. (2017) Tangible trauma informed care. *Scottish Journal of Residential Child Care,* 16, 1. Retrieved from: www.celcis.org/files/4214/9322/2681/2017_Vol_16_1_Johnson_D_Tangible_Trauma_Informed_Care.pdf

Kendrick, A., Walker, M., Barclay, A., Hunter, L., Malloch, M., Hill, M., and McIvor, G. (2008) The outcomes of secure care in Scotland. *Scottish Journal of Residential Child Care,* 7, 1. Retrieved from: www.celcis.org/files/2414/8475/3535/2008_Vol_07_1_Kendrick_Walker_Barclay_Hunter_Malloch_outcomes_of_secure_care.pdf

Kibble (2015) *Profile of young people at Kibble.* Paisley: Kibble Education and Care Centre.

Kilbrandon (1964) *Report by the Committee appointed by the Secretary of State for Scotland.* Edinburgh: Her Majesty's Stationery Office. Retrieved from: www.gov.scot/Publications/2003/10/18259/26879

McIntosh, K. (2016) *Why Scotland can improve outcomes for New Zealand's children in care.* Blog on the Centre for Youth and Criminal Justice website. Retrieved from: www.cycj.org.uk/how-scotland-can-improve-outcomes-for-new-zealands-children-in-care/

McAra, L., and McVie, S. (2010) Youth crime and justice: key messages from the Edinburgh Study of Youth. Transitions and crime. *Criminology and Criminal Justice,* 10, 2, 179–209.

McAra, L., and McVie, S. (2013) Delivering justice for children and young people: key messages from the Edinburgh study of youth transitions and crime. *Justice for young people: Papers by Winners of the Research Medal,* 3–14.

McAra, L., and McVie, S. (2017) Developmental and life-course criminology: Innovations, impacts and applications. In A. Liebling, S. Maruna, and L. McAra (Eds), *Oxford handbook of criminology.* Oxford: Oxford University Press.

Millham, S., Bullock, R., and HosieK. (1978) *Locking up children: Secure provision within the child-care system.* Farnborough: Saxon House.

Moodie, K., and Gough, A. (2017) *Chief social work officers and secure care.* Glasgow: Centre for Youth and Criminal Justice. Retrieved from: www.cycj.org.uk/wp-content/uploads/2017/05/Chief-Social-Work-Officers-and-secure-care-report.pdf

Murray, K., McGuiness, P., Burnam, M., and McVie, S. (2015) *Evaluation of the whole system approach to young people who offend in Scotland*. Scottish Centre for Crime and Justice Research and Scottish Government. Retrieved from: www.gov.scot/Resource/0047/00479272.pdf

Riddell, S. (2009) Social justice, equality and inclusion in Scottish education. *Discourse: Studies in the Cultural Politics of Education*, 30, 3, 283–296. Retrieved from: www.docs.hss.ed.ac.uk/education/creid/Projects/16xi_ESRC_Pub_SocJus_sr.pdf

Scottish Government (2013) *Scotland's future: your guide to an independent Scotland*Edinburgh: Scottish Government. Retrieved from:www.gov.scot/resource/0043/00439021.pdf

Scottish Government (2017) *Education outcomes for looked after children 2015/16*. Edinburgh: Scottish Government. Retrieved from: www.gov.scot/Resource/0052/00521222.pdf

Scottish Government (2018) *Children's social work statistics*. Retrieved from: www.gov.scot/Topics/Statistics/Browse/Children/PubChildrenSocialWork

Scottish Institute for Residential Childcare (2005) *Secure in the knowledge: perspectives on practice in secure accommodation*. Glasgow: SIRCC. Retrieved from: www.celcis.org/files/2314/3878/4209/secure-in-the-knowledge-perspectives.pdf

Scottish Parliamentary Corporate Body (2016) *Legislative Consent Memorandum (Children and Social Work Bill, lodged by John Swinney in the Scottish Parliament)*, January. Retrieved from: https://publications.parliament.uk/pa/bills/cbill/2016-2017/0121/LCM-S05-7.pdf

Shaw, T. (2007) *Historical abuse in residential child care in Scotland 1950–1995*. Edinburgh: Scottish Government.

Simpson, S., and Dyer, F. (2016) *Movement restriction conditions (MRCs) and youth justice in Scotland: are we there yet?*Glasgow: Centre for Youth and Criminal Justice. Retrieved from: www.cycj.org.uk/wp-content/uploads/2016/10/MRCs-and-Youth-Justice-in-Scotland-2.pdf

Smith, M., and Milligan, I. (2005) The expansion of secure care in Scotland: in the best interest of the child? *Youth Justice*, 4, 3, 178–190. Retrieved from: https://pure.strath.ac.uk/portal/files/67592940/Miligan_Smith_ECP_2006_From_welfare_to_correction_a_review_of_changing_.pdf

Smith, S., Dyer, F., and Connelly, G. (2014) *Young men in custody: a report on the pathways into and out of prison of young men aged 16 and 17*. Glasgow: Centre for Youth and Criminal Justice. Retrieved from: www.cycj.org.uk/wp-content/uploads/2014/09/Young-men-in-custody-research-report.pdf

Sturgeon, N. (2017) *The 15th Kilbrandon Lecture* (online transcript). University of Strathclyde and Scottish Government. Retrieved from: https://news.gov.scot/speeches-and-briefings/kilbrandon-lecture-strathclyde-university

UNESCO (1960) *Convention against discrimination in education*. Paris: UNESCO. Retrieved from: http://portal.unesco.org/en/ev.php-URL_ID=12949andURL_DO=DO_TOPICandURL_SECTION=201.html

Vaswani, N. (2014) *Speech, language and communication difficulties*. Glasgow: Centre for Youth and Criminal Justice. Retrieved from: www.cycj.org.uk/wp-content/uploads/2014/10/SLCN-report.pdf

Vaswani, N. (2018) *Adverse childhood experiences in children at high risk of harm to others. A gendered perspective*. Glasgow: Centre for Youth and Criminal Justice. Retrieved from: www.cycj.org.uk/resource/adverse-childhood-experiences-in-children-at-high-risk-of-harm-to-others-a-gendered-perspective/.

7
EDUCATION FOR U.S. YOUTH IN SECURE CARE

The sum of the parts is not whole

Deborah K. Reed

It is estimated that approximately 50,000 young people (referred to in this chapter as *youth*) are held in juvenile justice facilities and shelters (collectively referred to here as *secure care*) each day in the United States (Puzzanchera and Hockenberry, 2015). These court-involved youths can enter secure care in different ways that may depend upon their family histories, their level of criminal behaviour, the local law enforcement and judicial authorities' approaches, the state in which they enter the system, and even their citizenship status. While in secure care, youth are still entitled to a free basic education – one that would be of similar quality to the education they would receive in their public schools (U.S. Department of Education, 2014). However, under Title 1 of the U.S. Elementary and Secondary Education Act of 1965 (amended in 2015 as the Every Student Succeeds Act), the students' circumstances classify them as being at risk of academic failure.

Indeed, the majority of court-involved youth perform significantly behind age-matched peers in reading (Flynn, Ghazal, Legault, Vandermeulen, and Petrick, 2004; Houchins, Jolivette, Krezmien, and Baltodano, 2008) and drop out of school at far higher rates than their peers who are not in secure care (Bruskas, 2008; Cavendish, 2014). Yet, the educational services provided have a history of being inadequate and disjointed (Leone and Wruble, 2015). Some of the challenges to improving the education stem from the different contexts in which the services are provided. There are a range of dispositions for youth cases, but this chapter will focus on secure placements where youth both reside and attend school. Specifically, the pathways explored here are: sheltered youth (those in foster care and unaccompanied minor immigrants), detained youth, youth in juvenile corrections, and youthful offenders in the adult criminal system. As depicted in Figure 7.1, there can be movement among the pathways, thus multiplying the number of educational systems involved in any one case.

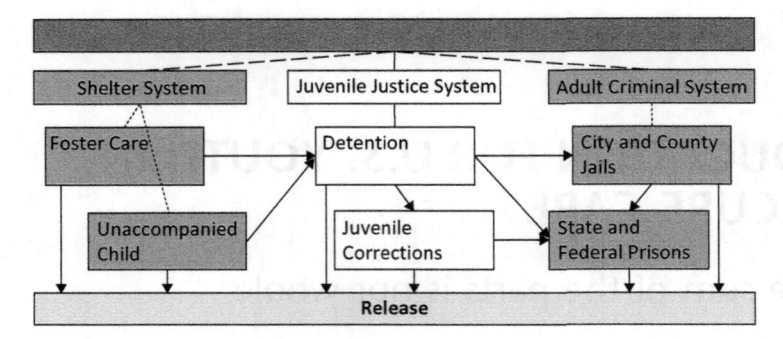

FIGURE 7.1. Potential secure care placements and movement among the settings for court-involved youth

Sheltered youth

Shelters and group homes are not intended as punitive placements but are a safe option for housing about 14% of the nearly half a million children in the U.S. foster care system (U.S. Department of Health and Human Services, 2016). The shelters become a form of confinement in that they have strict rules regarding visitation, when the youth may leave the grounds, how they must behave and interact while housed there, and under what circumstances they will be released. Although many sheltered youth will continue to attend their public schools during the day, some facilities assume responsibility for the educational services.

The different school setting adds to the challenges of transitioning to shelter because each school change that a child in care experiences has been associated with a 4- to 6-month loss in academic achievement (Emerson and Lovitt, 2003). This is due, in part, to the difficulty in sharing records across institutions and misalignment of curriculum from school to school. Accordingly, recommendations for improving the education provided to sheltered youth include formalising interagency data sharing plans, conducting and disseminating research on promising practices for overcoming educational barriers, adding school accountability for the performance of students in the system, and building educators' capacity to meet the needs of court-involved youth (Center for the Future of Teaching and Learning at WestEd, 2014).

A different form of shelter is provided for immigrant children who are apprehended on the U.S. border but are unaccompanied by an adult. According to publicly available statistics provided by U.S. Customs and Border Protection (2016), the number of unaccompanied alien children taken into custody each year since 2012 has fluctuated from a low of approximately 39,000 to a high of about 69,000. There are about 150 shelters throughout the U.S. dedicated to residential care for unaccompanied children, and all sheltered youth are prevented from leaving the facilities until they are reunited with a responsible family member or other adult sponsor. If a family member or adult sponsor cannot be located, a child may be placed in foster care. Release or placement occurs, on average, within 35 days of arrival and is granted as a temporary placement until the courts determine whether the child can remain in the country. U.S. law entitles all children, no matter their immigration status, the right to an elementary and secondary education. Therefore, educational services are provided within the shelter but are limited to English language learning or recreational activities. As with U.S.-born sheltered youth, the limited services and associated outcomes for students are due, in part, to the lack of records and the transient nature of the classroom population (Maxwell, 2014).

Regardless of their citizenship status, sheltered youth often have experienced trauma and exhibit an increased risk for criminal behaviour (Lee, Courtney, and Tajima, 2014). Sometimes, the offenses seem associated with their initial placement in a shelter. For example, children exposed to drug use, sexual abuse, or violence are more likely to engage in those behaviours themselves – including with other children (Dishion and Tipsord, 2011). However, some offenses are indicative of broader mental health issues, such as a female juvenile who was charged with murdering a foster care provider (Shahid, 2011). Once a crime is committed (other than entering the country illegally, in the case of the unaccompanied children), the youth can be arrested and transferred to the juvenile justice system.

Detained youth

After arrest, the local law enforcement agency has some discretion as to whether or not the youth should be referred to juvenile court. About 68% of arrests are sent to the courts, and about half of those advance to formal legal proceedings (Sickmund and Puzzanchera, 2014). Predispositional youth, or those awaiting court hearings, can be held in detention facilities if it is believed they: (a) are unlikely to appear for their hearing, or (b) pose a risk to themselves or others. In fact, the majority of detained youth are held predisposition (Snyder and Sickmund, 2006).

Although designed for short-term stays, often an average of 14 days (Gonsoulin, Clark, and Rankin, 2015), youth may be detained for a year or more if they have been charged with a serious crime. During predisposition, they cannot have contact with anyone else being held at the facility who also stands accused of involvement in the same crime. In addition, other youth regularly rotate through the facility and are intermingled with those who are detained predisposition. About 30% of the detention centre population is held short-term for violating court orders, committing a technical probation violation (e.g. not abiding by an imposed curfew, truancy, alcohol possession), or angering their adult caretakers (Lubow, 2005). These stays may last only a few days but could occur repeatedly (Bond-Maupin and Maupin, 2009). In addition, some youth are detained postdisposition, or after being found guilty in court and sentenced for a criminal offense. This can occur when a placement in a long-term correctional facility has not yet been determined or when the sentence imposed is a short-term detention. These circumstances combine to make the school schedule driven by security and management concerns rather than by the educational needs of the youth (Krezmien and Mulcahy, 2008).

Detained youth tend to be the most highly transient among the court-involved population, so the educational challenges associated with records transfer in secure care are magnified in detention facilities. Administrators also report that there is little accountability for adhering to state or federal educational laws and that they face more variation in students' learning needs, fewer resources for meeting those needs, and more frequent interruptions for legal meetings or diagnostic testing than youth in long-term commitment facilities experience (Koyama, 2012). There are many uncertainties for the detained youth because they often do not know how long they can expect to be there or what will happen to them when they leave the facility

It is recommended that detention facilities carefully plan lessons on high priority skills (i.e. literacy, numeracy, and current events) that can be delivered during the first few days of a student's arrival and generate a feeling of academic success (Leone and Fink, 2017). However, the challenges that detention centre teachers face can de-incentivise the planning of any quality lessons. Rather, teachers may take an expedient approach to education by handing out packets of work that keep the students busy (Reed and Wexler, 2014). Packets of worksheets completed in isolation are not likely to improve any student's academic knowledge or skills, but many detained youth have reported being confused about what they were supposed to be doing with the worksheets and afraid to 'disturb' the teacher by asking for help while she was at her desk (Reed and Wexler, 2014). One student in Reed and Wexler's observation study was a Mexican national who had been caught trafficking drugs across the U.S. border. He would have been treated as an unaccompanied child had he been apprehended simply entering the country illegally. However, the possession of drugs for distribution resulted in a 30-day sentence to juvenile detention instead. When interviewed, this student described how all he could do every day was read the Bible because it was the only book in the facility that was written in Spanish. He sat in the educational classes, but he could not complete any of the packets that were provided only in English. He stated, 'I haven't learned anything in here' (Reed and Wexler, 2014: 201).

On the day that he was interviewed, this youth was scheduled for release and asked the researchers what that meant would happen to him. No one had explained the procedures, so the researchers inquired with the facility staff on his behalf. The staff explained that the student would be taken in a van to the border and released to cross back into Mexico on his own. When asked whether anyone would attempt to notify a family member as would have happened had he been treated as an unaccompanied child, the staff answered, 'No'. The researchers pressed about the safety of leaving the student alone at the border to find his way home and were told, 'Well, that's how he got here' (Anonymous, personal communication, March 6, 2012).

This may have been an extreme case, but it highlights the disconnectedness of different institutions serving different functions in the secure care system. Youth who move from detention to commitment facilities can face a similar lack of transitional assistance. One commitment facility administrator has referred to the detention centres as his 'feeder schools', meaning that the detention centres are a type of pipeline that feeds students into the commitment facility school

(Anonymous, personal communication, May 17, 2017). Despite viewing the system in this way, the administrator had no idea what curriculum the detention centres used or what data they gathered on the youth. There was no structure for communicating across the facilities as students received a postdisposition placement.

Youth in corrections or commitment facilities

About 26% of U.S. juvenile court cases result in commitment to a juvenile correctional facility, but not all of these facilities maintain the level of security that detention centres do (Sickmund and Puzzanchera, 2014). Many appear more like open campuses, whereas detention centres commonly are surrounded by secure fencing and have a single entry-exit point with a controlled access. Typical lengths of stay in postdisposition commitment facilities are six months or longer, so there is an expectation that youth will make measurable academic progress while there (Gonsoulin et al., 2015).

Commitment may be the first time in many years that some students have attended school consistently (Balfanz, Spiridakis, Neild, and Letgers, 2003). Hence, educators have an opportunity to capitalise on the structured and secure environment to help students accomplish academic goals. Indeed, students interviewed while in a commitment facility have expressed a firm desire to earn their high school diplomas and continue on to post-secondary training (Reed and Wexler, 2014). Moreover, some students interviewed by Reed and Wexler commented on how getting sentenced to a commitment facility actually improved the educational services they received. As one student expressed, 'I feel like I'm getting more support here than, like, I would be in a regular school' (p. 202).

The longer lengths of stay make it more feasible to conduct research on educational interventions in commitment centres than in shorter-term secure care settings. A recent meta-analysis of studies found positive and statistically significant effects from two types of interventions: (a) computer-assisted instruction for increasing students' reading comprehension and (b) personalised learning for improving diploma completion and post-release employment (Steele, Bozick, and Davis, 2016). One of the advantages of education in the facilities is that the class sizes purposefully are kept small to maintain security. For example, Wilkerson, Gagnon, Mason-Williams, and Lane (2012) reported a mean of 12 students per class. Therefore, the opportunity exists to offer personalised learning in which the educational programme is specially tailored to each student. In addition to meeting individual needs, the practice also is recommended for keeping students engaged and motivated (Gonsoulin et al., 2015).

Computer-assisted and personalised learning approaches keep students separated and working individually. This may be appealing from a security standpoint, but it may not provide the diversity of experiences that would normally be expected of adolescent students and that have been found to improve academic outcomes (Wexler, Reed, Pyle, Mitchell, and Barton, 2015). Despite concerns about having youth in corrections interact with each other (Gatti, Tremblay, and Vitaro, 2009), students participating in studies of academic interventions have reported that they prefer to complete learning activities collaboratively and benefit from doing so (Wexler, Reed, Barton, Mitchell, and Clancy, 2018). However, peer-mediated instruction is rarely implemented in juvenile corrections (Wilkerson et al., 2012), and security staff may feel compelled to disrupt efforts to implement these kinds of learning activities (Wexler et al., 2018). Alternatively, security staff could play an instrumental role in planning the instruction by helping teachers think through the design of lessons and taking positive and proactive steps to prevent difficulties.

Finding ways to support the academic achievement of youth in commitment facilities is critical to their long-term success. Unfortunately, commitment facilities reportedly provide fewer hours of instruction per week than typical public schools, and they have fewer math and science course offerings in particular (U.S. Department of Education, Office for Civil Rights, 2016). Research suggests that those who make more academic progress have a greater likelihood of returning to school after release and a reduced risk for reoffending (Blomberg, Bales, Mann, Piquero, and Berk, 2011). Furthermore, Blomberg et al. found those with better post-release school attendance who did recidivate were arrested for less serious crimes than youths who did not return to school or did not attend school regularly. Thus, current guidance documents stress the importance of carefully planning transition services that will include educational goals, such as earning course credit and meeting the same accountability measures that students who are not court-involved must meet (e.g. Council of State Governments Justice Center, 2015; Gonsoulin et al., 2015).

Yet, transition planning within a commitment facility is not a guarantee that youth will have an easier path to re-entry. Public schools or other receiving institutions must be willing to honour the academic accomplishments earned in the commitment facility. According to the Georgetown Law Human Rights Institute (2012), U.S. public schools tend to create barriers to the reintegration of students post-release, such as by transferring them to other campuses (on the basis of protecting the safety of other students) or denying credit for assignments or full classes completed while in juvenile corrections. In addition, not all youth leave a juvenile commitment facility to return to their communities. Some are transferred to adult corrections at the age of 18 under blended sentencing laws that can be imposed in 31 states, and all states but New York allow judicial or prosecutorial discretion in charging youth as adults or imposing adult sentences for serious crimes (Sickmund and Puzzanchera, 2014).

Youthful offenders in the adult criminal system

Youthful offenders, those age 17 or younger held in an adult correctional facility, make up roughly 1% of the population in U.S. jails and prisons (Carson and Anderson, 2016; Minton and Zeng, 2015). The numbers have been declining markedly since about 2009, but still amount to approximately 4,200 youth in city or county jails and another 1,000 in state or federal prisons. As with juvenile corrections, educational programmes for incarcerated adults are viewed as critical to successful post-release outcomes such as reduced recidivism and increased employment (Batiuk, Lahm, McKeever, Wilcox, and Wilcox, 2005; Davis, Bozick, Steele, Saunders, and Miles, 2013).

Four types of programmes are prevalent in adult corrections (Reed, 2015). The first, adult basic education, offers literacy and maths instruction for individuals performing at very low levels. It may serve as an initial step for youthful offenders attempting to earn a high school diploma through equivalency test preparation, the second type of correctional education. In turn, a high school diploma would permit the youth to participate in the third type of programme, postsecondary education. These programmes usually offer liberal arts credits toward an associate degree, but inmates may have access to online classes for a four-year or advanced degree. Finally, vocational or career and technical education programmes allow youth to prepare for skilled trades such as plumbing, construction, or auto repair.

Although there are some concerns about the instructional or programmatic quality, participants have reacted positively to these opportunities to work towards educational goals (Tewksbury and Stengel, 2006). Unfortunately, legislation has restricted youthful offenders' access to some postsecondary and vocational education programmes. Under the Higher Education Opportunity Act of 2008, those who have been convicted of sexually violent crimes, murder, or criminal offences against minors are prohibited from participating in the Grant to States for Workplace and Community Transition Training for Incarcerated Individuals Program. Anyone age 17 or younger who was prosecuted and sentenced as an adult is quite likely to have committed one of those types of crimes. Consequently, youthful offenders would not be able to attain much more than a basic education or high school equivalency.

This is a challenging conundrum of education for court-involved youth. If they had been treated as juveniles, the secure care facility would have been obligated to educate them in some way to prepare for their transition back to the community. But because they were treated as adults, the youthful offenders became barred from services that would help them the most in gaining an equal footing with entry-level job seekers against whom they will be compared after their release.

Future directions for education in secure care

Ensuring a quality education in secure care can seem like a daunting task. When asked how to improve the system, one of the detained youth in an observation study commented, 'Honestly, I wouldn't know [what to change]. It seems like a little too complicated, thinking of all the, like, different things you would have to learn for every single person' (Reed and Wexler, 2014, p. 205). Understanding the unique learning needs of court-involved youth is important—as is having empathy for their tumultuous circumstances. After all, it is difficult to acquire new information or concentrate on academic tasks when experiencing physical or mental distress (Smith and Ayres, 2014).

More organised efforts to reduce the problems associated with the transition process would be helpful in lowering the stress experienced by the youth and, relatedly, that of their teachers. Specifically, there need to be more formalised requirements for coordinating across the various parts of the U.S. secure care system. Each component is overseen by a different entity with no official mechanism for data sharing among agencies or developing a common plan for educating the youth they serve. Law enforcement agencies have been creating information exchange models since September 11, 2001, to track criminal activity. It should not be an insurmountable problem to develop a common portal for tracking educational records once a youth became court-involved, thereby eliminating the frequent complaint that lack of information delays or prevents the provision of appropriate educational services.

Data sharing would be a first step in creating a coherent system, but the data will mean little from one institution to the next if each continues creating its own academic programme. An alternative might be for the courts to require the creation of an educational plan at the point a youth is taken into secure care that outlines the core coursework and overall educational milestones for the student in a manner similar to the Individualized Education Program required under the federal Individuals with Disabilities Educational Improvement Act of 2004. All facilities could have access to the plan and the student's progress on it through the data sharing portal, and all parts of the system then could work in a unified manner to carry out the plan.

Conclusion

Although there are different entry points (foster care, unaccompanied minor, detention) and pathways through the U.S. secure system (temporary hold, interagency transfer, juvenile commitment, adult criminal system), court-involved youth face similar challenges in maintaining their educational progress. Specifically, there are systemic problems with the following:

- sharing academic records;
- providing consistent curricula across settings;
- prioritising individual learning goals;
- ensuring access to quality instructional opportunities;
- considering educational needs when making placement and transition plans.

Secure care settings are intended to protect or rehabilitate youth who have experienced trauma and exhibited risk for not thriving. These are some of the most vulnerable youth in our society, and the current approach to their education and care is not successful enough to argue against putting forth effort to improve it. No matter the number of logistical challenges to creating a unified system, the consequences for not doing so remain high—first and foremost for the individual children entrusted to the state's care but also to the health and wellbeing of society as a whole (National Conference of State Legislatures, 2011). When courts become involved, there should not be youth who think as one stated, 'They just put me in a class with all the other kids who misbehaved. No one cared' (Anonymous, personal communication, March 14, 2012).

References

Balfanz, R., Spiridakis, K., Neild, R.C., and Letgers, N. (2003) High-poverty secondary school and juvenile justice systems: how neither helps the other and how that could change. *New Directions for Youth Development*, 99, 71–89.

Batiuk, M.E., Lahm, K.F., McKeever, M., Wilcox, N., and Wilcox, P. (2005) Disentangling the effects of correctional education: are current policies misguided? An even history analysis. *Criminal Justice*, 5, 1, 55–74.

Blomberg, T.G., Bales, W.D., Mann, K., Piquero, A.R., and Berk, R.A. (2011) Incarceration, education and transition from delinquency. *Journal of Criminal Justice*, 39, 355–365.

Bond-Maupin, L.J., and Maupin, J.R. (2009) The mis(uses) of detention and the impact of bed space in one jurisdiction. *Juvenile and Family Court Journal*, 53, 3, 21–31.

Bruskas, D. (2008) Children in foster care: a vulnerable population at risk. *Journal of Child and Adolescent Psychiatric Nursing*, 21, 2, 70–77.

Carson, E.A., and Anderson, E. (2016) *Prisoners in 2015*. Washington, DC: U.S. Department of Justice, Office of Justice Programs, Bureau of Justice Statistics. Retrieved from: www.bjs.gov

Cavendish, W. (2014) Academic attainment during commitment and postrelease education-related outcomes of juvenile justice-involved youth with and without disabilities. *Journal of Emotional and Behavioral Disorders*, 22, 41–52.

Center for the Future of Teaching and Learning at WestEd (2014) *Addressing the invisible achievement gap: the need to improve education outcomes for California's students in foster care, with considerations for action*. Santa Cruz, CA: CFYL. Retrieved from: www.cftl.org

Council of State Governments Justice Center (2015) *Locked out: improving educational and vocational outcomes for incarcerated youth*. New York, NY: CFTL. Retrieved from: https://csgjusticecenter.org/

Davis, L.M., Bozick, R., Steele, J.L., Saunders, J., and Miles, J.N.V. (2013) *Evaluating the effectiveness of correctional education: a meta-analysis of programs that provide education to incarcerated adults*. Washington, DC: RAND Corporation and the Bureau of Justice Assistance, U.S. Department of Justice.

Dishion, T.J., and Tipsord, J.M. (2011) Peer contagion in child and adolescent social and emotional development. *Annual Review of Psychology*, 62, 189–214.

Elementary and Secondary Education Act 1965. Pub. L. No. 89–10, §79, Stat. 27.

Emerson, J., and Lovitt, T. (2003) The educational plight of foster children in schools and what can be done about it. *Remedial and Special Education*, 24, 199–203.

Every Student Succeeds Act 2015. Pub. L. No. 114–195, 20 U.S.C. §6301 et seq.

Flynn, R.J., Ghazal, H., Legault, L., Vandermeulen, G., and Petrick, S. (2004) Use of population measures and norms to identify resilient outcomes in young people in care: an exploratory study. *Child and Family Social Work*, 9, 65–79.

Gatti, U., Tremblay, R. E., and Vitaro, F. (2009) Iatrogenic effect of juvenile justice. *Journal of Child Psychology and Psychiatry*, 50, 991–998.

Georgetown Law Human Rights Institute (2012). *Kept out: barriers to meaningful education in the school-to-prison pipeline*. Washington, DC: GLHRI. Retrieved from: http://www.law.georgetown.edu

Gonsoulin, S., Griller Clark, H., and Rankin, V.E. (2015) *Quality education services are critical for youth involved with the juvenile justice and child welfare systems*. Washington, DC: National Evaluation and Technical Assistance Center for Children and Youth Who Are Neglected, Delinquent, or At-Risk (NDTAC).

Higher Education Opportunity Act 2008. Pub. L. 110–315, 122 Stat. 3457–3459, codified as amended at 20 U.S.C. §1151.

Houchins, D.E., Jolivette, K., Krezmien, M.P., and Baltodano, H.M. (2008) A multi-state study examining the impact of explicit reading instruction with incarcerated students. *Journal of Correctional Education*, 59, 65–85.

Individuals with Disabilities Educational Improvement Act 2004. Pub. L. No. 101–476, 20 U.S.C. §1400.

Koyama, P. R. (2012) The status of education in pre-trial juvenile detention. *Journal of Correctional Education*, 63, 1, 35–68.

Krezmien, M.P., and Mulcahy, C. A. (2008) Literacy and delinquency: current status of reading interventions with detained and incarcerated youth. *Reading and Writing Quarterly*, 24, 219–238.

Lee, J., Courtney, M., and Tajima, E. (2014) Extended foster care support during the transition to adulthood: effect on the risk of arrest. ChildrenandYouthServicesReview, 42, 34–42.

Leone, P., and Fink, C. (2017) *Raising the bar: creating and sustaining quality education services in juvenile detention, first edition*. National Technical Assistance Center for the Education of Neglected or Delinquent Children and Youth (NDTAC). Retrieved from: www.neglected-delinquent.org

Leone, P.E. and Wruble, P.C. (2015) Education services in juvenile corrections: 40 years of litigation and reform. *Education and Treatment of Children*, 38, 587–604.

Lubow, B. (2005) Safely reducing reliance on juvenile detention: a report from the field. *Corrections Today*, 67, 5, 66–72.

Maxwell, L. A. (2014) Schools brace for influx of immigrants. *Education Week*, 33, 36, 1–19.

Minton, T.D., and Zeng, Z. (2015) *Jail inmates at midyear 2014*. Washington, DC: U.S. Department of Justice, Office of Justice Programs, Bureau of Justice Statistics. Retrieved from: www.bjs.gov

National Conference of State Legislatures (2011) *Juvenile justice guidebook for legislators*. Washington, DC: NCSL. Retrieved from: www.ncsl.org

Puzzanchera, C., and Hockenberry, S. (2015) *Census of juveniles in residential placement*. Washington, DC: National Center for Juvenile Justice, Office of Juvenile Justice and Delinquency Prevention. Retrieved from: www.ojjdp.gov

Reed, D.K. (2015) A synthesis of the effects of correctional education on the academic outcomes of incarcerated adults. *Educational Psychology Review*, 27, 537–558.

Reed, D.K. and Wexler, J. (2014) 'Our teachers...don't give us no help, no nothin': juvenile offenders' perceptions of academic support. *Residential Treatment for Children and Youth*, 31, 188–218.

Shahid, A. (2011) New Mexico teens, Alexis Shields, Desiree Linares kill foster mom, Evelyn Miranda, then flee cops. *New York Daily News* [online], 11 June. Retrieved from: www.nydailynews.com

Sickmund, M., and Puzzanchera, C. (2014). *Juvenile offenders and victims: 2014 national report*. Pittsburgh, PA: National Center for Juvenile Justice

Smith, A., and Ayres, P. (2014) The impact of persistent pain on working memory and learning. *Educational Psychology Review*, 26, 245–264.

Snyder, H., and Sickmund, M. (2006) *Juvenile offenders and victims: 2006 national report*. Washington, DC: U.S. Department of Justice, Office of Justice Programs, Office of Juvenile Justice and Delinquency Prevention. Retrieved from: www.ojjdp.gov

Steele, J.L., Bozick, R., and Davis, L.M. (2016) Education for incarcerated juveniles: A meta-analysis. *Journal of Education for Students Placed At Risk*, 21, 65–89.

Tewksbury, R., and Stengel, K. M. (2006). Assessing correctional education programs: The students' perspective. *The Journal of Correctional Education*, 57, 1, 1–25.

U.S. Customs and Border Protection (2016) *United States Border Patrol Southwest family unit subject and unaccompanied alien children apprehensions fiscal year 2016*, October 18. Retrieved from: www.cbp.gov

U.S. Department of Education (2014) *Guiding principles for providing high-quality education in juvenile justice secure care settings*. Washington, DC: U.S. DoE. Retrieved from: www2.ed.gov

U.S. Department of Education, Office for Civil Rights (2016) *Protecting the civil rights of students in the juvenile justice system*. Washington, DC: U.S. DoE. Retrieved from: www2.ed.gov

U.S. Department of Health and Human Services (2016) *The AFCARS report: preliminary FY 2015 estimates as of June 2016*. Washington, DC: U.S DoHHS. Retrieved from: www.acf.hhs.gov

Wexler, J., Reed, D.K., Barton, E.E., Mitchell, M., and Clancy, E. (2018) The effects of a peer-mediated reading intervention on juvenile offenders' main idea statements about informational text. *Behavioral Disorders., 43, 290-301. doi: 10.1177/0198742917703359*

Wexler, J. A., Reed, D.K., Pyle, N., Mitchell, M., and Barton, E.E. (2015) A synthesis of peer mediated academic interventions for secondary struggling learners. *Journal of Learning Disabilities*, 48, 451–470

Wilkerson, K.L., Gagnon, J.C., Mason-Williams, L. and Lane, H.B. (2012) Reading instruction for students with high-incidence disabilities in juvenile corrections. *Preventing School Failure*, 56, 219–231.

PART III
Case examples and models of practice

8

'BEHIND THE HEADLINES, INSIDE THE WALLS – TEACHING BRITAIN'S HIDDEN CHILDREN'

Perspectives and practices within the secure children's homes network

Melanie Prince, Aileen Conlon, Marc Herbert, Phillippa Brooks and Sarah Douglas

There are 15 secure children's homes in England and Wales. Some are all welfare units, some are Youth Custody Service (YCS) units, and some a mixture of both. Some units take a mix of boys and girls and some are single sex. Each unit has its own ethos, its own nuances, and its own approach. However, the children we teach have all, we feel, been let down by the system that is supposed to help them. Many of our pupils have experienced severe stress-induced depression, anxiety, or dissociation and at least one exclusion from not only mainstream, but also alternative educational provision, sometimes at several points. In their academic careers, at some point, they may come to the belief that if they consistently fail within systems and institutions where other children thrive and succeed, the problem isn't the systems; it's them. Some might say that school is for the successful and that alternative education is for failures. It is easy to see how children become disillusioned and disengaged.

When a child arrives at a school in the secure estate, they are at rock bottom. Although we may think we can imagine the life that has led them to us, we cannot experience it as they have. We can read about the chronic levels of serious neglect, the systematic and sustained physical, emotional, and sexual abuse, the exploitation of their naïve child-like thought processes and decision-making capacities, which draw them in, and then trap them in cycles of extreme danger. We can certainly empathise, but we cannot know what it feels like to be that child who, at every stage of their lives, has been surrounded by adults, including professionals, and most certainly teachers, charged with helping them and keeping them safe, but, for numerous and complex reasons, have been unable to. Imagine thinking 'it's me. It's my fault'. Because when systems, the familial and institutional, are operating in a way that other children around them thrive and succeed, at some point, on some level, the child may understandably blame themselves.

The British Association of Social Workers, through a research study by Brown et al. (2016), assert that, when assessing a child's risk in relation to becoming a victim of child sexual exploitation (CSE), work largely focuses on the child but that situational, environmental, and perpetrator/potential perpetrator factors were rarely considered. They state that:

> A focus on assessing an individual's risk of CSE can lead to victim-blaming, particularly where risks are narrowly linked to individual behaviours. Apart from having serious negative impacts on children, victim-blaming undermines good practice around CSE as it obscures important contextual factors and the role of perpetrators in manipulation and abuse.
>
> *(Brown et al., 2016)*

The larger social narrative around children, but specifically teenagers, can indeed compound the view that they are to blame for their abuse because they have made 'lifestyle choices' as opposed to being exploited, and their anti-social behaviour seen as a causal factor, rather than a symptom of, their abuse and exploitation.

In a report commissioned by the Children's Society in 2014, several recommendations are made with regards to the way that cases of CSE and abuse are investigated and prosecuted, including how the prosecution system move away from an over-reliance on the victim to a clearer focus on the perpetrator and the evidence that agencies have gathered. Still, as professionals and agencies work together to get to grips with one form of abuse, adult perpetrators simply find more and different ways to exploit and abuse the vulnerable child, such as what has recently become known as 'County Lines'. In the Home Office review in 2015, strategies that 'work' to prevent gang involvement, youth violence, and crime attempt to intervene early and change the attitudes of the children deemed to be at risk, thereby making *them* responsible for whether or not they become involved in gangs, violence, and crime, rather than looking at approaches to systematically root out the adults who are responsible for grooming children into this lifestyle.

Whether young people arrive in a secure children's home because they have been sentenced by the courts for a criminal offence, or placed by the courts on a welfare order, there is another level of trauma around this process over which the child is powerless. As professionals who work with these young people every day, we see chronologies of chronic and sustained abuse, neglect, and harm, often unconnected to the reason why the courts have finally placed them in our care.

To enable young people to see the beginnings of success, there must be a clear distinction drawn between the failure as being the mainstream model itself and the failure being in *how it has been applied*. Our educational model is aimed at teaching our pupils that they can succeed at school and we start to rebuild their identity as a learner.

According to Department for Education national data published in January 2017, there are almost 16,000 pupils on-roll at pupil referral units – and another 22,000 in other local authority alternative provision. On top of that, there were another 10,000 pupils with subsidiary registrations at pupil referral units (PRUs) (i.e. pupils on the rolls of schools and attending a PRU for some of the time), Whether or not these units are currently meeting the educational needs of these young people is hard to establish, but in launching the government's inquiry into alternative provision in September 2017, Robert Halfon MP, Chair of the Education Select Committee, said: 'Students in alternative provision are far less likely to achieve good exam results, find well-paid jobs or go on to further study. Only around 1% of young people in state alternative provision receive five good GCSEs' (UK Parliament, 2017).

Sadly, this cannot be a surprise given that the new GCSE system and the very way that it has been designed demands continuity, in both provision and progress, if there is to be any hope of success. Increasingly, the system of assessment that now exists assumes a continuous and seamless trajectory of learning and the ways progress can and must be achieved which culminate solely in a summative assessment where the pupil is ranked competitively against their peers. This is arguably a serious and significant general failure, but for our most vulnerable and disadvantaged learners in secure children's homes it is even more problematic.

In his launch statement in 2014, the then Secretary for Education, Michael Gove, spoke passionately about the changes being made, stating that they were more ambitious with 'greater stretch for the most able' and that they had been specifically designed to provide further challenge to those aiming to achieve top grades. Not once were the most vulnerable or the least able acknowledged.

At this point, the task for us as teachers of these young people is not to dissect why both the mainstream and alternative models have, in our opinion, failed to work, but it is to acknowledge that they have and to recognise the time and focus we have with our learners is critical. To apply an analogy, their education is in 'intensive care'; with the right treatment it may recover, but when the damage that has placed them there has been so significant, there can be no guarantees.

In an academic year there are 190 days. That means that over a child's secondary school career they should receive 950 days of learning. An average length of stay in a secure children's home is around 158 days, with some young people on three-month orders being with us only 90 days. The time they spend with us can be short and our approach must be fit for purpose.

All 15 secure children's homes in England and Wales meet regularly and are in contact with each other through the Secure Accommodation Education Network. This enables us to act as critical friends for each other, to offer peer support and have a voice at the end of the telephone in what can be an isolating educational environment for us to work. We collate educational data so that we can measure and analyse the progress of students that spend time in the secure estate. We have had the opportunity to work closely with Ofsted in reviewing and revising the framework against which we are inspected. We are all inspected annually but, overall, we find Ofsted supportive and understanding of the starting points of our students and the myriad of needs and difficulties we have.

In this next section we present case examples of some of the SCHs in the network and the work taking place with learners.

Aycliffe

Aycliffe is licensed by the Department of Education to provide a home for up to 38 young people between the ages of 10 to 18 years, or over 18 years where it is deemed by the professionals involved that they are particularly vulnerable when transferred to another facility. The home is also registered with Ofsted. Eighteen places are commissioned via a contract with the Youth Custody Service (YCS) with the remaining places being used by local authorities across the country to accommodate young people on welfare grounds; these include children who have experienced, or at risk of experiencing, CSE and children who have been groomed into criminal gangs and been exploited by them. As a multi-agency centre, there is an inbound mental health team, substance misuse team, and a physical nursing team. The school in the centre follows the typical structure and routines of the secondary model.

As the largest secure children's home in England and Wales, in the academic year 2016–2017, we welcomed 74 young people into school. Of these young people, 60 were in Key Stages 4 or 5, but 80% of them were working within Key Stage 1 to 2 age-related expectations in English and Maths. No learner arrived working within the upper range of Key Stage 4 expectations, i.e. Level 2 or old A★–C range at GCSE. Initial assessments by specialist teachers revealed significant gaps in learning that could not be attributed to a lack of ability. It is rare that we admit a child who has been attending and succeeding within the mainstream system. Just as there are gaps in learning, there are gaps in educational chronologies where, after exclusions and attempts at alternative provision have been unsuccessful, no school or alternative setting was able to accommodate or meet the complex and challenging needs of the child as a learner.

Exploiting the educational 'norms'

It has been an active decision to create a model based on a traditional secondary school, where the day is structured into 50-minute lessons and pupils move around the building between subject specialist teachers and classrooms, have learning targets, work towards age appropriate and relevant accreditation, choose vocational options, and there are clear expectations of positive behaviour. Teachers are active in their responsibility for ensuring that they create the conditions where pupils can learn, and, despite difficulties and setbacks, there are clear long-term goals for *each child*; not simply short-term goals for each lesson. The focus of the teacher, and the main concern of the school leaders, is the child and within this context we see young people begin to have those first experiences of success and, more importantly, have that success rewarded.

Last year, a decision was made that we would specifically open our doors to young people who needed to be accommodated specifically for welfare reasons, but because of the high levels of risk that their behaviours presented could not be placed elsewhere in the secure estate. These young people are amongst the most complex and challenging learners in the country. How would we successfully enable these young people to access our model, and, in fact, should we commence down this route? Our conclusion was yes. These children had as much right to the opportunity to succeed as everyone else; creating the conditions that would enable this would be where the work would be concentrated.

As an example, L is in Year 9 and was admitted to us in November 2017 due to the risks he posed to both himself and other people in the community. He was frequently missing from home with over 50 missing person (MISPER) reports filed in a three-month period, including overnight, and he has subsequently made disclosures about his exposure to sexually harmful behaviour. L has a prolific history of offending behaviour and exhibited extremely complex and dangerous sexualised behaviours and sought to cause himself serious hurt and harm. L has witnessed domestic violence from a very young age and this appears to have caused significant emotional harm, including attachment issues and difficulty processing emotional responses. He was placed in the care of the local authority in 2016 after a family member was no longer able to care for him. A placement was found, but L was removed by his father shortly afterwards. He was at significant risk due to domestic abuse and exposure to substance misuse so was returned to the placement on an interim care order.

As his new school, we were given the following chronology:

- February–August 2015 – L had a place at a Behaviour Support Unit within a PRU. This broke down after assaults on staff.
- September 2015 – The plan was for L to receive 1:1 sessions with staff in his care home.
- October 2016 – L was to receive two hours tuition a day (2:1 staffing) with a plan for possible reintegration into the PRU.
- An update to the report stated that the PRU was no longer an option due to further serious assaults on staff. L to remain on local authority roll and be provided with alternative provision.

Naturally, L was significantly behind national age-related expectations for learning.

L was extremely anxious and withdrawn when he arrived and presented a level of paranoia about how he would be perceived by other young people due to his history, and consequently responded aggressively towards the assistant head when he first arrived. As this relationship developed, L agreed to try a one-to-one music lesson as this was his favourite subject, only entering the school building once other young people were already in class. This first attempt resulted in L asking to return to the house immediately due to his anxiety. This was not perceived as an issue; he had already achieved something by simply deciding to commit to coming into school. The next step was to try again, and L achieved two successful one-to-one lessons with the specialist music teacher. With L's agreement, we then introduced another young person, with whom L felt comfortable, and then at his request he successfully attempted a small group session with four other pupils. When the group increased to five due to a new admission, L became anxious again and refused to attend. The assistant head worked with him, suggesting a group change, but L was determined he wanted to try again. He then progressed from only attending music, to trying PE, where he has excelled in trampolining. His risk assessment originally meant he could not attend food technology lessons despite wanting to, but his behaviour improved significantly meaning that this could be changed, and he now attends and engages extremely well in this subject.

From January, L has been fully integrated into the school community. He attends assemblies and group events, which have included two sports and team building days, where he was placed in a new/unfamiliar group, specifically to stretch and challenge his social skills, and this was a real success. He has been awarded Student of the Week twice. L has met his target in Maths, which was set at two levels above his initial assessment score and he is currently producing a piece of creative writing in English that he is taking his time over and will only share when it is completed. To see work that he has produced, amended, and then redrafted, demonstrates his commitment to his learning and progress. Week on week, the number of learning targets L has met have increased, but if there is a dip, we now know that L has the resilience to give it another go.

Recently L's mother emailed our assistant head teacher:

> My son was out of school for a number of years prior to being sent to you. He never started secondary school – sat at a desk willing to participate in education was unheard of. Today during my visit to see him I was shown all his certificates for positive engagement within the school routine as well as also pupil of the week which he was presented with today – to say I am proud is an understatement. To see him achieving academically is a massive positive, I can't thank the education department enough for all the work they have done with my son as I'm seeing things I never thought I'd see – thank you!

Again, it has been an active decision to base our behaviour management system on positive reinforcement, including the use of systems such as Student of the Week, Special Mention Certificates, and points that are usually found within a primary model. They are appropriate to our learners as not only are they familiar with them, they may represent either the last time they were successful at school, or they were deemed unsuccessful because they did not receive them. By allowing them to experience success within structures and models that they are familiar with means that they will hopefully begin to realise that they *can* be successful at school; not only can they be, but they *are* learners. They are just like other children.

Aldine House

Aldine House was purpose designed and built as a secure children's home and opened in February 1997. Aldine House currently accommodates a maximum of eight children, male and female, between the ages of 10 and 17. The children and young people who are placed at Aldine House come from all parts of England. They require a safe and controlled environment in which to challenge their attitudes and behaviours that have put them, other people, and their community at high risk. Children and young people are also accommodated at Aldine House due to the extreme risks posed to them by others and their community.

In the majority of cases, the children and young people placed at Aldine House have previously been subjected to many professional interventions that have ultimately failed to keep them or others safe. It is the purpose of Aldine House to keep them and the public safe.

Staff at Aldine House create a therapeutic environment in which children are made to feel safe and are, subsequently, able to develop strong relationships. These relationships allow children to work with staff to challenge the negative aspects of their attitudes and behaviour. We are extremely passionate and committed to ensuring that all young people make progress. This is not an easy process and often requires reflection, strategy, momentum, and a great deal of energy.

In summary, working with our young people has many stages. In the most extreme and complex cases, our young people arrive in a state of anxiety. They are hostile towards their learning and cannot invest in the process, demonstrating highly interrupted learning patterns and disruptive habits which will enable them to intentionally leave learning. Many young people wrestle with themselves as they begin to be subject to the 'dance of attunement'. Once the relationships become more established, the young people are conflicted; there is a natural trust which develops which is contrary to the previous experiences of the young people. That is to say, they leave behind a rhetoric which states 'I don't want to do anything; I hate education and feel vulnerable when I have to engage in it as I don't feel I have anything productive to offer (strengths)' and are able to adopt a positive approach which states 'I am happy to give this a go!' This is truly the process which enables the teaching and learning exchange to take place. What sounds romantic and easy really isn't. It requires resilience and direction, clear boundaries, and consistent challenge.

It is explained to new staff that successful teaching in a secure children's home relies on the ability to manage the behaviour. If behaviour is not challenged at the earliest point with a low-level prompt, then the riskier behaviour is inevitable. Young people need to have confidence that the staff who are working with them in the classrooms can keep them safe when they exhibit the behaviour which would satisfy the young people learning in a secure setting. We are not practitioners who would ever be able to say 'and now I have seen it all!'; rather, we are professionals who are ready to respond to the often bizarre and risky occurrences in the context of a planned lesson. The lessons need to be captivating and equitable with learning in the community. It should be ambitious and exciting. The lesson itself may have almost 40 variations, taking a different direction with the flicker of a young person needing a movement break, making an inappropriate comment, or 'over-sharing' with the group. In this sense, teaching at the unit requires the ability to take the role of stand-up comedian, red-coat entertainer, teacher, pastoral manager, corporate parent, advocate, and so on. The strategies needed to engage young people need humour, light and shade, distraction, challenge, and bravery. We ask, how are the young people to make academic progress and return to the community if they do not make progress with their social and emotional aspects of learning?

We believe that if young people do not have the skills to be able to undertake learning in a productive way, then this does not mean that they should never have the opportunity to practise this. They should have the opportunities to undertake this learning in a more structured way to enable them to learn the skills to be able to achieve that safely.

We are extremely fortunate to work with young people who have taught us a great deal about what is needed in this context. Education at this unit is organic and raw. It is intimate. We do not have professional distance, which pushes the young people away. We draw them in with our quirks and anecdotes.

A young person said to a staff member during a young person's panel,

> You seem okay to us, but let me tell you this ... we are not interested in your personal problems. Don't take this job and tell us that you can't do the job because you are getting a divorce or moving to a new house or having a baby. We have our own issues.

The response was 'I've just moved to a new house and am not planning to move again, I have been married for a long time and am not planning to get divorced and I have finished growing my family'. In short, what was being conveyed was, I understand what this job entails, and I can make a commitment (to grown up choices and to you). A job in a secure children's home is a life-style choice. The needs of the young people do not finish at the end of the school day.

Unit B operates as one team. Education is part of the offer for young people. All members of the team may have a different area of training or expertise but, ultimately, we are in the house to meet the needs of the young people. As one team.

There are many young people remembered fondly. It has been a privilege to meet them. They surprise themselves with the progress they make and the qualifications they leave with. They are able to return to the community and make positive contributions. We are proud of the contribution which young people make to education and there is a culture of high expectations for learning in the home. Occasionally, new young people will say 'I'm not going to school; I don't do school' and I always smile when the other young people say 'Why? You'll really like it. They won't put you on the spot and make you feel like a dickhead'.

Atkinson Children's Home

The Atkinson Children's Home is a small secure home which presently has capacity for 10 young people, rising to 12 after April 2018. The home is a welfare only setting, offering therapeutic care through on-site CAMHS provision and highly trained staff with experience of using the PACE technique to support the therapeutic style of Dyadic Developmental Psychology. We work with young people aged 13–17, both boys and girls, who have suffered from a range of different traumas including loss and bereavement, neglect, domestic violence, and other forms of abuse. Many of them have mental health difficulties as a result. These young people often have not attended school for some time, on average over a year, and therefore need to be reintroduced to school life gradually. At least 80% of all our young people have a language and communication need, and roughly 50% of our cohort at any one time will have a range of additional educational needs, including ADHD and ASD, learning disabilities, sensory processing difficulties, and dyslexia. The average stay for the young people is around three months. In that time, we aim to identify their educational needs, apply for an EHC plan, if they don't already have one, and help them make enough progress so that they can gain qualifications in English and Mathematics and any other appropriate subject areas.

Helping young people to understand and manage their emotions

At this unit, our overarching ethos is to help young people manage their emotions. We have a nurturing style of parenting as all our young people are placed here for welfare reasons. Having a CAMHS team on site and a core of long-term, mature members of staff also helps to create a nurturing, family feel. All staff have had Dyadic Developmental Practice training and have a PACE style of parenting (playful, accepting, curious, empathetic) to de-escalate young people, and the regularly scheduled direct work sessions between keyworkers and their key children mean that we can do lots of 1:1 work on emotional literacy and helping them to manage their emotions.

Within the school, we also take on board this ethos through our negotiated, child centred learning, where we help young people to make decisions that have thought behind them rather than acting impulsively. This helps to take time to think, however briefly, before reacting emotionally to situations. We try hard to embed the British values of mutual respect and tolerance and democracy within our curriculum and working practices and hope that this becomes part of our young people's personal values too.

One case example was B. He was 13 years old when he joined us and is now 14. He was initially removed from his mother's care at 22 months due to neglect. Mum was a heroin user. His paternal grandmother and aunt tried to care for him in between being taken into care but struggled with his behaviour. His father was in and out of his life and B suffered physical abuse related to dad's drinking. B was known to be associating with older young people and open to criminal exploitation from the age of seven.

B was taken into care again in 2016 and was placed in a residential school after being excluded. At this point he was using cannabis. B has had a Statement of

Special Educational Needs since 2012 and this has now been converted into an EHC Plan. B's main areas of need are:

- Speech and language – B has previously been in a language unit and struggles with receptive language, especially when agitated.
- He has a poor working memory (0.3 percentile) and an IQ of 62.3.
- B was diagnosed in 2017 with ADHD and ODD but until coming to the Atkinson Home had refused medication.
- B has had extreme early childhood trauma, compounded by later traumas, and has disrupted attachment difficulties, which affects his ability to trust adults and follow directions.

B initially struggled to attend any lessons without becoming abusive or violent. B's timetable was therefore completely individualised: he was taught on his own, initially in non-school areas and then later in school classrooms. Each morning's lesson was reduced from 45 minutes to 20, with incentives and instant rewards in place if he managed to stay focused during that 20 minutes. Each lesson was separated by some form of physical activity, such as football or basketball, and the non-essential lessons that he struggled with were replaced by physical activities like gardening and forest school so that he learnt soft skills like appropriate communication, responsible working, and empathy. B would be forewarned if there are changes to his day and the key phrases have been 'flexibility', 'pupil led learning', and 'every day is a new day'.

B has been taught by specialist subject teachers since his arrival. We had very clear expectations and made sure to explain what he would be learning, and what was required in order for us to count it as a successful lesson. His ADHD and poor working memory were juxtaposed in that he needed frequent switches of activity in order to maintain his attention, but his poor working memory meant that he required lots of repetition in order to embed any new concepts. Therefore, the teacher had to be very intuitive to his changing needs and change their plans dynamically to maintain his involvement in the lesson. In some cases where he was required to listen to information on a piece of software and answer questions on it in order to gain his basic food hygiene certificate (so he could do practical cooking), we have had to deconstruct the computer programme and present the information in completely different ways in order for B to be able to access it and gain the knowledge required in order for him to cook safely.

When B first arrived, he was reluctant to attend education and his aggressive, disruptive behaviour meant that he had to be educated off the school corridor for a short period of time. B had education staff working with him during this time and education and care staff worked together to help him regular his behaviours and emotions. B still struggles to get up for school and his attendance remains at around 70%, an improvement from his initial attendance of around 5%. This must be seen in context, however – he has had extended periods of time within his life when he was receiving no formal education and this escalated once he went into Year 7. B has had his attendance incentivised and we have set up meetings with B, his tutor, and his keyworker to discuss how best we can help him attend school. B particularly enjoys Lego and his timetable has now got reward time featuring Lego embedded within it.

Clare Lodge

This secure children's home is a medium sized, female welfare only unit. The average length of stay is 181 days and the average age of those placed is 16 years. We provided places for 45 children during the last academic year. We provide a therapeutic, nurturing environment specialising in CSE and we now have an increasing number of mental health referrals. The service provides an intensive in-house psychiatric and psychological provision. Young women placed here may have extensive histories of abuse and sexual exploitation, poor attachments, drug and alcohol misuse, mental health issues, and self-harm.

In recent years, there has been increased referrals for those with complex mental health difficulties who have shown high levels of self-harm and risky behaviours. Approximately 50% of the girls are under the care of the psychiatrist receiving psychoactive medication in order to help them manage emotional dysregulation, ADHD, PTSD, or sleep difficulties. This has presented high levels of self-harm and risk and it is necessary to put in a range of risk management strategies on both individual and group basis to manage this safely.

Nearly all our students arrive with a history of educational failure and exclusion. They all have extremely low self-esteem and see no worth in themselves and often have no desire to engage in education. They also often have attachment issues, have suffered trauma, and are unable to regulate their emotions. However, none of our students are placed with us because of their inability to engage in education. They have experienced chronic neglect, systematic and sustained physical, emotional, physical, and sexual abuse that has led, understandably to difficulties coping in a 'normal' school environment. They have usually had multiple placements – in different parts of the country, reinforcing attachment difficulties. It would be difficult for any child to readjust to different education settings, but for those who have experienced such trauma in their early lives it is nigh on impossible.

We have also made the conscious decision to create a model in this unit that is based in the educational 'norm' of a traditional secondary school, but with the flexibility that will cater for the individual. The day is structured into six 45-minute lessons, with pupils moving from class to class, with subject specialist teachers. There are no more than four students in a class, with an experienced and qualified teacher and support from a teaching assistant at all times.

Our curriculum consists of:

- Core subjects – English, Mathematics, and ICT.
- Subjects designed to encourage healthy lifestyles – PE/PSHE/cookery/child development.

- Vocational subjects and a careers education, information, advice, and guidance (CEIAG) programme (including carefully planned 'work experience' placements for half day/one day at a time) to improve employability prospects.
- Creative subjects such as art and drama offer a more therapeutic alternative. There is an individualised life skills programme, designed to assist those whose next placement is semi-independent or independent living.
- We are keen to offer 'off timetable' opportunities for teachers and students to build relationships without the pressures of academic related pressures.

Our students still arrive with a feeling of educational failure and often do not want to engage. The teachers must have expert subject knowledge, effective planning, constructive use of assessments, ability to understand the nuances of behaviour management within the therapeutic environment of the home, act as good role models, offer a range of tasks and activities, that suit different learning styles in short bursts, have enthusiasm, presence, and motivational ability, have resilience and the ability to be flexible as the secure children home environment changes very quickly.

The behaviour management approach we use is the ARC framework (Attachment, Regulation, and Competency). The ARC framework is built around the following core targets of intervention (Table 8.1).

These targets are addressed in 'client' and 'system-specific' ways, with an overarching goal of supporting the child and family to engage thoughtfully in the present moment (Trauma Experience Integration).

Across targets, *Routines and Rituals* and *Psychoeducation* are integrated as crosscutting elements of intervention.

In this section we present the example of X. X suffered from neglect (physical and emotional). Her local authority had concerns around her social vulnerability and risk of being sexually exploited. She also had a history of offending and violent behaviour, assaulting staff and other students. She had been in another secure unit in the past and arrived with us at the age of 15 years 9 months. She had an EHC plan with special needs relating to behavioural, social, and emotional difficulties. She had many fixed term exclusions from school and was being schooled on a 1:1 basis, for her own and others' safety. She would not engage in her education, would not answer any questions around education, and would not work in a group situation but she was clearly a bright girl. She enjoyed art, food technology, and English, and soon made good progress in these areas. However, in maths lessons especially, she would misbehave in when other peers were present. She did not want to show that she was struggling, she was reluctant to listen to explanations and would often get confused when given explanations and not follow a

TABLE 8.1 The ARC framework

Attachment	*Regulation*	*Competency*
Caregiver affect management	Identification	Executive functions
Attunement	Modulation	Self-development
Consistent response	Expression	

process correctly as a result. She had a very bad relationship with the maths teacher at that time and was very aggressive to her. We felt that whilst we were 'getting through' in some subject areas, maths remained an issue, and if she was to fulfil her potential later in life, it was important to break down this barrier. We put in a programme of 1:1 maths lessons, with a higher level teaching assistant who was persistent and understanding. We did not replace maths lessons, but instead stuck to a timetable every day with a dogged persistence. Without the fear of failure in front of others, and with carefully planned, fully differentiated lessons that involved short tasks and careful explanations, we were able to slowly introduce her back to the full class. At the end of her stay, she achieved a Level 2 in Functional Skills in both English and Mathematics, she had a work experience at a local publishing company, and she wrote a story that was published in a young writers' competition. She is now attending college and has also secured employment.

Lansdowne

Lansdowne is a local authority run home in East Sussex. It is modern, purpose-built, and physically secure. It provides care for up to seven young people, aged 10 to 17. Our ethos is child-focused and homely.

Each young person has a care plan ensuring support around agreed areas of work to meet education and health needs. They are encouraged to take part in individual and group work designed to develop understanding and skills which will equip them once the terms of their secure order are met. The nurturing environment and skilled staff ensure good outcomes for our residents; they develop positive relationships and feel supported to invest in themselves during their time here.

The welfare provisions within the secure estate care for young people with histories of extreme chaos. Many have had troubled upbringings and suffered neglect or physical abuse which, in turn, has meant the formation of survival strategies ultimately leading to behaviours such as drug use, sexual exploitation, and involvement with gangs. A natural result being a young person who has disengaged from the education system, for whom learning has little value and whose aspirations are significantly limited

On arrival at their new placement a young person is typically in crisis and it is the role of the multi-disciplinary team to stabilise the young person and quickly establish a sense of safety. Early intervention from health professionals can address the issues of drug withdrawal or infection, but key at this stage is for the new resident to be looked after, fed, clothed, and rested.

Our ethos is to support each young person in the often extremely emotional journey towards self-worth. To create positive relationships, to develop the skills enabling positive decision making, and to support the confidence to re-engage in education as a route to a successful and fulfilling future.

The unit makes provision for a very small number of young people aged 11–17, irrespective of gender. The balance between creating a home and providing a tightly structured, carefully regulated living environment is often difficult but it is this balance that enables residents to thrive. The school is an integral part of the home provision and soon after admission all young people are expected to participate in the full time school schedule. The routine offered by this is an important stepping stone in enabling young people to begin to regulate themselves.

The school focus is to develop core skills which underpin all future learning and serve to equip young people to embark on studies of age appropriate qualifications in subsequent placements. The timetable includes:

- Core learning – based around functional English and mathematics.
- Creative learning – including art and PE.
- Vocational learning – child development, cooking, hair and beauty.

All students work towards personal targets across the curriculum, which support development of transferable (soft) skills.

Through careful planning teachers ensure that students make rapid progress. Use of the Bloom's Taxonomy approach to establish lesson learning outcomes enables each young person to see how their skills, knowledge, and understanding develop into higher order processes. A high level of support is provided because class sizes are small. Many of our students have failed in a traditional mainstream setting because their needs could not be met in the size of class or establishment. We are able to rebuild learning confidence through our ability to rapidly respond to each young person's need for academic or emotional support within the classroom.

Significant progress is characteristic of young people within this setting. On arrival in school, each young person undertakes a range of baseline assessments. These include analysis of literacy and numeracy skills, reading and spelling ages as well as using the 'Myself as a Learner' scale. Many students are identified as having reading skills significantly below that expected for their age. To address this, we employ the 'Drop Everything and Read' approach. One-to-one time sharing a book with an adult is a novelty for many of the residents and the success of this approach is borne out when scores for exit assessments are analysed. Typically, in a typical four-month stay a young person can impact to make progress in their reading age.

Such individual support means that school staff rapidly identify specific learning needs. With one young person this was significant in their placement being successful (referred to in this section as C). As a 16-year-old, C was aware that her behaviour prior to admission had meant that she was now a school leaver with no qualifications. Whilst she aspired to work as a nursery nurse, her school career to date was now limiting the options available to her in achieving this goal. C struggled with very low learning confidence and she said she felt 'stupid'. Her reading age was measured at 11 years 11 months. Through 1:1 work, utilising the D.E.A.R (Dyslexic Education Association of R's) programme, the school identified indicators for dyslexia, a specific learning difficulty that impacts on reading as well as many organisation skills, time telling, and memory tasks. School sought support from C's local authority and she was formally assessed. Once she had received an explanation for her difficulties, C was able to approach learning with a new sense of confidence and she worked with staff to develop strategies. During her 25-week stay C improved her reading age by 1 year and 10 months and her spelling by 2 years and 2 months. The new positivity C felt about her learning encouraged her social worker to prioritise a suitable learning provision as part of her exit plan and, on departure, arrangements were in place for C to attend college with appropriate support, working towards her goal of childcare qualifications.

Conclusion

We would be content if all of the positives described above were the usual story. We cannot claim that all the children achieve success whilst with us, but what is especially frustrating is that those who have thrived in the context of secure children's homes leave us and soon lose their self-esteem or momentum. The educational progress made is lost. Why is this? All too often a next steps school or educational provision has not been identified at the point of leaving. Local authorities often have to contact hundreds of residential providers country wide before they find a 'suitable' provision and the search for a suitable school/educational provision is unfortunately but understandably at the bottom of the list. We have been the last resort in the young person's life – that radical intervention to ensure physical and emotional health and wellbeing –but, when this short stay comes to an end, the next step can be a 'panic provision'. Some children will return to the same systems that have failed them previously.

A good transition package is vital. Unfortunately, our assumptions are that children will move to their new and open setting, but with a fresh range of adults to mistrust. Transitions should be carefully planned by the multi-disciplinary team involved with the child. Education, care, and health should be in place before the move. There should be discussions and meetings between the secure children's home and the next provider, the child should agree to the move and have had opportunities to visit and begin to build relationships with the next set of adults that have the responsibility to look after them.

References

Brown, S., Brady, G., Franklin, A., and Crookes, R. (2016) *The use of tools and checklists to assess risk of child sexual exploitation: an exploratory study*. Coventry University. Retrieved from: www.csacentre.org.uk/research-publications/cse-risk-tools/explorator y-study-on-the-use-of-tools-and-checklists-to-assess-risk-of-child-sexual-exploitation

Department for Education (2017) *Who are the pupils in alternative provision?*Education Data Lab. Retrieved from: https://educationdatalab.org.uk/2017/10/who-are-the-pupils-in-a lternative-provision

House of Commons (2014) House of Commons Parliamentary Debates, 16 June.Retrieved from: https://publications.parliament.uk/pa/cm201415/cmhansrd/chan7.pdf

The Children's Society (2014) *Inquiry into effectiveness of legislation for tackling CSE and trafficking within the UK*. London: The Children's Society. Retrieved from: www.children ssociety.org.uk/sites/default/files/tcs/u44/sexual_offences_act_inquiry_submission_ -_the_childrens_society_final.pdf

UK Parliament (2017) *Committee calls for better support for foster carers and children in care*. Retrieved from: www.parliament.uk/business/committees/committees-a-z/commons-se lect/education-committee/news-parliament-2017/fostering-report-published-17-19

9

A SECURE CHILDREN'S HOME IN WALES

Care and educational provision from clinical, management, and educational perspectives

Richard Pates, Alison Davies and David Tiddy

This chapter describes a secure children's home, Hillside in Neath in South Wales. We explain the nature of this service, the type of problems we see, and the perspectives of three of the senior staff who work at the home: the clinical psychologist, the manager, and the education manager. To provide successful outcomes, we must ensure that management, care staff, clinical staff, and education staff are working together and have the same goals and receive similar training on important issues of child development and child management.

We currently have 16 welfare beds and six youth custody service beds, and these beds are constantly in demand. The atmosphere on first appearance is daunting. There are high wire fences, airlocks to come in and out, locked doors and staff with keys, and a very high staff:child ratio. It can seem like a prison. Children referred here are often frightened when they arrive because of the nature of the place but, as will be discussed, children often do not want to leave when their time comes for departure. It must be especially daunting for those children who come in on welfare orders and who have not committed an offence but are here because of potential danger to themselves and others: 'If I haven't committed a crime why am I being locked up?'

We have three residential units at Hillside, two of which have eight beds and one has six beds. They are mixed in terms of whether they are Youth Justice Board or Welfare referrals, male and female, and mixed abilities. The staffing level is about 2:1 on the units and we also have full time psychologists, a resettlement officer, a drugs worker, and a part time speech and language therapist. We have sessional time from psychiatry, a general practitioner, a nurse, and a dentist. We also have a school with 14 staff. We are well staffed and self-contained.

Who comes to us?

The young people who are referred to Hillside have an extremely varied profile. They range in age from 10 to 18, although we see few children under the age of 13. They come from a wide range of cultural, ethnic, or religious backgrounds and a broad range of intellectual abilities from those with learning disabilities to intellectually gifted children. They also range physically from small and underdeveloped to adult size children.

Most of the young people admitted to Hillside have missed on average two years' schooling before coming to Hillside. Pates and Hooper (2017) found that 38 of the 70 males and eight of the 32 females admitted had been assessed for a Statement of Educational Needs and more recently research (Harris et al., forthcoming) found that there was a significant difference between verbal and performance IQ in 46 children assessed, typically by around 12 points. This may affect their communication skills and their ability to understand instructions etc. We hypothesise that this is probably due to missing so much education and coming from an unstimulating intellectual environment where normal communication between parents and children is often lacking.

Except for a few young people referred as part of sentencing for crimes committed, nearly all the young people have attachment disorders in common. They come from backgrounds of physical, emotional, or sexual abuse, neglect, domestic violence, and serious substance use in the family and, as a result, have poor social functioning in society and difficulties with boundaries. They have been subject to few boundaries and inconsistent discipline. We see high levels of self-harm, drug use, actual or potential child sexual exploitation, and disturbed behaviour. Because of these attachment disorders and lack of normal childhood developmental experiences, they are often functioning at a lower emotional and social level than their chronological age.

The clinical perspective: issues and problems

What work do we do?

On admission the clinical staff complete a Summary of Needs and Responses (SONAR) which is a precis of the young person's history, their needs and relevant medical history, and risks the young person poses. This is to aid care staff in understanding how to handle the young person and it becomes a living document, which is amended as and when changes may occur. Within the first month, providing they are sufficiently settled, we administer a cognitive assessment unless they have had one in the past year and we have the relevant report. This is to aid care staff understand the levels of cognitive functioning in the young person and how to talk to them. We will also administer a Trauma Symptom Checklist for Children (TSCC) that will give some indication of the presence of anxiety, depression, anger, post-traumatic stress, and sexual preoccupations. This gives us some idea of the areas of concern on which we need to work. After the young person has been with us for three months we complete a Social and Emotional Development Level assessment (SEDAL) which helps us understand the emotional level at which the young person is functioning; many are functioning many years below their chronological age.

We recognise that coming to a facility like Hillside will be stressful and young people need time to settle. During that early period, behaviour may be more unsettled as they get used to the boundaries and rules of the place and get to know their peers and the staff. All the young people have individual plans worked out for them and will get professional help as needed.

Working with the Trauma Recovery Model (Skuse and Mathews, 2015), we need to recognise that the young people have missed the early stages of child development in terms of interaction, development of attachment, etc. Hillside is therefore a therapeutic environment where the care staff are the most important therapeutic agents as they are with the young people all the time and help them to develop boundaries, trust, and an appropriate way of behaving in the world and interacting with their peers and others.

We aim to help them develop through the stages that they have missed, develop trust in peers and adults, and take responsibility for their own actions. This is often at the most basic level for young people who have rarely been praised or even hugged, who have never had structured meal times or even a decent diet, no control of their media usage or bedtimes, and on top of this many have been abused or neglected so feel that the most important figures in their lives cannot be trusted. Care staff often become surrogate parents for the time the young person is with us and develop attachments for the first time in their lives.

What problems do they have?

A recent report from Public Health Wales on Adverse Childhood Experiences (Bellis et al., 2016) stated that the long term harm resulting from chronic stress on individuals, arising from abuse and neglect and exposure to domestic violence or individuals with substance use problems, will increase the chances of adopting health harming behaviours during adolescence, mental health problems, and diseases such as cancer, heart disease, and diabetes later in life. Adverse childhood experiences (ACEs) include verbal abuse, physical abuse, sexual abuse, parental separation, exposure to domestic violence, mental illness, alcohol abuse and drug use, and incarceration.

Forty-seven per cent of adults in Wales suffered at least one ACE. Compared with people with no ACEs, those with four or more ACEs are four times more likely to be a high risk drinker, six times more likely to smoke, 14 times more likely to be a victim of violence over the past 12 months, 15 times more likely to have committed violence against another person in the past 12 months, 16 times more likely to have used cocaine or heroin, and 20 times more likely to have been incarcerated at some time in their life (Table 9.1).

TABLE 9.1 Adverse childhood experience rates at Hillside compared to the Welsh population

	Hillside	Welsh population
0 ACEs	0%	53%
1 ACE	10%	20%
2–3 ACEs	26%	13%
4+ ACEs	64%	14%

At Hillside, the number of ACEs experienced is much higher than average Welsh families and even higher than children on the Welsh Child Protection register.

As can be seen from Table 9.1, the children have experienced severe traumatic experiences which inevitably affect their behaviour. As can be seen in Table 9.2, these figures are even worse than children on the Child Protection Register. Table 9.2 shows the level of exposure to domestic violence (66%), parental substance misuse problems (84%), and emotional neglect (62%).

Self-harm

Because of their early experience there is a high level of self-harm by some of the young people, especially the females. Common forms of self-harm are the tying of ligatures (one young woman tied over 700 in a period of six months), cutting, and swallowing items. Everything is done to try to alleviate self-harm, but it is impossible to remove all possible routes to self-harm unless the young person is isolated with no objects that could be used. Reasons for self-harm are varied but often it is

TABLE 9.2 Trauma history of children in SCHs compared to children on the Child Protection Register in Wales

	SCH	Child Protection Register Wales
Exposure to domestic violence	66%	21%
Reported sexual abuse	32%	7%
Reported physical abuse	44%	16%
Substance misuse problems	84%	★
Parental substance misuse	52%	★
Reported emotional neglect	62%	38%
Childhood sexual exploitation	34%	★
Sexually harmful behaviour	34%	★

★No data available

related to the feelings of worthlessness having been treated as being worthless for many years.

Substance use

In 2003, the Advisory Council on the Misuse of Drugs (ACMD) published a report, 'Hidden Harm – Responding to the needs of children of problem drug users', which highlighted for the first time that problematic drug use can and does cause serious harm to children at every age from conception to adulthood. They estimated that there were (at the time of the report) between 250,000 and 350,000 children of problem drug users in the UK and that number of affected children was only likely to decrease when the number of problem drug users decreases.

One of the conclusions of the report was that 'because of their numerous effects on the users' physiology and behaviour, drugs and drug taking have the potential to disturb every aspect of their child's development from conception onwards' and 'the extent of the damage and disadvantage varies enormously; however, we became convinced that the consequences for children are severe and long lasting'. The ACMD found that one-third of mothers and two-thirds of fathers no longer lived with their children and, the more severe the drug problem, the more they are likely to be separated from their children.

Many of the young people who come to Hillside have parents who have been using drugs from before they were born. We hear testimonies from the young people such as 'my mother would rather stick a syringe in her arm than talk to me' or where both parents have been so involved with drugs that the young person has become 'feral' and almost living outside the family. It is clearly been the case that damage has been done to these young people through neglect and the witnessing of parental drug use. In addition to this, many young people live with the effects of parental alcohol use with the concomitant neglect and violence associated with the abuse of alcohol.

Pates and Hooper (2017) in their review of young people admitted in 2014–2015 found that 59 of the 70 males used cannabis and 18 of the 32 females, and there was an increase in the use of new psychoactive substances (NPS). In 2015 the National Crime Agency (NCA) reported an increase (NCA, 2015) in the use of vulnerable young people to distribute drugs from larger cities (especially London) to smaller commuter towns, market towns, and coastal towns. We have noticed an increase in the involvement of young people referred to Hillside involved in drug running. We have also noticed an increase in young people referred who are involved in gangs (which often involve drugs and violence) particularly again from London.

Domestic violence

Domestic violence, and the witnessing of it, is a common theme to many of the young people's lives. According to the report on adverse childhood experiences

(Bellis et al., 2016), 16% of childhood households experienced domestic violence. What we observe in our young people are two major effects: a) growing up with violence being a common occurrence desensitises young people to the effects of violence and it becomes part of everyday life. They experience a very powerful effect of social learning which they then copy; and b) They see a parent being beaten by a partner, spouse, or step parent (usually but not always a male aggressor) and then try to intervene to protect the parent. The consequence of this happening frequently can lead to guilt about not being able to protect mum, or even, in severe cases, PTSD from the witnessing of the violence and being unable to protect her and when mother is away from them they worry about whether she is safe.

Sexual abuse and child sexual exploitation (CSE)

The report on adverse childhood experiences (Bellis et al., 2016) found that 24% of the people in their survey experienced early childhood sexual initiation (sexual intercourse before the age of 16), but this rose to 54% of those who had four or more adverse childhood experiences. Many of our young people, especially the females, have become sexually active at a very young age, often as young as 11 or 13. Many of them have been sexually abused, although this is not always disclosed, and a number of them have experienced rape either within the family or when absconding from care. Their perception of risk is very low and most of the females have the potential of sexual exploitation. They often don't see this as exploitation and say, 'it's my body to do what I want with' and do not appreciate the exploitative nature of these relationships or the legal aspects of a 13-year-old having sex with a 19-year-old man or often older than that.

The effects of sexual abuse are profound in terms of how a young person values their own body or their right not to be touched or abused. Most of our residents are adolescents and therefore sexual issues are of interest to them so we must not pathologise an interest in sex, but we must be able to separate what is normal and legal from what is illegal and abusive.

Labelling

The issue of diagnosing and labelling of young people is often very unhelpful. As can be seen from the details above, we deal with very damaged and distressed children. Many have attachment issues through having had little adequate parenting or a constant change of placements. We have young people with learning difficulties, but we often reassess after they have been stable at Hillside and find their potential higher than previously measured. A high percentage come in with a diagnosis of ADHD which, following observation and discussion, we feel to be a dubious diagnosis.

Requests for mental health assessments are frequent. Many referrers see the disturbed behaviours that are exhibited are symptoms of mental illness but often they are a result of the experience and background of the young person. Once they have settled we can deal with mental health problems without bringing in a Community Adolescent and Child Mental Health Service (CAMHS). We have our own clinical team with inhouse psychiatry and psychology, speech and language therapy, substance use worker, and a worker for childhood sexual exploitation and sexually harmful behaviour. The reason why we don't like these diagnoses is that once they are made the young person is labelled and the label will follow them through notes and referrals. We have quite frequently had a diagnosis of 'emerging personality disorder' for a young person who has a very disturbed background and that is frequently not only not the case but also this label will follow them throughout life.

Pates and Hooper (2017) reviewed the case notes of all young people admitted to Hillside during 2014 and 2015. Of the 102 admitted (70 males and 32 females) 45 of the males and 25 of the females (i.e. nearly 70%) had been referred to their local CAMHS service but, with the exception of ADHD (diagnosed in 26 of the males and two of the females) and eight males diagnosed with ODD or conduct disorder, only 24 had any other mental health diagnosis including autistic spectrum disorder (ASD). On observing the young people when they have settled, many of them show few signs of ADHD which we believe they have been diagnosed with because of troubled and difficult behaviour caused by childhood trauma and attachment problems. Some of them have had between 15 and 20 residential placements which will cause further attachment problems as each placement breaks down. In the past two and a half years, only four young people have had significant mental health problems requiring onward referral for mental health problems.

Interventions

As has been stated, the whole environment is designed to be therapeutic and the care staff who are with the young people most of the time provide a therapeutic milieu with regular meal times, staff they can trust (each young person has a key worker), boundaries, and a regular timetable plus activities in the holidays and at weekends.

Individual therapeutic interventions are designed for the individual young person's specific needs. These can range from art therapy, play therapy, simplified cognitive behavioural therapy, and even behavioural interventions and work on their specific issues.

The manager's story

I arrived at our children's secure home as the interim principal manager in May 2017. One could say I arrived 'by accident'! I was initially tasked to undertake a safeguarding review. The initial plan was to be seconded for three months from my existing role as the safeguarding lead for the local authority. Safeguarding is defined in Wales as the protection of children and the enhancement of their wellbeing. This is a statement which is absolutely integral to the work at our secure unit.

I was clear that this was a time limited and focused piece of work because running and leading the only secure children's home in Wales was not on my wish list of ten things I had to do before I reached retirement. In fact, running a children's secure home was not on my wish list of things to do at all.

My background was as a qualified social worker, a qualified teacher, and a previous children's guardian in the court arena. I had a strong family court background and for six years I had worked for Welsh Government, as an area director of the children and family courts advisory service. During the last seven years of my career I had been the head of safeguarding for three local authorities, with a remit of safeguarding children, safeguarding adults, and safeguarding in education.

With nearly 30 years post qualifying child protection and safeguarding experience, and 13 years as a senior manager I suppose, on reflection, it was a sound platform on which to be parachuted in to head a service that caters for the holistic needs of the most vulnerable and traumatised children in England and Wales; 24 hour days and 365 days a year.

The brief was to strengthen and promote the commitment to safeguarding in the secure estate in Wales by manging and reducing risk versus danger, to challenge and dispel the preconceived ideas that secure accommodation is the last resort for these 'dangerous and beyond control children' and ensure that the secure accommodation in Wales was respected and viewed as a children's home first and not a prison.

Within six weeks of arrival, I had taken stock. It was obvious that there was a huge legacy of tremendous work that had gone on before my arrival, but that this was a service that needed development and reviewing. There were excellent staff, but many were working unilaterally, and working in silos. I decided then that this was an incredible opportunity to take this secure provision in Wales forward. I am very proud that this secure children's home is the national provision in Wales, and we want to, as a team, develop it with further partnership collaboration to be a centre of excellence. We are someway along the trajectory of that journey, and I was fortunate enough to inherit the successes, but I have also had to address the challenges.

With a staff group of 161 and 22 young people, some with the most complex needs in society, this is one of the most exciting and challenging opportunities I have ever been offered. We are now also a key part of the larger Neath Port Talbot council and children's services under the social services and housing directorate headed by a new director who is keen to support the secure estate in his authority. Subsequently, this is integrating us both with local and national service resource and provision.

The core theme of everything in secure setting is managing risk alongside nurturing our young people. Social theorists have noted the increased preoccupation with risk in late modern society (Beck, 1992; Parton, 1996, 2006). There has been a tendency to identify and categorise risks in most spheres of human activity and governments, institutions, and workers are increasingly required to manage these risks. Horlick-Jones (2005) has noted how such preoccupations with the management of risk have affected professionals and organisations. Holland (2015) stated that professional discretion has increasingly been replaced by a preoccupation with procedures and the expectation of an audit trail for all actions. This is because organisations are concerned with managing the risk of damage to reputation as well as risks associated with their main tasks.

Manging risk in a secure children's home must be built into the psyche of all the staff employed there and is a skill that most people on the outside would find too difficult a task.

Subsequently, every operational person at Hillside needs to know how to assess 'risk' versus 'danger', whether in the residential unit in the school or in the clinical support team. Every operational person at the home needs to ensure risk management that keeps our young people safe from significant harm at all times whilst they are at the home and whatever their legal status, i.e. welfare or Youth Custody Service (YCS). To do this in our setting, which has a remit to provide education alongside our residential care setting takes a huge amount of skill and commitment, knowledge. Providing a seamless and outstanding service 'across the piste', while keeping children safe, is the focus of our work going forward.

The commitment and the vision I have now is that our young people are protected, are safe, will stabilise, will be nurtured and leave Hillside to return to their communities with a safety plan and a behaviour management assessment for them to acquire the long-term support they need in order to achieve positive and measurable outcomes. Our ambition is that they will receive an education tailored to their individual needs and that every young person will leave us with a recognised qualification. This involves a triangulation of care education and clinical support at our secure unit, the tripartite being the children's home (the units), the provision of education via our school, and our inhouse clinical support team; this consists of a clinical psychologist, a child and adolescent psychiatrist, two assistant psychologists, a speech and language therapist, a substance misuse councillor, and a sexually harmful behaviour, and CSE specialist worker from Barnardo's Better Futures project. An active offer of therapeutic support services alongside excellent care provision also makes us more attractive to the placing local authorities.

We are providing empirically based assessments to courts and are being recognised as experts in our field. The assessments of each part of the service complement and inform each other and we can measure exactly where our children are in terms of their education and emotional and cognitive development. We have successfully implemented the Trauma Recovery Model (TRM) (Skuse and Mathews, 2015) but are also now moving into another model which has been devised by our manager of clinical resources, Karen Wedmore, and her clinical team. This model is the Safety, Stability and Structure model (Wedmore, 2017) and incorporates incremental stages of the TRM recognising that children cannot progress unless the safety stability and structural needs in their lives are being met. It is based on a scoring matrix we use to find out where our young people sit in terms of their stability and emotional security that we can triangulate with all the assessments. It has a large section which is pertinent to educational needs being met and we feel enhances our overall assessments of our young people.

I have professional oversight of the whole of the service and its development and I must ensure that safeguarding is everybody's business. This phrase is borrowed from child protection terminology in the UK that child protection is 'everybody's business'. This phrase appears to have originated in Every Child Matters Programme in England, although the wording does not occur in the original Green Paper. It is now commonly used in local and national governmental and organisational statements about children's safeguarding.

In terms of education, we must ensure that the children placed at our secure unit have a right to and will receive a good and diverse standard of education while they are placed with us, and that their emotional, cultural, educational, developmental, and safety needs are met during their stay. Some of the key themes run across all areas of the service and are safety, partnership and communication. Supporting young people through education, through the residential home, and through the clinical services cannot be done in isolation or unilaterally.

Since being in post I have had to evaluate our position in the market place. We are a self-funding organisation with a zero budget within the local authority. Our financial viability in the market place is also a key consideration; nevertheless, despite being in a sellers' market, the welfare of young people placed there is, and will always be, paramount (Children Act, 1989).

Key aspects of service provision have been reviewed, their value has been established, and room for improvement identified. Clinical support services have been strengthened, a new rota implemented and the statement of purpose has been amended. Education provision continues to go from strength to strength and is in line with the Charlie Taylor recommendations (2016). Furthermore, we have aligned the peer safeguarding review in education in our secure unit with the rest of the safeguarding checks and balances in the local authority. The review highlighted that, although we have made significant progress, managing provision has become more demanding. There is always room for improvement and managing risk versus danger is a key player in the paradigm.

Managing risk in a secure educational setting

In terms of what our young people may have experienced before they arrived at our unit, I have developed a list to highlight some of the negative experience our young people may have been subjected to prior to arrival. This list is neither mutually exhaustive or exclusive, but one child will have experienced many of these things before being placed; these children are traumatised, scared vulnerable, sad children, they are not mad or bad.

Our children may:

- be the subject of child protection investigations
- have been physical, emotionally or sexually abused
- be looked after children, had frequent moves or many placement breakdowns
- have experienced domestic abuse, racial abuse, homophobia
- be young carers

or have:

- misused substances
- had episodes of going missing
- been a victim or perpetrator of child sexual exploitation
- experienced compromised parenting
- mental health issues
- displayed offending behaviour or sexually harmful behaviours
- no educational attainments
- non-school attendance.

Local authorities have frequently tried everything else and expect a secure unit to 'fix the problem'. They also expect the young person for whom they have corporate parenting responsibility to receive a good education, and we aim to please!

The education manager's story

Teaching in a national secure children's home is not for everyone, but if you are interested in making a significant impact on the lives of the most traumatised young people in the country, it can be the most rewarding experience of your career.

The terms 'school' and 'headteacher' are often used in conjunction with secure children's homes, but the truth is that our school is not officially classed as a school. It's defined as an educational placement in a social service setting, and the headteacher is the education manager. The education staff at Hillside are all very experienced educationalists and our current staff comprises of seven teachers including one deputy head teacher and one head teacher (teachers' specialisms include mathematics, English, ICT, PE, modern foreign languages, and technology). Additionally, we have one higher level teaching assistant and six learning support assistants. When a young person has need of more support, we are able to bring in additional 1:1 learning support assistants to maximise the progress of that individual young person. The lessons delivered in the academic year 2016–17 included: English, literacy, maths, numeracy, science, information communication technology, careers, pastoral social health and environment, physical education, food technology, independent living skills, art, thematic lessons, construction, Duke of Edinburgh Award, child care, guitar lessons, hair and beauty, fitness, European studies, cake decorating, design technology, street art/murals, parenting skills, jewellery making, motor vehicle maintenance, games, radicalisation and racism, crime and consequences, Phoenix Course, Welsh, and finally Spanish. Consequently, teachers here have to be multi-skilled and flexible ... we are a 'Jack of all trades', perhaps, but also master of many!

The school is structured so that four classes run in parallel for six 45-minute periods plus a form period/tutorial session daily within a fortnightly timetable. The day is divided into three main parts and the day starts with the core subjects of maths, English, science, and ICT. After morning break up there are thematic lessons, PSE, and careers lessons. Hillside has moved away from discrete humanities lessons in line with the recommendations that Donaldson made in his report 'Successful Futures' (2015) to a more thematic approach. This is not yet statutory in Wales, as we are in a transition period, but we expect it to be made statutory in the near future. After lunch the more kinaesthetic/vocational lessons where young people are given choices take place. There is a whole school assembly every Friday afternoon where we celebrate successes. There are 12 classrooms and other specialist teaching areas such as DT workshops, food technology room, ICT suite, and sports hall.

Many challenges face teachers working in the secure estate and these are no different in Wales. The young people bring with them many behaviours that, when together in a class, the resulting mix can be extremely volatile and challenging. And while the Youth Custody Service young people know why they are placed in the secure estate and know when they are leaving the Section 25, the Welfare young people may disagree with the reason for secure placement and do not know when they are leaving and where their next placement may be.

A young person's duration of stay can vary from a few hours to several years, but a typical period would be 14 weeks. This means that we cannot hope to emulate the structures and programmes of study found in a mainstream setting. The class will be comprised of young people of varying ages, varying abilities, and different start dates. Conventionally, organisation within settings might be undertaken according to ability as in a mainstream school but we must group young people where they are least likely to play off one another. Some young people arrive with drug or alcohol dependency, may have been physically, psychologically or sexually abused, and may also be violent. We also find that many learners arrive at our school with very little meaningful information about their previous education attainment.

As in every secure children's home, there may be tensions between care staff and education if both teams do not work together closely and we work hard to minimise these and integrate both parts of the service. Good teaching often involves taking risks; this is at odds with the ethos of the secure estate which errs towards being totally risk adverse. Procedures and policies inside a secure children's home can also be very restrictive and frustrating for a newly arrived teacher, as safety and security trump all other educational concerns.

An issue that all teachers may have faced at one time or another is that the non-teaching adults' view of school is often clouded by their own experiences behind the desk or through interactions with their own children's schooling. Colleagues in a 'professional parenting' role can have a skewed vision of what education is and little or no knowledge of how learning is achieved. Observers will see education as a process that is applied to a young person, where as we in the profession know it is a collaborative endeavour between the teaching staff and the learners.

We have no lone teaching; there would always be one teacher and one learning support assistant in every classroom. Staffing can therefore be a huge issue as all staff require specialist training and induction to work in our secure children's home, which in turn makes it very difficult to simply bring staff in to cover for absent colleagues. The easiest solution to this problem was to 'borrow' care staff who are less experienced in the role of a learning support assistant. This also created a further problem for care staff reducing their available staffing and increasing pressures for care colleagues. There are also many locked doors in secure children's homes and teachers must lock themselves in their classrooms with the pupils, and this is something that not everyone is comfortable with.

But despite these challenges we have been able to make huge progress, creating a warm and nurturing environment for all our young people that meets the requirements of placing authorities and regulatory bodies with every young person re-engaging with school and leaving with recognisable qualifications. Exam success is essential in helping us to increase pupil's feelings of self-esteem and self-worth especially as most of our young people on arrival are certain that school was not for them.

Often the young person is in a state of crisis when they are sentenced, and regularly arrive late at night from court many miles away into what appears from the outside to be a cold, austere, frightening institution. In the first few days of a young person's stay, secure children's homes can feel a long way from home, a long way from normality, but school brings normality to an abnormal situation as all young people have had some previous experience of school.

We aim to put the learners at the centre of everything we do. Our curriculum is broad and balanced, with enough flexibility to create an individualised curriculum, with young people able to make choices over some of their lessons. We have a school council that meets every five weeks which ensures that the 'pupil voice' is heard and recognised.

Life for a young person in a secure children's home can be very 'boring' to them so we aim to make each school week different from the previous week by celebrating many different festivals, themes, and occasions whether it be Christmas or Diwali, Comic Relief or MacMillan coffee mornings. We have enterprise weeks, Duke of Edinburgh expeditions, sports days, and vocational weeks. We also work with a wide range of outside agencies, such as Mid and West Wales Fire Service, who provide a very successful firefighter cadet type programme called the Phoenix course. We now have young people who enjoy coming to school especially as there are rewards to be gained from engaging fully in the school day. Reintroduction into education is possibly the most important thing that we can achieve, as most of the young people have totally disengaged from school prior to arrival.

We seldom receive any useful data on prior educational attainment. Education staff carry out a battery of tests, including WRATs 4 (wide ranging achievement test, fourth edition), which gives us an accurate assessment of our young people, and by retesting prior to discharge, we can show progress. For the school year 2016–2017 for an average of 37 young people, we were able to show significant progress: three years increase in reading age, 3.5 years increase in comprehension, and 4.2 years increase in maths age. Working in conjunction with our clinical team and care team, who compile the young person's chronology of events and a full assessment of their cognitive and emotional states, we can 'see the whole child', and not just the presented behaviours.

Our educational team has developed a strong 'esprit de corps', where they socialise together. The staff team have even requested a staff uniform! This team spirit can be infectious, and it is perhaps best demonstrated by their 'can do attitude' which is essential as it can be all too easy to find an excuse for not doing something out of the norm.

We have sufficient staff so that we can extract pupils for 1:1 support, and to cover absent colleagues without impacting on our care colleagues. Our previous staffing structure worked on paper but seldom in practice. In fact, all the learning support assistants (LSAs) are able to work additional shifts if they want to as care officers, so helping to bridge the gap between care and education. Unlike many mainstream schools, all our LSAs have additional responsibilities and are an integral part of the team.

A unique feature of Hillside Education is working in partnership with our local mainstream secondary school, which allows us to rotate staff out who disclosed that they felt 'burnt out'. We are also able to call upon specialist subject support from the school and additional support from the local authority. This has meant that all young people following GCSE courses prior to admission can continue to follow most GCSE courses due to this ongoing external support. Our staff also benefit from the in-service training organised by the mainstream school.

Whilst working in silos must be avoided at all costs, those working as part of the education team need the freedom to work independently within the centre free from micromanagement. We always seek to involve care staff in various activities to establish improved communication, better team work, and for all staff to be able to celebrate the significant successes that our young people make. The best secure children's homes minimise these issues by having a unified leadership team with a shared vision for the home, communicating readily with each other, and having managers who are keen to support each other. I know that we as a children's home, through both care and education staff, make a major difference to most, if not all, of our young people, and this has been the most challenging and the most rewarding phase of my career.

Conclusions

What outcomes do we see?

One problem that faces us is the unrealistic expectations of those who refer. We are dealing with the most difficult and damaged young people in the country who have often suffered years of neglect abuse and have few attachments to anyone. We do not work miracles and the problems these young people have take time to turn around. We are often expected to have them for so short a time that, realistically, little work can be done. The young person needs to settle before they can be properly assessed, and any work can realistically take place. But we get asked to do things in short time scales and with an expectation that the young person will turn out 'normally'.

What we often find is that young people, who hate being here to start with, will not want to leave when their time comes to move on. They have become settled, find they are in a safe place, and with people who are predictable and who they can trust. It is scary to go back out into that big uncaring world. But while here they do form attached relationships with staff and, although they will test these out to see if they are rejected, we do not discharge children before the dates set by the courts; the young people are never rejected by us.

In terms of measurable change, we notice a dramatic decrease in major and minor incidents over three months, a steady decrease in self-harm, they will begin to trust staff and often go on to disclose abuse and trauma that they have been too frightened to disclose previously. They often make dramatic improvements in their educational attainments through an increase in reading, writing, spelling, comprehension, and numeracy levels, and they have the opportunity, via our resettlement officer, to look at the future: which may be college, housing, or a job. We recognise the need to develop more sophisticated outcome measures both during their stay with us and six months after having left. Therefore, we are planning a major piece of research to provide objective measurable outcomes to demonstrate the value of the secure children's home.

A report recently published by The National Association for Youth Justice compared secure training centres and young offenders institutions with secure children's homes and stated the following:

> YOIs and STCs have repeatedly shown themselves to be incapable of caring for vulnerable children, especially those whose behaviour might often be challenging. They should therefore be abolished forthwith. Conversely, the performance of Secure Children's Homes, at their best, demonstrates that a model of secure accommodation based on a child care ethos can provide a safe environment that has the potential to minimise the damage caused by custody while preparing children for a positive future on release.
>
> *(Bateman, 2016)*

We do not believe in original sin, we believe all children are born equal, and it is their early experience that becomes the moulding factor in their lives. This facility is good at the difficult job they do, but staff need time and patience especially from referrers. These are not 'naughty kids' as they are often described, just very distressed and disturbed young people who are often in this situation through no fault of their own. The Jesuits used to say, 'give me the child by the age of 7 and we will give you the man'. The reality is that by the age of seven it is often too late. Children who have been neglected, abused, and left without human contact or love will react from a young age. We can help reverse some of these problems but only with full co-operation from referrers in terms of timing and expectations.

References

Advisory Council on the Misuse of Drugs (2003) *Hidden Harm – responding to the needs of children of problem drug users: a report of the Advisory Council on the Misuse of Drugs.* London: Home Office.

Bateman, T. (2016) *The state of youth custody. A report for the National Association for Youth Justice.* London: National Association for Youth Justice.

Beck, U. (1992) *Risk society: towards a new modernity.* London: SAGE Publications.

Bellis, M.A., Ashton, K., Hughes, K., Ford, K., Bishop, J., and Paranjothy, S. (2016) *Adverse childhood experiences and their impact on health-harm in behaviours in the Welsh adult population.* Public Health Wales and Centre for Public Health/Liverpool John Moores University.

Children Act 1989. London: The National Archives [Online]. Retrieved from: www.legislation.gov.uk/ukpga/1989/41/section/31

Donaldson, G. (2015) *Successful futures: a report on the curriculum and assessment arrangements in Wales.* Cardiff: Welsh Assembly.

Harris, R., Pates, R.M., and Barratt, H. (forthcoming) *Differences in verbal and performance IQ in a group of traumatised children.*

Horlick-Jones, T. (2005) On 'risk work': professional discourse accountability, and everyday action. *Journal of Health, Risk and Society,* 7, 3, 293–307.

Holland, S. (2015) *Public health ethics.* Oxford: John Wiley and Son.

National Crime Agency. (2015) *NCA intelligence assessment: county lines, gangs and safeguarding.* London: NCA.

Parton, N. (1996) Social work, risk and the 'blaming society'. In N. Parton (Ed.), *Social theory, social change and social work.* Brighton: Psychology Press.

Parton, N. (2006) *Safeguarding children: early intervention and surveillance in a late modern society.* Basingstoke: Palgrave Macmillan.

Pates, R.M., and Hooper, K. (2017) Drug use and mental health in a secure children's home. *Advances in Dual Diagnosis,* 10, 2, 71–80.

Skuse, T., and Mathews, J. (2015) The trauma recovery model: sequencing youth justice interventions for young people with complex needs. *Prison Service Journal,* 220, 16–25.

Taylor, C. (2016) *Review of the Youth Justice System in England and Wales. A report for the Ministry of Justice.* London: MoJ.

Wedmore, K. (2017) *The safety, stability and structure model.* Unpublished report.

10

ALIGNING WITH THE CHAOS AND NAVIGATING THROUGH THE TRAUMA

Deirdre McConnell, Kate Brown, Yanela Garcia and James Stephens

A different kind of therapy space: first impressions

The room isn't quiet or private. Through the window in the door, the reception can be seen where music is blaring from the television, and in the next room another young person is escalating into a loud confrontation. There's a camera in the corner keeping a watchful eye on my safety, which is not something I'm used to and do query as a therapist, but this is not my normal territory and so I will adhere to the structural boundaries already in place. I'm beginning to question how therapeutic this space can really be. How am I going to build a sense of safety and create a place for recovery for clients who are caught up in criminal activity, teetering on the edge of custody, and potentially dangerous? For them, am I just another appointment, another professional they must talk to? With confidence wavering, I nervously await the opening of the door.

It is 25 minutes into the dramatherapy session and the young person hasn't arrived at the Youth Justice office. The hour ends, and the door doesn't open. The surveillance camera witnesses the waiting, the setting up of carefully considered materials and games, as well as the packing up. At this point my experience of the young person consists of ticks indicating symptoms of stress on a referral form, a detailed history of multiple traumas and criminal offences, and a voice over the phone stating they will 'definitely attend'.

The offences committed have led these young people to become entrenched within the legal system. Their lives are often a whirlwind of chaos. It appears to us that, with a heavy reluctance and a hard-exterior display of defensive behaviours, they hide and protect their multiple layers of trauma, abuse, and pain. Their arrival at the Youth Justice offices is not the beginning of their stories. Their narrative, up to this point in their lives, has become locked away and fiercely guarded. The therapeutic process needs to delicately peel away this hardened exterior, explore the factors that propelled them towards this trajectory, and then to set them on a more positive path.

Somehow, we need to gain their trust and build and nurture a therapeutic alliance so that together we can navigate to the beginning of their stories. If they can understand the 'What, Why and How'[1] within their narratives, they may be able to begin a new story for themselves (Lovett, 2015).

Navigating stories

New beginnings and personal stories have been at the heart of our work

In the early 2000s, the Labour Government's Every Child Matters Agenda (ECM) heralded a host of initiatives aiming to improve the lives of children. The serious case review of Victoria Climbie's killing alerted professionals to systematic failings and the need to work far more closely to safe-guard children. ECM encouraged innovative approaches across a wide range of school and community settings. The Emotional and Trauma Support (ETS) team was born in this period, financed by the Children's Fund. It has worked since then in partnership with other services, especially schools, developing an expertise in working with children who have experienced overwhelming distress in relation to past life events.

Starting in 2002, ETS laid a strong foundation in its work with trauma, initially with refugee and asylum-seeking children and their families and, later, with other children. Safety at every level is paramount in trauma recovery. Physical, emotional, and psychological safety – all essential – are made possible by the provision of safe spaces, authentic therapeutic relationships, and appropriate support at supervisory and systemic levels. ETS originally started its therapeutic work with an educational psychologist, an art therapist, a counsellor, and a horticulture therapist. For the new narrative to emerge, making sense of experience in a meaningful way, safety, and attachment (the powerful antidotes to trauma) are required. When an environment conducive to being heard, being witnessed, is provided, children become able to express themselves in whatever way feels right for them. Words were not necessary, and language was not a barrier. The children were able to communicate through a different modality, using innate creativity to understand better what they were experiencing both in their bodies and minds and in their everyday living. They were given the emotional support to help them move forward.

Since 2008, ETS has been commissioned directly by schools and local authorities and the development of the work across several phases has been analysed elsewhere (McConnell, 2012). In some cases, intensive therapeutic support has been provided to families who need to overcome complex, seemingly intractable situations, where children have been out of school for extended periods, potentially heading for looked after child status or custody. Working with families in parallel with children is sometimes a necessity to achieve sustainable change. This can present challenges and nowhere more than in the youth justice context where some families with multiple social stressors resist support for a variety of reasons. They are living the experience too. However, some families can respond positively to the support which is offered. As well as being concerned for the safety and wellbeing of their child, they may be targets of abuse themselves.

How did we start working with the Youth Justice Service?

ETS was commissioned in 2016 for an initial six months to deliver therapeutic support to young people, to help them 'desist from offending behaviours, improve engagement in rehabilitation and employment and gain improved resilience and self-confidence'[2](HMIP, 2016). Action research methodology was applied using a *plan-do-review* process. Two ETS dramatherapists delivered the interventions and reflected weekly through a team approach with the team leader and assistant lead. External clinical supervisors also met with each dramatherapist individually. Therapeutic material was analysed alongside logistical and systemic issues to correlate key themes between therapists and caseloads.

The flexibility of the dramatherapists and the modality have been pushed to new limits within this working environment. With children and adolescents, the testing of boundaries is an inevitable and necessary stage within the process. The therapist becomes the container and they will maintain boundaries to create safety for the client. Once established, the trust and relationship can start to develop. However, for clients who have not experienced a safe home and lack a consistent primary caregiver, implementing boundaries does not always build a sense of safety. For them, adults may well be perceived as inherently unsafe, so an adult being pleasant and caring towards them can be a threat in a different way. They can be so hyper-vigilant that they are in a constant state of arousal, alert for potential dangers and ready for fighting or flight.

Starting point

Potential participants are referred for therapeutic support by their youth justice caseworker and an initial meeting is held with the caseworker acting as a transitional person. Each worker had his or her own approach to building relationships, modelling care and sensitivity, and taking into consideration the potential of a perceived threat which the children would be likely to feel at the prospect of another professional trying to work with them. Many young people approached the therapist with caution and apprehension. The therapy was not a formal requirement of the young person's order but could be used as an alternative to the work of their assigned caseworker. Encouraging the young people to make decisions on what would be most helpful to them was a starting point in regaining agency over their situations. This resulted in a change in their perception of the therapist, who was now seen as a person offering supportive flexibility rather than, as previously, punitive rigidity. The young people were viewed as expert in their own experience of the criminal justice system and any issues around their order would be listened to. However, the role of the therapist was maintained by refraining from using any legal language or processes. The caseworker would clarify or enforce the terms of their order if necessary.

Setting up 'therapeutic contracts' was important. These were considered an agreement and a commitment to find a way of working together. Many individuals would comment on their difficulty with the contract before agreeing to it. After all, the contract acts as container and these young people may never have felt the safety of a containing place or person before. Lack of internal safety and inability to be contained has in fact most likely led them to a point where they were on the path to potential custody. These conversations, in which we agreed how the therapist and the young people should work together, helped to give them a clearer notion of their own individuality along with a better insight into their own motivation. We looked at the many systems surrounding the young person to ensure that he or she, through being the greatest stakeholder in their journey, would be at the centre of the process. As therapists, we agreed to be consistent but understood that the young person might be ambivalent throughout this process.

The lack of trust and pain they feel around adults can play out straight away, projecting all their internal trauma on to the therapist. No matter how far along the therapeutic process we were, we could never assume that we had their full trust. The closer you got to their inner world the more they would push you away, continuously working on the edge of risk. The potential risk to therapist, the perceived risk to the young person of building a relationship, and the implications this could have all need to be taken in consideration. Any interruption to the process can reinforce old scripts that they cannot trust adults and they are not safe.

And how do we work with that? This is a question we continue to ask. Initially it was painstakingly slow and immensely challenging. Pushing past the offences, the defiance, the DNAs, the breaching, and the anger was difficult and time-consuming. On every occasion where a young person did not arrive for an appointment, we used the time to reflect on our approach, to work with it, and to stay with the process. One young person was surprised when he arrived to find his therapist present and waiting, even after he had missed four consecutive sessions. This became a pivotal moment within their alliance as it enabled him to move to the next phase of the therapy process. Seeing the therapist's commitment made him feel valued and it challenged his own commitment to the therapy.

Working with real life dramatically

Dramatherapy is a form of psychological therapy in which all of the performance arts are utilised within the therapeutic relationship. Dramatherapists are both artists and clinicians and draw on their trainings in theatre/drama and therapy to create methods to engage clients in effecting psychological, emotional and social changes. The therapy gives equal validity to body and mind within the dramatic context; stories, myths, playtexts, puppetry, masks and improvisation are examples of the range of artistic interventions a Dramatherapist may employ. These will enable the client to explore difficult and painful life experiences through an indirect approach'.

(British Association of Dramatherapists, 2018)

'Don't tell me: show me!'

We have the opportunity within creative arts therapies to talk, or not talk, to be, or play, or not play. The space invites the client to experience a different state of being, but we first must identify their 'play language'. Understanding what type of play language will aid the young person's process is key to beginning the dramatherapy journey and this may be present immediately or take several weeks to emerge. The therapist may decide to present a number of materials for the individual to choose or present one method and work with the response of the individual. The responses to what is not used can be equally powerful as to what *is* used.

Keeping going with creativity is vital. Whether the child is explicitly acknowledging or 'acting out' their situation, the dramatherapists would work towards a dramatic or metaphorical frame. In moving from real life into a dramatic space, an opportunity arises to work in safety with past trauma and new possibilities, often at the same time. It was interesting to note that once an appropriate metaphor or dramatic space had been created, usually jointly by the therapist and the young person, it could be used both as a way of safely examining negative past experiences and envisioning future more positive ones. Enabling the imaginary space can provide instant relief from the overwhelming pain of trauma; however, there is a need to move aspects of the imaginary space into permanent fixtures within the young person's real world to support long term change.

Developmental trauma

The young person's 'acting out' behaviour may seem an easy starting point for therapy and the reason why they are asked to attend. This behaviour itself is of course a form of communication. Multiple traumatic events can alter the child's brain development in early childhood or, as Perry and Szalavitz (2006) put it, experience can become biology. Without a safe base and a consistent care-giver a child will struggle to build his or her own identity and lack the skills to form future healthy attachments. A single traumatic event within a child's life can have adverse effects on their behaviour and emotional wellbeing. The young people that become embroiled within the Youth Justice System have experienced not one but multiple traumas and are still currently entangled within them, living in chaos and reliving traumatic experiences daily. Van der Kolk introduced the diagnosis of Developmental Trauma Disorder in 2009 to assist clinicians to better understand the presentations and realities of children and adolescents exposed to 'chronic interpersonal trauma'[3] (2014). The young people who do eventually walk through the door are not merely offending youths who should be approached with caution. They are also traumatised children with a fragmented sense of self, emotionally immature, academically behind, and with little or no support networks around them. They are lost within an adult world that they don't fully understand or have the skills and resilience to cope with. Their development has been hindered by their traumatic experiences. The therapy process allows us to revisit missed milestones to help reshape and repair early experiences to alter the young person's perspective and to start the healing process.

Sophie was 13 years old at the time of referral and had been arrested over 20 times, predominantly for theft and assault. Historical domestic violence was reported in the family home between Mum and various partners. Recognised as the victim of emotional abuse and neglect, she was on a Child Protection Plan and in addition had been permanently excluded from school for assaulting a teacher. During her process a consistent theme has been the need to be nurtured. She often displayed regressive behaviour, such as sucking her thumb and curling up on her chair. Within attachment theory Bowlby states that a safe base is provided by the care-giver within early child development, to reassure the child and maintain a sense of safety, helping them to thrive. When a person has suffered traumatic experiences in early childhood and has an insecure attachment, he or she may seek out nurturing roles and attempt to create real life safe spaces outside of their family dynamic. They may achieve temporary gratification by aligning themselves with peers who are part of the criminal world, as in some way they are having their needs met. Often, they have role models who are further along the trajectory than they are themselves, but with low self-worth and confidence, they struggle to identify genuine friends and their vulnerabilities may be exploited.

The developmental model within dramatherapy is rooted in the developmental stages of early childhood and parallels the way children learn to play. It focuses on three important stages: Embodiment, Projection, and Role – EPR (Jennings 2011).[4] Using projective play, Sophie was able to put elements of her life into the narrative. The story dice she used within a session provided enough therapeutic distance to allow her to explore current and difficult feelings around her own relationships within the safety of metaphor. Simply asking her about her current situation with her mother would have triggered an angry response and may have resulted in a shut down in communication. However, distancing herself from the actual situation with the use of a character within a story helps her to explore this in a safer, less threatening way. She can communicate difficult feelings without feeling vulnerable.

Sophie[5]

> Sophie chose to begin the story and rolled the story dice showing 3 images. A tree, a plane and a clock. Without hesitation, she began telling a story about herself and how she was lost in a forest where she found a clock that showed she only had 3 minutes left until her mum would be leaving to catch a plane to Australia. She gets home but dad tells her that mum has already left. So, she runs out the house to try and catch her, only to find mum is sat up on a rainbow. She finds a compass to show

her the way to mum and gets in a car but can't drive, so she gets on a bee that flies her up to the rainbow. On her way there a man tries to warn her she's on a dangerous path and heading to a dangerous windy tree. Suddenly an arrow shoots at her and she falls off the bee and lands in the flowers that surround a big castle. A beetle takes her to the hospital to fix her sore foot. Mum comes to visit her and then takes her home. The end.

The difficulties within her relationship are articulated through the fairytale imagery she creates. The obstacles she faces in the story directly correlate with her continuous battle to gain her mother's time and attention. In reality, their relationship is a juxtaposition of love and angry hostility, yet through the use of story Sophie was able to recognise her longing for mum to find her and the need to be taken care of. The therapy space provides the client with a safe, consistent, and non-threatening environment that can contain difficult material and yet be a place of calm within a chaotic world. As the therapist in this case was female, it was important to recognise the young person's provocative language and defensive manner as purposeful attempts at creating conflict by transferring on to the therapist the role of argumentative mother. The therapist can be an appropriate nurturing figure but needs to remain consistent and boundaried, promoting positive adult relationships and providing the safety and security that has previously been disrupted in early development. The therapist's efforts can be immediately rejected, as these young people need to feel needed and will often want to be persuaded to stay in the therapy space.

Using these methods, Sophie was able to become more aware of her emotional needs and began to think more reflectively. Within the sessions she took ownership of her successes and expressed the desire to maintain them. Her perspective shifted slightly so she was able to explore new scripts, make attempts to alter her behaviour, and to break the repetitive cycle of offending she was currently stuck in. With her growth in confidence and self-worth she began to identify previous associates who could prevent her from achieving her new goals. She was able to recognise that they were attempting to sabotage her, but refused, as she said, to let them 'bring her down to their level'. Sophie is currently in education and has not reoffended for nearly a year.

Handling dynamite

The testing of boundaries never actually comes to an end; every peeling away of a layer reveals new information and instigates movement within the process. The closer the therapist gets, the more vulnerable the client feels; consequently, defences become alerted and this can result in further challenges and further testing out of the relationship. This can take the form of a sudden refusal to participate, verbal aggression or an abrupt departure from the therapeutic space. As Cordess points out, being listened to and heard has just not been part of the life experience of many 'wayward youngsters' (2002: 76) and so, paradoxically, it is often actually more confusing and more difficult to cope with than the negative attitudes with which they are more familiar.

Developing a way to navigate through certain conversational barriers was a skill that required fine tuning. A stiffening of the shoulders or a sudden sharp look was enough to indicate that defences had been triggered. During these moments the therapist needs to tread very carefully and delicately manoeuvre themselves away from potential eruption. The process can feel like handling dynamite, trying not to set it off yet attempting to transfer it delicately and safely to a place where it can access the therapy. This meant that initially the sessions lacked fluidity, as the therapist had continuously to shift to realign with the client. For them, we were invading their space and attempting to know them. Once their guard came up you had to find another way in.

Joint reflective practice is crucial. Going through this journey with a colleague was a well-needed source of support and comfort, as we compared notes and worries throughout this parallel process. Reflecting within the team as well as having separate clinical supervision supplied us with our own safety network. The *plan-do-review* approach became a system for ourselves that enabled continuous reflective thinking, supportive consultation, and an adaptive process. Creating a bespoke service that integrated the rigidity of the legal system with therapeutic alignment to build a supportive infrastructure around the young person was a challenge but well worth it.

Many of the young people who accessed therapy were overwhelmed by the chaotic environments in which they lived and to which they would return after their sessions. Therapists working with the youth justice population will be familiar with individuals arriving for sessions and bringing this chaos with them. Whilst child protection processes and the criminal courts may decide that a child needs to be removed from home, for his or her own safety and/or to protect others, the therapist's role is to work with the young person where he or she is, physically and emotionally, at the time of the encounter. Many dramatherapists work with the notion of remaining with the chaos, rather than becoming a 'helper'. Our aim is to assist the individual to access their own inner resources. To do this requires creating a liminal space – a threshold between the old world of uncertainty and abuse and a new one of hope and achievement – where healing can take place and new possibilities can be explored. Paolo et al. describe the liminal as 'a pause in everyday life in which habitual behaviours, attitudes and beliefs can be transformed' (2005: 45) For change to occur, therefore, individuals must reflect upon their own sense of self and may need to begin this process by 'restructuring (their) old identity'. Moving flexibly in dramatherapy sessions between real life and dramatic play can assist young people to come to a better understanding both of who they are and who they want to be.

Ben

Ben had attended ten dramatherapy sessions and often arrived frustrated. He would talk about giving up on his referral order and not caring about going to prison. In the first few sessions the therapist would listen to Ben's frustrations and his story started to emerge. He began talking openly about not wanting to follow the trajectory of his violent step-father but recognised the anger they both shared. Ben spoke about the domestic violence at home. Angry at his past, his current relationship with his mother and his youth offending order, he felt that his life was unpredictable and out of control.

> Ben arrived at his eleventh session and appeared low. He felt that he was stuck in the area he lived in and that he needed to protect himself across different 'territories' pretending to be someone else in each of the places defined/controlled by local gangs. Ben was invited to explore his changing roles across these real-life territories by arranging small objects. He chose a selection of buttons, representing figures in his life and spread them across the table in relation to one another, with himself in the middle. He categorised them as safe, unsafe and 'snakes in the grass' for people he could not trust, all the while being careful not to name any of his associates or the 'snakes'. The unsafe buttons dominated the table and his sense of being stuck laid out in front of him. The safe people formed a separate smaller space on the table and were seen as belonging to 'different world' from that of criminal activity – it was a place where Ben could have aspirations for himself. He smiled when talking about these safe figures and said he felt a more relaxed and 'lovable' self when there. This shift in presence was noticed by the therapist and Ben was asked to share his future aspirations and give voice to his loveable self.

The therapist felt in a dilemma – would it be helpful to assist the client to change the internal working model that states 'I cannot trust adults and the world is unsafe' when this very model was true to his present life, maintained his hypervigilant state, and therefore, in important ways, kept him safe? Abandoning it might lead to life improvements, but, given the actual situation he was in and considering the risks it presented, it was easy to see why he was reluctant to adopt it. He has needed to protect himself to survive, and even now the same approach helps him to avoid exploitation and to keep safe in his community. Greater insight into his past and its connection with his present situation would help him face both with a different perspective. This was what the dramatherapy sessions were intended to provide, but it was a real challenge to find an opening to that liminal space mentioned above where past traumas and future aspirations could be considered together, with both pointing to a positive outcome.

Over the next few sessions a dialogue between these two worlds was explored through projective play. The role of 'survivor of the snakes' came up against the 'loveable self' which was a reflection on his need to be looked after and to play, the early childhood processes he missed. There were times of confusion when hypervigilance and destruction crept into the safe world and when these projected roles became embroiled in the unsafe world. It wasn't that Ben didn't care about his future; he clearly did. He began to view himself as a survivor of abuse and to connect with the 'loveable' self, or, as the therapist suggested, a child who wants to play, feel safe, and to relate to others. Together Ben and the therapist considered his inner world conflicts and the outer world struggles. An idea of what a good life might consist of gently emerged. Reconsidering his initial view that prison was the only way forward, Ben became more motivated and hopeful about his future. He arrived at his last few sessions with updates on the steps he was proposing to take to further education and sporting activities, at the same time as distancing himself from the 'snakes'. He was not exactly rejecting his situation, but he was certainly reframing it.

These dramatherapeutic processes introduced distance between Ben and real life. Ben played out his physical and emotional worlds but was not consumed by them. He was able to gain different perspectives to identify signs of exploitation and situations that could put him at risk of harm from the view of the loveable self or loving and caring towards self as it later became. There was deeper trauma work that allowed his pain and distress to be voiced to move forward to a new future.

Finding metaphors for real life

Some young people are unable to work within their reality through directive methods. It may be too complex, too painful, or there may not be words for those experiences. Dramatherapists aid those young people to search for meaningful metaphors in these circumstances and respect their readiness to let somebody witness the inner world which they are trying desperately to protect.

> Darren would not talk in his first therapy session. Any questions were responded to with a clear 'no' or 'nah'. In his second session, he was asked to pick an image he was drawn to. He took the pile of images and looked through them. After 30 minutes of organising and mapping out images in silence, whilst the therapist witnessed, he presented a complex representation of his internal sense of self and his external world. At the centre of these images was a spider's web, representing his struggle to navigate childhood on his own after being neglected and moving through the care system. Surrounding this image, feelings in relation to his offending behaviour were represented through a riot, an uplifted tree with exposed roots and a crooked ladder. With regret of his actions he labelled himself as a criminal and thought he would always been seen by others in the same way. His therapist felt the next step could be to give a voice to these aspects of self. His sense of self appeared fragmented.
>
> Darren had a gift for rapping and a sense of musicality. He would often 'beatbox' along to the music on his phone on arrival to his session. The therapist encouraged Darren to work with his talents and in a rap battle with the therapist he improvised 'I build walls, walls so high, walls that keep me safe at night'.

Co-creation and ever shifting mediums can allow meaningful metaphors to be identified. At times there are direct correlations between the client's thoughts, and feelings and his/her behaviour. Metaphors like the wall and the spider's web provide safe holding for such trauma-focused work to take place and can guide individuals to a place of insight and healing. To reconnect with those aspects of self that are hidden, damaged, or voiceless, the inner world is expressed, often unconsciously through the play, metaphors, and move towards their consciousness and ability to make sense and find the words to articulate his experiences.

Darren's process expressed his lack of trust. It is not the therapist's task to chip away at the wall, but rather to assist the young person to explore the wall from its foundations. For Darren his raps transformed from explicit anger, to rapping about loss, pain, and being sorry for committing his crime.

Darren made good progress with the support of the therapy and the sensitive work of the team around the child. He said towards the end of therapy, 'I've always been on the line between making the right choices and going to jail. I now want to make the right choices. I don't want to go to jail.' He had been successful in passing exams and would be starting at college soon.

Our links with education have been strong and we have had the opportunity to work in a number of pupil referral units where young people are engaged in individual programmes.

From working with feeling to accessing the school curriculum

Madu

Madu was a 13-year-old boy with a learning difficulty. His order was based around sexually harmful behaviour. It caused significant distress to the family, uprooting them from their home to a different area of the city. Dad's job had to change. If Madu is going to be out of the house or education for more than 12 hours, they must report to the police station beforehand, but his father does not wish to do this because of the shame he feels. As a consequence, Madu's life experiences over the last two years have become very restricted and he has not had opportunities to be in social situations, which is really important for his development, learning, and life skills.

> After therapy had been going on for about six months, teaching staff would comment on the sounds coming from the room. It transpired that our exploration of sound and voice carried through the school. An English teacher said that she wanted to do some Shakespeare with Madu. She seemed excited but very nervous and didn't know how to go about it. She spoke to me because she knew I am a dramatherapist. She had also heard the creative energy coming out of the room! We talked about Othello, and aspects and themes that Madu might connect with. Also, about delivery, how to engage him creatively with English as a subject to support his academic attainment. She had many of the answers, it was just highlighting them, bringing them to awareness and having a sounding board. A month later, I had finished a session

with Madu and where I leave there is a sitting area. Madu was there, with three teachers around him. I was signing out and the teacher asked Madu if he could recite some of Othello for me. He responded by reciting the first four lines. After we praised him, because it was fantastic, he then continued into the next few verses. Then the teacher tried to join in, and she stumbled upon her words and he took over and continued.

The teacher felt as much sense of achievement as Madu did. Not only had he achieved academically, but the relationship had progressed too using Shakespearean language and theatrical expression.

Collaborative working

For the arts therapies to be effective, certain core requirements need to be in place. In addition to fluidity and dynamism of the creative medium, as our case studies show, space and time boundaries to protect confidentiality are crucial. All these ingredients help the young people feel cared for and psychologically safe to embark on their inner work. They need to feel held attentively in the mind of others. While being conceptually firm, these boundaries can also be very flexible and bespoke – in time and space. To arrive at collectively understood, creative, and efficient solutions to these boundary problems, close collaboration is required and a high level of trust between all concerned.

Collaborative working has been a feature of school-based ETS interventions and in the youth justice service collaborative working became more intense, involving a dynamic network of people, comprising therapists, team leader and assistant team leader, caseworkers, youth justice managers, teachers, and the external supervisors of the two therapists.

Figure 10.1 aims to show our model of working. Through regular reflective practice we identified six principles underpinning our therapeutic work. These will continue to serve as the basis for future development within the youth justice context.

Six principles were identified:

- **Client-centred/young person at the centre/unconditional positive regard** – We approach the client without judgement through acceptance and support regardless of what they say or do.[6] The young person's voice and own agency was central to planning their intervention.
- **Alignment** – The role of the therapist within the youth justice system is challenging. These environments are usually associated with punishment and attendance is considered a requirement. These associations can also be placed upon the therapy sessions and it is the therapist's job to shift this perspective and clarify his or her role. We work alongside the young person, outside the criminal justice system yet with one foot within it, to build the young person's agency to desist. Our relationship with the client is a core consideration within

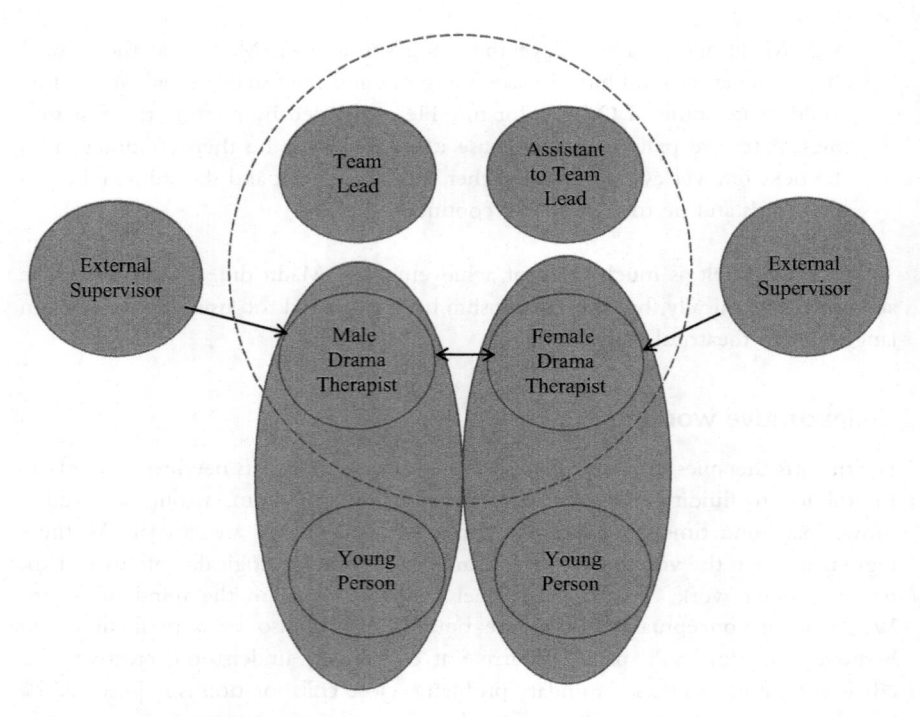

FIGURE 10.1 Supervision and managerial model for the therapy

sessions and within supervisory exploration. The notion of a 'thread' linking the therapist with the client became a powerful metaphor within clinical reflection.
- **Flexibility and boundaries** – Therapists working with young offenders within the community will often question their own boundaries in relation to the clients' need for a dynamic approach that includes place and time. With commitment and consistency being two key difficulties with engagement, we identified citywide therapeutically safe places for each client (and therapist) so the relationship became the container upholding the required boundaries whilst meeting the client's need for flexibility.
- **Systemic approach** – Consideration is given to multiple systems and their interplay with one another. Professionals such as teachers and youth justice caseworkers work towards specific goals such as educational engagement, and having an insight into the child's inner world, their motivations and defence systems can be an important factor in the achievement of such goals. It is challenging for the young person to manage appointments, juggle commitments and requirements of the criminal order. They can often feel 'over-worked' by endless appointments with 'another worker'. Careful consideration with a coordinated team approach is required to ensure support is not duplicated or overwhelming as this can result in disengagement. Information sharing amongst education, health, and social care staff is essential to

improve engagement, identify goals, and provide a better understanding of the young person's situation.
- **Engaging parents** – Opportunities to reduce risks and improve wellbeing are significantly increased when parents can be a part of the process. For each young person, there was a process of seeking consent from a parent or carer. If this was not obtained, the reasons would be explored before deciding if the individual has Fraser competence, permitting them to consent for themselves. It is not always in the child's best interest to involve the parent, but wherever possible it *was* a key part of the referral process.
- **Time considerations** – The young person's order is a possible indicator of the likely length of the intervention and this is discussed with the young person in the first meeting. We found building on their success through short incremental moments of engagements could potentially allow their own intrinsic motivation to emerge. Over the 18-month period we are considering, the length of interventions ranged from, at the lowest end, a single session and, at the highest, weekly sessions over the full 18 months.

Outputs and outcomes

In our work with youth justice over one year, we worked in 13 different venues, including youth justice offices, pupil referral units, and independent alternative education providers. Each therapist worked one day per week for the first year. We worked with 27 young people, 8 female and 19 male, aged from 12 to 18 years and received assessment/therapeutic interventions ranging from one week to 33 weeks (Table 10.1).

The main aim was to help the young people desist from reoffending. Research shows that 68% of children released from custody reoffend within a year (Beyond Youth Custody, 2015). Of the young people we worked with, 25% reoffended but the reasons for arrest were, for example, breaches rather than aggression towards others. Youth justice managers who accessed official records to obtain this statistic noted that these offences were not considered grave and that they felt significant improvements had been gained from the ETS input.

Our work aimed at early intervention, to stop the revolving door process whereby young people offend, are arrested, given orders, enter the youth justice system, complete their order – then offend again and the cycle repeats. We found that trauma

TABLE 10.1 An overview of the interventions provided in one year

Contact type	Level of support	No. of young people
Introduction	1 meeting	5 young people
Assessment	1–2 sessions	9 young people
Short Term	3–6 sessions	7 young people
Medium Term	7–20 sessions	8 young people
Long Term	21+ sessions	3 young people

is a trajectory into the youth justice system and needs to be dealt with, to stop this cycle. Research has already shown that 91% of young offenders have experienced abuse or loss, and that incidence of learning disabilities and mental ill health is significantly higher in the offending population (Wright and Liddle, 2014).

As practitioners working in education, several children were known to us years ago at primary age, when therapeutic interventions were advised by teachers, but resources were not available because of the cost implications. Years later, these same children, after exclusion from primary and secondary schools, had entered the youth justice system. It seems clear that if trauma-focused support had been provided throughout their school career, their entry to the youth justice system could have been prevented. We hope that our work in schools more widely, and in youth justice services, may contribute to trauma-informed practice in youth justice and impact on educational engagement and outcomes for the current generation of children with similar life experiences and needs.

Notes

1 Within the work at Youth Justice we found trauma and attachment issues to be the most predominant. Lovett explores through many clinical examples how to process or 'un-tangle' the trauma-attachment knot which has provided further insight into our work.
2 At the outset of our work the HM Inspectorate of Probation's document on Desistence Theory and its application (or not), across Youth Offending Teams (YOTs) provided a starting point for our work. It is worth noting that in some local authorities, the term YOT has been replaced by the term Youth Justice. In September, the Youth Justice Board produced a briefing paper, *In-brief: Trauma-informed Youth Justice*, recognising the need to make the link between childhood trauma and young people's behaviours and, by extension, the impact of trauma on their capacity to desist.
3 Van der Kolk's work has inspired us for many years. A training he delivered in London in 2005 was critical in the formation of the team's work. Entitled 'The understanding and treatment of post-traumatic stress disorder: The vital role of body, movement and imagination', the training had huge relevance to our practice of the arts therapies with children and young people affected by trauma. His recent book (2014) is a comprehensive overview of how traumatic memory is stored in the body, and how it can be worked with effectively towards recovery
4 Sue Jennings has been a pioneering dramatherapist across the UK and Europe for over 40 years. She developed the Emodiment-Projection-Role (EPR) paradigm in the 1970s and 1980s whilst working with parents and children. This model offers the field of dramatherapy a basis for assessment and intervention when working with traumatised children, young people, and adults from a developmental play perspective.
5 Sophie is not the young person's real name. Likewise, further on in the text, to protect confidentiality Ben, Darren, and Madu are not the young people's real names.
6 The core conditions of Carl Rogers' counselling theory include empathy, congruence, unconditional positive regard.

Acknowledgements

We would like to express our appreciation to all the young people for sharing their stories with us. Thank you for sticking with it. Thanks are due to the Head of Youth

Justice service whose dynamic vision led to the commissioning of this work and to all the managers and caseworkers who embraced the opportunity to work with us in a truly collaborative way. We would also like to thank the therapists' supervisors; Roland Javanaud who kindly provided an external perspective on this article; and Karen Lake.

References

Beyond Youth Custody (2015) *Effective resettlement of young people: lessons from beyond youth custody*. Nacro, University of Salford, and the University of Bedfordshire.

British Association of Dramatherapists Website. *(2018)*. Retrieved from: www.badth.org.uk

Cordess, C. (2002) Building and nurturing a therapeutic alliance with offenders. In M. McMurran (ed.) *Motivating offenders to change: a guide to enhancing engagement in therapy* (Wiley Series in Forensic Clinical Psychology). Chichester: John Wiley and Sons Ltd., pp. 75–86.

Her Majesty's Inspectorate of Prisons (2016) *Desistence and young people: an inspection by HMI Probation*. London: HMIP.

Jennings, S. (2011) *Healthy attachments and neuro-dramatic play*. London: Jessica Kingsley.

Lovett, J. (2015) *Trauma-attachment tangle: modifying EMDR to help children resolve trauma and develop loving relationships*. London: Routledge.

McConnell (2012) The cave and the dome: safe enough spaces for transformative creativity, a study of how a project sustained itself through economic crisis. Unpublished MA dissertation.

Paolo, J.K., Levine, E.G., and Levine, S.K. (2005) *Principles and practice of expressive arts therapy: towards a therapeutic aesthetics*. London: Jessica Kingsley.

Perry, B., and Szalavitz, M. (2006) *The boy who was raised as a dog and other stories from a child psychiatrist's notebook*. USA: Perseus Books.

Van der Kolk, B. (2005) Developmental trauma disorder: towards a rational diagnosis for children with complex trauma histories. *Psychiatric Annals*, 35, 5, 401–408.

Van der Kolk, B. (2014) *The body keeps the score: brain, mind and body in the healing of trauma*. London: Penguin.

Wright, S., and Liddle, M. (2014) *Young offenders and trauma: experience and impact. Beyond youth custody*. Nacro, University of Salford, and the University of Bedfordshire.

Youth Justice Board (2017) In-brief: trauma-informed youth justice. Retrieved from: https://yjresourcehub.uk/our…for…/588_5e9a4cdcfa738eb6db35fbaaac85d872.html

11

THE NATURE-BASED RESIDENTIAL TREATMENT CENTRE AS AN ALTERNATIVE MODEL FOR MEETING THE NEEDS OF CHILDREN AND YOUNG PEOPLE

Steven Klee, Joanna L. Becker and Miyako Kinoshita

This chapter describes a case example of alternative secure accommodation that uses nature-based educare to treat children with complex social, emotional, and learning difficulties and provides a different perspective and way of perceiving the needs of children and young people. Green Chimneys is a residential treatment centre (RTC) in Putnam County, New York, in the United States which provides a unique, multi-faceted, intensive therapeutic programme for children age 6–13. Green Chimneys accommodates over 200 children who have significant psychiatric histories; half of the students are in secure, residential care and half of the students attend a day treatment programme and return home daily. Green Chimneys is a rural facility that is also a farm, founded on the belief that children benefit from interaction in nature and that the needs of children and young people with significant emotional and behavioural difficulties can be addressed by creating and nurturing connections to the natural world.

Green Chimneys opened in 1948 as 'The Green Chimney's School for Little Folk'; a private school providing academics, recreation, and a loving environment for children, with the unique experience of interacting with and caring for animals, being outdoors, and providing nature-based learning experiences. In the early 1970s Green Chimneys became a non-profit treatment centre and school for children who required a specialist setting because of their emotional, behavioural, and learning difficulties. Although the types of children that have been cared for at Green Chimneys over the years has changed, the basic treatment philosophy has remained consistent. The Farm and Wildlife Centre that is part of Green Chimneys houses 300 domesticated animals and wildlife species. The nature-based educational classes combine with the animal-assisted activities and therapy to provide an enriched therapeutic milieu for the children.

Pathways to Green Chimneys

There are many commonalities experienced by the children treated at Green Chimneys on the path towards residence at the facility. All the residents have had previous psychiatric hospitalisations. While the average number is two, some have had seven or eight prior psychiatric admissions. The vast majority of children are on psychotropic medications. The average child enters on three medications and many are taking up to six or seven medications upon admission. Loss and separation are major factors in their lives. Many of these children have been shuffled from one placement to another because of their behaviour. Those who remain with their biological families have experienced many school changes. Many of the children have documented trauma histories, while others have been traumatised by witnessing aggression or through the many separations from their families. All the children at Green Chimneys are emotionally dysregulated. They appear to be at an 'emotional simmering point' throughout most of the day, and it takes only a minor issue to move this to an emotional boil. The children at Green Chimneys also usually enter with significant academic delays. This may be due to a concurrent learning disorder or possibly due to the inconsistent school attendance their behavioural problems have produced.

For a child to enter into residential care at Green Chimneys there needs to be an agreement between the parents/guardians and the child's school district that this level of secure care is needed. It is generally the case the child has been demonstrating problems both at home and at school and previous attempts at management in a less restrictive setting have been unsuccessful. The children enter with a vast array of psychiatric diagnoses ranging from affective disorders to externalising disorders to developmental delays. Most children enter with several Diagnostic and Statistical Manual of Mental Disorders (DSM-5) diagnoses. Despite the wide range of presenting problems, the most common issue that drives the move towards residential care is aggressive behaviour. This is not the kind of aggression others perceive to be associated with delinquency or conduct disorder. To the contrary, the view is that they are fragile children with poor impulse control and limited ability to modulate their emotions, which then leads to aggressive/destructive behaviour that is problematic for their teachers, peers, parents, and siblings.

More and more children are entering the facility with a diagnosis of autism spectrum disorder. For these children, additional attention to sensory needs is required. In addition, many of the children have co-morbid medical issues to go along with their emotional difficulties. The most common medical issues include enuresis, asthma, seizure disorders, injuries due to self-abuse, severe constipation, and obesity (the latter two issues are often side effects of the psychotropic medications).

Trauma-informed practice at the facility

Staff at Green Chimneys use trauma theory in their work with children (the idea that traumatisation has occurred and both internal and external resources are inadequate for the individual to cope with perceived external threat leading to an impact on both a biological and behavioural level in arousal and self-regulation). Trauma can cause serious ruptures in interpersonal relationships and the expression is often strong emotional reactions and aggressive behaviour towards others or oneself in social situations. The therapeutic programme at Green Chimneys is an example of trauma-informed practice and, as such, focuses on teaching emotional regulation and social skills while emphasising warm, accepting relationships between the residents and all the staff members.

Knowing that the separation from home to enter a residential facility for an indeterminate period can be traumatic, staff strive to create an atmosphere where the child can feel safe. Towards this end, a trauma informed care model has been adopted that seeks to provide a place where the children can heal and grow. Trauma informed care means understanding how a child's past experiences informs and guides as to the best type of care and treatment for that child in the present. Whether there is a documented trauma history or just the multiple attachment disruptions, the goal is to minimise the opportunities for re-traumatisation while creating opportunities for the child to succeed using therapeutic physical and outdoor activity. The children are encouraged to be active, to engage in traditional sports, to take part in outside recreation, to participate in year-round gardening and undertake work at the farm, and be involved in the wildlife programme.

Children in residential care have experienced a host of failures before their removal from their community. Because the focus has been on their behavioural and emotional difficulties, they begin to doubt whether they have any positive qualities. It is, therefore, imperative that opportunities for them to succeed are provided. This may take the form of encouraging an academic strength or succeeding socially by mentoring a younger child. Others find success through a job role, an art or music project, a presentation, or a relationship with a staff member. Children who have academic difficulties can instead excel in nature-related activity; for example, a child struggling with literacy can demonstrate their academic capabilities by naming every bird in the wildlife centre and their eating habits.

Regardless of DSM-V diagnoses or disability classification, all students at Green Chimneys possess deficits in the development of social-emotional skills. Chronic behaviour problems related to emotional dysregulation and volatility are the primary reason for children to be referred to Green Chimneys. Poor impulse control, high emotional reactivity, and limited ability to cope with stressors are pervasive problems for students at Green Chimneys. Students show immature and/or maladaptive coping strategies for managing intense emotions. Such coping strategies might include tantrums, self-injury, running away, and aggression toward others (verbal and physical).

Although all students show marked delays in social-emotional functioning, the student population at Green Chimneys is heterogeneous in terms of all other areas of development. Based on IQ scores, the overall cognitive functioning of students ranges from Intellectual Impairment (1st percentile) to Superior Intellectual functioning (98th percentile). Most students also show uneven development of intellectual skills within their own individual profiles. Many students possess significant delays in working memory (the ability to remember and manipulate information in one's mind) and processing speed (the ability to efficiently perform simple tasks). Underlying cognitive weaknesses are viewed as having a wide impact on children's functioning in areas that range from academic progress, to remembering the steps of daily living tasks, to completing tasks within a reasonable amount of time.

The variability in IQ scores is representative of the variability seen in other areas of functioning, such as speech and language ability, motor skills, and self-care skills (adaptive skills). Outside of psychological disorders, language and communication disorders are very common in the student body. Students with language and communication disorders may struggle to communicate thoughts and ideas, to make requests, and to understand instructions from others; all of which can trigger children to experience episodes of extreme frustration and volatility. Communication disorders can also include poor development of nonverbal language ability, which manifests as students who are unable to accurately read body language or understand/use gestures to communicate at an age-expected level. Delays in motor development are also common, with many students qualifying for occupational therapy to address delays in fine and gross motors skills and/or sensory integration.

Individualised treatment programmes

Due to the complex and variable profiles of Green Chimneys students, an emphasis is placed on individualised treatment programmes. Since psychological and behavioural disorders are the principal reason for referral, all students receive individual counselling services provided by a social worker, mental health counsellor, or school psychologist. Counselling services include scheduled individual therapy sessions at least once per week as well as crisis intervention services. Treatment approaches vary based on a student's symptoms and an effort is made to use evidenced-based treatments, especially cognitive-behavioural models. Since emotional reactivity and behaviour problems frequently interfere with the development of social relationships, students also participate formal and informal group counselling. Some students participate in limited-time groups that help with management of specific issues, such as dealing with the death of a family member, divorce, or adoption.

With a few exceptions, the tuition of students attending either the Therapeutic Day Programme (TDP) or the Residential Treatment Centre (RTC) is funded by each student's local school district with additional county and state funds contributing to the daily rate. As per United States Federal law, students with disabilities are entitled to a free education in a setting that both allows them to access the curriculum and that can accommodate and remediate their areas of need (IDEA, 2004). To this end, every student who attends Green Chimneys has an Individualised Education Programme (IEP), which is a legal document outlining the child's classification of disability, personal strengths, and educational needs. The need for an IEP is established when a team of educators, psychological professionals, and parents agree that a child possesses a difficulty or disability that significantly interferes with functioning in academic, social, or adaptive domains.

The IEP works as a central document that serves both as a place for recording a student's history of performance and needs, and a place to document student progress throughout the school year. At least once per year, the IEP is reviewed by a team comprised of a child's parents, teacher, therapist, home school district, and any additional service providers involved in meeting a student's needs. It is at that time that the team evaluates the child's current strengths and weaknesses and yearly goals are established. Outside of the annual meeting, the IEP can be amended at any point with agreement on the part of the treatment team. At least every three years, every student undergoes standardised psychological, cognitive, and academic testing for evaluating the child's abilities in comparison to the normative population and to evaluate individual growth. Students with deficits in language and/or motor skill development also receive comprehensive standardised evaluations in their area(s) of need.

With respect to the provision of treatment, the most useful components of the IEP are the inclusion of information about the child's present levels of functioning across developmental domains and the yearly goals for each area of need. The IEP goals are divided into sections based on developmental domains. Although the goals must be agreed upon by the entire treatment team, they are written by a specialist in each domain. For example, a special education teacher sets the academic goals, while the therapist selects the social-emotional goals. A key component of IEP goals is that they represent behaviours that are both observable and measurable. The requirement that goals be observable is necessary to allow for objective evaluation of the child's progress. Accordingly, the provision that goals must be measurable allows service providers to collect and review data of student progress. Progress monitoring data has become a central means for reviewing the effectiveness of treatments across school settings. Service providers are expected to use progress data to make decisions about whether to continue with an intervention plan or adjust, such as changing approaches or altering the frequency or duration of treatment.

Another service common to all students is placement in a special education classroom. Each classroom is staffed by one special education teacher and two teaching assistants. Most students are behind grade-level in respect to academic skills. Academic delays are attributable to a combination of factors such as co-morbid learning disorders, attention-deficit hyperactivity disorder, cognitive impairments, and disruptions in formal school due to hospitalisations or suspensions. While teaching the standard curriculum, teachers also provide academic accommodations and tailor lessons to individual needs, as required by each student's IEP. Given that students are placed at Green Chimneys by their school districts, it follows that there is often an emphasis on academic growth, particularly on the part of parents and the home school district. Every treatment team faces the challenge of discovering the balance between a push for academic growth and the need to maintain a child's emotional stability.

Transition to adulthood

In 2015, the residential programme was expanded to include an additional unit designed for adolescents preparing to transition into adulthood. The need for such a unit is based on the realisation that the transition from a highly structured, residential treatment centre to adult life in the community is often a jolting experience for young adults. The unit's programming places an emphasis on promoting independent living skills that will be important for success across domestic, social, and occupational settings. Students learn to do grocery shopping, to review bills, and to use public transportation. They also receive job coaching, including the 'soft skills' needed for interviewing and maintaining appropriate work relationships. Regardless of a student's diagnoses, there is a realisation that some degree of impairment will be present across the lifespan. As such, students are encouraged to practise and get comfortable with advocating for their special needs.

Family involvement

For all students in the residential programme, discharge to the family home or another less restrictive setting is a primary goal. Parents are viewed as essential to the child's treatment and success after discharge. As such, family therapy and frequent interactions between parents and children are encouraged. Participation in family therapy is strongly encouraged, however it is not mandatory. Parent involvement in therapy varies greatly, with some parents participating in weekly therapy and others opting not to participate at all. Monthly parent training seminars are also offered to help parents develop parenting skills for managing challenging behaviours at home and in the community. Students with severe emotional disorders can be very difficult to parent effectively. It is common for families to experience years of discord and volatile interactions between family members, so intensive therapy to establish new patterns of interaction is an important part of treatment. There is a clear understanding that successful residential care must include a transfer of the gains made in the residence to the child's home and community. To develop new ways of relating to one another, families must spend time together. After a two-week acclimation period, students in the residential programme begin going home every other weekend and for holidays. As students show gains in their ability to manage their behaviour, the frequency of visits increases. Parents are also able to visit their children on site or take them off grounds.

Discharge from the residential treatment centre

There is no single criterion that indicates a student's readiness to be discharged from the RTC. Instead, the decision to discharge students from the RTC is based on a range of factors. Each student's readiness is evaluated individually and on an on-going basis. Following treatment in the RTC, most students can transition to a less intensive programme, often a therapeutic day school. A key piece of any recommendation to a day programme is whether the student can consistently maintain emotional and behavioural control in the community and family settings. Other factors are considered, such as the accessibility of social services in the community, the family's access to social supports, parental involvement in treatment. A child's age, cognitive functioning, and diagnosis are all considered when exploring discharge eligibility. There is a subset of children who suffer from psychiatric or behavioural disorders not well-treated in the RTC. For those children, therapists seek out placements in more intensive programmes, such as long-term psychiatric hospitalisation. Regardless of the discharge plan, all children and families participate in discharge preparation sessions with therapists who help them locate and contact service providers, such as psychiatrists, therapists, and any available social services.

Features of the farm at the residential treatment centre

One major advantage of our treatment milieu is the accessibility of the animals and outdoor spaces throughout the campus grounds. The decision to integrate nature-based programmes across the campus is based on a belief that animal-assisted treatments may be more easily disseminated to children than traditional therapeutic interventions. Although a review of research on the effectiveness of animal-assisted interventions is beyond the scope of this chapter, there is a growing body of research indicating that interactions with animals are associated with reductions in stress, increased language use, and increased social engagement (Hergovich, 2002; Friesen, 2009; Beetz, 2011). Anecdotally, staff at the facility report that children are naturally drawn to animals and that they often describe the animals as calming and as understanding friends. The concept that interactions with nature are therapeutic, restorative, and serve as a 'jumping off' point to future healthy relationships is at the core of the Green Chimneys philosophy. The commitment to nature-based programming is further highlighted by the fact that, unlike other educational and therapeutic services that are supported by tuition rates, the farm programme is an unfunded programme that continually needs outside donations and grants to remain viable.

The success of the programme over the last 70 years is, at least in part, due to the positive human animal interactions that in turn have a positive impact on the child's overall treatment goals. The purpose of the farm is to offer campus-wide support, including to the school, clinical departments, residences, and staff. The farm is a central part of the therapeutic milieu and the nature programmes taking place are more than petting an animal. Rather, interactions are purposefully created to address student's social-emotional, educational, and vocational goals. The farm department not only provides educational and therapeutic activities to children, it also is a resource that all staff at Green Chimneys are able to utilise in their interaction with children.

The farm consists of five different areas and specially trained staff in each area to ensure successful programming and assurance for safety. Each area has different and unique differences in animal care, management, and the outside agency that oversees programme. The farm director and two managers oversee the whole department which consists of 18 staff and 12 interns who are placed in each area. The teaching barn maintains over 150 domesticated animals traditionally associated with farms and small pet species. The staff in the teaching barn consists of an animal care taker who has a background and education in livestock management, a New York State licensed teacher as a farm teacher, and an evening programme facilitator. The programme follows strict regulations from United States Department of Agriculture (USDA) as a licensed exhibitor and is informed by 4H youth programmes and Farm Based Education Association's activity guidelines. The facility is also a Premier Accredited Centre of the Professional Association of Therapeutic Horsemanship International (PATH) and Green Chimneys operates a diverse equine education and interaction programme in a modern, large, 22-horse stall barn and various adjacent pastures and paddocks. There are riding instructors and a stable manager, all of whom hold nationally recognised certifications in therapeutic riding instruction. The vision of the programme is that children are exposed to horsemanship, vocational education, and academics through their interaction with horses. Riding, driving, stable management, and therapeutic activities with horses serve to support students' primary educational and therapeutic goals.

The Paul C. Kupchok Wildlife Rehabilitation Centre at the facility features over 50 permanently disabled or imprinted raptors and other wildlife. The wildlife centre is licensed by the U.S. Fish and Wildlife Service and the New York State Department of Environmental Conservation to maintain and rehabilitate birds of prey. The centre treats, rehabilitates, and releases injured, orphaned, or distressed raptors, and occasionally some songbirds and small mammals. The wildlife education centre also is home to several exotic reptiles, amphibians, and insects. It is important to understand that the animal species in this specialty area are generally not appropriate for traditional human animal environments and it is only due to special permits and licenses and highly trained and certified animal specialists that the centre is able to structure meaningful interactions in ways that are safe and ethical for both children and animals. The programme at the centre is to educate children about the impact of humans on the natural environment, resources, and the responsibility humans have of caring for others. It sets a clear boundary between wildlife and domesticated/companion animals (for example, wild animals are never given names in the centre). Though children love the birds and animals in this area, they interact with them respectfully and offer minimum contact.

In 2014, a shelter dog interaction programme was established on site. The shelter dog programme brings carefully screened shelter dogs to Green Chimneys to be cared for and socialised by the students. The selection and training of these dogs is under the auspicious of All About Dogs, Inc., which is the animal shelter programme partner. Consisting of various sizes, ages, and breed types, the dogs are specially chosen for apparent health and soundness of temperament and are in residence at Green Chimneys for six weeks. The children learn to socialise and train the dogs on basic obedience using scientifically sound, positive training methods. An inter-departmental trained staff team cares for the dogs during their stay with children, and currently there are over 100 staff members on campus who have completed training to work with children in this way. The dogs are fully integrated and incorporated into the school, residential units, recreation, and therapeutic services. The benefit of working with screened shelter dogs is that any child can make a difference in each dog's life and have a meaningful role. Children also learn information that are helpful in managing their own pets at home, which is vital as many students have dogs at home and are likely to be dog owners in the future.

The provision of horticulture also offers a unique opportunity that complements the animal programmes. Working with plants, soil, and insects provides a dynamic sensory experience; and plants offer delayed gratification and patience, while animals often offer immediate response and reaction. There are two gardens: one focused on education of children, and one focused on vocation and production. The staff includes a New York State certified teacher, a horticulture therapist, and an organic gardener. The focus is on the process of growing, and staff incorporate many academic topics and vocational skill trainings into their time in the garden. Often children learn to appreciate fresh produce and learn healthy eating habits.

Children access the farm in many ways. The organised and scheduled programmes include group farm, wildlife, equine, gardening, and dog educational classes, and 1:1 learning opportunities called 'Learn and Earn' which offer over 170 students a week the opportunity to care for animals and plants, as well as after school and evening programmes, animal-assisted therapy with social workers, psychologists, occupational therapists, and speech language pathologists. Staff members from childcare, clinical, and education departments also access the farm as needed. There are places they can go without specialists, and training is available upon request to anyone who is interested in working with certain animals or part of the farm.

Animal-assisted therapies

A unique aspect of the provision at Green Chimneys is the degree to which therapists collaborate with professionals across farm and nature-based departments to better engage students in treatment. Prior to their admission, students tend not to have responded to traditional interventions. Alternative approaches are, therefore, warranted as many students display behaviours that are resistant to change and difficult to treat. Through collaboration with experts in animal and nature-based activities, clinicians can design sessions that are highly engaging and still address treatment goals. For example, a therapist might focus on tolerance for frustration by asking a student to work through increasingly challenging handling skills with a miniature horse, while offering in vivo coaching for the use of socially appropriate coping skills. Therapy sessions at the farm or garden offer many benefits not readily available in a therapist's office or counselling room. Animals help calm a child in crisis and to reinforce a child's behaviour through additional contact with the animals. Students can participate in multisensory experiences, seek support from the animals, and practise new skills without fear of judgement from peers. As with all interventions, therapists help students adopt strategies for generalising new skills from session to everyday life.

Impact of nature-based programmes on school staff

In addition to promoting student growth, the nature-based programmes are viewed as a support for staff as well. Anyone working with children and families with special needs, especially those in frequent states of crisis, is susceptible to experiencing high levels of stress. Staff members in all departments are encouraged to be aware of their own stress management needs, and to take steps to maintain appropriate self-care. To this end, many staff members seek out animal interactions, often through the shelter dog programme, to help themselves stay grounded. It is also common to see employees taking walks through the farm or on the trail to clear their minds. The accessibility of the farm programme is an asset for staff, allowing employees of Green Chimneys to get the benefit of much needed restorative breaks.

Implementation of human-animal interactions

For residential treatment centre to incorporate animals, there are many considerations to ensure positive, safe, and meaningful interactions between students, staff, and animals.

Animal background, training, conditioning, and handling

It is a priority that animals at the facility enjoy interacting with children and are not stressed by the contact that they may have with children. Many of our children's activities are created to care for animals and meet the needs of the animals in residence. However, this environment can be stressful to animals that are timid, scared, and not properly trained to be around children. Monitoring the amount of contact an animal has with people, scheduling a rotation so that animals get to have time in a quiet environment without contact, and providing environmental enrichment programmes for animals are examples of our conditioning programme. We spend much time educating staff in and out of the farm department to ensure there is consistent handling, and cooperation with protocols to ensure the safety and well-being of all involved.

Understanding the children's behaviour and needs

Many of our children gravitate towards the animals and nature but have limited experience with animals or growing plants. Fear, curiosity, and intimidation are very common feelings for the children, and these are expressed behaviourally in several different ways. Our children often have sensory integration issues and therefore are very sensitive to smell, noise, and visual stimulations. The staff are trained to understand the children's needs in groups and individual sessions to select the most appropriate animals for that child and need of the individual and/or groups can be different. The flexibility and the understanding of animals' behaviour and temperament are critical to facilitate a productive activity, as is training in both animal behaviour and children's behaviour. Behaviour management is required for all staff members who facilitate either individual or group activities for children and animals. Often, a class that has a lot of energy ends up working with larger animals or do some work outside. Larger animals can tolerate movements and active students better than small animals do. Assessment and monitoring happens with every animal interaction to ensure safety for people and animals and to meet the student's needs.

Making the learning fun and meaningful

Incorporating animals into social situations and teaching makes activities fun and meaningful. Traditional learning environments are often stressful, and many of the children at Green Chimneys had negative experiences in school settings. Children are naturally curious, and most are positively drawn to the animals. This makes the environment a more relaxed one and offers multiple opportunities for learning and therapy that can be explored very organically. The Nature Based Programmes can enhance multiple therapy goals and academic subjects simultaneously. Experiential aspect of the environment allows students to learn using their stronger senses. At the same time, the environment satisfies some of the children's sensory and emotional needs, enabling them to participate in, follow, and understand the lesson. We have also found that the children tend to be much calmer and under better behavioural control when interacting with the animals. Given this, they may be more receptive to both academic and social learning. Camels offer many adaptations that are visible to the children. Children have shown a particular interest in camels and understand how they must behave near them to keep everyone safe. If they are calm and safe, they can look at the camel's eyes closely to see two sets of lashes they developed. They can touch the hump to feel the fat, they can observe and touch their feet that are developed to deal with snow and sand. They also have callus on their stomach and hocks to allow them to sit for a long time. Children regulate their behaviour as they want to participate. When they are in a calm state, they can learn in an experiential way while being able to work with peers and monitor their own behaviour.

Relationship model and the well-being of the animals and environment

The philosophy of Green Chimneys is that interactions between children and nature are the basis of positive relationships, interconnection, and compassion. Children want to be gentle because they care about the animals. Children desire to learn about animals because they like to take care of them. Learning that animals are sentient beings with feelings and recognising signs of animal cognitions, intelligence, and emotions allows students to be empathetic. Interactions are designed to help animals or work alongside them rather than 'using' animals for our gain. For example, when a child rides a horse, the skills are taught in a way that children understand the clear communication and correct aides to work with the horse instead of making a horse 'go'. The child will spend time observing horses in the herd, and spend time grooming and caring for it to develop a bond with it. Similarly, there is a deep respect of the natural environment and plants, giving careful considerations so that we learn from them without harm or destruction.

A restorative approach is also taken. An example of the restorative approach in this context is how social workers and a group of adopted children from Russia together cared for orphan lambs. The children participated in raising the lambs while social workers connected the experience to the attachment issues that they were experiencing. Another example relates to two miniature horses: a mother and son. A social worker observed that the younger horse often pushed his mother around. She worked with a teenage boy who had a difficult relationship with his mother and conducted family sessions with his mother with the miniature horses. The student recognised certain behaviours of the young horse and identified with him and sometimes behaved similarly. The student participated in training the young horse with the therapist learning his own self-awareness and regulation.

Children who are inappropriate with animals

Although many children at Green Chimneys are at high risk for showing inappropriate behaviours toward animals due to severe emotional disorders and exposure to domestic violence, the frequency of such incidents is low. Any child who is admitted with a history of harming animals, or who demonstrates any aggression or inappropriate behaviour toward animals while admitted to the RTC, is evaluated by an interdepartmental committee consisting of clinical and farm staff. Since animal welfare is valued greatly, the committee evaluates even minor behaviours, including gestures or verbalisation of a wish to hurt an animal. The assessment includes an evaluation of the child's risk for future harm, protective factors, and history of trauma. Recommendations are then provided to the child's treatment team. The philosophy at Green Chimneys is not to keep a child away from the animals but rather to find ways to continue to allow interaction in a safe manner.

Green Chimneys was founded on the philosophy that children benefit from their interaction with nature. While there have been enormous changes to the facility, to the staff and to the programme, 70 years later this philosophy has not changed and there are many examples from over the years of how this approach has changed lives for the better. The animals and gardens are an integral part of the therapeutic milieu but our learning how to better integrate the nature-based programmes with our therapeutic and educational programmes continues. Staff in the facility are more aware of national and international research in human-animal interaction and are now conducting their own studies to contribute to the evidence-base. In a world in which communication and learning is indoors and electronic, there is a renewed commitment to offering our children the opportunity to learn outside the classroom or therapy office. The nature-based programmes offer the children an opportunity to grow socially and emotionally. They offer an opportunity for a child to feel accepted and competent. Such positive, successful experiences go a long way towards countering the trauma and failures these children experienced prior to their residential placement.

References

Beetz, A., Kotrschal, K., Turner, D.C., Hediger, K., Uvnäs-Moberg, K., and Julius, H. (2011) The effect of a real dog, toy dog and friendly person on insecurely attached children during a stressful task: an exploratory study. *Anthrozoos*, 24, 4, 349–368.

Education of Individuals with Disabilities Education Act 2004. 20 U.S.C. § 1400. Retrieved from: https://www.gpo.gov/fdsys/granule/USCODE-2011-title20/USCODE-2011-title20-chap33-subchapI-sec1400

Friesen, L. (2009) Exploring animal-assisted programmes with children in school and therapeutic contexts. *Early Childhood Education Journal*, 37, 4, 261–267.

Hergovich, A., Monshi, B., Semmler, G. and Zieglmayer, V. (2002) The effects of the presence of a dog in the classroom. *Anthrozoos*, 15, 1, 37–50.

PART IV
Inclusion and voice

12

YOUTH VOICE AND PARTICIPATION IN SECURE SETTINGS FOR YOUNG PEOPLE

Caroline Lanskey

This chapter discusses the role of youth voice and participation in secure settings. It describes the development of student and pupil voice initiatives in mainstream education and the debates surrounding their aims and values. It gives examples of existing participatory activities for young people in secure institutions and reflects on why they have received comparatively less attention than in other educational settings. It considers what further spaces there are for young people's voices to be heard within the acoustic of secure environments identifying the conditions and values that underpin voice activities and their wider implications for interactions between staff and young people. It outlines possibilities for further participatory activities in secure settings that schools have successfully applied but cautions against idealism. Reflecting on the successes of the Consulting Pupils about Teaching and Learning Network, it identifies the possibility of establishing a youth voice and participation network across secure settings for the sharing and dissemination of experiences and ideas.

Supported by children's rights' frameworks (e.g. United Nations Convention on the Rights of the Child, 1989), student voice has become integral to educational practice in England and Wales (Mitra et al., 2014). Although long associated with progressive education ideals since the beginning of the 20th century, student voice initiatives gained new energy and direction in the 1990s. Through research and educational partnerships arising out of the Consulting Pupils about Teaching and Learning Network – part of the ESRC funded Teaching and Learning Research Programme – a 'new order of experience' (Rudduck and Flutter, 2000) was established as students started to participate in strategic decisions on the educational and the communal life of the schools. The practices gained political support. A policy consultation paper: 'Working Together: Giving Children and Young People a Say' was published (Department for Education and Skills, 2004) and measures of student participation were incorporated into the Office for Standards in Education

(Ofsted) framework for school inspections (Ofsted, 2000). There was a strong international interest in youth voice too, for example, in the US (e.g. Mitra 2008; Cook-Sather, 2002), in Australia (e.g. Holdsworth, 2000), in Chile (e.g. Prieto, 2001), and in Nicaragua (e.g. Shier, 2010).

With the rise of participatory activities in the arena of education, there was quickly a need to distinguish between different types of initiative taking place under the title of 'student voice' or similar. Educators looked to a parallel field of research on children's participation in citizenship activities. Roger Hart's ladder of child participation (1992: 2), itself modelled on an earlier model of adult participation developed by Arnstein (1979), identified a hierarchy of child participatory activities ranging from: 'manipulation' (by adults) to 'child initiated, shared decisions with adults'. Shier (2001) subsequently identified pathways that led from minimal participation (children being listened to) to children sharing with adults power and responsibility for decision-making.

Drawing from this earlier work, Rudduck devised a ladder of participation for educational settings (2001: 3). It identified activities ranging from: listening to students (students as a data source) to students playing a joint role in decision making with teachers. Fielding developed a similar typology of student participation set within an explicitly democratic framework which, at its highest level, extended beyond collaborative decision-making to a shared commitment to and responsibility for 'the common good' (Fielding, 2011a: 11). The aim of all these models was to provide an analytical lens through which practitioners could evaluate their existing practices and identify new possibilities for youth voice activities. Criticisms about the relative merits of participatory activities implied by the 'ladder' concept were met with an analogy to a painter, who used different rungs on the ladder for different tasks (Shier, 2010).

Fielding (2011a) proposed that the popularity and take up of student voice initiatives into mainstream educational practice could be understood in terms of the wide variety of purposes to which 'the personal' and 'functional' dimensions of student voice were put. He drew attention to two common but contrasting approaches to schooling: a neo-liberal market-led orientation and a person-centred democratic one. In the neo-liberal model, students are viewed as individual consumers or customers who need to make informed choices about their learning, often with a view to their future employment, and schools are ranked competitively against each other in performance league tables. Student voice in this model is relevant because 'in listening to students the school becomes a more accountable and more effective learning organisation' (2011a: 9) which strengthens the performance of the school. In contrast, a person-centred democratic perspective of schooling concerns 'fundamental questions to do with how we become good persons' and promote 'human flourishing' (Fielding, 2011b). Drawing on the writings of the philosopher John Macmurray, he argued that from this perspective a school's main task is one of 'developing an inclusive, creative society through a participatory democracy'. In this model, student voice is important:

not so much through representative structures (though it will have these and operate them well), but rather through a whole range of daily opportunities in which young people can listen and be listened to, make decisions and take a shared responsibility for both the here-and-now of daily encounter and for the creation of a better future.

(Fielding, 2011b)

Underpinning the debates on these models was a view that student voice was gaining 'mile-wide' promotion with only 'inch-thick' understanding (Rudduck, 2006: 133). Educational communities were urged to consider why they wanted to develop student voice activities and what the associated risks and benefits were (Rudduck, 2006).

Youth voice and participation in secure setting

There has been some uptake of participatory initiatives for young people in secure establishments; young offender institutions (YOIs), secure training centres (STCs), and secure children's homes (SCHs). In today's settings, consultation activities have been arranged by education departments, in others, by the organisation's management.[1] In one YOI the education department ran annual consultations with young people about the provision of education and provided feedback on the action that was taken as a result (see Lanskey, 2015). Trainee councils have operated in some STCs, providing feedback on their experiences of custody, and in STCs and SCHs young people have been involved the recruitment of new staff. In other settings, however, there are few internally structured opportunities for young people to express their views. Lanskey (2010) reported that, in some young offenders institutions, the only structured channel for communication with the management was for complaints. Otherwise, young people's voices are heard through external channels, through the work of research and consultancy organisations (see for example User Voice, 2011; Little, 2015) and through inspection reports (see for example Kennedy, 2013; Elwood, 2013). The majority of these activities can be placed at the lower rungs of the participatory ladder with young people acting as a data source. Why, in comparison to schools and colleges, has there been relatively little systematic take up of participatory activities for young people in secure settings?

Understanding the silences

Like many developments in mainstream educational practice, the transfer of student voice initiatives to secure settings has not been immediate (see Taylor, 2016) and it is possible to identify system specific factors that have played a role; there is an absence of policy incentives to consult with young people as well as potential barriers related to the ideology and organisation of custody which serve to subdue young people's voices. It is also relevant to consider the potentially negative legacies of young people's past educational experiences, including with earlier student voice activities as well as their social and linguistic confidence.

Historically, education in secure institutions for young people has been provided by organisations outside of the mainstream secondary education sector (Lanskey, see Chapter 2, this volume). They have commonly been placed under the jurisdiction of government justice departments rather than education departments. Although some administrative and legislative bridges have been built between the sectors, such as the Apprenticeships, Skills, Children and Learning Act in 2009, secure institutions have had a history of working slightly apart educationally and of developing their own working practices.

There are international quality benchmarks such as the *European rules for juvenile offenders subject to sanctions or measures* (Council of Europe, 2009) which emphasise the importance of children's voices being heard in decisions made about them in custody and which identify the need to provide support on how to make complaints for children who may not have the skills or knowledge to do so through formal channels. Such rules reinforce Article 12 of the United Nations Conventions of the Rights of the Child which outlines the right of all children to have a voice in decisions made about them. However, such rules set out minimum standards rather than potential remits and are not therefore on their own sufficient to encourage action beyond the specified baseline. The absence of legislative incentives and systematic networking opportunities between secure organisations and school communities may have limited the spread of new educational ideas and practices so that the participatory initiatives that exist in the secure estate are the result of the vision of individuals working within particular establishments.

From an organisational perspective, there are challenges in settings where young people are only resident for a short period in contrast to school communities where staff–student relationships and communications can develop and build over a period of years. Short-term residencies in secure settings may mean that young people do not see action taken on the basis of consultation or research activities before they leave. The opportunity for building capacity for regular participatory activities within the organisation is also reduced. There are challenges too when custodial settings have limited resources to operate more than the basic requirements of a secure regime.

Youth voice initiatives have implications for power relationships which may not appear to sit well with discipline and control agendas in secure establishments. As Wegerif notes: 'To enter into dialogue is to surrender some autonomy and allow the possibility of learning something which is the possibility that you will change' (Wegerif, 2016). Researchers in schools have identified defensiveness from teachers about the power shifts implicit in listening and responding to student suggestions for classroom practice (McIntyre and Pedder, 2001). Bragg (2001) notes the discomfort of 'the voices we don't want to hear' and that seem 'incomprehensible, recalcitrant or even obnoxious (2001: 70). The mutual preparedness to listen, to acknowledge others' views, to modify one's position if necessary, and to collectively agree action may be seen as both a challenge and a strength of youth voice activities.

There are also potential ideological tensions between student voice interests and policy approaches towards young people in custody. The principle of 'lesser eligibility' (where those who have committed a crime should not enjoy better opportunities than those who have not) is no longer an explicit policy with regards to young offenders as it has been in the past (see Carlebach,

1970); however, the Prison Service Instruction (PSI 38/2010) which requires governors of public sector YOIs to consider how the media would react to educational activities they run is arguably its most recent reconfiguration. Prison managers' assumptions of populist punitive (Bottoms, 1995) views on punishment and reform may confine conceptual horizons for young offenders' educational experiences in custody, with limits being placed on what is considered 'appropriate' activity for young people who have broken the law (Lanskey, 2011).

It is also relevant to consider the influence of young people's earlier experiences of consultative or participatory initiatives in schools. As many young people in secure settings have had negative experiences of schooling they may well have been the ones whose voices were not heard. Such experiences of marginalisation maybe class-related, racialised, and/or gendered. The implicit hierarchy of valuing students within school communities has been evocatively captured by one African American student in a study by Silva:

> We got squeaky wheels and flat tires ... Some smooth white walls rollin' their way right to college, gettin' oil all the way. And then the rest of us ... flat tires! Bumpin' on down the road, making all sorts of crude noises. Probably fall off real soon anyway. Ain't worth the grease'
>
> *(Silva 2001: 95)*

MacBeath et al. (2003: 42) noted that the students who were more likely to be involved in participatory activities were the more articulate ones which left others 'ironically, feeling disenfranchised in an initiative specifically designed to empower them'. Participatory activities may in this way reinforce rather than undo divisions between students in schools.

A further point is that criminological research has not engaged with young people's voices in the same way as educational research has done. It has focussed on the voice of the young person in the legal decision-making process (Ronner, 2002) and less on the role of voice in the secure settings. An exception is the work of Bryan and colleagues who have drawn important attention to the high levels speech, language, and communication difficulties among young offender populations in custody (Bryan, 2004; Bryan et al., 2007). Their findings are relevant for understanding some of the dispositional and skills-based barriers to participatory activities by young people in secure institutions. Rudduck and Fielding (2006: 227) acknowledge that youth voice activities require 'a degree of social confidence and of linguistic competence that not all students have' and argue the need to ensure fair distribution of resources to provide the conditions for equal participation.

Sounding out possibilities

Given the arguments outlined above, it does not seem so surprising that few opportunities for the voices of young people within the acoustic of the institution have developed. Nevertheless, the following section considers why youth voice initiatives have a potentially strong role to play in secure environments.

Rudduck and Flutter's (2000) discussion of the role of student voice in school improvement identified a basic principle for consultation; young people have expert knowledge of their feelings and attitudes towards learning and of the type of teaching and educational environment they find helpful. They can offer important insights into their individual learning preferences, their classroom experiences, and more general educational issues e.g. evaluation and assessment processes. Consultations on these matters have multiple potential benefits. The process can give students a stronger sense of their identity as learners which can help them to better manage their own learning (Lanskey and Rudduck, 2010).

The knowledge generated through the process is equally informative to teachers who can use it to shape and develop their own practice: 'the achievement of voice is mutual, and teachers who help students to find student voices will discover that their own voices are clearer and stronger in the process' (Lincoln, 1995: 93). Education departments can benefit from these insights too in evaluation and planning activities. From this perspective, consulting young people can be seen not as a peripheral activity but as integral part of improving the processes of teaching and learning in secure settings.

As mentioned earlier, the remit of student voice activities can extend beyond the educational sphere to inform institutional practice also. Young people in secure settings will have unique perspectives on the staffing and the daily regime. Matheson's consultation of young people's views of what makes a good officer in a young offender institution, for example, established a set of principles that young people considered to be important which could inform future staff training and recruitment policies (Matheson, 2016).

On a more general level, such participatory activities can generate an arena for the practice of democratic citizenship. Through participatory activity young people may develop a sense of confidence in their ability to engage with those in authority and to influence leadership decisions. For example, Fielding (2001a) describes an initiative at Sharnbrook Upper School in Bedfordshire where students conducted research projects on the experiences of trainee teachers, on the school's assessment and profiling system, on aspects of careers education, on the quality of school meals, on the life skills programme, and on the impact of student voice activities themselves. Over a two-month period they collected and analysed data and presented a report to various forums – students, teachers, parents – with recommendations for future action. These recommendations were then discussed and follow up action was collectively agreed. Such experiences of collaborative information gathering, deliberation, and decision-making position young people as 'citizens of the now' as 'subjects of their present lives' (Invernizzi et al., 2008: 6) as well as providing a model for their citizenship of the future. They can give students a sense of their own political agency and sense of self-worth as they see their own actions having an impact on issues that matter to them.

Genuine consultation and collaborative decision-making may lead young people to feel more positive about teachers and managers who facilitate such activities.

Perceptions of the legitimacy of authority flow from such meaningful dialogue. Consultation need not therefore jeopardise authority structures within educational environments, rather it might strengthen relationships between young people and educators and others holding authority in the secure environment. As Rudduck and Flutter have found, young people 'who feel they are respected as individuals and as an institutional and social group are likely to feel a greater sense of respect ... (and) are less likely to disengage' (Rudduck and Flutter, 2004: 107).

Re-shaping and expanding the acoustic of the secure setting

The transformative potential of such participatory activities is contingent, however, on several factors from the substance and process of conducting youth voice activities to the broader organisational context in which the activities take place. Rudduck (2006) identifies three conditions for the development of participatory activities: *climate, reciprocity,* and *valuing social or civic skills*.

Climate

Rudduck (2006) argues that the principles of trust and openness characterise climates where student voice thrives. Whether within the classroom or the setting, young people need to feel confident that they can offer their views freely and without recrimination. Dialogue that is mutually respectful takes time to build. To create the conditions for trusting and open dialogue, other forms of interaction between staff and young people within the institution will need to be in harmony with the values of student participation. There are implications therefore for institution-wide policies such as those relating to discipline, diversity, or safeguarding.

Reciprocity

According to Rudduck (2006), the development of youth participatory activities can be constrained by traditional conceptions of childhood as synonymous with immaturity. In addition to these limiting perspectives, as mentioned earlier, some negative perceptions of young offenders and punitive views of the purposes of custody may create additional barriers in secure settings. Participatory activities require teachers and other staff within the setting 'to see young people differently, to recognise different capabilities and to believe that they can offer insightful comments that can make a difference'. And there is an equivalent condition for young people: 'But it is also about young people seeing educators differently, with both parties believing that they can have open and constructive dialogue about their work' (2006: 141).

The valuing of social or civic skills

In settings where student voice is valued, education is understood as more than the acquisition of academic and or vocational skills. It also encourages the development of qualities associated with democratic participation such as understanding the viewpoints of others, a willingness and capacity to negotiate, and a preparedness to offer and to accept help. These qualities are valued in interactions within the classroom, within the wider environment of the secure setting, and for their relevance for young people's future lives.

With these three conditions in place, consideration also needs to be given to the substance and process of participatory activities in order that they are fully inclusive and address issues that matter to young people. Fielding warns that:

> Students will soon tire of invitations (a) to express a view on matters they do not think are important, (b) are framed in a language they find restrictive, alienating or patronizing, and (c) that seldom result in actions or dialogue that affects the quality of their lives.
>
> *(Fielding, 2004: 306–307)*

What is important is that young people recognise that their views and recommendations are taken account of and responded to and that they are not 'merely treated as minor footnotes in an unaltered adult text' (Fielding and Prieto, 2002: 20).

Many of the activities that have been pioneered in schools have potential applications to secure settings. The nine schools involved in the research conducted by MacBeath et al. (2001) had developed various forums for student voice, from pair work and discussion groups in class to representative councils at form, year, and school level. Some students were representatives on national bodies such as a youth parliament. Within the classroom students worked in pairs to review and support each other's learning, and to identify effective approaches to working. They were involved in the review of specific subjects and the improvement of IT facilities. Within the wider school community, students were involved in the appointment of new teachers, annual teaching and learning and curriculum reviews, the formulation of the school development plan, and the development of new policies such as equal opportunities, health and safety, and drug use. They jointly organised conferences and proposed and developed new projects: setting up a radio station, out of hours study support, and charity events. In MacBeath et al.'s research students' views were collected in several different ways. In one school visual display, drama and role play were used alongside more conventional questionnaires. Photographs taken by students have been used to show areas of the school where students felt safest from bullying.

In the choice of approach, clearly, contextual factors need to be taken into account. Lanskey (2007) found that in one school, where the concern was that voices could be marginalised, surveys of all young people approaches were preferred. Raymond (2001) identified a staged engagement with student voice in her school, moving from giving students questionnaires to complete to working with students to design questionnaires and analysing results. As students became more confident and competent in research skills they started to collaborate on and eventually design their own research projects.

Conclusion

From the research projects linked to the Consulting Pupils Network, toolkits were developed which offer advice to practitioners interested in setting up student voice activities (MacBeath et al., 2003; Fielding and Bragg, 2003). They include examples of the range of activities: ways in which young people's voices can be elicited and integrated into decision-making in different arenas within the school community. They offer advice too on the management of activities including peer support activities and representative channels such as student councils.

There is much potential for the transfer of such initiatives to secure settings. Beyond the contribution of young people's opinions to external evaluations by inspection and research organisations, possibilities for the expression of young people's voices exist within class groups, in residential units, on organisational committees within the secure setting, and on national bodies, such as the Youth Justice Board. Young people's views could be elicited through questionnaire-based approaches, writing-based approaches (e.g. open written questions, sentence completion, evaluation logs), talk-based approaches (conversations, discussions, interviews), and image-based approaches (drawings and paintings, photographs, posters).

The promise of young people's participatory activities however needs to be tempered with a pragmatic realism. Lefstein (2006) warns of the danger of the idealisation of dialogue, which masks the difficulties in capturing multiple diverse voices and that assumes a single, uncomplicated 'given' voice rather than one that is constructed through particular relationships and contexts (Morgan, 2009). It is also relevant to consider the assumptions and expectations underpinning participation whether it is about building democratic fellowship or about developing self-reliance and expertise in self-direction. Masschelein and Quaghebeur argue that participation always 'prescribes a certain participatory identity, a certain way of being for the subject that involves not only the government of the self as a participant but the consideration of the other as participant also' (2005: 56).

It follows that youth voice activities have the potential to be empowering or controlling, depending on the social and political values that shape the context in which they operate (Lawson, 2011). It is important therefore to be mindful of the aims of youth voice activities and the extent to which wider contextual dynamics are oriented towards supporting them. Young people learn about how they are valued through communications in and outside of the classroom, through the formal and communication challenges of the institution (Lanskey, 2016), and valuing voice in one context and not another is likely to generate doubts about the sincerity of the organisational commitment to youth voice. Fielding (2001b) proposes two key questions in this regard: Do we need new structures? Do we need new ways of relating to each other?

Wider attitudinal or structural barriers need not however preclude all forms of youth voice activity. Following Unger (1987), we can falsely assume the necessity of completely changing the whole system for action to occur. Within a single secure organisation, it may be that the education department provides the starting opportunity for a shift in practice, starting small and then building up. Arnot et al.

argued that 'fairly simple consultation strategies—with individuals and with groups—can produce a lot of useful ideas; and it is probably sensible for schools and teachers to start with such simple strategies' (2004: 89).

Small initiatives that have positive outcomes may serve to reduce anxiety and build support. More broadly, a mapping of what is already taking place would establish a baseline from which to move forward. Following the example of the Consulting Pupils Network, a forum for practitioners and researchers could be set up to share experiences exchange ideas and to develop alternative ways of interacting that give young people the tools and space to be agents of change to improve their lives and to the lives of others.

Note

1 In schools young people are defined as 'students' whether in or outside the classroom. The potential remit of student voice activities in secure settings extends therefore beyond the education department to the wider organisational community. The term 'student' is used interchangeably with 'young people' and 'youth' in this chapter to signal that participatory activities extend beyond the formally defined educational remit of the secure institution.

References

Arnot, M., McIntyre, D., Pedder, D., and Reay, D. (2004) *Consultation in the classroom: developing dialogue about teaching and learning.* Cambridge: Pearson Publishing.

Arnstein, S.R. (1979) Eight rungs on the ladder of citizen participation. *Journal of the American Institute of Planners*, 35, 4, 216–224.

Bottoms, A.E. (1995) The philosophy and politics of punishment and sentencing. In C.M.V. Clarkson and R. Morgan (Eds), *The politics of sentencing reform.* Oxford: Clarendon Press, pp. 17–50.

Bragg, S. (2001) Taking a joke: learning from the voices we don't want to hear. *Forum*, 43, 2, 70–73.

Bryan, K. (2004) Preliminary study of the prevalence of speech and language difficulties in young offenders. *International Journal of Language and Communication Disorders*, 39, 391–400.

Bryan, K., Freer, J., and Furlong, C. (2007) Language and communication difficulties in juvenile offenders. *International Journal of Language and Communication Disorders*, 42, 5, 505–520.

Carlebach, J. (1970) *Caring for children in trouble.* Abingdon: Routledge.

Cook-Sather, A. (2002) Authorizing students' perspectives: toward trust, dialogue, and change in education. *Educational Researcher*, 31, 4, 3–14.

Council of Europe (2009) *European rules for juvenile offenders subject to sanctions or measures.* Strasbourg: Council of Europe Publishing

Department for Education and Skills (DfES) (2004) *Working together: giving children and young people a say.* London: DfES.

Elwood, C. (2013) *Children and young people in custody 2012–13. An analysis of 12–18-year-olds' perceptions of their experience in secure training centres.* London: HM Inspectorate of Prisons/Youth Justice Board.

Fielding, M. (2001a) Students as radical agents of change. *Journal of Educational Change*, 2, 2, 123–141.

Fielding, M. (2001b) Beyond the rhetoric of student voice: new departures or new constraints in the transformation of 21st century schooling? *Forum*, 43, 2, 100–110.
Fielding, M. (2004) Transformative approaches to student voice: theoretical underpinnings, recalcitrant realities. *British Educational Research Journal*, 30, 2, 295–311.
Fielding, M. (2011a) Student voice and the possibility of radical democratic education: re-narrating forgotten histories, developing alternative futures. In G. Czerniawski and W. Kidd (Eds), *The student voice handbook: bridging the academic/practitioner divide*. Bingley: Emerald, pp. 3–17.
Fielding, M. (2011b) Student voice and inclusive education: A radical democratic approach to intergenerational learning (La voz del alumnado en una escuela inclusiva). *Revista Interuniversitaria de Formación del Profesorado*, 70, 25, 1. Retrieved from: https://aufop.blogspot.co.uk/2010/08/michael-fielding-student-voice-and.html
Fielding, M., and Bragg, S. (2003) *Students as researchers. Making a difference*. Cambridge: Pearson Publishing.
Fielding, M., and Prieto, M. (2002) The central place of student voice in democratic renewal: a Chilean case study. In M. Schweisfurth., L. Davies, and C. Harber (Eds), *Learning democracy and citizenship: international experiences*. Oxford: Symposium Books, pp. 19–36.
Hart, R. (1992) *Children's participation: from tokenism to citizenship*. UNICEF Innocenti Essays, 4. International Child Development Centre of UNICEF.
Holdsworth, R. (2000) Schools that create real roles of value for young people. *UNESCO International Prospect*, 3, 349–362.
Invernizzi, A. and Williams, J. (Eds) (2008) *Children and citizenship*. London: Sage Publications.
Kennedy, E. (2013) *Children and young people in custody 2012–13: An analysis of 15–18-year-olds' perceptions of their experiences in young offender institutions*. London: HM Inspectorate of Prisons/Youth Justice Board.
Lanskey, C. (2007) Student autonomy in schools: contemporary and earlier thinking and practice. Unpublished PhD dissertation.
Lanskey, C. (2010) Citizenship education for young people in secure institutions in England and Wales. *Educação, Sociedade and Culturas*, 30, 41–56.
Lanskey, C. (2011) Promise or compromise? Education for young people in secure institutions in England. *Youth Justice Journal*, 11, 1, 47–60.
Lanskey, C. (2015) *Education pathways of young people in the youth justice system: a case study* (Final Report). Cambridge: Institute of Criminology.
Lanskey, C. (2016) Formal and informal learning in custodial settings for young people. *Prison Service Journal*, 226, 3–7.
Lanskey, C. and Rudduck, J. (2010) Leadership and student voice. In *International Encyclopedia of Education* (3rd edn). Boston: Elsevier.
Lawson, T. (2011) Empowerment in education: liberation, governance or a distraction? A review. *Power and Education*, 3, 2, 89–103.
Lefstein, A. (2006) Dialogue in schools: towards a pragmatic approach. *Working Papers in Urban Language and Literacies* 33. London: Kings College.
Lincoln, Y. (1995) In search of students' voices. *Theory into Practice*, 34, 2, 88–93.
Little, R. (2015) Putting education at the heart of custody? The views of children on education in a young offender institution. *British Journal of Community Justice*, 13, 2, 27.
MacBeath, J., Demetriou, H., Rudduck, J., and Myers, K. (2003) *Consulting pupils: a toolkit for teachers*. Cambridge: Pearson Publishing.
MacBeath, J., Myers, K., and Demetriou, H. (2001) Supporting teachers in consulting pupils about aspects of teaching and learning and evaluating impact. *Forum*, 43, 2, 78–82.

Masschelein, J., and Quaghebeur, K. (2005) Participation for better or for worse? *Journal of Philosophy of Education*, 39, 1, 51–65.

Matheson, H. (2016) What makes a good prison officer? Perspectives of young men in HM YOI Polmont. Unpublished Masters Thesis.

McIntyre, D., and Pedder, D. (2001) How teachers respond to and use pupil perspectives to improve teaching and learning. Paper presented at the Annual Meeting of the American Educational Research Association, Seattle.

Mitra, D.L. (2008) *Student voice in school reform: building youth-adult partnerships that strengthen schools and empower youth*. Albany, NY: SUNY Press.

Mitra, D., Serriere, S., and Kirshner, B. (2014) Youth participation in US contexts: student voice without a national mandate. *Children and Society*, 28, 4, 292–304.

Morgan, B. (2009) 'I think it's about the teacher feeding off our minds, instead of us learning off them, sort of like switching the process around': pupils' perspectives on being consulted about teaching and learning. *Curriculum Journal*, 20, 4, 389–407.

Office for Standards in Education, Children's Services and Skills (2000) *Evaluating educational inclusion: guidance for inspectors and schools*. London: HM Stationery Office.

Prieto, M. (2001) Students as agents of democratic renewal in Chile. *Forum*, 43, 2, 87–90.

Raymond, L. (2001) Student involvement in school improvement: from data source to significant voice. *Forum*, 43, 2, 58–61.

Ronner, A. D. (2002) Songs of validation, voice, and voluntary participation: therapeutic jurisprudence, Miranda and juveniles. *U. Cin. L. Rev.*, 71, 89–114.

Rudduck, J. (2001) The ladder of pupil participation. *Consulting Pupils Network Newsletter* No. 1. Retrieved from: www.consultingpupils.co.uk/resources/Newsletter%201.pdf

Rudduck, J. (2006) The past, the papers and the project. *Educational Review*, 58, 2, 131–143.

Rudduck, J., and Flutter, J. (2000) Pupil participation and pupil perspective: carving a new order of experience. *Cambridge Journal of Education*, 30, 75–89.

Rudduck, J., and Flutter, J. (2004) *How to improve your school*. London: Continuum.

Rudduck, J., and Fielding, M. (2006) Student voice and the perils of popularity. *Educational Review*, 58, 2, 219–231.

Shier, H. (2001) Pathways to participation: openings, opportunities and obligations. *Children and Society*, 15, 107–117.

Shier, H. (2010) 'Pathways to participation' revisited. In B. Percy-Smith and N. Thomas (Eds), *A handbook of children and young people's participation: perspectives from theory and practice*. Oxon: Routledge, pp. 215–229.

Silva, E. (2001) Squeaky wheels and flat tires: a case study of students as reform participants. *Forum*, 43, 2, 95–99.

Taylor, C. (2016) *Review of the Youth Justice System. An interim report of emerging findings*. London: Ministry of Justice.

Unger, R.M. (1987) *False necessity: anti-necessitarian social theory in the service of radical democracy*. Cambridge: Cambridge University Press.

United Nations (1989) *Convention on the rights of the child*. United Nations: Geneva.

User Voice (2011) What's your story? Young offenders' insights into tackling youth crime and its causes. Retrieved from: www.uservoice.org/wp-content/uploads/2011/03/User-Voice-Whats-Your-Story.pdf

Wegerif, R. (2016) What is dialogic space? Blog, 5 February [online]. Retrieved from: www.rupertwegerif.name/blog/what-is-dialogic-space.

13

CHILDREN'S VIEWS OF EDUCATION IN A YOUNG OFFENDERS INSTITUTION

Ross Little

This chapter draws on children's views of education in a young offenders institution (YOI) to explore education provision in the youth secure estate from their perspectives. It builds on research undertaken by the author in a YOI, findings from which have been previously published (Little, 2015b). The chapter highlights how listening to the experience of children in prison helps to understand how education provision could be improved to better achieve its objectives. Children themselves are a useful source of information about their previous educational experiences, the effectiveness (or otherwise) of current provision, and which improvements should be considered. For some children, the most meaningful experiences of education and learning come from informal opportunities to engage with new subjects, ideas, and practices.

In the YOI where the research took place, the *Raptor* project stood out as an educational opportunity in which the children felt they had positive opportunities for learning, the potential for increasing levels of commitment and responsibility, and, eventually, opportunities to leave the prison for short periods of time. This type of learning opportunity was the exception in the YOI, not the norm, but is suggestive of the type of educational experience that could help some of the most vulnerable children move on from negative prior experiences of formal education. The chapter lastly considers recent policy developments and the opportunities, and challenges, for delivering educational opportunities for children in YOIs. Education in prison has been on the policy agenda of recent governments. The Taylor Review of the Youth Justice System (and the associated government response) and its proposal for a new form of custody for children based on principles of education and health and the Coates Review of education in prison have been the most recent manifestations of this. Prior to this, the United Kingdom coalition government between 2010 and 2015 sought to make significant changes to the composition of the youth justice secure estate in England and Wales. They proposed a new network of secure colleges, the first of which was planned for 2017 on a site in Leicestershire (Ministry of Justice, 2014a).

The apparent motivation for this supposedly new approach was the poor level of education in prisons for children. The government response to the consultation on their Transforming Youth Custody Green Paper (Ministry of Justice, 2014b) highlighted several particularly concerning findings in relation to the educational achievements of children in prison:

> Latest figures suggest 86% of young men in Young Offender Institutions (YOIs) have been excluded from school at some point, and over half of 15–17 year olds in YOIs have the literacy and numeracy level expected of a 7–11 year old. Research also indicates that 18% of sentenced young people in custody have a statement of special educational needs.
>
> *(Ministry of Justice, 2014b: 3)*

Educational provision within YOIs and secure training centres is hampered by challenges that make it difficult for children to engage in education (Houses of Parliament, 2016). The issue of prior negative experiences of formal education was repeatedly found amongst the participants in the current research. This is a key consideration when thinking about how 'education' or 'learning' opportunities are organised and delivered in custodial establishments for children.

About the research

This chapter draws on research undertaken by the author when working as part of the 'U R Boss project', a youth justice participation project funded by the Big Lottery Fund and hosted by The Howard League for Penal Reform. Access to YOIs for the purposes of research, information gathering, or discursive, participatory work can be very challenging. The author of this chapter's involvement in a Youth Justice Board working group on access to college education for children in prison, also attended by senior staff from young offender institutions, helped facilitate access to a YOI. The aim of the research was to find out what children's experiences of education in a YOI were like from children themselves.

There were three methodological elements to the research: a questionnaire, a discussion group, and one-to-one interviews with individual children accommodated on different wings of the prison, including one on the Care and Separation Unit.

The questionnaire asked participants 18 questions about: the type of educational activities they were involved in at the YOI, whether they were in education prior to entering the YOI, whether they had ever been excluded from education, about their educational qualifications, what courses they had been on at the YOI, what kind of help and support they had received to help them find education and employment, what kinds of education and employment plans they have for after the YOI, potential barriers to these plans, and what else the YOI might do to help them. Eighty-five questionnaires were distributed by YOI staff at the end of June

2012. Respondents filled in the questionnaire of their own volition. These were either handed directly to young people attending education classes in the YOI during the final week of June 2012 or placed under their cell door. Forty-seven questionnaires were returned by participants (a response rate of 55%). There was no extra support provided for filling out the questionnaire. Whilst respondents did not need to write much, they would have needed to be able to read the questions. Not every participant responded to every question, so question response numbers reported in this chapter may not always equal 47.

Five discussion groups were facilitated over three days in July 2012. Each lasted up to two hours, the duration of the morning and afternoon education slots, to fit in with the prison regime. There were 24 discussion group participants in total with an average of five children attending each discussion group. Themes explored were the same as those covered by the questionnaire with scope for the discussion to flow in ways determined by the participants. Because the groups were live discussions, the precise nature of conversation varied between the different groups and depended on the level of engagement of the participants, their curiosity and degree of comfort with the set-up and their fellow participants. Each of the discussions was facilitated by two members of staff from the U R Boss project. One facilitator tended to facilitate discussion while the other was responsible for note-taking. The purpose of the project and the commitment to anonymity of participants was explained to each group. These groups lasted one or two hours each, focused on exploring the questions, and were carried out with a member of YOI staff present. The presence of the YOI staff member was a condition of the discussion groups taking place and may have impacted on the responses of some of the children.

Also completed were four interviews with individual children on three different wings, including one on the Care and Separation Unit, colloquially known as 'The Seg' owing to the segregation of its inhabitants from the mainstream YOI population. These individuals had been deemed unsuitable for group work by the management team. These individual sessions took place subject to the agreement of the individual child. Whether or not they were asked to participate would have been the decision of the senior member of prison staff facilitating the research. The research may have therefore excluded the involvement of children experiencing the most difficulties in the prison at the time. YOI staff were not present for these meetings with young people. A brief outline of the context for each of the four children interviewed in segregation appears at several points in the text, relating to points made about experiences of, or attitudes towards, education in the YOI.

Taken together, the research engaged with up to 75 children detained in the YOI, around half of the population there at the time. The reason it is not possible to be precise about the number of different individuals engaging with the research is because there was no way of matching discussion group participants to questionnaire respondents. Individuals attending the discussion groups were asked whether they had completed the questionnaire but only half a dozen indicated that they had. Findings from the questionnaire, discussion groups and interviews were presented to the management team at the YOI later in the same year. In terms of how the sample was selected, questionnaire respondents did so of their own volition and returned completed questionnaires in a blank envelope. Potential participants for the discussion groups were recruited from education classes.

It should be noted that the research took place before some of the effects of the government's budget reductions had impacted on staffing levels across the secure estate and before the YOI was 're-rolled' to become an adult prison the following year.

Summary of findings

The following section summarises some of the findings from the report, highlighting key themes and points for thinking about the broader role that education in prison can play for children in prison. The findings are drawn from responses to the questionnaire, the discussion groups, and the interviews. Key findings discussed here include:

- Perceptions and experiences of education. Many of those that engaged with the research stated that their prior experiences of education had been extremely negative. Despite this, education and qualifications remained important to their perceived chances of subsequent employment. The issue of choice is important here. If children are expected to willingly engage in education provision, the choice provided needs to be meaningful.
- There are variety of practical barriers that limit access to children's choices.
- Partly because of the barriers, the way education is provided in prisons does not engage children as well as it might.
- The children's experiences of education in prison raise questions about the nature of education provision in the 'secure estate'.

Before exploring these themes further, it is worth considering the context in which these children are participating (or not) in education, particularly their previous experiences of education.

Pre-custody education experiences

Consistent with previous literature (Cripps and Summerfield, 2012; Houses of Parliament, 2016; Ministry of Justice, 2016b), a disrupted experience of education prior to entering custody was a common theme with young people who participated in the work. Of 45 respondents, nine out of ten (89%, 40) had been excluded from education, 63% of which were permanent exclusions. This compares with around 3–5% of the general population (Houses of Parliament, 2016). This was consistent with the findings from the focus groups, in which nearly all respondents reported having been excluded from mainstream education, and the larger sample size in a study by Cripps and Summerfield (2012). Over a quarter (27%, 12) of 45 questionnaire respondents said they were last in school aged 14 years or under. The remaining 33 respondents said they were last in school aged 15 years or over. In terms of the institutions they had been excluded from, the questionnaire identified that nearly all those that had been excluded (38 out of 40) were from a school. Seven of the 40 had been excluded from a pupil referral unit and three had been excluded from a further education college. In the first focus group, all four participants had been excluded from school, two of them permanently, one of these stating that 'I was excluded almost every day'.

Some participants expressed a lack of interest or engagement in structured or formal education and had clearly had prior negative experiences of classroom environments. Others recognised that they had missed out by being excluded from education previously: 'I kept getting kicked out ... I didn't like people telling me what to do. I wasn't interested in school at the time. Now I'm older I think differently' and 'I got kicked out in Year 9. I lost focus. I was intelligent. I never got into trouble with the police until I went to a PRU' and 'It was fun at the time, but I didn't realise 'til it was too late ... You end up chilling with your pals on the street and you have spare time on your hands and you end up getting in trouble'.

In one of the focus group sessions, all five participants were unanimous in the belief that education provision at the YOI could not make a difference to them. One had strong views that education was just a waste of time relative to his goal of earning money: 'You don't need education in your life, you need money.'

Another participant qualified this by saying that education in custody could make a difference, but only if the support provided is sufficient: '[Education can't make a difference] unless you're on a long sentence ... I've had help and completed Level 2 Horticulture'. Overall, most participants' lives had been characterised by unhappy, irregular, and/or inconsistent experiences of education. More than four in 10 participants (20, 43%) did not state any previous educational attainment.

Choice

Given the frequency of negative prior experiences of education, it is unsurprising that respondents tended to have low expectations of the education they would receive in prison. However, the issue of meaningful choice and activity were themes that respondents returned to consistently in the discussion groups. The questionnaire findings indicated that participants felt able to choose which courses they wanted to study: 38 respondents said they were able to choose what course they wanted to study, 30 of whom said that they were able to get on to the course they wanted to. Four respondents said they were not able to choose their course of study and five did not respond to this question. However, the group work allowed more discussion about the extent of the choice that participants could exercise in practice. Whilst individuals had been asked for their preference about which courses they most wanted to attend, the type of course available limited their options considerably at the time: 'I didn't get the choice I wanted, which was radio, media and gym. Instead I got Maths, English and ICT' and 'I wanted to construction but had to do maths instead. Then I went on radio' and 'I wanted to do mechanics but had to do education ...'

Some participants had strong ideas about what they wanted to study or train in and had been left disappointed by the restricted options available: 'When I first came in I wanted to do geography, history and German but they don't do them here' and 'There should be more education – more options available ... a barbering course – there has to be one person who can do hair properly here – the hairdresser who comes here has one hour to do everyone on the whole wing. Plumbing. Woodwork' and 'I wanted to do languages but there was only one copy of the Spanish CDs in the library and it wasn't there'.

Choice was particularly constrained if participants already had attained GCSEs. Twelve respondents said they had GCSEs, eight of whom said they had five GCSEs graded A★ to C. Five respondents had NVQ Level 2 or a BTEC First Diploma. Three respondents had a NVQ Level 1 or a BTEC Introductory Diploma. A common response referred to the lack of education provision for those willing and able to study beyond GCSE level: 'It's good quality [the education], but only up to GCSEs' and 'If you've done GCSEs, or if you don't want to do them, there isn't much else. If people are working at their age-level and they've done GCSEs then they're at a disadvantage' and 'Yes [there was a choice], but I've done most of my GCSEs already'.

Discussion group participants commented that doing higher qualifications is possible, but that this was subject to having sufficient self-confidence and self-motivation: 'You can do distance learning – Open University. That's alright but you have to feel confident'.

In addition to possessing this self-discipline in the prison environment, it was also necessary to have access to a teacher qualified to teach above GCSE level. This relied on more external factors, such as good fortune: 'I'm doing AS Maths and I can only do that cos there's someone who can teach me that here'.

There was a lack of consistency regarding access to a suitably qualified tutor. Without this support, one boy explained that he found the prospect of self-directed learning in prison too daunting to contemplate: 'They offered me A-levels; I refused to do it. I work better face-to-face. They only offered me study on my own, without a teacher'.

These experiences raise important points about the lack of support available for the significant minority of children in prison who do have a track record of educational achievement. Or as the Taylor Review of Youth Justice subsequently put it: 'There is also not sufficient provision for high-ability children who are capable of getting the top grades in their GCSEs and to go on to take A-levels and prepare for university' (Ministry of Justice, 2016b: 39).

This is similar to the situation for many prisons in the adult secure estate struggling to provide meaningful educational opportunities to men and women across a wide spectrum of educational achievements and different motivations to learn (Prisoner's Education Trust, 2014).

One participant suggested the idea of 'taster courses', to give people choice about what they might want to do more of and ultimately help people 'to find their own path'. A conversation with senior staff highlighted the administrative barrier to making curriculum changes. For example, if the YOI wants to make a change to the curriculum this must be agreed with the education service provider, together with the Education Funding Agency (the Department for Education's delivery agency for funding and compliance) and the Youth Justice Board (YJB). One focus group participant noted a recent change to the curriculum that meant he could no longer access his chosen subject of drama: 'My plans? Performing arts [in response to a question about what he wants to do at college]. But drama isn't on the curriculum now ... It used to be.'

It is worth noting here that because there are multiple stakeholders involved in contemporary YOI education provision (including the institution, central government department, the Education Funding Agency, and the education provider) changes to education provision in YOIs can be very difficult to bring about.

Barriers

In addition to some restrictions on the practical choices they could make, participants identified different types of barriers, including their difficulty in concentrating in the prison environment, especially if they felt others were being disruptive: 'I can't focus. You need to put people that do want to work in a place they can concentrate' and 'Here I've found I can't really learn ... I just can't concentrate' and 'I just don't like being in groups really. Don't like being around other people.'

These responses raise fundamental questions about what education provision really means for these children in prison. It is perhaps worth reminding ourselves about the day-to-day lived reality for children in prison. Drawing on research presented in *Life Inside*, a report on the daily lives of 15–17 year old males in prison, it is clear that around half have experienced time in care, or substantial social services involvement, compared to 3% in the general population (NACRO, 2003, cited by The Howard League for Penal Reform, 2010). A quarter of the boys report suffering violence at home and one in 20 report having been sexually abused (YJB, 2007). Three in ten boys report having a recognised mental health disorder (YJB, 2005) compared to one in ten in the general population (ONS, 2005, cited by The Howard League for Penal Reform, 2010: 8). Relationships with others can therefore be affected.

As recent inspection reports have shown, the levels of self-harm, suicide, and general violence have increased considerably in YOIs in recent years (Her Majesty's Inspector of Prisons, 2014; 2015a; 2015b). In July 2017, the Chief Inspector of Prisons was moved to state that 'The current state of affairs is dangerous, counterproductive and will inevitably end in tragedy unless urgent corrective action is taken' (BBC News, 2017).

A key barrier identified by participants was the nature of their risk assessment, which could severely limit their educational options: 'I have a high-risk assessment, so there's not much I can do. I can do different stuff but it's all based around education (not practical activities). I don't wanna do education. I kick off a lot and just walk out' and 'I'm high risk. I can't do things like mechs (car mechanics) and cookery ... I want to do cooking ... I do FLL (Foundation Life Learning) instead' and 'I put down for horticulture when I arrived – I was low risk when I arrived. I waited 2 and-a-half months for nothing'.

Nine respondents to the questionnaire said they had barriers getting in the way of them making plans for education and training. Reasons given were related to being in prison itself, to their offence, to mental health problems, a lack of GCSEs, or issues with their Youth Offending Team. Only four respondents stated that there were no barriers getting in the way of their plans for education or training. A psychological barrier to engaging with education for some was that they had bigger problems to worry about, including family issues and/or no accommodation on release. For example, when asked about his plans following release, one boy stated: 'I ain't got nowhere to go when I come out. Accommodation is a big problem for me. I don't know where I'm gonna live'.

Issues, such as uncertainty about where they are going to live after being in the YOI, can affect how children feel about themselves, their lives, and their perceptions and motivations about education and learning. Those children experiencing some of the biggest barriers to accessing education in the short term were those receiving education on unit or 'Ed on Unit'. The research included interviews with four young people receiving 90 minutes of education in their cells each day, Monday to Friday: 45 minutes in the morning, 45 minutes in the afternoon.

The following biographies of four individual boys outline something of their experiences relating to education and have been interspersed throughout the remainder of this article. The first outlines a little of the context for 'Chris',[1] for whom education was a distant concern, at least partly because of his fears about his own personal safety in the prison environment.

Chris – 15-year-old black male from London

Chris was receiving education separately in the segregation unit for his own protection. He had experienced difficulties in the YOI due to his recorded gang affiliations with other inmates. He received two 45-minute sessions each day, one in the morning and one in the afternoon. One session focussed on English tuition and the other focussed on mathematics tuition. Chris had previously been permanently excluded from school. He had been in a pupil referral unit before being remanded to HMYOI Feltham. From there he had been transferred to this current YOI.

For Chris, formal education barely featured on his personal radar, despite its daily presence in his life, at least on weekdays: 'I don't feel settled here so I'm not even thinking about education.' Chris explained that he had other things to worry about, namely his own personal safety, before concerning himself with his educational development. A bigger issue for him was the lack of physical activity available as part of the regime in segregation: 'You're not allowed to go to the gym on this unit'. The distance between his present state and voluntary engagement in education or some form of productive learning appeared to be great. This was in contrast with Paul, an older boy also receiving education segregated from the rest of the prison community.

Paul – 17-year-old white male from Kent

Paul was receiving education on unit due to his own disruptive behaviour in group classes. Like the others we spoke with receiving education on unit, he received two 45-minute sessions of tuition each day; once in the morning, once in the afternoon. At the time of the research, he was working towards Mathematics Level 1 and English Level 2.

Paul had only been at the YOI for one month having recently been transferred from a secure training centre. Like the vast majority of the boys who participated in the research, he had previously been excluded from school. He had then been sent to a pupil referral unit but stopped attending when he was 15 years old.

Despite these prior negative experiences, Paul was relatively optimistic about the education provision he was receiving in the segregation unit and in the prison more generally: 'The subjects I'm doing here will be helpful for me'.

Concerns about accommodation in the community following a spell in prison was an issue for some boys. For others, there were concerns about the consequences for their education when they moved on to their next, adult, prison. Transfer of records between institutions can be delayed and incomplete at times and continuity of education provision for individuals can suffer (Ofsted, 2010). This was indeed related to one of David's concerns as a 17-year-old in the segregation unit soon to 'celebrate' his birthday.

David – 17-year-old, white male from Kent

Like Paul, David was receiving education on unit because he had assaulted someone in the YOI. He was unique amongst the boys in segregation at the time for studying towards his Economics GCSE. Whilst it initially appeared that this was a subject he had himself chosen, he was disappointed that his choices were constrained by the limitations of what could be offered by the available tutor: 'I can only do what the one-to-one tutor can offer'.

Prior to his spell in a YOI, David attended a pupil referral unit for about a year. His main concern in relation to his education was his impending move to a different prison, particularly as this would be his first experience of an adult prison: 'I'd like to go back to mainstream education in (this) prison but I'm 18 so I'll get shipped out to a different prison soon'.

Despite efforts by the institution to get each of these segregated children engaged in education, each discussed their disengagement from education both before and during their time in prison. This is problematic when it is clear the re-offending rate by under 18s leaving YOIs is so high. Of those released from custody during 2015/16, 68.7% were reconvicted within 12 months, an increase of 1.5% on the previous year (Youth Justice Board/Ministry of Justice, 2017). Ofsted's review of arrangements for learning in custody and on release found that children often did not have personal education plans on arrival in prison and that arrangements to continue education when they returned to the community were unsatisfactory (Ofsted, 2010).

One of the main topics of conversation in the discussion groups focusing on education was food, hunger and nutrition. This echoed the findings from *Life Inside* (The Howard League for Penal Reform, 2010) where one of the most frequently voiced concerns of boys in prison was the amount and quality of the food on offer. Together with the hypermasculine context and the frequent threat of violence, the lack of food was a recurring theme amongst the discussion group participants. Each of these elements fundamentally impacts on what and how individuals learn in such environments.

The most positive comments by children about the educational opportunities available in the YOI were reserved not for the formal education classes but the Raptor project. This project allowed the children to work with, and care for, birds of prey living at the prison site. Responses from participants who had been involved with the project were extremely positive. For example, Matt, one of the four children interviewed in segregation, was extremely enthusiastic about this project.

Matt – 17-year-old white male from Kent

Matt was receiving education on unit for a month or two due to his vulnerability to attack from others being held in the same prison. He felt the need to complete GCSE English so that he would have three GCSEs and thus be eligible for a mechanics course. For him, the experience of education in the segregation unit appeared to be an opportunity to focus in a way that had not been possible in the mainstream education provision: 'I got more done in Ed on Unit than in class'. He was also unique amongst the boys in prison in expressing a preference for more exam-based assessment for courses. Despite this, his real passion, the thing that had really captured his imagination, was the Raptor project, which sought to build skills and confidence in the boys through working with birds of prey: 'Raptor is one of the best things I've done since I've been here ... On Raptor, I'm learning something new, I never knew it existed before'.

That these comments were made by a child who had been receiving one-to-one education segregated from the rest of the YOI population highlights its potential for engaging even some of the most vulnerable and disaffected children in prison. Another participant in one of the discussion groups was also very enthusiastic about the Raptor project: 'Raptor is [the best thing offered here] – it's unique – you can't do it at any other prison'.

In addition to enthusiasm from the children held in the YOI, staff at the YOI were also proud of the project and the attention it had received from outside the prison in the community. As visitors enter the prison, colourful promotional material about the project had been placed in a prominent position. In addition to on-site activities, some children in the YOI had been allowed out on release on temporary license (ROTL) to attend local events with the birds of prey. Ofsted was also sufficiently convinced about the educational value of the project to present it as an example of good practice:

> [it] ... uses care and display of predatory birds to engage young people who traditionally don't engage in learning activities. The Raptor Project builds self-confidence, personal development and team-working skills and improves academic skills such as English and mathematic.
>
> *(Ofsted, 2014)*

It is important to note that only a small number of children could be involved in the Raptor project. Three survey respondents stated that they had been involved with Raptor. One discussion group participant and one interviewee stated that they had been part of the project. An associated problem of the project's desirability, was that it could only be available to a small number of children in the YOI at any one time. In addition, the children had to have retained 'gold' status for a certain period of time, which involved maintaining an excellent behaviour record. This was a challenge for some of the children especially those for whom confrontation was a regular occurrence. Together with food, a child's current earned privilege status was one of their main concerns for day-to-day living in the prison.

The link identified by Ofsted between informal learning opportunities in the prison environment and educational skills is an interesting one. It could not be confirmed by the current research but if enthusiasm for engaging in an activity is a proxy measure for subsequent involvement and success, then it was clear that the feelings of those engaged in the Raptor project were exceptionally positive relative to other learning opportunities available.

In his review of youth justice, Charlie Taylor cautions against taking the 'easy option' of placing 'children only in the classes or the courses that they enjoy most' (Ministry of Justice, 2016b: 39). The review highlights the importance of good levels literacy and numeracy.

> There is lots of vocational training happening in custody, but there needs to be a sufficient focus on the building blocks of English and maths as well. There are few jobs now that do not require good levels of literacy and numeracy. However they arrive, children must not leave custody still unable to read.
>
> *(Ibid.)*

There is no denying the importance of these skills in the contemporary workplace, or life in general. However, engaging some children in the custodial environment in formal education requires a degree of self-esteem and confidence in the classroom that is best built through more informal educational and learning opportunities. As Warr argues:

> In order for prison education to work efficiently and to serve the interests of the prisoners, the institution and the wider public we need to move away from the current disciplinary practices and ideologies that exist within prison education and instead re-privilege those skills that arise when learning occurs

for learning's sake ... [it] is only when we move beyond these destructive ideologies and simple binary outcomes that we will acquire a prison education system that truly delivers pedagogically informed transformations.

(Warr, 2016: 18)

Concluding comments

Whilst most of the participants in the research were mostly relatively content with the educational options available, it was clear that a range of barriers restricted considerably the educational offer in practice. Some of the children involved in the research were not able to contemplate engagement in education whilst other more pressing issues concerned them. It is also reasonable to suggest that children who participated in the research are generally likely to have been amongst the more sociable and engaged in the institution. Relatedly, children who did not participate are likely to have been experiencing other barriers to their engagement in education.

Opportunities to learn informally, building confidence, self-esteem, and learning in a way that felt different to the traditional classroom were crucially important for some respondents. Equally, opportunities for learning that go beyond GCSE level are important for some participants.

It is important to recognise that a focus on 'education' can be rather limited and limiting. A fuller, more meaningful discussion needs to consider the opportunities for 'learning' in the prison environment. This perhaps leads us to question more directly what it is that children are likely to learn in environments that the Chief Inspector has referred to as 'dire', in which 'tragedy' is 'inevitable' (BBC News, 2017). With the persistently high levels of re-offending by children leaving custody, it is also reasonable to ask the question about what our government has learnt in recent years about the impact of custody on children's willingness and ability to learn. Perhaps, more pertinently, it is reasonable to ask what the experience teaches children who go into custody.

In the best circumstances, there were opportunities for those motivated individuals who are academically talented and who are able to concentrate in an environment as hostile to positive learning experiences as a YOI. There were also positive experiences for those able to get one of the limited places on the Raptor project. It is important to note that this type of informal alternative learning opportunity was, and remains, rare. Since the institution re-rolled as an adult prison, the Raptor project has not been replicated in another YOI.

With a political environment that values decreasing the expenditure per head for children in custody, the education and learning opportunities available to children in custody have not been expansive in recent years. The educational offer needs to go beyond a focus on English and mathematics, involving greater breadth and further development. Educational experiences in YOIs are highly unlikely to be rehabilitative if welfare needs and issues are not recognised as part of the learning that children are engaged in.

Note

1 As with other names used in this chapter, Chris is not his real name.

References

BBC News [online]. (2017) Youth custody centres so unsafe a tragedy is inevitable. Retrieved from: www.bbc.co.uk/news/uk-40644383

Cripps, H., and Summerfield, A. (2012) Resettlement provision for children and young people and the care of looked after children in custody: findings from two HMIP thematic reviews. *Prison Service Journal*, 201, 31–38.

Her Majesty's Inspector of Prisons. (2014) Unannounced inspection of HMYOI Feltham. Retrieved from: www.justiceinspectorates.gov.uk/hmiprisons/wp-content/uploads/sites/4/2015/01/Feltham-A-CYP-web-2014.pdf

Her Majesty's Inspector of Prisons (2015a) Report on unannounced inspection of HMYOI Glen Parva. Retrieved from: www.justiceinspectorates.gov.uk/hmiprisons/wp-content/uploads/sites/4/2014/08/Glen-Parva-Web-amended-2014.pdf

Her Majesty's Inspector of Prisons (2015b) Report on unannounced inspection of HMYOI Wetherby. Retrieved from: www.justiceinspectorates.gov.uk/hmiprisons/wp-content/uploads/sites/4/2015/06/Wetherby-web-2015.pdf

House of Commons Hansard Debates (2014) *Mike Kane (Wythenshawe and Sale East), Member Environmental Audit Committee, Criminal Justice and Courts Bill Deb*, 20 March, c283. Retrieved from: www.publications.parliament.uk/pa/cm201314/cmpublic/criminaljustice/140320/pm/140320s01.htm#14032080000055

Houses of Parliament Parliamentary Office for Science and Technology (2016) Education in youth custody. POST Briefing for Parliamentarians. Retrieved from: http://researchbriefings.parliament.uk/ResearchBriefing/Summary/POST-PN-0524#fullreport

Legislation.gov.uk Website (2015) *Criminal Justice and Courts Act 2015*. Retrieved from: www.legislation.gov.uk/ukpga/2015/2/contents/enacted/data.htm

Little, R. (2015a) Participation and practice in youth justice. *Eurovista*, 3, 3. Retrieved from: http://euro-vista.org/eurovistavol3–3

Little, R. (2015b) Putting education at the heart of custody? The views of children on education in a YOI. *British Journal of Community Justice*, 13, 2, 27–46.

Ministry of Justice (2014a) Major economic boost as Wates is chosen for secure college design and build (Press Release), 8 June. London: MoJ. Retrieved from: www.gov.uk/government/news/major-economic-boost-as-wates-is-chosen-for-secure-college-design-and-build

Ministry of Justice (2014b) Transforming youth custody – government response to the consultation. London: MoJ.

Ministry of Justice. (2016a) *Proven reoffending statistics quarterly: July 2013 to June 2014, Table C2b*. London: Ministry of Justice. Retrieved from: www.gov.uk/government/collections/proven-reoffending-statistics

Ministry of Justice (2016b) *Review of the Youth Justice System in England and Wales by Charlie Taylor*. Retrieved from: www.gov.uk/government/uploads/system/uploads/attachment_data/file/577103/youth-justice-review-final-report.pdf

Ministry of Justice (2016c) *The government response to Charlie Taylor's Review of the Youth Justice System presented to Parliament by the Lord Chancellor and Secretary of State for Justice by Command of Her Majesty*. Retrieved from: www.gov.uk/government/uploads/system/uploads/attachment_data/file/576553/youth-justice-review-government-response.pdf

Ministry of Justice (2016d) *Understanding the educational background of young offenders: joint experimental statistical report from the Ministry of Justice and Department for Education.* London: Ministry of Justice. Retrieved from: www.gov.uk/government/uploads/system/uploads/a ttachment_data/file/577542/understanding-educational-background-of-young-offenders-full-report.pdf

Ministry of Justice (2016e) *Unlocking potential: a review of education in prison by Dame Sally Coates.* London: MoJ. Retrieved from: www.gov.uk/government/uploads/system/uploa ds/attachment_data/file/524013/education-review-report.pdf

National Youth Agency (2011) *Participation in youth justice: measuring impact and effectiveness.* Leicester: NYA.

Office for Standards in Education, Children's Services and Skills (2010) *Transition through detention and custody: arrangements for learning and skills for young people in custodial or secure settings.* London: Ofsted.

Office for Standards in Education, Children's Services and Skills (2014) *Improving skills for vulnerable, disengaged young people* (Ofsted Research and Analysis), 4 June. Retrieved from: www.gov.uk/government/publications/improving-skills-for-vulnerable-disenga ged-young-people

ONS (2005) *Mental health of children and young people in Great Britain.* London: Department of Health.

Parliament UK (2015) *Criminal Justice and Courts Bill returns to the Lords PLA report – theory of change.* Retrieved from: www.parliament.uk/business/news/2014/june/lords-criminal-jus tice-and-courts-bill

Prisoners' Education Trust (2014) *Brain cells: listening to prisoner learners* (3rd edn). Retrieved from: https://fbclientprisoners.s3.amazonaws.com/Documents/Reports/PET%20Brain% 20Cells%203%20Report%20LR.pdf

Tay, L., and Diener, E. (2011) Needs and subjective well-being around the world. *Journal of Personality and Social Psychology,* 101, 2, 354–365.

The Howard League for Penal Reform (2010) *Life inside: a unique insight into the day to day experiences of 15–17 year old males in prison.* London: The Howard League for Penal Reform. Retrieved from: https://d19ylpo4aovc7m.cloudfront.net/fileadmin/howard_lea gue/user/pdf/Publications/;Life_Inside_2010.pdf

U R Boss project blog [online]. (2015) Retrieved from: www.urboss.org.uk/blog

Warr, J. (2016) Transformative dialogues: (Re)privileging the informal in prison education. *Prison Service Journal,* 18–25.

Youth Justice Board (2005) *Mental health needs and effectiveness of provision for young offenders in custody and in the community.* London: Youth Justice Board.

Youth Justice Board (2007) Accommodation needs and experiences. Retrieved from: http s://assets.publishing.service.gov.uk/government/uploads/system/uploads/attachment_da ta/file/354901/yjb-accommodation-needs-experiences.pdf

Youth Justice Board (2014) *Custody and resettlement: Section 7 case management guidance.* London: Youth Justice Board. Retrieved from: www.gov.uk/government/publications/custody-a nd-resettlement/custody- and-resettlement-section-7-case-management-guidance

Youth Justice Board/Ministry of Justice (2017) *Youth justice statistics 2015/16.* Office for National Statistics. Retrieved from: www.gov.uk/government/uploads/system/uploads/a ttachment_data/file/585897/youth-justice-statistics-2015-2016.pdf

14
SAFEGUARDING CHILDREN IN THE YOUTH JUSTICE SECURE ESTATE

Katharine Evans

This chapter will consider implications associated with the duty to safeguard and promote the welfare of children under Section 11 of the Children Act 2004, when deprived of their liberty and placed within young offender institutions (YOIs) and secure training centres (STCs). Statutory guidance as issued by HM Government (2015: 5) defines safeguarding and promoting the welfare of children as:

1 protecting children from maltreatment
2 preventing impairment of children's health or development
3 ensuring that children are growing up in circumstances consistent with the provision of safe and effective care
4 taking action to enable all children to have the best life chances.

Protecting children from maltreatment

Abuse constitutes maltreatment of a child which involves inflicting harm that may include *physical abuse, emotional abuse, sexual abuse,* or *neglect,* or the failure to act to prevent harm to a child (HM Government, 2015).

Physical abuse

According to the HM Chief Inspector of Prisons (2017a), there is no provision within the youth justice custodial estate deemed safe to hold children and young people; violence and intimidation have been described as 'a feature of life in YOIs' (p. 62) and STCs have been deemed to be insufficiently safe with high levels of violence. What has emerged is a youth justice secure provision that is described as dangerous, violent, and unsafe (see for example Local Government Association, 2017; Longfield, 2017; Taylor, 2016a; Wightwick, 2017). In addition to rising violence within youth justice secure settings, concerns have been raised about underreporting of this issue and a lack of nationally coordinated efforts to remedy the status quo (HM Chief Inspector of Prisons, 2017a). One explanation for the rising violence is the increase in the proportion of young people in custody for violent offences; cumulatively, violence against the person, robbery, and sexual offences constitute 68% of offences resulting in custodial sentences (Youth Justice Board and Ministry of Justice, 2017); overall we are seeing a decrease in the number of young people placed within such settings, however young people accommodated have been imprisoned for more serious and violent offences. The current trend is that violence within YOIs is escalating, with a total of 2,900 assaults recorded for the year ending 2016, of which 1,700 incidents constituted assaults against young people. HM Chief Inspector of Prisons (2017a) has reported that 29% of children in YOIs have been victimised by peers and highlighted instances where victim support was lacking, inadequate, and did not meet the needs of children.

Further to children's experiences of physical abuse perpetrated by peers are implications associated with children being exposed to violence and the way in which such behaviours may become normalised and a part of everyday institutional life. Exposure to violence is a risk factor associated with youth offending and violent behaviour (Tsang, 2017; Wilkins et al., 2014; Wright and Liddle, 2014) and further, a link between violent victimisation and offending has been established (Cops and Pleysier, 2014; Owen and Sweeting, 2007). Exposure to violence has been shown to have an acute and lasting effect on aggression (Kirk and Hardy, 2012) and contributes to wider adverse effects on health and welfare outcomes, including as a causal factor of fear, anxiety, depression, suicide ideation, and decline in educational engagement and achievement (Seal et al., 2014). Young people within the secure estate often have a history of abuse and exposure to violence (British Medical Association, 2014; Jacobson et al., 2010; Taylor, 2016a); the reinforcement of this cycle of violence and abuse within secure settings serves only to amplify the harm caused to children. Within a child protection context, the legal definition of harm includes 'impairment suffered from seeing or hearing the ill-treatment of another' (Children Act 1989, Section 31). Thus, keeping young people safe from peer violence emerges as a primary safeguarding challenge within the secure estate, a concern that must extend beyond protecting children from physical peer abuse to include the statutory duty to protect children from the harmful outcomes associated with normative exposure to such violence.

Emotional abuse

Emotional abuse is defined as 'the persistent emotional maltreatment of a child such as to cause severe and persistent adverse effects on the child's emotional development' (HM Government, 2015: 92); examples of emotional abuse include causing children to feel fearful, serious bullying, setting developmentally inappropriate expectations, and preventing participation in opportunities for learning and social interaction. Within the context of the secure estate, one of the most significant issues that falls within the definition of emotional abuse relates to children living in fear of harm and victimisation. Increased levels of violence have resulted in 41% of young people feeling unsafe, this issue having greater prevalence among young people with disabilities (HM Chief Inspector of Prisons, 2017a) and mental health issues (Taflan, 2017). HM Inspectorate of Prisons describes bullying and intimidation as a 'regular feature of life' (Simmonds, 2016: 16), whereby 31% of children have reported being subjected to verbal abuse and 18% subjected to threats and intimidation by peers. In a study examining fear of bullying among adult and juvenile prisoners, Chan and Ireland (2009) found that half of their participants reported having fear of being bullied, with verbal aggression representing the most common concern. Gooch and Treadwell (2015) identified verbal abuse, intimidation, and threats to be significant causes of fear and helplessness; wider outcomes associated with bullying include emotional distress, self-harm, disengagement, social isolation, and withdrawal. Furthermore, young people were found to employ self-isolation as a strategy to avoid victimisation, an approach that fails to alleviate feelings of fear and may contribute to increased anxiety and further deterioration of emotional health and wellbeing. Further evidence of this issue has been presented by the European Committee for the Prevention of Torture and Inhuman or Degrading Treatment or Punishment (CPT) (2017), who found that exposure to high levels of peer violence in Cookham Wood YOI left many children too afraid to leave their cells. These issues are exacerbated by the fact that relatively few young people would consider reporting victimisation within the secure estate; Simmonds (2016) found that only 28% of young people would report victimisation to staff within YOIs, and, according to HM Chief Inspector of Prisons (2017a), just one in five young people believe that staff would take any report of victimisation seriously.

The use of solitary confinement represents another widely reported feature of life within the secure estate that may constitute a form of emotional abuse under the statutory definition. Separation involves placing young people in isolation which may involve placement in cellular confinement or segregation units, segregation units being unique to YOIs (Children's Commissioner, 2015). The Carlile Inquiry was launched to investigate the use of solitary confinement, restraint, and strip-searching of children in secure settings and whether such issues constitute child abuse (Lord Carlile of Berriew, 2006). The Inquiry highlighted a number of observations, including the use of solitary confinement as a form of punishment, instances where young people were segregated for periods of up to a month, and stark conditions 'which in effect were inducements to suicide' (p. 62). Although the Inquiry concluded that 'the use of segregation units in prisons is wrong on moral grounds' (p. 65) and made a series of recommendations to improve practice, no explicit judgement was made in relation to establishing whether such practices constituted child abuse. Nearly ten years later, the Children's Commissioner (2015) conducted an investigation into isolation practices and found that children in YOIs were being held in isolation for weeks, identifying cases of boys spending less than one hour per day outside their cell, and that a majority of young people interviewed had experienced at least one week of continual isolation. Further concerns extended to isolation conditions such as the size of cells, the absence of meaningful activity, limited opportunity for physical activity, and sporadic access to education; HM Chief Inspector of Prisons (2017a) has raised particular concerns about the impact of such lack of activity upon children placed in isolation over prolonged periods of time.

Interestingly, the primary reason for children not attending education while in the secure estate is attributed to their time spent in segregation (The Parliamentary Office of Science and Technology, 2016). Many children placed in isolation often demonstrate higher levels of vulnerability, for example, children with suicide risk are 50% more likely to be isolated (Howard League for Penal Reform, 2016) and children with learning disabilities, experience of the care system, or history of trauma are the most likely to experience isolation (Children's Commissioner, 2015). There is broad acknowledgement that isolating children under such conditions compounds their difficulties and adversely affects emotional wellbeing and mental health (British Medical Association, 2014; Children's Commissioner, 2015; CPT, 2017; Howard League for Penal Reform, 2016; Youth Justice Board, 2011). The potential for harm includes psychological effects (for example anxiety, depression, anger, paranoia or psychosis, cognitive disturbances, and self-harm) and physiological effects (for example insomnia, weight loss lethargy, tremulousness, and broader physical stress responses) (see Lee, 2016; Méndez et al., 2016; Shalev, 2008). In addition, children are particularly vulnerable to permanent developmental damage by being denied opportunity for rehabilitation, psycho-social and identity development, educational opportunities, skills acquisition, and access to treatment and support (Birckhead, 2015; Simkins et al., 2012).

There have been repeated calls by the United Nations and others for an absolute ban on the isolation and confinement of children because the damage and harmful outcomes associated with such practice may amount to cruel, inhuman, and degrading treatment (see, for example, Children's Commissioner, 2016; CPT, 2017; Howard League for Penal Reform, 2017; Méndez, 2011; Owen and Goldhagen, 2016). In a High Court legal challenge brought by the Howard League for Penal Reform (2017), the case of a young offender subjected to prolonged isolation and confined to his cell for over 22 hours a day in Feltham YOI was found to be unlawful. The ruling was based upon a failure to provide a minimum of 15 hours education per week; however, this judgement fell short when considering solitary confinement as degrading and inhuman treatment. The CPT (2017) have deemed that isolating young people under such conditions does amount to inhuman and degrading treatment, having observed boys as young as 15 being held in their cells for 23.5 hours per day for weeks on end at Cookham Wood YOI. Despite growing evidence of the detrimental effects and harmful outcomes associated with the prolonged solitary confinement of children, this remains routine practice within the youth justice secure estate.

Neglect

Neglect is defined as 'The persistent failure to meet a child's basic physical and/or psychological needs, likely to result in the serious impairment of the child's health or development' (HM Government, 2015: 93) and may involve a failure to

- provide adequate food, clothing and shelter
- protect a child from physical and emotional harm or danger
- ensure adequate supervision (including the use of inadequate care-givers)
- ensure access to appropriate medical care or treatment.

The definition extends to include 'neglect of, or unresponsiveness to, a child's basic emotional needs' (HM Government, 2015: 94).

Provide adequate food, clothing, and shelter

The provision of a healthy and balanced diet is crucial to children's development (Chambers, 2011) and is a determinant of health, contributing significantly to mental, emotional, and physical wellbeing (HM Inspectorate of Prisons, 2016a). The Prison Rules (1999, in HM Inspectorate of Prisons, 2016a: 4) stipulate provision of three wholesome meals per day that offer sufficient quantity, nutrition, and variation, while being well prepared. Despite this, the provision of poor quality food and insufficient portion sizes for young people in custody has been highlighted as a significant issue amid reports that children within the secure estate are frequently left hungry (British Medical Association, 2014; Chambers, 2011; HM Inspectorate of Prisons, 2016a; Willow, 2015a). Chambers (2011) argues that there is a systemic failure to provide appropriate budgets for food, with HM Inspectorate of Prisons (2016a) reporting a trend of declining expenditure with as little as £1.87 spent per prisoner, per day in some institutions. Furthermore, HM Inspectorate of Prisons (2016a) have highlighted a range of additional concerns, including food being served cold, undercooked or overcooked, poor provision for prisoners with medical, religious, or ideological requirements, and cases where children go up to 20 hours between meals. Cumulatively, these issues are indicative of a secure estate that exposes children in their care to *food insecurity* (see for example Dowler and O'Connor, 2012; Harvey, 2016; Taylor and Loopstra, 2016), which has been established as a risk factor for poor physical health outcomes, emotional and mental health issues, behaviour problems, and lower educational attainment (Chambers, 2011; Child Poverty Action Group, 2016; Harvey, 2016). There is growing evidence that the secure estate is failing to meet the basic material needs of children, including reports of deteriorating physical conditions that pose health and safety risks to children and staff (HM Chief Inspector of Prisons, 2017a; 2017c). Examples of living conditions observed at Wetherby YOI and Parc YOI include cramped cells, inadequately screened toilets, poor ventilation, and a lack of basic items such as curtains; children at Wetherby YOI are deprived of essential clothing (HM Chief Inspector of Prisons, 2017c; 2017d). Furthermore, communal areas have been described as 'grubby' or 'shabby' across YOIs (HM Chief Inspector of Prisons, 2016; 2017b; 2017c), with some accommodation deemed to be run down and poor. There also emerges a reoccurring theme surrounding restricted access to washing facilities and cleaning products (British Medical Association, 2014; HM Chief Inspector of Prisons, 2017c), limited access to showers (HM Chief Inspector of Prisons, 2017b; 2017d; 2017e; Taflan, 2017; Gyateng et al., 2013) and prevalence of dirty cells (HM Chief Inspector of Prisons, 2017c; 2018), inevitably impacting upon personal hygiene, dignity, and wellbeing.

Protect a child from physical and emotional harm or danger

Children within the secure estate are entitled to child protection intervention and to be safeguarded from harm (HM Government, 2015); by incarcerating children, the state assumes responsibility for protecting and promoting the welfare of the child (British Medical Association, 2014). The painstaking work of Willow (2015a; 2015b) has highlighted grave concerns about the abuse of children and systemic failures to protect them from harm within secure settings. This work included freedom of information requests to local authorities which revealed a history of inconsistent and apathetic investigation of safeguarding referrals despite high rates of injury caused by self-harm, assaults, and staff use of force; within a five-year period, only one serious case review had been initiated in respect of a child death in custody. The lack of independent scrutiny was raised as a particular concern as serious case reviews for children are required only in instances where a child has been subjected to significant harm or concerns exist about the effectiveness of joint working to safeguard children (Willow, 2015b). Following allegations of child abuse at Medway STC as exposed by BBC Panorama (2016), the Medway Improvement Board (2016) raised similar concerns regarding poor inter-agency coordination and referral processes, describing local authority scrutiny of safeguarding arrangements as *'insufficient'* across all STCs (p. 37). Medway Safeguarding Children Board claim to have had no safeguarding concerns about Medway STC prior to the BBC Panorama broadcast, despite having received a significant number of referrals that were subsequently dismissed on the grounds that there was no CCTV evidence to substantiate children's claims of abuse. The Youth Justice Board, responsible for commissioning and overseeing the youth justice estate at the time, had over the previous seven years received a total of 35 whistle blowing documents from parents, professionals, and staff referring to corruption and inappropriate treatment and behaviour toward children in STCs across the country; the Youth Justice Board had provided 'very little evidence that a serious attempt had been made to organise the accumulated evidence or analyse the data' (p. 41). The Medway Improvement Board (2016) subsequently called for an independent body responsible for the scrutiny of safeguarding arrangements and to reduce dependency upon internal assessments of safeguarding issues through ensuring external oversight.

More recent inspection reports suggest very little progress has since been made in strengthening safeguarding arrangements within the secure estate. Ofsted (2017a) deemed the safety of children at Medway STC as 'inadequate', highlighting a failure of the local authority and police public protection units to re-establish clear referral processes and described a 'legacy of arrangements that are not satisfactory or compliant with statutory guidance' (p. 8). Wider reported issues included inconsistent child protection records, insufficient recording of information, poor escalation arrangements, and omitted referrals where relevant thresholds had been met. Provision for the safety of children at Oakhill STC has also been judged 'inadequate' (Ofsted, 2017b); issues exposed include ineffective managerial oversight of safeguarding arrangements and inadequate staff responses to abuse, neglect, and wider safeguarding issues that place children at risk of significant harm. This report further provided examples of breaches to statutory safeguarding duties, such as the failure to refer a child's allegation of being subjected to multiple assaults by a member of staff to the local authority designated officer. Failures to protect children from harm are not limited to STCs within the youth justice system. Following a visit to Cookham Wood YOI, the CPT (2017) raised concern regarding child allegations of staff violence and abusive behaviour, some resulting in external referral or internal disciplinary proceedings, but several which had resulted in no recorded action whatsoever. HM Chief Inspector of Prisons (2018) has since identified a number of further issues at Cookham Wood, including the lack of local authority representation at safeguarding meetings, the absence of procedure for notifying local safeguarding children boards of serious incidents (and found evidence of two such unreported incidents), lack of clarity around interdisciplinary safeguarding responsibilities, and incomplete records of incidents involving staff use of force. At Parc YOI, inspectors have raised concerns about deteriorating safeguarding practice: inadequate oversight and resolution of incidents, poor attendance at safeguarding meetings, and inconsistent external scrutiny of cases involving allegations against staff (HM Chief Inspector of Prisons, 2017c). These concerns were echoed at Wetherby and Keppel YOI, where inspectors further observed deterioration in child protection arrangements, including poor record keeping, delays to investigations, failures to act to prevent harm, and that 'the inconsistent use of body-worn video cameras by staff from all areas frustrated investigations into maltreatment' (HM Chief Inspector of Prisons, 2017d: 24).

Children in the secure estate are unlikely to use internal complaint procedures and lack confidence in the system (Medway Improvement Board, 2016; Prisons and Probation Ombudsman, 2015; Youth Justice Board, 2011); a number of causes have been identified including concerns that complaints would be doctored or ignored, not be taken seriously, dealt with unfairly, or result in reprisal and punishment (see Ofsted, 2017b; Prisons and Probation Ombudsman, 2015; Taflan, 2017; Youth Justice Board, 2011). Investigation outcomes from Medway STC demonstrate that such perceptions held by children represent legitimate and substantiated concerns. The Medway Improvement Board (2016) found evidence of poor internal investigation (alongside allegations not being investigated at all), falsification of records, intimidation of whistle blowers, the use of safeguarding plans as a means to punish children, and staff activity to manipulate and deter children from complaining. Young people are most likely to report mistreatment by staff to a solicitor, primarily due to their status as being independent of the prison (Prisons and Probation Ombudsman, 2015). However, Willow (2015b) has pointed out that legal aid reforms in recent years have limited children's access to recourse when mistreated in custody, and that this represents 'a very serious attack on child protection given continuing concerns about the use of restraint in custody, and the known difficulties abused children in closed institutions have in accessing outside help' (p.8). This issue has been further highlighted by Crook (2017), who has expressed concern about the number of children disclosing safeguarding issues to the Howard League for Penal Reform legal team. They report increasingly making safeguarding referrals, including allegations of harm inflicted by staff responsible for children's care. Furthermore, they have received hostile calls from secure estate staff in attempts to undermine and discredit children and their claims of abuse. The failure to protect children from harm as exposed at Medway STC does not appear to be unique to any single organisation. The proliferation and diversity of reported failures reflects the prevalence of a culture that is not only negligent in promoting the welfare of children, but one that is contrary to the spirit of child protection which should lie at the very heart of the system.

Ensure adequate supervision

Within the context of safeguarding children, the concept of supervision generally refers to such issues as setting rules and boundaries, providing guidance, and knowing the whereabouts of a child; a failure of supervision may involve abandonment or leaving children in the care of inappropriate carers (Raws, 2016). Conditions within the secure context reflect a polarised position to this notion by imposing a regime that is founded upon constant and strict supervision within an environment concerned with controlled regulation of activity, time, and space. It is the *adequacy* of supervision within this extreme context that is critical because a large proportion of the people charged with the care of these children hold a primary role to enforce rules and enact control (Taylor, 2016a). From a safeguarding perspective, authoritarian parenting (involving setting high levels of demand and control while offering little warmth and acceptance) and exposure to extreme parenting environments have been associated with a range of negative outcomes including aggression, anti-social behaviour, and emotional and mental health problems (Earle, 2013; O'Connor and Scott, 2007). In terms of the quality of supervision within the youth justice estate, there are growing concerns regarding the suitability and calibre of staff and their ability to meet the needs of children that represent the most vulnerable, challenging, and troubled in society; most notable are reports that staff are ill-equipped and lacking the required skills, knowledge, and experience to fulfil their roles (Medway Improvement Board, 2016; Ofsted, 2017c; Taflan, 2017; Taylor, 2016a; Youth Custody Improvement Board, 2017). The youth justice estate is also subject to understaffing and retention issues (HM Chief Inspector of Prisons, 2017a; Taylor, 2016a), undermining capacity to address rising violence and resulting in staff feeling unsafe and demoralised (Youth Custody Improvement Board, 2017). These staffing issues have a considerable impact upon children who have to spend more time in their cells and experience deterioration of access to education, health, and wider services (Taylor, 2016a). Staffing shortages have also impacted upon children's relationships with and access to responsible adults, for example, Taflan (2017) has reported a decline in the number of children having designated key workers and an increased number of children feeling they have no one to turn to for help and support. The allocation and role of key workers is particularly significant within the secure estate as they are seen to be impartial, separate to the prison system, and providers of advocacy support for young people (Prison and Probation Ombudsman, 2015). What is happening reflects a perverse amplification of authoritarianism; the consequence of insufficient staffing levels, inadequate supervision, and a failure to maintain safety is the escalation of control, restriction, and regulation, thus culminating in a harsher regime concerned with containment and risk management rather than rehabilitation and child welfare. As noted by Gooch (2016), such approaches serve only to exacerbate children's 'pains of imprisonment' (p. 292).

Ensure access to appropriate medical care or treatment

Young people within the youth justice secure estate represent a demographic group with disproportionately high levels of physical, emotional, and mental health needs, often entering the system with conditions that have previously been undiagnosed or untreated (British Medical Association, 2014; Royal College of Paediatrics and Child Health, 2013). Primary physical health problems include sexually transmitted infections, blood-borne viruses, dental issues, visual and auditory impairment, and long-term conditions such as asthma, diabetes, and epilepsy (NHS England, Youth Justice Board and Public Health England, 2016). Substance misuse represents a primary health issue, with 31% of young people entering YOIs having a drug problem upon arrival (Taflan, 2017). Young people with disabilities are also disproportionately represented (Council for Disabled Children, 2017); 27% of young people in STCs and 19% in YOIs consider themselves to have a disability (Taflan, 2017). However, it is worthy to note that such official figures are based upon self-reports rather than objective measures or assessment. There is also a growing body of evidence highlighting significant prevalence of neurodevelopmental disorders such as learning disability, attention deficit/hyperactivity disorder, autistic spectrum disorder and communication disorders; the latter having greatest prevalence estimated between 60–90% of young people in custody (Hughes et al, 2012; Hughes and O'Byrne, 2016). Young people within the secure estate are also up to eight times more likely to have traumatic brain injury which can result in problems with memory, concentration, emotional awareness, impulse control, and social judgement, as well as being associated with broader issues including neurodevelopmental disorders, mental health issues, and substance misuse (Williams and Chitsabesan, 2016). In terms of mental health, just over one in four young people in YOIs self-report having an emotional or mental health problem, however, this figure is far surpassed by findings from a Young Minds study which identified high rates of co-morbidity, with 80% of young people in the secure estate having two or more mental health disorders (Campbell and Abbott, 2013). Despite the complex health needs of children in custody, there are consistent reports that these needs are often not being met (British Medical Association, 2014; Lennox, 2014; Medway Improvement Board, 2016; Williams and Chitsabesan, 2016; Youth Custody Improvement Board, 2017); young people in custody experience difficulties in accessing medication, nurses, doctors, dentists, and experience delays of transfer to mental health services (see British Medical Association, 2014; HM Chief Inspector of Prisons, 2017a; 2017c; Taflan, 2017). The potential for harm associated with problematic access to health services within the secure estate appears to have been subject to limited scrutiny, which in itself is a significant cause for concern considering the vulnerability and complexity of needs among young people within such settings.

Neglect of, or unresponsiveness to, a child's basic emotional needs

According to Maslow (1943), basic emotional needs include safety (personal security, health, and wellbeing), esteem (self-esteem, acceptance, and being valued by others) and social belonging (family, friendships, and intimate relationships); failing to meet these needs is the most common factor in cases of child maladjustment and psychopathology. The ability to develop and maintain reciprocal and loving relationships forms part of widely adopted definitions of mental health and wellbeing; this is a key indicator, as well as risk factor, for child and adolescent mental health (Earle, 2013; National Institute for Health and Care Excellence 2013). Family dynamics also represent a significant risk factor associated with youth offending, including such issues as impoverished parental involvement, poor family bonding, family conflict, and intrafamilial maltreatment and abuse (Hawkins et al, 2000; Jacobson et al, 2010). It may therefore not be surprising that 38% of young people in the youth justice secure estate have been in local authority care (Simmonds, 2016), or that 72% of these young people have experienced abuse and 57% have experienced significant loss (Boswell, 1996 in Wright and Liddle, 2014). Family stability and support is of paramount importance as expressed by children (Gooch, 2016; The Children's Society, 2017) and a lack of family contact and support undermines mental health, emotional wellbeing, and leaves children feeling isolated within the secure estate (British Medical Association, 2014). Maintaining contact with family and friends emerges as a significant issue for young people within secure settings, with 56% of boys in YOIs reporting that contact with family is problematic; only a third receive visits from friends or family on a weekly basis (Taflan, 2017). Young people have also reported difficulties with accessing telephone calls and there is a significant decline in the number of boys who have daily use of a telephone (HM Chief Inspector of Prisons, 2016; HM Chief Inspector of Prisons, 2017b; Taflan, 2017). Further difficulties include delays in the allocation of telephone personal identification numbers, resulting in new arrivals being unable to call home for up to three weeks (HM Chief Inspector of Prisons, 2016).

There is also a growing trend of young offenders being accommodated further away from home; the Youth Justice Board and Ministry of Justice (2018) attribute this to a range of factors including a shortage of available local placements and placement capacity to manage risk or meet the needs of individual young people. HM Inspectorate of Prisons (2016b) has published a thematic report about the *impact of distance from home on children in custody* raising notable concerns about the negative outcomes and difficulties this issue presents to young people, particularly in relation to maintaining relationships with family and carers. The report proposes that accommodating children far from home presents unnecessary barriers and undermines children's rights to regular and frequent visits when deprived of their liberty under United Nations human rights standards. Findings from this thematic review demonstrate a direct link between the distance from home and the number of visits young people receive from family, friends, and community-based professionals involved with their care: 'Those children held furthest from home (over 100 miles) frequently said that their parents either no longer visited or visited monthly or less' (p. 22). Many young people have also raised concerns about the cost, travelling times, and arduous journeys faced by their families when visiting. Findings from this report and others (see Children's Commissioner, 2017) highlight the significant potential for negative outcomes associated with disrupting family and community ties, thus affecting the vulnerability, loneliness, mood, and behaviour of young people, while undermining parental or carer involvement and support, community resettlement, and desistance. For children looked after by local authorities, this issue is particularly acute, as they are significantly less likely to receive weekly visits (HM Chief Inspector of Prisons, 2017a) and may have a greater reliance upon support from community-based professionals. However, young people's access to support within the secure estate is in decline as previously described, with limited and inequity of access, contact, and support from professionals including mentors, key workers, personal officers, chaplains, and external agencies such as Childline and Samaritans (HM Chief Inspector of Prisons, 2016; Taflan, 2017).

Sexual abuse

There exists limited reliable evidence relating to coercive sex and peer sexual violence in prisons in the UK (Howard League for Penal Reform, 2015). However, there is recognition that peer sexual abuse constitutes almost half of all known cases within children's residential institutions, and that this issue is often overlooked (Timmerman and Schreuder, 2014). According to HM Inspectorate of Prisons, 1% of children in YOIs and STCs have reported being sexually abused by peers (Taflan, 2017); however this figure is based upon children's self-reports and is unlikely to reflect an accurate measure because of children's reluctance to report peer sexual abuse to staff (Howard League for Penal Reform, 2015). Boys are particularly unlikely to disclose sexual abuse because of social norms associated with masculinity and fear of labelling; for these reasons, incidents are sophisticated and carefully concealed (Gooch and Treadwell, 2015) and boys are considered to be a 'hidden group' due to acute under-reporting of this issue (Fox, 2016: 15). The number of children in custody for sexual offences is increasing and this discrete cohort constitutes 9% of the secure estate population (Youth Justice Board and Ministry of Justice, 2018). This is significant because children who may be vulnerable to sexual abuse and exploitation are accommodated alongside children with histories of sexually harmful behaviour. Children who engage in sexually harmful behaviours have often themselves been victims of sexual abuse, and furthermore, boys have been found to be particularly vulnerable to peer-sexual exploitation in gang situations (Fox, 2016). This is particularly salient amid growing concerns surrounding gang-related problems within the secure estate, with 47% of children experiencing gang-related difficulties upon arrival (Taflan, 2017). The Howard League for Penal Reform (2015) have concluded that a secure estate consisting of large, closed institutions with high levels of violence, poor staffing ratios, and shared cells amplifies the risk of sexual abuse and exploitation of children by their peers.

Children in the secure estate have reported being sexually abused by staff, this issue also affecting 1% of children (Taflan, 2017). This figure is likely to reflect the tip of the iceberg as the majority of institutional child sexual abuse cases are not reported and the issue is believed to be extensive (Kaufman, 2016; Mcalinden, 2006). The Howard League for Penal Reform (2015) has concluded 'It is complacent to assume that staff cannot sexually abuse children in prisons in England and Wales' (p. 8). Willow (2015a) has chronicled an extensive number of cases in which secure estate staff across a range of institutions have been sacked, charged, or convicted as a consequence of inappropriate sexual contact, sexual offences, or possessing, making, or distributing indecent images of children. Operation Hydrant, the national policing response to historic institutional child abuse in England and Wales, currently has open cases relating to 34 prisons/YOIs which are subject to police investigation (National Police Chief's Council, 2017). According to the Independent Inquiry into Child Sexual Abuse (2018), children in the secure estate are particularly vulnerable to sexual abuse and little is known about the extent to which institutions have enacted their duty to protect them. Lack of access to and separation from family is seen as a particular vulnerability factor; in addition, children may be targeted where they are seen as 'problem children' or stigmatised by an organisation as this compromises their credibility and the subsequent likelihood of being believed (National Crime Agency, 2013: 16). Children with a history of sexual abuse are particularly vulnerable to re-victimisation (Fisher et al., 2017), as noted by Lord Carlile of Berriew (2006), 'Many children in custody have experienced past sexual abuse, often by adults ostensibly in positions of authority' (p. 47). Children with disabilities such as behavioural disorders, communication disorders, and intellectual disabilities are also at increased risk of sexual abuse (Kaufman et al, 2016), these issues being particularly prevalent among the secure estate population (see Hughes et al., 2012; Hughes and O'Byrne, 2016).

Children in the secure estate are unlikely to disclose sexual abuse perpetrated by staff as consistent with reasons for not reporting other forms of institutional abuse already discussed elsewhere in this chapter. However, within the specific context of sexual abuse, there exist additional barriers such as fear of increased abuse and retribution, because perpetrators within these settings are seen to hold complete power over children (Mcalinden, 2006; National Crime Agency, 2013). Perpetrators will seek to manipulate institutional conditions and environments that provide opportunity for sexually abusing children (Kaufman, 2016; Mcalinden, 2006), particularly where there exist significant power differentials between children and institutional staff (Kaufman et al., 2016) and where 'the organizational culture itself may be conducive to abuse of power and erosion of the primary functions of care and protection' (Mcalinden, 2006: 353). Cultural issues within institutions that influence the prevalence of child sexual abuse include poor leadership, ineffective policies and procedures, poor staff training/supervision, and activities that discourage reporting (Kaufman, 2016; National Crime Agency, 2013); the prevalence of these issues 'facilitates a malign climate which colludes with those inclined to sexually abuse children' (National Crime Agency, 2013: 5). Further significant institutional conditions and practices that place children at risk of sexual abuse include routine use of force and reward schemes that can be manipulated to gain compliance or punish children as a means of coercion and control (National Crime Agency, 2013). Willow (2015a) has raised significant concern around practices for the strip searching in children within the secure estate, including the forcible removal of children's clothing while being restrained; such practices still remain prevalent within the secure estate (HM Chief Inspector of Prisons, 2017d). Strip searching is described as 'a manifestation of power relations' which is demeaning and dehumanising to children (Lord Carlile of Berriew, 2006: 58) and the Howard League for Penal Reform (2016) have reported continually coming across cases involving the inappropriate strip searching of children within the youth justice secure estate.

Preventing impairment of children's health or development

There is overwhelming evidence that the incarceration of children is more damaging than rehabilitative, and the negative consequences are such that normal health, development, and transition into adulthood are impaired (Lambie and Randell, 2013). Aside from the high rates of pre-existing mental health problems and heightened potential for further exacerbation of such conditions within the secure estate, are issues directly attributed to the hostility, stress, and toxicity of the secure environment; the British Medical Association (2014) describes the placement of children within prison environments as detrimental to mental health, wellbeing, and emotional development and highlight a range of psychological responses including elevated levels of anxiety, depression, and subsequent difficulties with attention, empathy, emotional cognition, and the ability to form social bonds. The Youth Justice Board and Ministry of Justice (2017) have reported rising rates of self-harm, with 1,400 incidents recorded in the year ending 2016, an issue affecting 9% of children in the youth justice estate. However, Gyateng et al. (2013) suggest that recorded figures may be ambiguous and underestimated due to unclear or undetected cases; they found that secure estate staff estimate 75% of young people in STCs and 20% of young people in YOIs pose a risk to themselves. Jacobson et al. (2010) found mental health to be the primary health issue affecting children, with self-harm, suicide attempts, and the potential inability of a child to cope mentally or emotionally when placed in custody representing the most common practitioner concerns. According to a study conducted by Gyateng et al. (2013), youth offending team staff recorded concerns about the vulnerability of children if imprisoned in 59% of cases involving STC placement and 39% of cases involving YOI placement; furthermore, there existed a 23% margin of error whereby children identified as vulnerable by youth offending team practitioners had not been identified by secure estate staff. The Youth Custody Improvement Board (2017) have exposed a lack of information and analysis surrounding children's levels of need, specifically citing the failure to report on the prevalence, treatment and processes for assessing mental health needs as an example. These findings led the Board to conclude that

> in the Board's view there is not sufficient evidence to draw robust conclusions about the level of need in the estate, and the extent to which those needs are being addressed, despite the very small number of young people involved.
> *(Youth Custody Improvement Board (2017: 4)*

These issues suggest impoverished systems and practices in preventing detrimental outcomes on two counts; firstly, by failing to identify and respond to children's needs, and secondly by knowingly exposing children to harm associated with penal institutionalisation where there exist concerns about their emotional and mental ability to cope with placement in such settings.

Prison environments also offer impoverished conditions for supporting child development; there is universal acknowledgement that healthy adolescent development is best promoted through provision of diverse opportunities for learning and environments that nurture attributes such as self-efficacy, self-worth, morality, empathy, and interpersonal bonding (see for example Lerner et al., 2000; McNeely and Blanchard, 2009). The youth justice custody population largely consists of boys between the ages of 15–17 who have yet to reach emotional, social, and cognitive maturity (Howard League for Penal Reform, 2015; Youth Justice Board and Ministry of Justice, 2018) and this age range represents a significant developmental stage for independent functioning, moral correctness, emotional resilience, and identity formation (McNeely and Blanchard, 2009). In addition to being deprived of the conditions required for normal and healthy development, imprisoned children are particularly vulnerable to developmental delay or impairment as a consequence of prolonged exposure to social, environmental, and psychological stressors associated with such settings (British Medical Association, 2014); this includes potential for neurodevelopmental damage which often manifests as emotional and behaviour difficulties. Impairment to psychosocial development, including the ability to form and maintain relationships with others, affects transition into adulthood and capacity for community reintegration and resettlement (Lambie and Randell, 2013). The Howard League for Penal Reform (2015) have highlighted particular concerns about the impact of imprisonment upon boys' sexual development, sexual identity, and ability to form intimate or romantic relationships; furthermore, high levels of violence within the secure estate are cited as a risk factor for sexual aggression. In terms of physical development, recent evidence has shown that children within the youth justice estate are presented with limited opportunity for physical activity and exercise (CPT, 2017; HM Chief Inspector of Prisons, 2017; Gyateng et al. (2013); HM Chief Inspector of Prisons (2017a) has reported stark exercise yards and inadequate access in a majority of YOIs.

Ensuring children are growing up in circumstances consistent with provision of safe and effective care

The state has a duty to set the highest standard of care when children are deprived of their liberty (Lord Carlile of Berriew, 2006). Following a catalogue of inspection reports that expose failings across the system, the Youth Custody Improvement Board (2017) have observed 'a clear deterioration in the quality of provision' (p.1). Both the Youth Custody Improvement Board and the Youth Justice Board have conceded the secure estate is not fit for purpose and a failure to intervene to remedy this state of affairs. In terms of provision of *safe and effective care*, the treatment of children by staff consistently emerges as an area of concern (see for example CPT, 2017; Crook, 2017; Howard League for Penal Reform, 2016; Willow, 2015a). The Youth Justice Board have highlighted the importance of caring staff, positive relationships, and a child-centred culture within the secure estate. Relationships between staff and children in their care are instrumental to understanding children's needs, supporting behaviour management, and facilitating positive engagement in interventions including education, training, and employment; ultimately, children's experience of custody is determined by the nature of their interactions and relationships with staff (Gyateng et al., 2013). The formation of therapeutic alliances with practitioners has shown to have prominence for children who place particular value upon open, warm, and non-judgemental relationships (Adler et al., 2016). Children have also highlighted the significance of positive relationships with staff as a primary factor for preventing violence and deescalating conflict without use of force (Children's Rights Alliance for England, 2013). The quality of relationships between children and staff vary across the system; it is of concern that only 61% of children report that staff treat them with respect and furthermore that 32% of boys report having been victimised by staff (HM Chief Inspector of Prisons, 2017a). Figures for children's claims of victimisation have been observed as high as 60% at Parc YOI where inspectors further identified an institutional failure to investigate the cause, despite having previously recommended such action (HM Chief Inspector of Prisons, 2017c). The most common form of victimisation reported across YOIs is insulting remarks as experienced by 15% of boys, 8% report having been subjected to physical assault (including being hit or kicked), and 7% have reported being threatened or intimidated. Children primarily attribute being victimised by staff to having made a complaint; furthermore, only 28% of boys are willing to report victimisation (Taflan, 2017). The interplay between these issues is significant; where there exists a situation in which only a small minority of children are willing to report abuse or make a complaint, and staff victimisation (or fear of victimisation) operates as a deterrent to reporting, it stands to reason that very little is actually known about the extent and scale of institutional abuse within the youth justice secure estate.

Children with disabilities, from Traveller communities, and with Black, Asian and Minority Ethnic (BAME) backgrounds are overrepresented in the youth justice system and secure estate (see Council for Disabled Children, 2017; Taflan, 2017; The Traveller Movement, 2016; Youth Justice Board and Ministry of Justice, 2018). Many children have reported being victimised by staff on the grounds of such issues as their nationality, race, religious beliefs, sexual orientation, and disability (Taflan, 2017). Children with BAME backgrounds tend to report more negatively on their experiences of custody, particularly in such areas as relationships and respectful or fair treatment by staff; they are five times more likely to report being victimised by staff based on their race, ethnic origin, or religion and are significantly more likely to have been restrained or placed in isolation (HM Chief Inspector of Prisons, 2017a; Taflan, 2017). Gypsy, Traveller, or Roma children are twice as likely to report being subjected to staff threats and intimidation and three times more likely to report being physically abused by staff than other children (The Traveller Movement, 2016). Children with disabilities or emotional and mental health issues are also twice as likely to report being victimised by staff, particularly relating to insulting remarks or being threatened and intimidated (Taflan, 2017). Aside from such disparities in the experiences of children, HM Chief Inspector of Prisons (2017a; 2017c; 2017d) has highlighted failures in governance, monitoring, and investigation of equality and diversity issues; redeployment of Equality Officers, lack of monitoring data, and failures to monitor outcomes for children with protected characteristics. Wider issues exposed include poor identification of children with disabilities, lack of monitoring and provision for gay or bisexual children, poor management of discrimination reports, and, perhaps of greatest concern, incognisance over the disproportionate treatment of young people with protected characteristics in such areas as separation, privilege schemes, and use of force. Children's experiences and perceptions of discrimination have significant and adverse effects on their wellbeing; this includes detrimental effects to self-esteem, mental health and educational engagement, and may cause feelings of alienation and aggression (Marks et al., 2015). The prevalence of problematic relationships, poor or differential treatment by staff, and perceptions or experiences of discrimination and abuse thus inevitably contribute to the toxicity of the secure environment and the subsequent stress experienced by children affected by such issues. Furthermore, little improvement is being achieved in these areas; overall, the youth justice secure estate has achieved only 29% of inspection recommendations associated with ensuring children are treated with respect and human dignity (HM Chief Inspector of Prisons, 2017a).

Children within youth justice secure settings are routinely subjected to use of force by staff (Children's Commissioner, 2017); the Youth Justice Board and

Ministry of Justice (2018) have reported 4,600 known incidents across an average custody population of 868 children during the year ending 2017. During this same period, there were 70 incidents of use of force that caused injury requiring medical treatment, of which four were sufficiently serious to require hospitalisation. Use of force in the youth justice secure estate may be enacted through personal safety techniques for the purpose of self-defence or the protection of others, or as part of an approved system of restraint and behaviour management: minimising and managing physical restraint (MMPR). Any use of force must be deemed necessary, reasonable, and proportionate, and used only as a last resort; this may include use of ratchet handcuffs and other pain-inducing techniques (Ministry of Justice, 2014). However, this policy contravenes recommendations from the Carlile Inquiry which concluded that use of handcuffs and pain-inducing practices is unacceptable and may be unlawful (Lord Carlile of Berriew, 2006; 2016). Use of force by staff leaves children feeling frightened, helpless, and unsafe; it also causes anger, aggression, and violence with potential for triggering trauma associated with experiences of past abuse and sexual violence (Children's Commissioner, 2017). Following a freedom of information request by Caroline Willow, there has emerged evidence that use of some approved restraint techniques may result in catastrophic injury to children, with a 40% chance of causing severe disability or death (Allison and Hattenstone, 2016). Further, Willow (2015b) has pointed out that a third of MMPR techniques involve infliction of severe pain and that the approved system lacks legal assurance for use of such practices. The Children's Commissioner (2016) has asserted that 'only techniques proven to be safe for children should be used and pain should never be deliberately inflicted in order to restrain a child' (p. 16). HM Chief Inspector of Prisons (2017a; 2017d) has observed poor de-escalation of conflict, overuse, and unacceptable practice relating to use of force and restraint, misapplication and inappropriate use of pain-inducing techniques, and, perhaps most alarming, use of restraint and pain-inducing techniques during the forcible strip-searching of children. Furthermore, concerns have emerged surrounding governance and poor oversight of incidents, non-attendance of health staff or MMPR coordinators, lack of staff experience or training, and incomplete or missing paperwork relating to use of force; for example, almost 300 documents were found to be missing at Wetherby and Keppel YOI, leading inspectors to conclude that 'the level and extent of use of force remained unclear' (HM Chief Inspector of Prisons, 2017a: 63).

Taking action to enable all children to have the best life chances

The life chances of children are undermined by exposure to multiple disadvantage; greater accumulation and exposure to disadvantage is associated with poorer outcomes in adolescence and adulthood (The Children's Society, 2017). Poverty, education, and employment are considered to be primary indicators for children's outcomes and subsequent life chances (Child Poverty Action Group, 2016). Education is seen to offer 'a powerful tool' to break the cycle of poverty and disadvantage for individuals, families, and countries, while providing the greatest opportunity for children's development and wellbeing; it is under this rationale that children's right to education is enshrined within the United Nations Convention on the Rights of the Child (Unicef, 2015: 4). Education is also seen as a 'mediator of social mobility' (Richards et al., 2016: 13) and a range of indicators across the domains of socio-economic status, family life, behavioural issues, education, and occupational attainment interact to influence and shape life outcomes. Such indicators are largely synonymous with risk and protective factors associated with youth violence and offending; the accumulation and influence of detrimental individual, family, education, and neighbourhood factors (including poverty) emerge as predictors of troubled and troublesome childhoods that often transcend into adulthood (see for example Hawkins et al., 2000; Farrington et al., 2016). Education issues such as poor engagement, school commitment, and attainment are often associated with youth offending (Brazier et al., 2010; Holden and Lloyd, 2004; Knight, 2014; Youth Justice Board, 2006). Factors such as school exclusion, truancy, poor engagement, and low attainment appear particularly prevalent among children within the secure estate. Approximately 90% of boys in custody have experienced school exclusion and persistent absence from education, with 63% being permanently excluded and 73% reporting a history of truancy. The majority of children in the secure estate are educationally disengaged upon arrival, 90% not having attended school before they reached the age of 16 and 39% not having attended school since the age of 14 or younger (see HM Chief Inspector of Prisons, 2017a; Ministry of Justice and Department for Education 2016). The education attainment gap between children in the secure estate and their peers is extreme, for example, only 1% of children serving a custodial sentence of 12 months or less have achieved five or more GCSEs at grade A*–C (Ministry of Justice and Department for Education, 2016). Many children in the secure estate are 'reluctant learners' or apprehensive about education as a consequence of previous negative experiences (Taylor, 2016b: 18). Such negative encounters may be reinforced or further amplified where secure settings replicate traditional or conventional approaches to teaching and learning that have already failed children embroiled in the youth justice system (Little, 2015; Taylor, 2016a; Taylor, 2016b). Children have consistently expressed that education provision within the secure estate is under-resourced and poor (Youth Custody Improvement Board, 2017) and there exists 'little evidence of high quality provision' (p. 7). Ofsted (2017c) have described outcomes for children in STCs and YOIs as sometimes being 'extremely poor' (p. 18) and has judged all current STC provision to be inadequate or requiring improvement overall; furthermore, all providers share a requirement for improvement in the area of children's achievement (Ofsted 2017a; 2017b; 2017d). The prison environment does not present a context that is conducive to learning, as observed by the Youth

Custody Improvement Board (2017), 'the majority of classrooms the Board saw contained bolted chairs facing a board at the front, were uninspiring and the available equipment was poor' (p. 10). Furthermore, there have been a range of issues identified surrounding the provision of education, including problematic teaching methods, limited resources, poor management of behaviour and discipline, lack of aspirational cultures, poor progression opportunities, limited places, and a narrow curriculum to name but a few (see, for example, Lanskey, 2016; Little, 2015; Taylor, 2016a; Parliamentary Office for Science and Technology, 2016).

The current nature of the youth justice estate is such that a range of operational and structural barriers to children's participation in education have emerged. Secure settings are consistently failing to meet weekly education attendance requirements and have low overall attendance and engagement (see CPT, 2017; HM Chief Inspector of Prisons, 2017a; Howard League for Penal Reform, 2017). This issue is primarily attributed to staffing shortages, time spent by children in segregation, high levels of violence, and conflicting demands for health or legal appointments such as court appearances (CPT, 2017; HM Chief Inspector of Prisons, 2017a; Parliamentary Office for Science and Technology, 2016; Taylor, 2016a). Although a range of courses appear to be available in principle, these are not accessible to children in practice (CPT, 2017; HM Chief Inspector of Prisons, 2017a; Lanskey, 2016; Little, 2015). Cumulatively, these issues are particularly problematic because learning environments and children's perceptions of investment in their education are cornerstones of their engagement, school connectedness, commitment to learning, and subsequent attainment (Centers for Disease Control and Prevention, 2009; Public Health England, 2014). As noted by Lanskey (2016),

> through the range of courses available (in practice as opposed to on paper) and the quality of its delivery, young people learned the extent to which staff, the establishment and the criminal justice system as a whole were committed to their personal development.
>
> *(Lanskey, 2016: 4)*

Commentators have highlighted that barriers to children accessing education provision represents a failure to meet their needs, for example, Little (2015) found that children's engagement in education was undermined by preoccupation with concerns about issues such as personal safety and accommodation arrangements following release. There may also be further questions to be asked about the nature of children's educational needs and whether existing educational programmes are fit for purpose. Taylor (2016b) has pointed out that children's level of access and number of hours spent in education tell us little about the quality of education or outcomes achieved. Current discourse about education provision centres largely upon development of literacy and numeracy skills as stand-alone subjects or as integrated into vocational programmes (see for example Parliamentary Office for Science and Technology, 2016; Taylor, 2016a). This focus is driven by wider policies aimed at tackling low levels of basic skills among the adult population, whereby higher levels of literacy and numeracy attainment are associated with greater productivity, employability, welfare, and health outcomes (see for example Hume et al., 2018; Kuczera et al., 2016; Ofsted, 2013). This agenda also provides a strong foundation for the education of young offenders because literacy and numeracy skills are seen as essential to educational progression, entry into the labour market, and subsequent reduced recidivism (Brazier et al., 2010). However, considering the traumatic histories, behavioural difficulties, and developmental needs of children in the secure estate, available evidence suggests that targeted education programmes that offer focus upon social and emotional learning (self-awareness, motivation, self-control, social skills, and resilience) have greater significance for educational outcomes, life chances, and preventing violence and offending (Feinstein, 2015; Youth Justice Board, 2006). The Prisoner's Education Trust have called for a broader definition of education that extends to include life skills, integration of education and therapeutic interventions, and wider opportunities for learning (Taylor, 2016b); 'Education in isolation will not address all the underlying emotional, attachment and behavioural issues which are ingrained within young people because of their early year experiences' (p. 8). In view of children's life experiences and vulnerabilities, the National Association of Youth Justice have promoted a vision for secure care that combines high quality education, care, and promotion of healthy development in recognition that children must first be 'education ready' before they can successfully engage in education (Bateman, 2016: 8).

Following their time in custody; nearly 70% of children are reconvicted within a year of leaving the secure estate (Ministry of Justice 2016, in Prison Reform Trust, 2017). Such poor offending outcomes for children following resettlement is attributed to the failure of secure institutions to manage behaviour, provide education, and meet the needs of children (HM Inspectorate of Probation, 2015). Furthermore, a link between the harshness of the custodial environment and the likelihood of children reoffending upon release has been established; under such conditions, children are also more likely to subsequently engage in prolific and priority offending (Lotti, 2016). According to HM Chief Inspector of Prisons (2017a), there is an expectation that children spend ten hours out of cell per day and existing provision for this is inadequate in the majority of YOIs. This issue has also been observed by the CPT (2017) who called for urgent action to ensure greater involvement in purposeful activity such as education, rehabilitation, and preparation for release, along *with* 'considerably more time-out-of cell than currently provided' (p. 57). Although the vast majority of young people within the secure estate are allocated case workers, less than half believe their case worker has helped them prepare for release and only 41% of boys feel that they have a say about what will happen to them upon release (Taflan, 2017). HM Chief Inspector of Prisons (2017a) found that resettlement plans for children comprise generic targets that are not tailored to their individual needs and, further, that nearly half of children are not even aware of their personal plan. In a thematic review of resettlement services, HM Inspectorate of Probation (2015) found planning meetings to be ineffective, poor engagement of children and their parents/carers in the process, and a failure to organise education, training, or employment opportunities upon release. Children are often released from custody without transitional support or needs-led services in place; this includes appropriate accommodation arrangements and mental health provision. These issues have greater acuity for vulnerable children, including those with mental health problems, emotional or behavioural difficulties, or looked-after status, who experience the greatest anxiety and challenges with this regard (HM Chief Inspector of Prisons, 2017a; Taflan, 2017; Taylor, 2016a); Taylor (2016a) describes this issue as a break-down of access to support at the point of release. Children have expressed anxiety about release and their ability to cope and readjust to the outside world as a consequence of institutionalisation; experience of detention damages self-esteem, taints self-worth, and creates despondency about their future and reintegration into society (Children's Commissioner, 2017). Such concerns are legitimate in view of the fact that the stigma associated with offending, incarceration, and subsequent requirements for disclosure of criminal records ultimately has an adverse effect upon access to housing, education, and employment into adulthood (House of Commons Justice Committee, 2017).

Conclusion

The evidence presented indicates that there are widespread and systemic failures to promote the welfare of children and safeguard them from harm within the youth justice secure estate; this extends to every aspect of the statutory definition. By exposing children to such environments and the conditions that exist within them, authorities are knowingly subjecting children in their care to harm associated with maltreatment, lack of safety, ineffective care, and impairment to health, development, and subsequent life chances. These issues represent a catastrophic failure of child protection whereby children are not only likely to suffer significant harm but are known to be suffering significant harm. The statutory duty is clear; the *failure to act* to prevent harm to a child constitutes abuse, and those who have a stake in a system that is known to be detrimental and harmful to children are complicit.

References

Adler, J.R., Edwards, S.K., Scally, M., Gill, D., Puniskis, M.J., Gekoski, A., and Horvath, M.A.H. (2016) *What works in managing young people who offend? A summary of the international research*. London: Ministry of Justice.

Allison, E., and Hattenstone, S. (2016) Approved restraint techniques can kill, MoJ found. London: The Guardian. Retrieved from: www.theguardian.com/uk-news/2016/dec/05/approved-restraint-techniques-can-kill-children-moj-found

Bateman, T. (2016) The state of youth custody. National Association of Youth Justice Briefing [Online]. Retrieved from: http://thenayj.org.uk/wp-content/uploads/2016/10/NAYJ-Briefing-State-of-Youth-Custody-2016.pdf

BBC Panorama (2016) Teenage prison abuse exposed [Online]. Retrieved from: www.bbc.co.uk/programmes/b06ymzly

Birckhead, T.R. (2015) Children in isolation: the solitary confinement of youth. *Wake Forest Law Review*, 1, 5.

Brazier, L., Hurry, J., and Wilson, A. (2010) *Post-16 education and training provision for young people involved with crime* (Literature review). London: National Research and Development Centre for Adult Literacy and Numeracy.

British Medical Association (2014) *Young lives behind bars: the health and human rights of children and young people detained in the criminal justice system*. London: British Medical Association. Retrieved from: www.bma.org.uk/collective-voice/policy-and-research/equality/young-lives-behind-bars

Campbell, S., and Abbott, S. (2013) *Same old ... the experiences of young offenders with mental health needs*. London: Young Minds.

Centers for Disease Control and Prevention (2009) *School connectedness: strategies for increasing protective factors among youth*. Atlanta: Department of Health and Human Services. Retrieved from: www.cdc.gov/healthyyouth/protective/pdf/connectedness.pdf

Chambers, J. (2011) Enough on their plate. Food in young offender institutions for 15–17 year old boys. *Prison Service Journal*, 197, 53–56.

Chan, J.P.K., and Ireland, J.L. (2009) Fear of bullying among adult, young and juvenile prisoners: Its association with perpetration, victimization and behavioural predictors. *International Journal of Prisoner Health*, 5, 4, 223–232.

Child Poverty Action Group (2016) *Life chances indicators*. London: Child Poverty Action Group. Retrieved from: www.cpag.org.uk/sites/default/files/Life%20Chances%20Indicators%20-%20CPAG%20Recommendations.pdf

Children Act 1989. London: The National Archives [Online]. Retrieved from: www.legislation.gov.uk/ukpga/1989/41/section/31

Children Act 2004. London: The National Archives [Online]. Retrieved from: www.legislation.gov.uk/ukpga/2004/31/section/11

Children's Commissioner (2015) *Isolation and solitary confinement of children in the English youth justice secure estate*. Sheffield: Office of the Children's Commissioner. Retrieved from: www.childrenscommissioner.gov.uk/wp-content/uploads/2017/06/Unlocking-Potential-supporting-research.pdf

Children's Commissioner (2016) *UN Committee on the Rights of the Child Examinatiom of the Fifth Periodic Report of the United Kingdom of Great Britain and Northern Ireland. UK Children's Commissioners' recommendations May 2016*. Sheffield: Office of the Children's Commissioner. Retrieved from: www.niccy.org/media/2461/uk-childrens-commissioners-final-recommendations-crc-examination-of-the-uk-2016.pdf

Children's Commissioner (2017) *Children's voices. A review of the evidence on the subjective wellbeing of children in detention in England*. London: Children's Commissioner for England. Retrieved from: www.childrenscommissioner.gov.uk/wp-content/uploads/2017/11/CCO-review-of-evidence-on-the-subjective-wellbeing-of-children-in-detention-in-England-2.pdf

Children's Rights Alliance for England (2013) *Ending violence against children in custody Speaking Freely England Research Report*. London: Children's Rights Alliance for England. Retrieved from: http://crae.org.uk/media/26345/CYP-research-report.pdf

Cops, D., and Pleysier, S. (2014) Usual suspects, ideal victims and vice versa: the relationship between youth offending and victimization and the mediating influence of risky lifestyles. *European Journal of Criminology*, 11, 3, 361–378.

Council for Disabled Children (2017) *Young people with SEN in the secure estate* [Online]. Retrieved from: https://councilfordisabledchildren.org.uk/our-work/adulthood/policy/young-people-sen-secure-estate

Crook, F. (2017) *Safeguarding*. Howard League for Penal Reform [Online]. Retrieved from: https://howardleague.org/blog/safeguarding/

Dowler, E.A., and O'Connor, D. (2012) Rights-based approaches to addressing food poverty and food insecurity in Ireland and UK. *Social Science and Medicine*, 74, 1, 44–51.

Earle, J. (2013) Emotional and behaviour problems. In G. Foyle and V. Nathanson (Eds), *Growing up in the UK. Ensuring a healthy future for our children*. London: British Medical Association.

European Committee for the Prevention of Torture and Inhuman or Degrading Treatment or Punishment (2017) *Report to the Government of the United Kingdom carried out by the European Committee for the Prevention of Torture and Inhuman or Degrading Treatment or Punishment (CPT)*. Strasbourg: Council for Europe.

Farrington, D.P., Ttofi, M.M., and Piquero, A.R. (2016) Risk, promotive, and protective factors in youth offending: Results from the Cambridge study in delinquent development. *Journal of Criminal Justice*, 45, 63–70.

Feinstein, L. (2015) *Social and emotional learning: skills for life and work*. London: Early Intervention Foundation. Retrieved from: www.eif.org.uk/publications/social-andemotional-learning-skills-for-life-and-work/

Fisher, C., Goldsmith, A., and Soares, C. (2017) *The impacts of child sexual abuse: a rapid evidence assessment*. London: Independent Inquiry into Child Sexual Abuse. Retrieved from: www.iicsa.org.uk/document/iicsa-impacts-child-sexual-abuse-rapid-evidence-assessment-full-report-english

Fox, C. (2016) *'It's not on the radar'. The hidden diversity of children and young people at risk of sexual exploitation in England*. Ilford: Barnardos. Retrieved from: www.barnardos.org.uk/it_s_not_on_the_radar_report.pdf

Gooch, K. (2016) A childhood cut short: child deaths in penal custody and the pains of child imprisonment. *The Howard Journal of Crime and Justice*, 55, 3, 278–294.

Gooch, K., and Treadwell, J. (2015) *Prison bullying and victimisation*. Birmingham: Birmingham Law School, University of Birmingham. Retrieved from: www.birmingham.ac.uk/Documents/college-artslaw/law/Prison-Bullying-and-Victimisation.pdf

Gyateng, T., Moretti, A., May, T., and Turnbull, P. J. (2013) *Young people and the secure estate: needs and interventions*. London: Youth Justice Board for England and Wales.

Harvey, K. (2016) 'When I go to bed hungry and sleep, I'm not hungry': children and parents' experiences of food insecurity. *Appetite*, 99, 1, 235–244.

Hawkins, J.D., Herrenkohl, T.I., Farrington, D.P., Brewer, D., Catalano, R.F., Harachi, T. W., and Cothern, L. (2000) *Predictors of youth violence. Juvenile justice bulletin*. Washington DC: Office of Juvenile Justice and Delinquency Prevention.

HM Chief Inspector of Prisons (2016) *Report on an unannounced inspection of HMYOI Cookham Wood*. London: HM Inspectorate of Prisons. Retrieved from: www.justiceinspectorates.gov.uk/hmiprisons/wp-content/uploads/sites/4/2017/01/Cookham-Wood-Web-2016.pdf

HM Chief Inspector of Prisons (2017a) *HM Chief Inspector of Prisons for England and Wales annual report 2016–17*. London: Her Majesty's Inspectorate of Prisons. Retrieved from: www.justiceinspectorates.gov.uk/hmiprisons/wp-content/uploads/sites/4/2017/07/HMIP-AR_2016-17_CONTENT_11-07-17-WEB.pdf

HM Chief Inspector of Prisons (2017b) *Report on an unannounced inspection of HMP/YOI Feltham (Feltham B – young adults)*. London: HM Inspectorate of Prisons. Retrieved from: www.justiceinspectorates.gov.uk/hmiprisons/wp-content/uploads/sites/4/2017/06/Feltham-B-Web-2017.pdf

HM Chief Inspector of Prisons (2017c) *Report on an unannounced inspection of juvenile unit at HMYOI Parc*. London: HM Inspectorate of Prisons. Retrieved from: www.justiceinspectorates.gov.uk/hmiprisons/wp-content/uploads/sites/4/2017/04/Parc-Web-2017-1.pdf

HM Chief Inspector of Prisons (2017d) *Report on the unannounced inspection of HMYOI Wetherby and Keppel*. London: HM Inspectorate of Prisons. Retrieved from: www.justi

ceinspectorates.gov.uk/hmiprisons/wp-content/uploads/sites/4/2017/09/Wetherby-Keppel-Web-2017.pdf

HM Chief Inspector of Prisons (2017e) *Report on an unannounced inspection of HMYOI Werrington*. London: HM Inspectorate of Prisons. Retrieved from: www.justiceinspectorates.gov.uk/hmiprisons/wp-content/uploads/sites/4/2017/07/Werrington-Web-2017.pdf

HM Chief Inspector of Prisons (2018) *Report on an unannounced inspection of HMYOI Cookham Wood*. London: HM Inspectorate of Prisons. Retrieved from: www.justiceinspectorates.gov.uk/hmiprisons/wp-content/uploads/sites/4/2018/01/Cookham-Wood-Web-2017.pdf

HM Government (2015) *Working together to safeguard children. A guide to inter-agency working to safeguard and promote the welfare of children 2015*. London: The National Archives. Retrieved from: www.gov.uk/government/uploads/system/uploads/attachment_data/file/592101/Working_Together_to_Safeguard_Children_20170213.pdf

HM Inspectorate of Prisons (2016a) *Life in prison: food. A findings paper by HM Inspectorate of Prisons*. London: HMIP. Retrieved from: www.justiceinspectorates.gov.uk/hmiprisons/wp-content/uploads/sites/4/2016/09/Life-in-prison-Food-Web-2016.pdf

HM Inspectorate of Prisons (2016b) *The impact of distance from home on children in custody. A thematic review by HM Inspectorate of Prisons*. London: HMIP. Retrieved from: www.justiceinspectorates.gov.uk/hmiprisons/wp-content/uploads/sites/4/2016/09/The-impact-of-distance-from-home-on-children-in-custody-Web-2016.pdf

HM Inspectorate of Probation (2015) *Joint thematic inspection of resettlement services to children by youth offending teams and partner agencies. A joint inspection by: HM Inspectorate of Probation Care Quality Commission Ofsted*. Manchester: HM Inspectorate of Probation. Retrieved from: www.cqc.org.uk/sites/default/files/20150311_youth_resettlement_report.pdf

Holden, T., and Lloyd, R. (2004) *The role of education in enhancing life chances and preventing offending*. London: Home Office.

House of Commons Justice Committee (2017) *Disclosure of youth criminal records. First report of session 2017–19*. London: House of Commons. Retrieved from: https://publications.parliament.uk/pa/cm201719/cmselect/cmjust/416/416.pdf

Howard League for Penal Reform (2015) *Commission on sex in prison. Healthy sexual development of children in prison briefing paper 4*. London: Howard League for Penal Reform. Retrieved from: https://howardleague.org/wp-content/uploads/2016/03/Healthy-sexual-development-of-children-in-prison.pdf

Howard League for Penal Reform (2016) *The Carlile Inquiry 10 years on. The use of restraint, solitary confinement and strip-searching on children*. London: The Howard League for Penal Reform. Retrieved from: http://howardleague.org/wp-content/uploads/2016/06/Carlile-Inquiry-10-years-on.pdf

Howard League for Penal Reform (2017) *High Court declares a child's isolation and lack of education at Feltham prison unlawful*. The Howard League for Penal Reform [Online]. Retrieved from: http://howardleague.org/news/felthamsolitaryconfinementhighcourtjudgment/

Hughes, N., and Peirse O'Byrne, K. (2016) Disabled inside: neurodevelopmental impairments among young people in custody. *Prison Service Journal*, 226, 14–21.

Hughes, N., Williams, H., Chitsabesan, P., Davies, R., and Mounce, L. (2012) *Nobody made the connection: the prevalence of neurodisability in young people who offend*. London: Office of the Children's Commissioner. Retrieved from: www.childrenscommissioner.gov.uk/wp-content/uploads/2017/07/Nobody-made-the-connection.pdf

Hume, S., O'Reilly, F., Groot, B., Chande, R., Sanders, M., Hollingsworth, A., Ter Meer, J., Barnes, J., Booth, S., Kozman, E., and Soon, X. (2018) *Improving engagement and attainment in maths and English courses: insights from behavioural research. Research and project report*. London: Department for Education Behavioural Insights Team.

Independent Inquiry into Child Sexual Abuse (2018) The sexual abuse of children in custodial institutions [Online]. Retrieved from: www.iicsa.org.uk/investigations/sexual-abuse-of-children-in-custody-including-medomsley-youth-detention-centre

Jacobson, J., Bhardwa, B., Gyateng, T., Hunter, G., and Hough, M. (2010) *Punishing disadvantage a profile of children in custody*. London: Prison Reform Trust. Retrieved from: www.prisonreformtrust.org.uk/portals/0/documents/punishingdisadvantage.pdf

Kaufman, K., Erooga, M., Stewart, K., Zatkin, J., McConnell, E., Tews, H., and Higgins, D. (2016) *Risk profiles for institutional child sexual abuse. A literature review*. Sydney: Royal Commission into Institutional Responses to Child Sexual Abuse. Retrieved from: https://aifs.gov.au/publications/risk-profiles-institutional-child-sexual-abuse

Kirk, D.S., and Hardy, M. (2012) The acute and enduring consequences of exposure to violence on youth mental health and aggression. *Justice Quarterly*, 1–29.

Knight, V. (2014) Framing education and learning in youth justice in England and Wales: some outcomes for young offender intervention. *British Journal of Community Justice*, 12, 1, 49–67.

Kuczera, M., Field, S., and Windisch, H. C. (2016) *Building skills for all: a review of England. Policy insights from the survey of adult skills*. Paris: Organisation for Economic Co-operation and Development. Retrieved from: www.oecd.org/unitedkingdom/building-skills-for-all-review-of-england.pdf

Lambie, I., and Randell, I. (2013) The impact of incarceration on juvenile offenders. *Clinical Psychology Review*, 33, 448–459.

Lanskey, C. (2016) Formal and informal learning in custodial settings for young people. *Prison Service Journal*, 226, 3–7.

Lee, J. (2016) Lonely too long: redefining and reforming juvenile solitary confinement. *Fordham Law Review*, 85, 2, 845–876.

Lennox, C. (2014) The health needs of young people in prison. *British Medical Bulletin*, 112, 1, 17–25.

Lerner, R.M., Fisher, C.B., and Weinberg, R.A. (2000) Toward a science for and of the people: promoting civil society through the application of developmental science. *Child Development*, 71, 1, 11–20.

Little, R. (2015) Putting education at the heart of custody? The views of children on education in a young offender institution. *British Journal of Community Justice*, 13, 2, 27–46

Lord Carlile of Berriew. (2006) *An independent inquiry into the use of physical restraint, solitary confinement and forcible strip-searching of children in prisons, secure training centres and secure children's homes*. London: Howard League for Penal Reform. Retrieved from: http://howardleague.org/wp-content/uploads/2016/03/Carlile-Report-pdf.pdf

Lord Carlile of Berriew. (2016) Carlile Inquiry – 10 years on. *Prison Service Journal*, 226, 27–30.

Local Government Association (2017) Councils call for urgent action to improve safety in youth offending institutions. Local Government Association [Online]. Retrieved from: www.local.gov.uk/about/news/councils-call-urgent-action-improve-safety-youth-offending-institutions

Longfield, A. (2017) Damning description of youth detention system highlights need for urgent action from Ministry of Justice. Office for the Children's Commissioner [Online]. Retrieved from: www.childrenscommissioner.gov.uk/2017/07/18/damning-description-of-youth-detention-system-highlights-need-for-urgent-action-from-ministry-of-justice/

Lotti, G. (2016) *Tough on young offenders: harmful or helpful? Warwick Economics Research Papers*. Coventry: Department of Economics, University of Warwick.

Marks, A.K., Ejesi, K., McCullough, M.B., and Coll, C.G. (2015) Developmental implications of discrimination. In M.E. Lamb, and R.M. Lerner (Eds), *Handbook of child psychology and developmental science* (7th edn). New York: John Wiley & Sons, pp. 324–365.

Maslow, A.H. (1943) A theory of human motivation. *Psychological Review*, 50, 370–396.

Mcalinden, A. (2006) 'Setting 'em up': personal, familial and institutional grooming in the sexual abuse of children. *Social and Legal Studies*, 15, 3, 339–362.

McNeely, C., and Blanchard, J. (2009) *The teen years explained: a guide to healthy adolescent development*. Baltimore: Center for Adolescent Health at Johns Hopkins Bloomberg School of Public Health.

Medway Improvement Board (2016) Final report of the Board's advice to Secretary of State for Justice [Online]. Retrieved from: www.gov.uk/government/uploads/system/uploads/attachment_data/file/523167/medway-report.pdf

Méndez, J. (2011) Solitary confinement should be banned in most cases, UN expert says [Online]. Retrieved from: www.un.org/apps/news/story.asp?NewsID=40097#.WgGnK5S7XZ4

Méndez, J.E., Papachristou, A., Ordway, E., Fettig, A., and Shalev, S. (2016) *Seeing into solitary: a review of the laws and policies of certain nations regarding solitary confinement of detainees*. New York: United Nations Office of the High Commissioner for Human Rights.

Ministry of Justice (2014) *Use of force – implementation of minimising and managing physical restraint*. London: Ministry of Justice. Retrieved from: www.justice.gov.uk/downloads/offenders/psipso/psi-2014/psi-06-2014-use-of-force-in-yp-estate.pdf

Ministry of Justice and Department for Education (2016) *Understanding the educational background of young offenders*. London: Ministry of Justice. Retrieved from: www.gov.uk/government/uploads/system/uploads/attachment_data/file/577542/understanding-educational-background-of-young-offenders-full-report.pdf

National Crime Agency (2013) *CEOP thematic assessment – the foundations of abuse: a thematic assessment of the risk of child sexual abuse by adults in institutions*. London: National Crime Agency. Retrieved from: www.nationalcrimeagency.gov.uk/publications/49-ceop-institutions-thematic-assessment/file

National Institute for Health and Care Excellence (2013) *Social and emotional wellbeing for children and young people*. London: National Institute for Health and Care Excellence. Retrieved from: www.nice.org.uk/guidance/lgb12/resources/social-and-emotional-wellbeing-for-children-and-young-people-pdf-60521143067845

National Police Chief's Council (2017) *Operation Hydrant Statistics. Operation Hydrant – quarterly statistics – breakdown of live investigations up to and including 31 March* [Online]. Retrieved from: www.npcc.police.uk/Hydrant/Hydrant%20stats%2018%204%2017.pdf

NHS England, Youth Justice Board and Public Health England (2016) *Improving health and wellbeing services for children placed in the children and young people's secure estate*. London: NHS England. Retrieved from: www.england.nhs.uk/commissioning/wp-content/uploads/sites/12/2015/04/yjb-phe-parts-agree.pdf

O'Connor, T.G., and ScottS.B.C. (2007) *Parenting and outcomes for children*. York: Joseph Rowntree Foundation.

Ofsted (2013) *Improving literacy in secondary schools: a shared responsibility*. Manchester: Ofsted. Retrieved from: www.gov.uk/government/publications/improving-literacy-in-secondary-schools-a-shared-responsibility

Ofsted (2017a) *Inspections of secure training centres. Inspection of Medway STC*. Manchester: Ofsted. Retrieved from: www.justiceinspectorates.gov.uk/hmiprisons/inspections/medway-secure-training-centre-6/

Ofsted. (2017b) *Inspections of secure training centres. Inspection of Oakhill*. Manchester: Ofsted. Retrieved from: www.justiceinspectorates.gov.uk/hmiprisons/inspections/oakhill-secure-training-centre-5/

Ofsted (2017c) *The annual report of Her Majesty's Chief Inspector of Education, Children's Services and Skills 2016/17*. London: Ofsted. Retrieved from: www.gov.uk/government/uploads/system/uploads/attachment_data/file/666871/OfSted_Annual_Report_2016-17_Accessible.pdf

Ofsted (2017d) *Inspections of secure training centres. Inspection of Rainsbrook*. Manchester: Ofsted. Retrieved from: https://reports.OfSted.gov.uk/sites/default/files/documents/secure-training-centre-reports/rainsbrook/Rainsbrook%20STC%20OfSted%20report%20June%202017%20%28PDF%29.pdf

Owen, M., and Goldhagen, J. (2016) Children and solitary confinement: a call to action. *Paediatrics*, 137, 5, 1–3.

Owen, R., and Sweeting, A. (2007) *Hoodie or goodie? The link between violent victimisation and offending in young people: a research report*. London: Victim Support. Retrieved from: www.victimsupport.org.uk/sites/default/files/Hoodie%20or%20goodie%20report.pdf

Prison Reform Trust (2017) *Prison: the facts. Bromley Briefings Summer 2017*. London: Prison Reform Trust. Retrieved from: www.prisonreformtrust.org.uk/Portals/0/Documents/Bromley%20Briefings/Summer%202017%20factfile.pdf

Prisons and Probation Ombudsman (2015) *Why do women and young people in custody not make formal complaints?* London: Prisons and Probation Ombudsman. Retrieved from: www.ppo.gov.uk/app/uploads/2015/03/Why-do-women-and-young-people-in-custody-not-make-formal-complaints_final.pdf

Public Health England (2014) *The link between pupil health and wellbeing and attainment A briefing for head teachers, governors and staff in education settings*. London: Public Health England. Retrieved from: www.gov.uk/government/uploads/system/uploads/attachment_data/file/370686/HT_briefing_layoutvFINALvii.pdf

Raws, P. (2016) *Understanding adolescent neglect: troubled teens. A study of the links between parenting and adolescent neglect*. London: The Children's Society. Retrieved from: www.childrenssociety.org.uk/sites/default/files/troubled-teens-full-report-final.pdf

Richards, L., Garratt, E., Heath, A.F., Anderson, L., and Altintaş, E. (2016) *The childhood origins of social mobility: socio-economic inequalities and changing opportunities*. London: Social Mobility Commission. Retrieved from: www.gov.uk/government/uploads/system/uploads/attachment_data/file/528315/The_childhood_origins_of_social_mobility.pdf

Royal College of Paediatrics and Child Health (2013) *Children and young people in secure settings*. London: RCPCH. Retrieved from: www.rcpch.ac.uk/system/files/protected/page/Healthcare%20standards%20A4%20report%20pages%20english%20compressed%20FINAL.pdf

Seal, D., Nguyen, A., and Beyer, K. (2014) Youth exposure to violence in an urban setting. *Urban Studies Research*, 1–11.

Shalev, S. (2008) *A sourcebook on solitary confinement*. London: Mannheim Centre for Criminology, London School of Economics.

Simkins, S., Beyer, M., and Geis, L.M. (2012) The harmful use of isolation in juvenile facilities: the need for post-disposition representation. *Washington University Journal of Law and Policy*, 38, 241–287.

Simmonds, J. (2016) *Children in custody 2015–16. An analysis of 12–18-year olds' perceptions of their experiences in secure training centres and young offender institutions*. London: National Archives. Retrieved from: www.justiceinspectorates.gov.uk/hmiprisons/wp-content/uploads/sites/4/2016/11/Children-in-Custody-2015-16_WEB.pdf

Taflan, P. (2017) *Children in custody 2016–17. An analysis of 12–18-year-olds' perceptions of their experiences in secure training centres and young offender institutions*. London: HMIP. Retrieved from: www.justiceinspectorates.gov.uk/hmiprisons/wp-content/uploads/sites/4/2017/11/6.3903_HMIP_Children-in-Custody-2016-17_FINAL_WEB_221117.pdf

Taylor, A., and Loopstra, R. (2016) *Too poor to eat. Food insecurity in the UK*. London: Food Foundation. Retrieved from: http://foodfoundation.org.uk/wp-content/uploads/2016/07/FoodInsecurityBriefing-May-2016-FINAL.pdf

Taylor, C. (2016a) *Review of the youth justice system in England and Wales*. London: Ministry of Justice. Retrieved from: www.gov.uk/government/uploads/system/uploads/attachment_data/file/577103/youth-justice-review-final-report.pdf

Taylor, C. (2016b) *Great expectations. Towards better learning outcomes for young people and young adults in custody*. London: Prisoner's Education Trust.

The Children's Society (2017) *Good childhood report 2017*. London: The Children's Society. Retrieved from: www.childrenssociety.org.uk/sites/default/files/the-good-childhood-report-2017_full-report_0.pdf

The Parliamentary Office for Science and Technology (2016) *Education in youth custody*. London: Houses of Parliament. Retrieved from: http://researchbriefings.parliament.uk/ResearchBriefing/Summary/POST-PN-0524

The Traveller Movement (2016) *Overlooked and overrepresented: Gypsy, Traveller and Roma children in the youth justice system*. London: The Traveller Movement. Retrieved from: http://travellermovement.org.uk/wp-content/uploads/Overlooked-and-Overrepresented-Gypsy-Traveller-and-Roma-children-in-the-youth-justice-system.pdf

Timmerman, M.C., and Schreuder, P.R. (2014) Sexual abuse of children and youth in residential care: an international review. *Aggression and Violent Behavior*, 19, 6, 715–720.

Tsang, S. (2017) Troubled or traumatized youth? the relations between psychopathy, violence exposure, posttraumatic stress disorder, and antisocial behavior among juvenile offenders. *Journal of Aggression, Maltreatment & Trauma*, October, 1–15.

Unicef (2015) *Education*. New York: United Nations Children's Fund. Retrieved from: www.unicef.org/publicpartnerships/files/2014_Annual_Results_Report_Education.pdf

Wightwick, A. (2017) More than 100 violent assaults have taken place at a Welsh young offenders unit. *Wales Online* [Online]. Retrieved from: www.walesOnline.co.uk/news/wales-news/more-100-violent-assaults-taken-12908450

Wilkins, N., Tsao, B., Hertz, M., Davis, R., and Klevens, J. (2014) *Connecting the dots: an overview of the links among multiple forms of violence*. Atlanta: Centres for Disease Control and Prevention, National Center for Injury Prevention and Control and Oakland: Prevention Institute. Retrieved from: www.cdc.gov/violenceprevention/pdf/connecting_the_dots-a.pdf

Williams, W.H., and Chitsabesan, P. (2016) *Young people with traumatic brain injury in custody. An evaluation of a linkworker service for Barrow Cadbury Trust and the Disabilities Trust*. London: Barrow Cadbury Trust.

Willow, C. (2015a) *Children behind bars: why the abuse of child imprisonment must end*. Bristol: Policy Press.

Willow, C. (2015b) The UK's compliance with the United Nations Convention on the Rights of the Child Evidence to the Joint Committee on Human Rights from Carolyne Willow. Children in custody [Online]. Retrieved from: http://www.parliament.uk/documents/joint-committees/human-rights/Carolyne_Willow_submission_090315.pdf

Wright, S., and Liddle, M. (2014) *Young offenders and trauma: experience and impact a practitioner's guide*. London: Beyond Youth Custody. Retrieved from: www.beyondyouthcustody.net/wp-content/uploads/BYC-Trauma-experience-and-impact-practitioners-guide.pdf

Youth Justice Improvement Board (2017) *Findings and recommendations of the Youth Custody Improvement Board. 24 February 2017*. London: Ministry of Justice. Retrieved from: www.gov.uk/government/publications/youth-custody-improvement-board-findings-and-recommendations

Youth Justice Board (2006) *Barriers to engagement in education, training and employment*. London: Youth Justice Board for England and Wales. Retrieved from: http://dera.ioe.ac.uk/7999/1/Barriers%20to%20ETE%20report%20FINAL.pdf

Youth Justice Board (2011) *Young people's views on safeguarding in the secure estate. A User Voice report for the Youth Justice Board and the Office of the Children's Commissioner*. London: Youth Justice Board for England and Wales. Retrieved from: http://dera.ioe.ac.uk/2201/1/Young_Peoples_Views_on_Safeguarding.pdf

Youth Justice Board and Ministry of Justice (2017) *Youth justice statistics 2015/16 England and Wales*. London: Ministry of Justice and Youth Justice Board.

Youth Justice Board and Ministry of Justice (2018) *Youth justice statistics 2016/17 England and Wales*. London: Ministry of Justice.

15

IDENTIFYING BARRIERS AND FACILITATORS FOR EDUCATIONAL INCLUSION FOR YOUNG PEOPLE WHO OFFEND

Practitioner and youth perspectives

Jenny Twells

Educational outcomes for youth offenders are frequently poor at a time when qualifications and good literacy and numeracy skills are increasingly important for employment. Young people within the youth justice system face multiple challenges which prevent them from accessing or succeeding in the education system: some will be disaffected, some will have their education disrupted by their offending, some may have special educational needs (SEN) issues or will be classified as not in education, employment, and training (NEET). This chapter looks at barriers and facilitators for youth offenders' engagement with education based on a study carried out in one inner London local authority (O'Carroll, 2016).

Empirical evidence demonstrates that there are significant factors that increase the risk of young people becoming involved with crime such as attachment and relationships/parenting difficulties, becoming a child looked after (CLA), mental health issues, substance misuse, special educational learning needs, and that interacting systems can be barriers for young people who have offended to engage back into education (Hayward et al., 2004). Therefore, it is important to acknowledge that young people involved with offending often experience a combination of multiple barriers. Young people involved in persistent offending are considered to be the most vulnerable, and, therefore, an understanding of the wider issues is important in trying to implement interventions to avoid offending and increase inclusion (Soloman, 2010).

Bronfenbrenner's (1979) ecological model can be helpful when exploring the multiple factors that exist in systems around a young person. This model divides the environment into five different levels and is used to explain how everything in a young person and their environment affects how they will grow and develop. For young people, it is the family, neighbourhood, and school environments that are fundamental for shaping development and Bronfenbrenner used the notion that these systems overlap and interact. Therefore, the interactions between the numerous overlapping systems can increase the likelihood of negative outcomes for youth offenders. This model was used in the study to try to explore and understand the interactions of these systems around youth offenders. This would then help identify the barriers and facilitators for young people involved in crime to achieve success in education.

The Risk Factor Prevention Paradigm (RFPP) (Farrington, 2000), currently the dominant discourse in youth justice, is also a mapping tool linking the risk factors for engaging in crime and implementing prevention methods to overcome them; this could be argued to be similar with identifying risk factors engaging with education. The aims of this study were to identify the reasons for educational underperformance and explore how to increase young offenders' successful participation and reintegration back into education. This was achieved using a mixed method approach which involved collecting quantitative data from the Youth Offending Service (YOS) Asset information (n=283), and qualitative analysis of interviews with professionals working within the YOS (n=7), education and training providers (n=7), and a sample of young people (n=7) known to the YOS. The YOS was based in an area of London with high levels of crime related to gang activity and multiple deprivation issues.

Results from the qualitative data are presented using two thematic maps (one for professionals and one for young people) produced during the thematic analysis. Each overarching factor or level has a number of sub themes and although the factors are presented separately (Figures 15.1 and 15.2), it is important to consider how they interlink and overlap.

Systemic factors from professional perspectives

Systemic factors represented themes that are related to organisational, cultural, legislative, and universal issues. Systemic factors identified by professionals identified themes of joined up working, communication, working to targets and deadlines, devolved budgets, and fragmented services and across borough challenges (Figure 15.3).

Professionals identified the reality of multiple professionals working within a climate of austerity and the pressures of working to targets and deadlines. This resulted in professionals feeling frustrated with the practical difficulties with working with reduced resources within the organisation. The professionals identified several issues relating to the challenges of working and communicating with multiple agencies such as different professional agendas and multiple locations of staff.

> Working in the YOT you find out there are five of us working with the young person, so you go hang on, do you mind if we sit down and have a talk about them and find out who is doing what?
>
> *(YOT worker)*

At the systemic level, all professionals mentioned: multi-agency challenges, services being cut or relocated within the council, and poor information sharing.

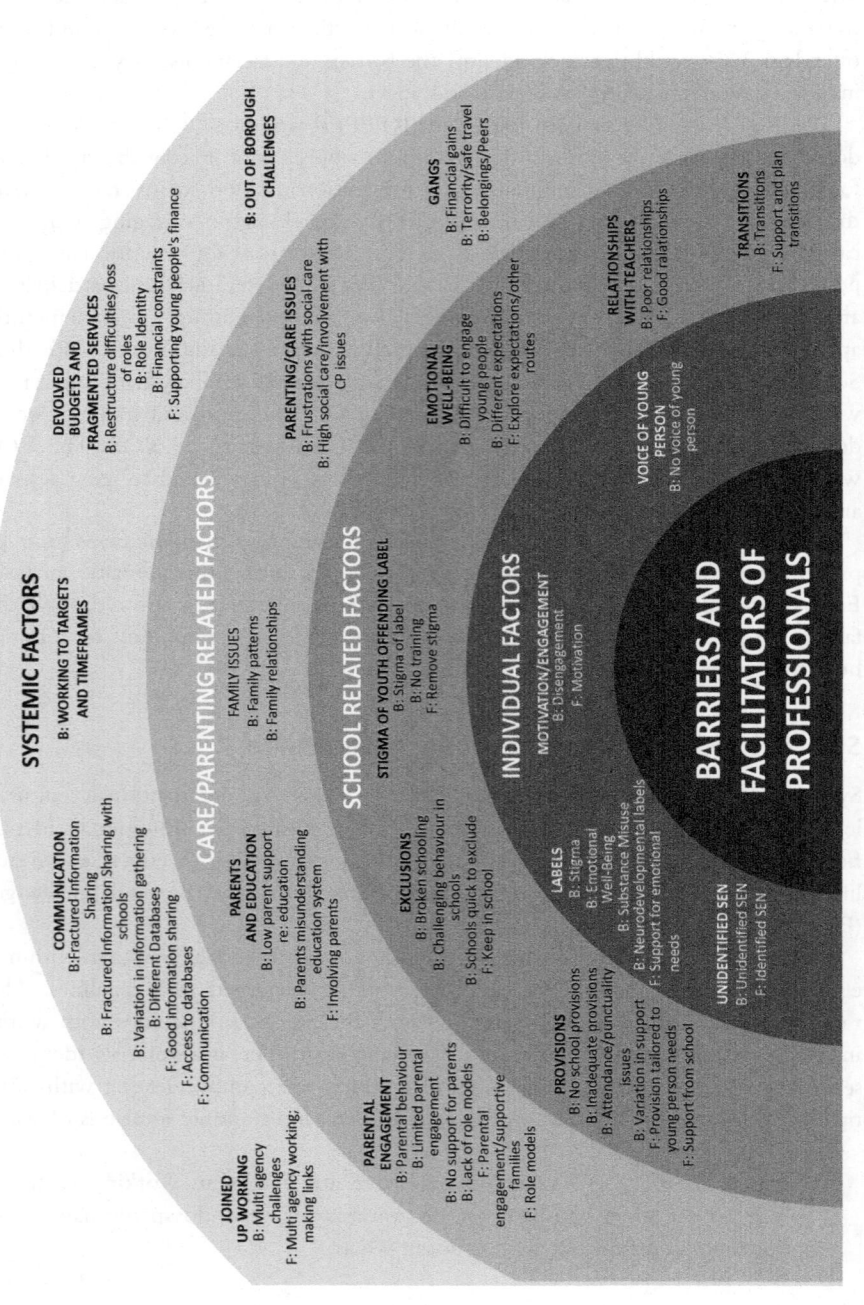

FIGURE 15.1 Barriers and facilitators: professional perspectives

SYSTEMIC FACTORS

- B: WORKING TO TARGETS AND TIMEFRAMES

COMMUNICATION
- B: Fractured Information Sharing
- B: Fractured Information Sharing with schools
- B: Variation in information gathering
- B: Different Databases
- F: Good information sharing
- F: Access to databases
- F: Communication

JOINED UP WORKING
- B: Multi agency challenges
- F: Multi agency working; making links

DEVOLVED BUDGETS AND FRAGMENTED SERVICES
- B: Restructure difficulties/loss of roles
- B: Role Identity
- B: Financial constraints
- F: Supporting young people's finance

- B: OUT OF BOROUGH CHALLENGES

CARE/PARENTING RELATED FACTORS

PARENTS AND EDUCATION
- B: Low parent support re: education
- B: Parents misunderstanding education system
- F: Involving parents

FAMILY ISSUES
- B: Family patterns
- B: Family relationships

PARENTING/CARE ISSUES
- B: Frustrations with social care
- B: High social care/involvement with CP issues

PARENTAL ENGAGEMENT
- B: Parental behaviour
- B: Limited parental engagement
- B: No support for parents
- B: Lack of role models
- F: Parental engagement/supportive families
- F: Role models

SCHOOL RELATED FACTORS

EXCLUSIONS
- B: Broken schooling
- B: Challenging behaviour in schools
- B: Schools quick to exclude
- F: Keep in school

STIGMA OF YOUTH OFFENDING LABEL
- B: Stigma of label
- B: No training
- F: Remove stigma

EMOTIONAL WELL-BEING
- B: Difficult to engage young people
- B: Different expectations
- F: Explore expectations/other routes

GANGS
- B: Financial gains
- B: Territory/safe travel
- B: Belongings/Peers

INDIVIDUAL FACTORS

PROVISIONS
- B: No school provisions
- B: Inadequate provisions
- B: Attendance/punctuality issues
- B: Variation in support
- F: Provision tailored to young person needs
- F: Support from school

LABELS
- B: Stigma
- B: Emotional Well-Being
- B: Substance Misuse
- B: Neurodevelopmental labels
- F: Support for emotional needs

UNIDENTIFIED SEN
- B: Unidentified SEN
- F: Identified SEN

MOTIVATION/ENGAGEMENT
- B: Disengagement
- F: Motivation

VOICE OF YOUNG PERSON
- B: No voice of young person

RELATIONSHIPS WITH TEACHERS
- B: Poor relationships
- F: Good relationships

TRANSITIONS
- B: Transitions
- F: Support and plan transitions

BARRIERS AND FACILITATORS OF PROFESSIONALS

FIGURE 15.2 Barriers and facilitators: young people's perspectives

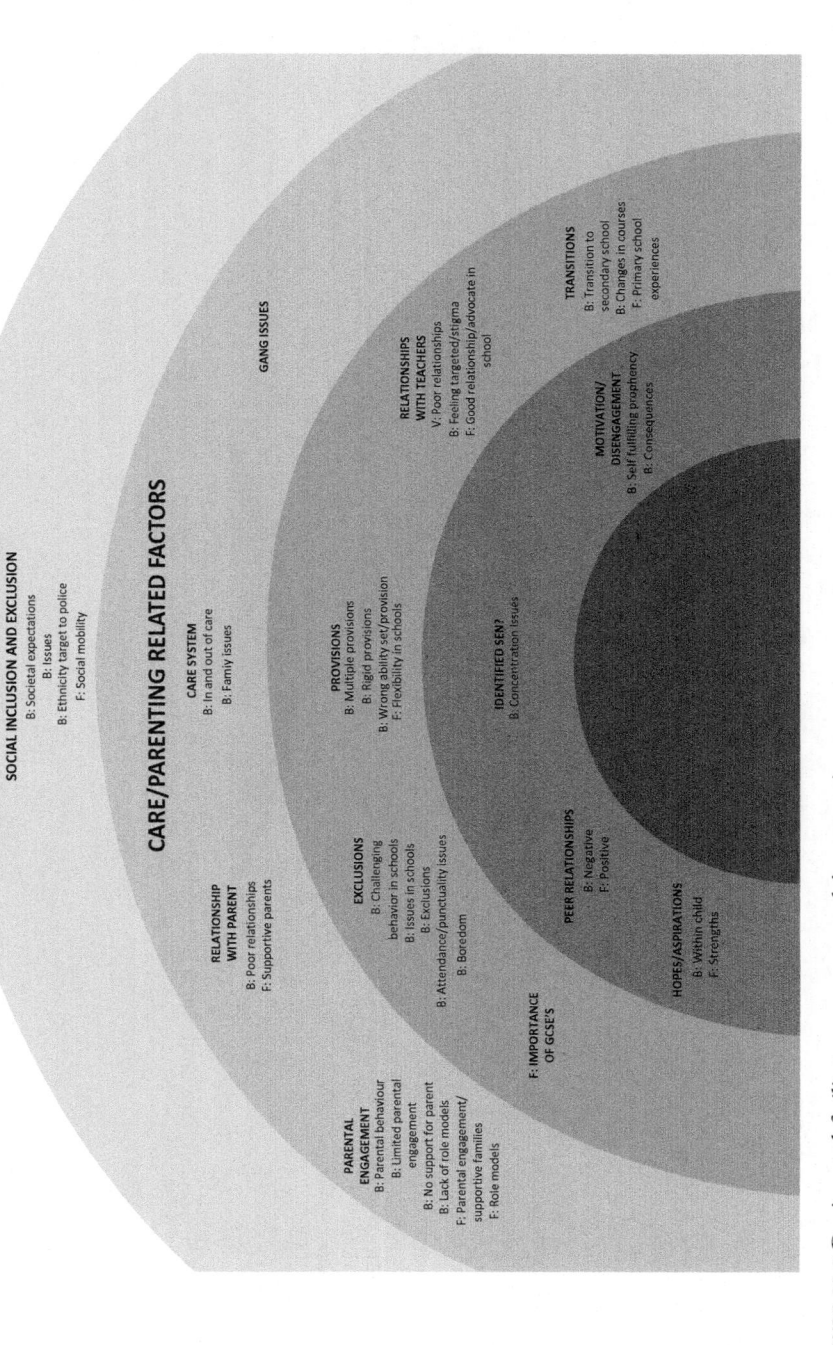

SYSTEMIC FACTORS

SOCIAL INCLUSION AND EXCLUSION
B: Societal expectations
B: Issues
B: Ethnicity target to police
F: Social mobility

GANG ISSUES

CARE/PARENTING RELATED FACTORS

CARE SYSTEM
B: In and out of care
B: Family issues

RELATIONSHIP WITH PARENT
B: Poor relationships
F: Supportive parents

PROVISIONS
B: Multiple provisions
B: Rigid provisions
B: Wrong ability set/provision
F: Flexibility in schools

EXCLUSIONS
B: Challenging behavior in schools
B: Issues in schools
B: Exclusions
B: Attendance/punctuality issues
B: Boredom

RELATIONSHIPS WITH TEACHERS
V: Poor relationships
B: Feeling targeted/stigma
F: Good relationship/advocate in school

IDENTIFIED SEN?
B: Concentration issues

PEER RELATIONSHIPS
B: Negative
F: Positive

MOTIVATION/DISENGAGEMENT
B: Self fulfilling prophecy
B: Consequences

TRANSITIONS
B: Transition to secondary school
B: Changes in courses
F: Primary school experiences

F: IMPORTANCE OF GCSE'S

PARENTAL ENGAGEMENT
B: Parental behaviour
B: Limited parental engagement
B: No support for parent
B: Lack of role models
F: Parental engagement/supportive families
F: Role models

HOPES/ASPIRATIONS
B: Within child
F: Strengths

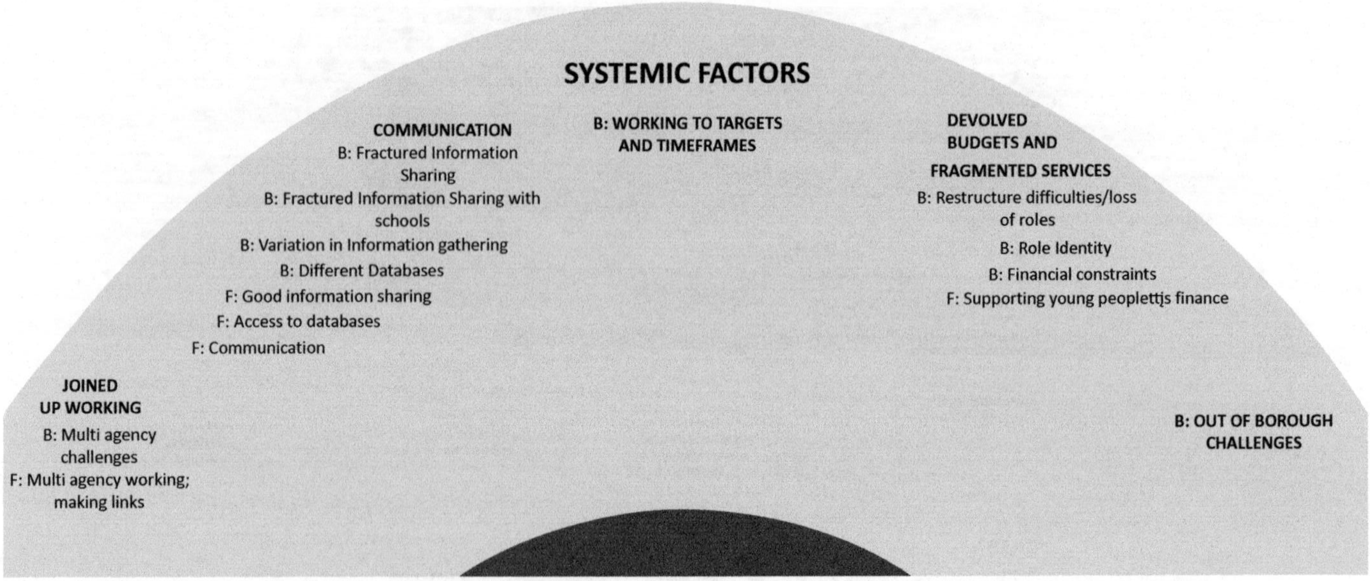

SYSTEMIC FACTORS

COMMUNICATION
B: Fractured Information Sharing
B: Fractured Information Sharing with schools
B: Variation in Information gathering
B: Different Databases
F: Good information sharing
F: Access to databases
F: Communication

B: WORKING TO TARGETS AND TIMEFRAMES

DEVOLVED BUDGETS AND FRAGMENTED SERVICES
B: Restructure difficulties/loss of roles
B: Role Identity
B: Financial constraints
F: Supporting young people's finance

B: OUT OF BOROUGH CHALLENGES

JOINED UP WORKING
B: Multi agency challenges
F: Multi agency working; making links

FIGURE 15.3 Systemic factors: professional perspectives

Successive reviews have repeatedly suggested problems with multi-agency working and system sharing (e.g. The Laming Reports, 2003; 2009) with different data systems, different terms, and poor quality of data collection and reporting. Within this local authority, there was a high turnover of staff with professionals having a high caseload, this further contributed to information getting lost and a difficulty sustaining and maintaining a structure in a context of restructuring and reorganisation. A previous study (Stephenson, 2006) has observed that, within the YJS, the focus of the work from each agency is on the young person and not on the systems around them. This structure of a disjointed multi-professional approach, where each agency has a focus on the young person with little communication between the multiple professionals, is evident in the present study. Furthermore, the restructuring difficulties and budget cuts resulted in confusion for professionals regarding their own responsibilities and the responsibilities of others, resulting in unnecessary tasks being completed such as duplication of work, for example, multiple professionals contacting schools for the same information.

Whilst it is important to tailor services to individual young peoples' needs, organisational structures do need to operate well at a broader systemic level if the complex network of services necessary to address those needs is to be managed effectively. Challenges associated with multi-disciplinary working can be overcome, for example, changes have been implemented to improve educational outcomes for CLA. This may be because there is a different social policy response to CLA than is evident in the YJS, following a growing body of literature, which revealed a systemic failure for CLA (DfES, 2000; DfES, 2003; DfES, 2006; DfES, 2007; DoH and DfE, 2009; DfE, 2010; DoE, 2011; DoH and DfE, 2014) but not for the YJS. Such policy reforms for CLA results in pressures on the professional network to have a robust system in place to work with vulnerable, complex and challenging young people. Therefore, this study could be argued to highlight that policy reform and robust systemic practice should also be in place for youth offenders.

Systemic factors from young people's perspectives

Systemic factors that the young people talked about involved how they feel within society and the impact this can have on them (Figure 15.4). The young people reported the negative view they perceive society has of them and the challenges they face within society either due to their ethnicity making them a target to authorities, worrying about other issues or having to rely on themselves to make a change.

> Like you hear it all the time like young people are so different, they're so rude, they don't want to do anything you tell them to.
>
> *(Year 11, alternative provision)*

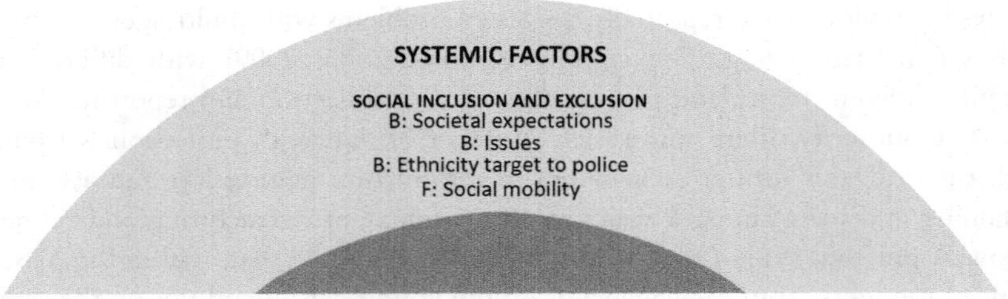

SYSTEMIC FACTORS

SOCIAL INCLUSION AND EXCLUSION
B: Societal expectations
B: Issues
B: Ethnicity target to police
F: Social mobility

FIGURE 15.4 Systemic factors: young people's perspectives

> Especially like us black boys as well, we're a target to police so I don't want him to be a target, if you get what I mean. Even though we're targets anyways, I don't want him to have a name … I don't want the police to know his name. The police know our names and it's not right, it's not nice to know like.
>
> *(Year 11, college)*

The importance of society's expectations of youth shouldn't be overlooked. Negative expectations or perceptions are likely to result in disengagement from society. Research by Bawdon (2009) showed that over half of stories about teenage boys in the National UK media were about crime, with common terms such as 'hoodie', 'louts', 'heartless', 'evil', and 'feral'. It also revealed that the best chance a teenager had of receiving sympathetic coverage was if they died. A practical danger of the currency of negative perceptions of youth is that it may undermine inclusion in mainstream educational provision.

One young person recognised that he wanted to change issues within society, which could be seen as a way of young people trying to overcome the barriers listed above:

> I don't want any little kid in this day and age to grow up and fear anybody, I don't want anybody to fear anybody. That's why I'm trying to change; I'm trying to change this circle, I'm trying to change.
>
> *(Year 11, college)*

Parenting and care related factors from the professional perspective

Within the parenting and care-related factor, professionals identified themes that were connected to professionals working with parents and families, social care, parents and their education understanding, family relationships, and gang related issues including the financial gains of crime and young people feeling a sense of belonging within a gang (Figure 15.5).

Professionals identified that working with and involving parents was considered vital; however, many barriers were cited as to why this was difficult to achieve in

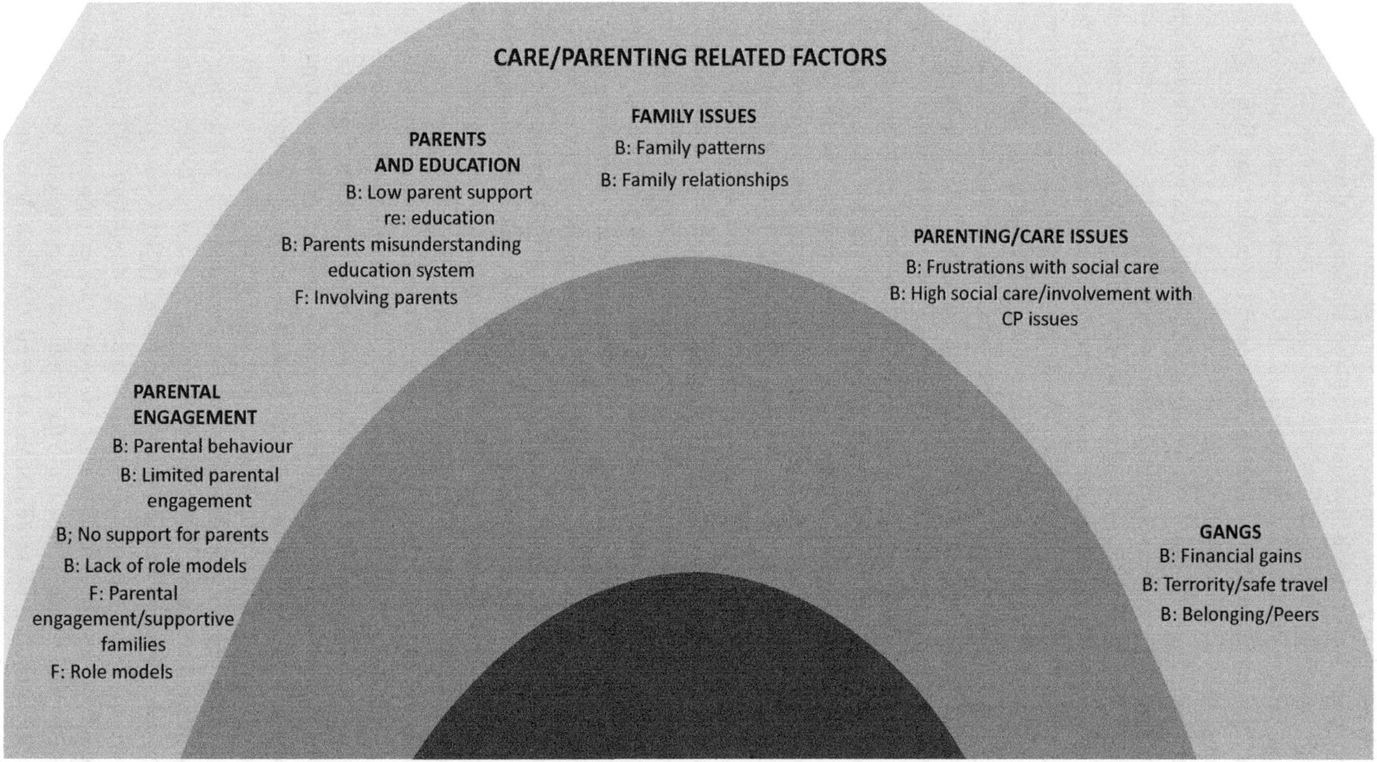

CARE/PARENTING RELATED FACTORS

FAMILY ISSUES
B: Family patterns
B: Family relationships

PARENTS AND EDUCATION
B: Low parent support re: education
B: Parents misunderstanding education system
F: Involving parents

PARENTING/CARE ISSUES
B: Frustrations with social care
B: High social care/involvement with CP issues

PARENTAL ENGAGEMENT
B: Parental behaviour
B: Limited parental engagement
B: No support for parents
B: Lack of role models
F: Parental engagement/supportive families
F: Role models

GANGS
B: Financial gains
B: Territory/safe travel
B: Belonging/Peers

FIGURE 15.5 Parenting and care related factors: professional perspectives

practice. Professionals reported that it could be very difficult to engage and involve parents with their work; the behaviour could be challenging from parents; the young people may often have a lack of role models and therefore have no or little support from parents. 'Because when you think about, certainly the youth offenders I know, how actively involved are their parents? I wouldn't say that involved and that supportive' (ETE worker).

Within the parenting and care level, when a good level of parental involvement was in place then this was considered a protective factor by both professionals and young people. The theme of repeating patterns of family issues or disengagement was apparent across both the education and social care systems; parental trust in the professional system may play a role here. Family patterns and family relationships led many professionals to feel that the young people had entrenched difficulties at home, such as witnessing domestic violence, substance misuse, mental health difficulties, absent family members, or parents facing homelessness. This resulted in many feeling that this created further complexities when supporting youth offenders to break a cycle. Many professionals reported a frustration with communicating and working with social care. Some expressed that they felt they were often having to do a social care role; or discussing concerns that social care was not working with youth offenders where they felt they should be especially with some of the issues mentioned above. However, most professionals reported that they felt the majority of youth offenders had child protection issues or high social care involvement, but they had little involvement with the social care professionals.

The parenting and care domain is significant as various studies have shown the risk and protective factors involved with family relationships with young people's wellbeing. Smith and Farrington (2004) looked at delinquency of children aged 12 and 13 years and found that the delinquent behaviour in young people was significantly related to family relationships and controls, with a strong association found with lower levels of parental supervision and their child's challenging behaviour. Furthermore, if a parent has problems of their own with education and/or offending then this could be a barrier for them being able to engage with their children's educational achievement. This is borne out by many studies such as Smith and Farrington (2004) and Thornberry (2010) where the engagement of parents is considered to be a protective factor in supporting young people. The idea of connectedness with parents (Grotevant and Cooper, 1986) as a positive factor against behavioural difficulties could present as some challenges for many young people involved in the YJS, where young people have a higher incidence of living with a relative/parental partner who has been arrested and 70% having social care involvement (Farrington, 1994; 1996; Sampson and Laub, 1993). Outcomes from a study commissioned by the Youth Justice Board (YJB) (Ghate and Ramella, 2002) showed the effectiveness of a Positive Parenting Programme (PPP) for parents of young people who are at risk or known to be engaged with offending. Therefore, it could be argued that the YJB should be supporting its own research findings as the majority of professionals reported the high level of social care involvement with the families they work with and the difficulty with engaging parents. This could be a resource and funding issue, as the local authority within the study had not recruited another parenting support role within the restructure and reorganisation, and therefore professionals within the YOS felt the strain of also trying to cover this role.

The gang lifestyle was reported by many professionals to provide a sense of belonging with peers, which was difficult for them to offer alternatives to young people.

> If you're looking for companionship and belonging and you're not getting it at home, being lured into a gang with offers of money or clothes or just a feeling of belonging, that's quite a pull for a young person. Some of our young people get pulled in that direction.
> *(Education, Training and Employment (ETE) worker)*

Furthermore, all the professionals mentioned that it was difficult for young people to prioritise education over the potential financial gains that gang involvement could offer them. The gang culture was also a major concern for professionals when working with youth offenders, and some of the young participants also mentioned the implications of such culture in their lives, for example, not being able to travel to some education or training facilities due to the area it was situated in being occupied by rival gang members. Youth gangs have gained increasing attention during the last decade, with youth surveys across the UK reporting that 2 to 7% of 10–19-year-olds report being a member of a gang (Nuffield Foundation, 2013; ONS, 2016). Research has consistently shown a link between gang membership, antisocial behaviour and offending (e.g. Thornberry et al., 2003). Gang membership is also more prevalent in areas of high socio-economic deprivation and unemployment and single parent families (The Centre for Social Justice, 2009) and may also be affected by racial inequality and ethnic oppression (Hagedorn, 2008). Research into gangs where young people are seen to join a gang for protection and where it is estate based, can result in postcode issues and violence (Hagedorn, 2008; Hallsworth and Young, 2008; Palmer 2009; Pitts 2007). The implications of gang involvement are problematic for professionals and young people.

Professionals have a pressure to provide education, training, or employment (ETE) for youth offenders and this can be problematic to find within their local area due to austerity cuts, but the young people may have issues with travelling safely to alternative provisions either within their borough or further afield, as expressed by both professionals and young people in the study. Some young people also spoke about not being able to attend an alternative provision due to their own or parents' concern of other gang members attending there. This results in a pressure on the local authority to try to secure additional provision to what they would normally offer young people and can then cause a delay for the young person in accessing ETE, which could manifest in further disengagement and motivation to engage.

Care and parenting related factors from the young people's perspectives

Care and parenting related factors represented themes that are related to young people's relationships with parents, families, parental engagement, social care, and gang related issues (Figure 15.6).

Although none of the young people interviewed were currently in the care system, two had been in care multiple times during adolescence, and only one of the young people interviewed lived with both parents with no social care involvement. Although the young people didn't directly talk about their experience of the care system, their explanations of multiple schools or missing school was due to moving locations or issues with family: 'I went to another school but because of what's been going on in my life, troubles and stuff, I had to leave that school' (Year 11, college).

Three of the young people spoke about fractured relationships with parents and four spoke about family that was supportive of them. The majority of boys interviewed spoke about gang related issues and how this can be a difficult issue for them to engage in some education settings due to travelling to a postcode where a rival gang territory is, or to get out of situations they are currently involved in due to dangers from rival gang members:

> Places that you can't go, even going outside to have a smoke or something, I don't know, or going to the shop, like simple things, going to the shop you have to look after your back, who's that, who's this, looking on buses 'cause you never know who's on that bus. I don't want my brother to have that fear.
> *(Year 11, college)*

Some young people spoke about the difficulty in resisting the financial gains that gang related crimes offered them as echoed by the professionals' views, which could affect them having difficulty with prioritising education:

> Yeah, if when I was younger, growing up I was going around with the older boys. I used to be fascinated seeing them with watches, cars, bags, money, I used to want to live that life but now it's not good, it's not good.
> *(Year 11, college)*

School related factors from the professional perspective

Within the school related factors professionals identified themes that were related to practicalities and practice within the education system such as supporting and planning transitions, school exclusions, disrupted schooling and challenging behaviour, the stigma of the youth offender label for young people, the difficulty of engaging young people with education due to their emotional wellbeing, and relationships with teachers (Figure 15.7).

CARE/PARENTING RELATED FACTORS

GANG ISSUES

CARE SYSTEM
B: In and out of care
B: Family Issues

RELATIONSHIP WITH PARENT
B: Poor relationships
F: Supportive parents

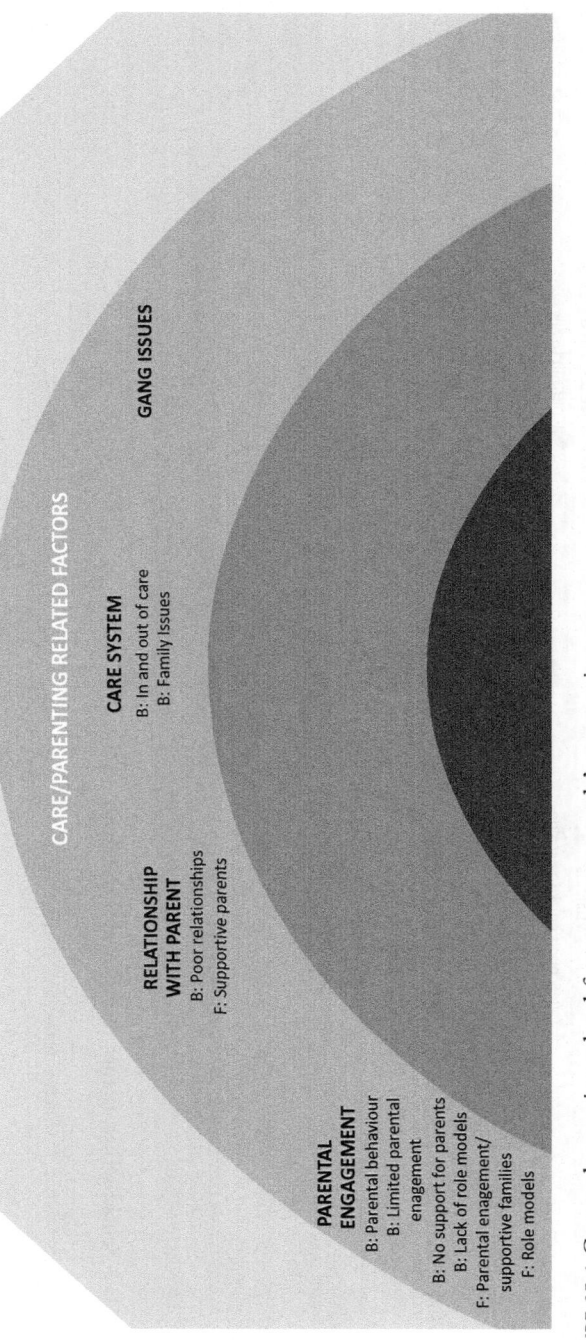

PARENTAL ENGAGEMENT
B: Parental behaviour
B: Limited parental enagement
B: No support for parents
B: Lack of role models
F: Parental enagement/ supportive families
F: Role models

FIGURE 15.6 Care and parenting related factors: young people's perspectives

STIGMA OF YOUTH OFFENDING LABEL
B: Stigma of label
B: No training
F: Remove Stigma

EXLUSIONS
B: Broken schooling
B: Challenging behaviour in schools
B: Schools quick to exculde
F: Keep in school

EMOTIONAL WELL-BEING
B: Difficult to engage young people
B: Different expectations
F: Explore expectations/other routes

RELATIONSHIPS WITH TEACHERS
B: Poor relationships
F: Good relationship

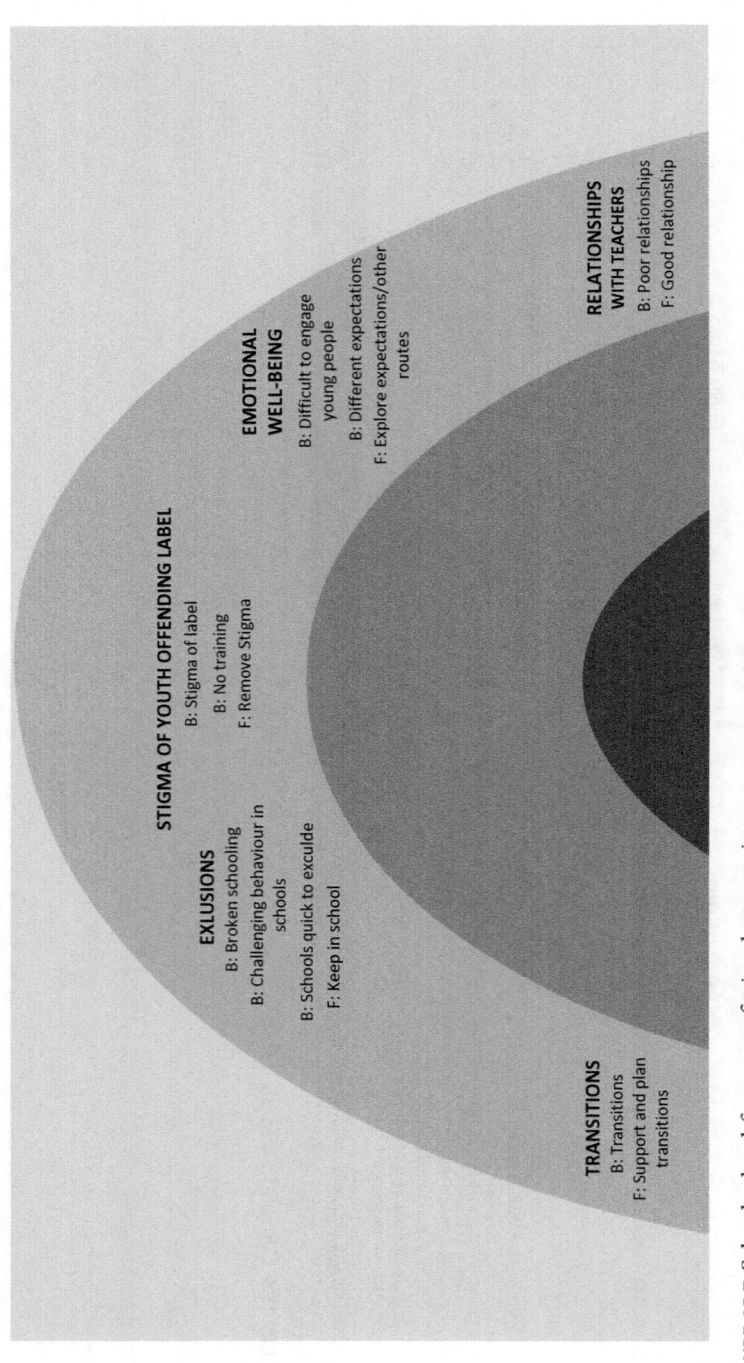

TRANSITIONS
B: Transitions
F: Support and plan transitions

FIGURE 15.7 School related factors: professional perspectives

Many professionals interviewed identified the frustration of inadequate or no provision suitable to meet the needs of many youth offenders at an organisational level:

> The lack of local accessible training programmes and educational settings in the borough ... so what we are finding is that the need is still there but we have to find it (education or training provision).
>
> *(YOS worker)*

> With this particular provision it's just there as a way of putting that group of young people somewhere to say that something is being done, but it doesn't necessarily mean that what's being done is meaningful.
>
> *(YOS worker)*

Professionals within the YOS reported a frustration with having appropriate provisions available and this is borne out in studies with YOTs struggling with issues of access to full time education, training, or employment for youth offenders (Stephenson, 2006). This pressure may be seen as linked to policy in the UK requiring at least 90% of youth offenders to be in suitable full time education, training, and employment (OLAS, 2004). Research from the YJB (2006) showed that only 35–45% of young people in the YJS were receiving full time education, training, or employment. Most professionals reported a weak link between schools or education settings and YOTs - or the YOT, which echoes Daniel et al.'s (2003) research indicating a cultural and structural mismatch between youth justice and education systems and YJB (2006) concerns that there is virtually no cross-pollination between education and youth justice.

Both professionals and young people reported many issues at the school related level, mainly around exclusions and disrupted education and stigma from professionals when working with youth offenders. Furthermore, professionals within education settings reported the difficulties of working with challenging behaviour and although the peak age for offending in the borough in the study was 14–16 years of age, many professionals reported the complex and long-standing issues for the young people prior to this age. Action for Children, Children's Society and National Children's Bureau recently published a report 'Losing in the long run' (2016) which calls on the government to renew its commitment to vital early intervention services that support children, young people, and families. The report shows that local authority spending on services for children, young people, and families has fallen by 31% between 2010–2011 and 2015–2016. Family support services have seen the biggest drop in spending including the Troubled Families programme. A high percentage of councillors (87%) reported that early intervention services are a high priority in their area, but 59% said there is a reduction in early intervention services. This could be pointing to a need for more preventative work with families happening earlier although austerity measures make this difficult currently. However, it is important to discuss that even if the families and young people attended early intervention programmes, problems can arise during adolescence and therefore may be needed at this age group too.

Findings from a Children's Society (2016) study showed that less than a third of teenagers reported that they were supported with education or emotional support which further highlights that this age group benefits from early intervention and professional intervention. This could be provided via an education psychologist training school staff around the physical and psychological stages that occur during adolescence, the prevalence of negativity accounts for teenagers, and an awareness of the YJS and the role of the YOS trying to bring the two services together.

School related factors from the young people's perspective

School related factors represented themes that are related to practicalities and practice within the education system including the importance for them to gain GCSEs, school exclusions and challenging behaviour in school, attending multiple provisions, relationships with teachers, and coping with transitions (Figure 15.8).

All but one of the young people reported multiple changes of school for a variety of reasons. These included moving locations, being excluded, the school arranging for the young person to have a managed move to another school, or the parent choosing to move their child to a different school.

> I've been to four different ones (PRUs). Two of them out of London. One was in north London and one was in (south coast) and then there are two other ones.
>
> *(Year 11, alternative provision)*

> I got kicked out of primary school, went into a PRU until secondary school, then by luck I got into a secondary school ... because of my behaviour I went into a course at another secondary school ... then I went to another school 'til the beginning of this year.
>
> *(Year 11, college)*

The majority spoke about the frustrations of being placed in the wrong ability set or provision, which they felt didn't stimulate or challenge them. Furthermore, the frustration of a rigid school or provision was expressed:

> yeah, anytime, even the mornings when you're just walking in, if your uniform wasn't correct, you're getting sent back home no matter how far you live ... Like they don't really care about your education 'cause uniform wouldn't mean that much ... yeah that's maybe why we failed.
>
> *(Year 12, NEET)*

But when schools had an understanding then they felt supported and willing to engage with them. Five of the young people had experienced multiple exclusions

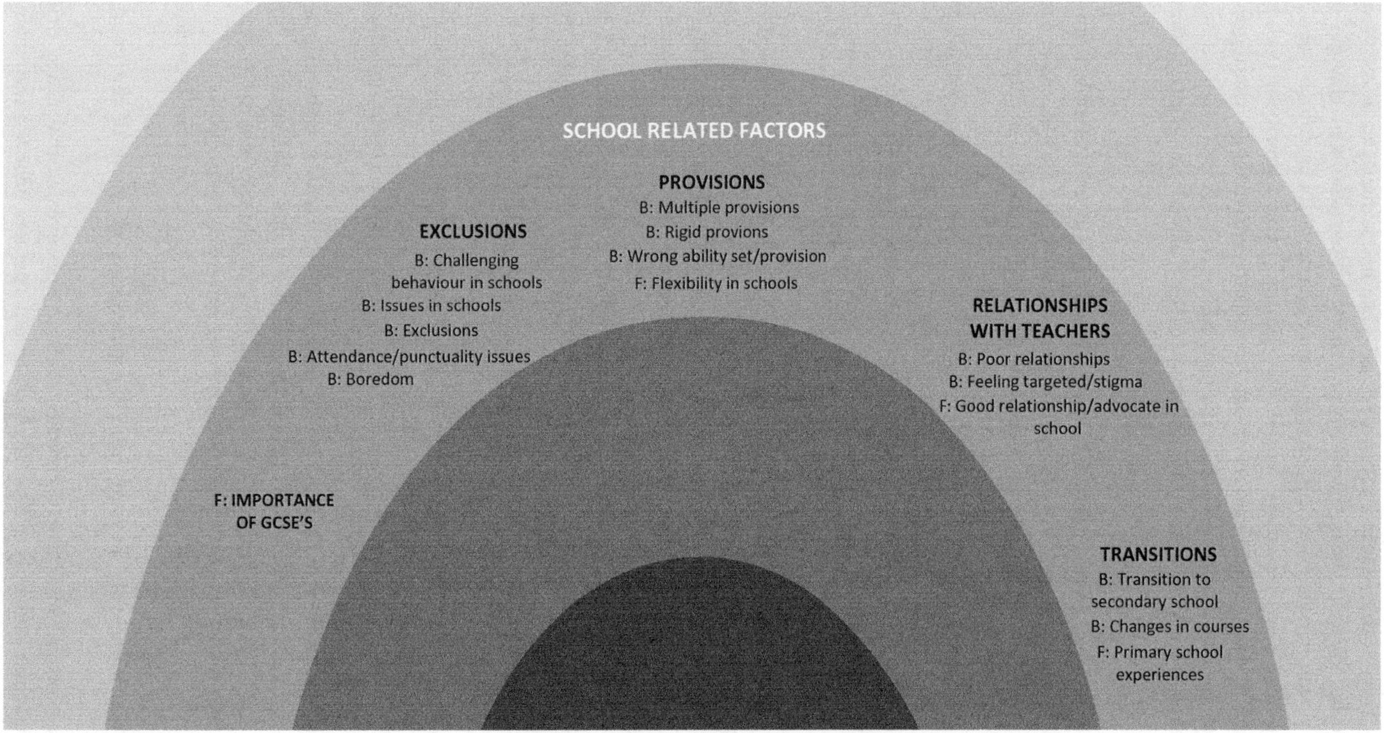

SCHOOL RELATED FACTORS

PROVISIONS
B: Multiple provisions
B: Rigid provions
B: Wrong ability set/provision
F: Flexibility in schools

EXCLUSIONS
B: Challenging behaviour in schools
B: Issues in schools
B: Exclusions
B: Attendance/punctuality issues
B: Boredom

RELATIONSHIPS WITH TEACHERS
B: Poor relationships
B: Feeling targeted/stigma
F: Good relationship/advocate in school

TRANSITIONS
B: Transtion to secondary school
B: Changes in courses
F: Primary school experiences

F: IMPORTANCE OF GCSE'S

FIGURE 15.8 School related factors: young people's perspectives

from schools. Two of these started at primary age. One had a managed move to an alternative setting and one young person experienced no exclusions or changes of schools. The young people did acknowledge their challenging behaviour in school and often reported how secondary school was 'boring'. The majority of young people also reported missing education or non-attendance either whilst waiting for a placement to be found or because they disengaged.

All the young people reported the importance they placed on gaining some GCSEs:

> No, I would like to take it (GCSEs) 'cause I know I'll need them for future. 'Cause I've got a cousin, she failed and then she's doing, she's 22 now and she's doing her GCSE's 'cause she needs them ... as long as that sits equal to a GCSE then I'm alright.
>
> *(Year 11, college)*

> I need GCSEs, yeah, 'cause if what I'm doing fails and I need GCSEs but I'm not really out trying to.
>
> *(Year 11, college)*

However, the changes in settings or courses that some young people experienced resulted in them having limited options in the qualifications they could achieve. Many of the young people reported positive experiences at primary school, however, they all reported the anxiety felt at transitioning to secondary school or how the secondary school experience was different from primary school.

Although many reported the difficult relationship they had experienced with teachers, they could name and remember a member of staff who encouraged and supported them.

The majority did report the stigma they felt from staff and being targeted:

> I dunno, like always on to me, I was like the first person they gave a warning to or something.
>
> *(Year 11, college)*

> I felt like I was always a target. That because of my behaviour from primary growing up, I always felt I was a target, 'cause I had a short like, anger ... my fuse was very short, the teachers knew that so they would take me the ... they would make up things and try to wind me up and stuff.
>
> *(Year 11, college)*

Stigmatisation was clearly an issue from the perception of many of the young people.

A study by Nottingham Trent University (YJB, 2006) revealed that fewer than half of head teachers and only a quarter of classroom teachers believed that mainstream schools were a suitable option for youth offenders when released from custody. This contrasted with views from further education colleges where two-thirds of their managers said they could offer suitable provision and welcomed more involvement with YOTs. The study reported that colleges are more receptive to work with youth offenders, as they may not have the same pressures as mainstream schools to produce increasing good exam qualification results.

This may highlight a relationship between the pressures that mainstream schools face when working with challenging pupils and the potential stigma attached to youth offenders engaging in mainstream education.

Individual factors from the professional perspective

Within the individual related factors professionals identified themes that were related to unidentified special educational needs, labels being attached to young people and the stigma of such labels, motivation and engagement with education, and the absence of the young person's voice in decisions being made about their education or training plan (Figure 15.9).

It is important to acknowledge that although not all youth offenders have problems engaging with education, there are some youth offenders who will be challenging to work with due to behaviour, disengagement, or several issues involved. The quotes below may demonstrate that professionals view the difficulty with the system being able to engage youth offenders with education, although it is important to acknowledge that some young people may be very difficult to engage and work with. However, as a service it is important that professionals can find the provision that meets the child's needs once the needs have been identified.

All professionals interviewed identified the reality and consequences of youth offenders having unidentified SEN:

> One of the young people come in today he's 17, he can't read or write, he's had no GCSEs. That stems from him having severe learning difficulties that were never picked up on.
>
> *(YOS worker)*

> Whether it's because they were causing agro at school, so it's the behaviour that's seen and not maybe the learning need.
>
> *(ETE worker)*

At the individual level, a theme of unidentified SEN was evident from the professionals, and although the young people didn't report any SEN concerns, the challenge of them achieving GCSEs when they had been placed in alternative provision was a concern for them. The literature details that there are a significant number of young people in the youth justice system who have identified or unidentified SEN (Berelowitz, 2011; ECOTEC, 2001; Farrington, 1996; Harrington and Bailey, 2005). This is also reflected by the quantitative and qualitative data in this study and confirms the findings from the Ofsted (2004) report which found

INDIVIDUAL FACTORS

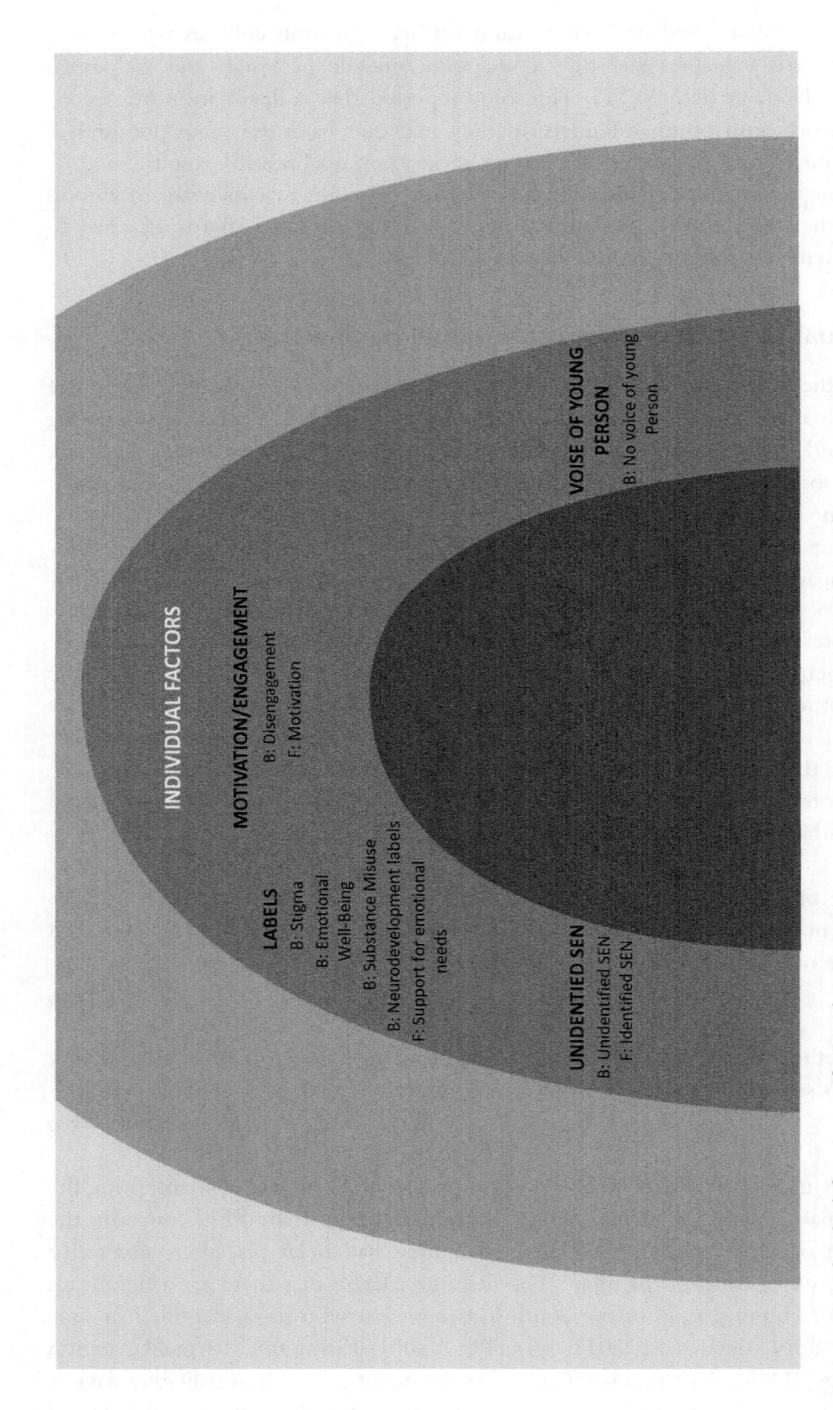

MOTIVATION/ENGAGEMENT
B: Disengagement
F: Motivation

LABELS
B: Stigma
B: Emotional Well-Being
B: Substance Misuse
B: Neurodevelopment labels
F: Support for emotional needs

UNIDENTIED SEN
B: Unidentified SEN
F: Identified SEN

VOICE OF YOUNG PERSON
B: No voice of young Person.

FIGURE 15.9 Individual factors: professional perspectives

that record keeping and detailed tracking of the educational needs of youth offenders is challenging. However, this problematic area has been overcome in the area of collecting data on CLA, which now has a systematic monitoring of the attainment level and academic or vocational progression of young people, but there is no such system in the YJS. Issues associated with assessing and recording the educational needs of youth offenders has been researched. Indeed, studies exploring the role of the Asset form as the data gathering system within the YJS have been critical of its use as a tick box exercise with a lack of a screening process, inadequate information, and a lack of confidence from some YOS staff with regard to educational issues (Welsh Assembly Government, 2009). The YJB (2006) report, which suggested that the educational demographics of young people in the YJS were largely unknown, could still be considered an issue ten years on from when that study was undertaken.

Individual factors from the young people's perspective

Individual factors represented themes that are related to the beliefs the young people have about themselves such as their hopes and aspirations, relationships with peers, identified SEN, and motivation and disengagement with education (Figure 15.10).

Many young people talked about their difficulties with learning in school and how they made sense of their SEN:

> I had a statement but ... yeah I did have one from primary, just something happened to it, I don't know.
>
> *(Year 11, college)*

> I didn't really like writing and all that ... He (tutor) tried to work with me and that and talk with me about my behaviour and tell me what I need to try to do and that.
>
> *(Year 11, tutoring)*

These quotes demonstrate that young people appear to have little understanding of their educational needs and that professionals could have focused on their behaviour over identifying any learning needs. Some young people also spoke about having trouble with concentrating, which again could be considered in relation to unidentified SEN or providing a label where other factors may be concerning the young person outside of the classroom.

Beliefs that young people held about themselves were also evident in some interviews. This theme exemplifies how internalised labels from the young person have been externally applied to them: 'I'm just a difficult child' (Year 11, college) and 'My school used to think I was bad' (Year 12, NEET).

All the young people shared their hopes and aspirations during the interview, these varied with some focusing on future careers, others on immediate

INDIVIDUSL FACTORS

IDENTIFIED SEN?
B: Concentration Issues

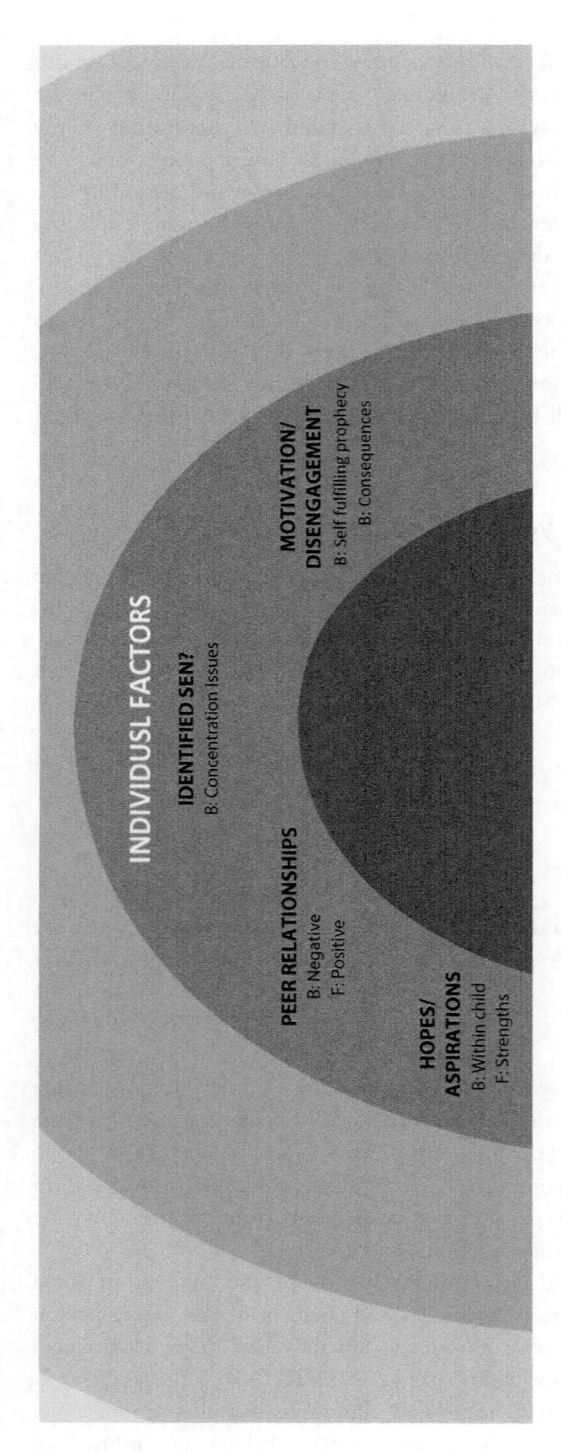

MOTIVATION/ DISENGAGEMENT
B: Self fulfilling prophecy
B: Consequences

PEER RELATIONSHIPS
B: Negative
F: Positive

HOPES/ ASPIRATIONS
B: Within child
F: Strengths

FIGURE 15.10 Individual factors: young people's perspectives

materialistic gains, others on future training. This may demonstrate the importance of involving the young people in discussing their aspirations to help motivate and plan with them the next steps and stages to achieve this. The findings demonstrate that some of the young people may need more support with identifying what they would like to do, or discussion about what they think is involved with the education or training course they talk about:

> I'm starting my own clothing brand ... I'm trying to be a successful business man ... I'm trying to do accessories as well, just a lot of things, just trying to make money.
>
> *(Year 11, college)*

> I'm trying to change, I'm trying to change this circle, I'm trying to change.
>
> *(Year 11, college)*

Findings from the quantitative data

The quantitative descriptive data from 283 young people known to the YOS over a three month period shows that the vast majority of the sample of young people open to the YOS during the three month period were black (n=259), male (n=212), aged between 14–16 years (n=155), and educated in a pupil referral unit (PRU) (n=42). This borough has a high proportion of BME young people within the YOS. In my sample it was 88% (n=259) but this is broadly similar to the local demographics (85% BME). However, this percentage is a much higher proportion than the national UK figures, where 82% are from a white UK background in the YOS with the national figure of 86% of the UK population described as White UK (ONS, 2011). The 14–16-year-old age group and males make up the largest proportion within the YOS and this is in line with national figures for youth offenders. At this age young people are going through developmental changes in adolescence, creating their identity and making plans for the future within their education settings to prepare for the ending of statutory education. This period of autonomy and gaining independence during adolescence is a time of increased vulnerability for disengagement from education, particularly when some teenagers have several issues to be dealt with at this time.

The data illustrates the vulnerabilities with this age group of young offenders in terms of education within alternative provision such as the PRU. This fits with previous literature on the associations between exclusions from school and offending behaviour and the concerns of detachment with education for this group (Daniels et al., 2003; YJB, 2006).

The data showed that the majority of above school age young people (n=66, 60%) had no provision recorded, which is consistent with national figures (National Audit Office, 2010). It is impossible to know if this number means they were NEET or the provision is not accurately recorded in the time of the data set being collected.

Missing data was a significant problem across the quantitative data and was also an issue when recording whether youth offenders had a statement of SEN. The categories of 'N/A', 'missing data' and 'not known' were all used on multiple occasions within the data and it is not clear how these items were defined by the various professionals using the system. The YJB (2006) study of a sample of Asset information provided on the SEN status of young people found that where information had been completed 25% reported a statement of SEN was present of which 75% had a statement of SEN. The Welsh Assembly Government (2009) reported that this discrepancy was due to the YOT practitioners completing Asset having limited expertise in SEN and identifying young people's needs in a subjective way.

The low number of statements with the higher reported difficulties with literacy and numeracy could suggest a raised level of need with the youth offending population that is not identified, which is also consistent with previous findings (Berelowitz, 2011; Department of Work and Pensions, 2012; Harrington and Bailey, 2005; Hughes, Williams, Chitsabesan, Davies and Mounce, 2012; YJB, 2006). These findings from the quantitative data are at odds with the qualitative data where many professionals spoke about youth offenders having identified learning needs. Furthermore, the levels of recorded exclusions would seem to suggest that there are problems and needs for most youth offenders.

The quantitative data also shows that the majority of young people did not report having poor relationships with teachers or experiences or having difficulties with peers such as bullying. These results are in contrast with the qualitative data.

Although the sample of young people interviewed was small and may not be representative, the discrepancy does raise issues regarding the validity of the Asset data. It is possible that this discrepancy could be due to how the data is collected but also who was asking the questions, for example, a young person may respond differently to a YOS case officer asking them a question as part of the Asset collection than to an education psychologist researcher asking them about their school experiences. It is also relevant to consider how terms such as poor relationships with teachers or peers were defined. Bullying is a vague term, and it is important to consider the social and psychological factors which might affect how willing a young person is to talk about such issues; young people could see this as a weakness or vulnerability to admit such things, or have fears of the negative repercussions of telling a professional such an answer. Or furthermore, the young person may not fully understand why such questions are being asked and therefore what happens to their answers.

Overall, the quantitative data showed that there is a problem with missing or unreliable data in this sample and it could be concluded that the quality of data is an issue. It is difficult to know how the YOS got their data, whether it was based on self-report or information from teachers or the local authority, or whether data was corroborated from other sources. This concern about data quality is echoed by some of the research. The YJB (2006) report that the educational demographics of young people in the youth justice system are largely unknown. Also, there is inadequate and missing information from the Asset collection, where the high level of discrepancy between youth offenders reported to have SEN from the number that actually had SEN was found to be due to YOS practitioners having limited experience in SEN and needs of the young person were subjective to workers perception (YJB, 2006; Welsh Assembly Government, 2009). However, the implications of not having accurate and effective identification of need are problematic for young people and the professionals working with them in the YJS. Furthermore, alongside the concerns of the quality of data collected and recorded, there is no such system for the monitoring and evaluating of educational progress made whilst young people are in the YJS. Some young people do have court orders for a considerable time within the YJS and monitoring attainment could be an indicator of what is, or is not, effective for their education. Having an agreed system of terms used and how to record data could help to gather accurate information to better meet the needs of young people.

The Office of the Children's Commissioner (Berelowitz, 2011) has raised concerns that considerable numbers of young people in custody may have undiagnosed neurodevelopmental disabilities, which may contribute to the behaviours that led them to offend. This study argues that early assessment, identification, and treatment could therefore potentially divert affected young people from the criminal justice system. One of the major potential weaknesses of longitudinal studies and youth offending is the emphasis upon individual characteristics with less emphasis upon social, political, cultural, and environmental factors, except for socio-economic status.

Another difficulty in studies is that record keeping and detailed tracking of education are impossible for youth offenders (Ofsted, 2004).

An education psychologist is well placed to help gather a holistic assessment of educational needs which is integrated with an assessment of behavioural, psychological, and emotional needs if the role is embedded within the YOS. This would support educational progress if the young person has their needs identified and support given to help any emotional needs, and furthermore is well placed to support an Education Health Care Plan (EHCP) application if required.

Summary

Examples of barriers and facilitators for educational engagement and inclusion for youth offenders were seen at all levels of the system. As previously discussed, there could be a lack of focus on the education of youth offenders due to a number of issues; the professional background of those involved with youth offenders within the YOS may not focus on education, professionals with an education background working within the education sector may not be trained to work with marginalised groups or may have external pressures that result in a difficulty working with young people with challenging needs, or even the organisational structure of where the YOS sits within the local authority could all be relevant. The poor outcomes of educational attainment for young people in the YJS seem to reflect a range of known risk factors, which results in a high level of vulnerability for these young people.

Pressures could be seen at each level of the system, and the context of austerity and a target driven culture are likely to have added to this. Throughout both sets of interviews a common thread was *relationships* and this was identified as a barrier and a potential facilitator at each level of the system. Relationships could be seen between limited research and practice, local authority and government drives, stigma, the multitude of professional involved, relationships with professionals and parents, young people and parents, teachers and professionals, teachers and young people. When good relationships are established then this can be a clear facilitator to helping young people to access and achieve in education. However, most professionals and young people cited fractured and difficult relationships at various levels of the system. Educational psychologists are well placed to work with the professional network involved to apply psychology at all levels to support the system.

In terms of the qualitative research findings, which explored the barriers and facilitators of educational inclusion for youth offenders, the findings echo previous findings, which point to systemic failure and social policy reform for CLA but no such coherent system for YJS. A strong supportive network was a protective factor, and this reinforces the idea that a good coherent system, with good working relationships, is crucial in supporting this vulnerable group of young people. When relationships are fractured, which can be an issue at each level of the system, this can be a massive barrier for youth offenders to engage and succeed with education. Therefore, this research would suggest that services around youth offenders should focus upon building and strengthening relationships at all levels of the system to facilitate these young people in accessing and achieving within the education system.

References

Action for Children, Children's Society and National Children's Bureau (2016) Losing in the long run trends in early intervention funding. Retrieved from: www.actionforchildren.org.uk/media/5826/losing_in_the_long_run.pdf

Bawdon, F. (2009) Hoodies or alter boys? What is media stereotyping doing to our British boys? *Women in Journalism, Echo*. Retrieved from: www.fionabawdon.files.wordpress.com/2011/02/wij_teenboys_report2.doc

Berelowitz, S. (2011) *'I think I must have been born bad': emotional well-being and mental health of children and young people in the Youth Justice System*. London: Office of the Children's Commissioner.

Bronfenbrenner, U. (1979) *The ecology of human development*. Cambridge, MA: Harvard University Press.

Centre for Social Justice (2009) *Dying to belong: an in-depth review of street gangs in Britain*. London: Centre for Social Justice.

Daniels, H., Cole, T., Sellman, E., Sutton, J., Visser, J., and Bedward, J. (2003) *Study of young people permanently excluded from school*. School of Education, University of Birmingham: Queens Printer.

Department for Education and Skills (DfES) (2003) *Every child matters*. London: HMSO.

Department for Education and Skills (DfES) (2006) *Care matters: transforming the lives of children and young people in care*. London: HMSO.

Department for Education and Skills (DfES) (2007) *Care matters: time for change*. London: The Stationery Office.
Department for Education (DfE) (2010) *Promoting the educational achievement of looked after children* (Statutory guidance for local authorities). Retrieved from: www.dcsf.gov.uk.
Department for Education and Skills and Department of Health (2000) *Guidance on the education of children and young people in public care*. London: DfES and DoH.
Department for EducationandDepartment of Health (2014) *Special Educational Needs and Disability Code of Practice: 0 to 25 years*. London: DfE and DoH.
Department of Education (2011) *The Munro Review of child protection: a child centred system (Final Report)*. London: The Stationery Office.
Department of Health and Department of Education (2009)*Statutory guidance on promoting the health and well-being of looked after children*. Nottingham: DCSF.
Department for Work and Pensions (2012) *Social justice: transforming lives*. London: The Stationery Office.
ECOTEC Research and Consulting (2001) *An audit of educational provision within the juvenile secure estates*. London: YJB.
Farrington, D.P. (1994) Early developmental prevention of juvenile delinquency. *Criminal Behaviour and Mental Health*, 4, 209–227.
Farrington, D.P. (1996) *Understanding and preventing youth crime*. York: Joseph Rowntree.
Farrington, D.P. (2000) Explaining and preventing crime – the globalization of knowledge: The American Society of Criminology 1999 presidential address. *Criminology*, 38, 1–24.
Ghate, D., and Ramella, M. (2002) *Positive parenting: the national evaluation of the Youth Justice Board's Parenting Programme*. Retrieved from: http://yjbpublications.justice.gov.uk/Resources/Downloads/PositiveParenting.pdf
Grotevant, H.D., and Cooper, C.R. (1986) Individuation in family relationships: a perspective on individual differences in the development of identity and role-taking skill in adolescence. *Human Development*, 29, 82–100.
Hagedorn, J. (2008) *A world of gangs: armed young men and gangsta culture*. Minneapolis, MN: University of Minnesota Press.
Hallsworth, S., and Young, T. (2008) Gang talk and gang talkers: a critique. *Crime, Media, Culture: An International Journal*, 4, 2, 175–195.
Harrington, R., and Bailey, S. (2005) *Mental health needs and effectiveness of provision for young offenders in custody and in the community*. London: Youth Justice Board.
Hayward, G., Stephenson, M., and Blyth, M. (2004). Exploring effective educational interventions for young people who offend. In R. Burnett and C. Roberts (Eds), *What works in probation and youth justice*. Cullompton, UK: Willan.
Hughes, N., Williams, H., Chitsabesan, P., Davies, R., and Mounce, L. (2012) *Nobody made the connection: the prevalence of neurodisability in young people who offend*. London: Children's Commissioner.
Laming, Lord (2003) *The Victoria Climbie inquiry. Report of an inquiry by Lord Laming*. Norwich: The Stationery Office.
Laming, Lord (2009) *The protection of children in England: a progress report*. London: The Stationery Office.
National Audit Office (2010) *The Youth Justice System in England and Wales: reducing offending by young people. Twenty-first report of 2010–2011*. Retrieved from: www.nao.org.uk/report/the-youth-justice-system-in-england-and-wales-reducing-offending-by-young-people/
Nuffield Foundation (2013) *Children and young people in gangs: a longitudinal analysis*. London: Nuffield Foundation.
O'Carroll, J. (2016) *Identifying barriers and facilitators for educational inclusion for young people who offend*. London: University College London.

Office for National Statistics (2011) 2011 census. Retrieved from: www.ons.gov.uk/census/2011census

Office for National Statistics Website (2014) Retrieved from: www.ons.gov.uk/dcp171776_355123.pdf

Ofsted (2004) *Out of school*. London: The Stationery Office.

OLAS (2004) *The offender's learning journey: learning and skills provision for juvenile offenders in England*. London: DfES.

Palmer, S. (2009) The origins and emergence of youth gangs in a British inner city neighbourhood. *Safer Communities*, 8, 2.

Pitts, J. (2007) *Reluctant gangsters: youth gangs in Waltham Forest*. Luton: University of Bedfordshire.

Sampson, R., and Laub, J. (1993) *Crime in the making: pathways and turning points throughout life*. Cambridge, MA: Harvard University Press.

Smith, C., and Farrington, P. (2004) Continuities in antisocial behaviour and parenting across three generations. *Journal of Child Psychology and Psychiatry*, 45, 2, 230–247.

Soloman, E. (2010) *Children and young people in the Youth Justice System: report of seminars organised by the All Party Parliamentary Group for Children 2009/10*. London: NCB.

Stephenson, M. (2006) *Young people and offending: education, youth justice and social inclusion*. Devon: Willan.

The Children's Society (2016) Understanding adolescent neglect. Retrieved from: www.childrensociety.org.uk

Thornberry, T.P. (2010) The causal impact of childhood-limited maltreatment and adolescent maltreatment on early adult adjustment. *Journal of Adolescent Health*, 46, 4, 359–365.

Thornberry, T.P., Krohn, M.D., Lizotte, A.J., Smith, C.A., and Tobin, K. (2003) *Gangs and delinquency in developmental perspective*. New York: Cambridge University Press.

Welsh Assembly Government (2009) *Analysis of support for young people with special educational needs in the youth justice sector in Wales*. Retrieved from: http://wales.gov.uk/docs/dcells/publications/111103senalysisrep09en.pdf

Youth Justice Board (2006) *Barriers to engagement in education, training and employment*. London: YJB.

PART V
Recommendations from research

16

RE-ENGAGING YOUNG OFFENDERS WITH EDUCATION IN THE SECURE CUSTODIAL SETTING

Adeela ahmed Shafi

This chapter is based on a doctoral research study completed in 2017 which focused on understanding the nature of disengagement in young offenders, offering a way to re-engage them with learning whilst incarcerated. The research was an ethnographic study conducted in one secure children's home in England, conducted in three phases. Phase I consisted of exploring the educational experiences of 16 young offenders. Phase II consisted of five in-depth case studies, each comprising an authentic inquiry process designed to begin with an authentic interest from the learner and to connect to a useful educational outcome. Phase III aimed to understand how the secure unit could facilitate re-engagement with learning. In its entirety the research generated data from 45 interviews, observations, and field notes with 16 young offenders, three teachers, three mentors, a head teacher.

Using three in-depth case studies from this research, this chapter illustrates how re-engaging young offenders with education and learning whilst in custody can be transformative, given the right conditions. Re-engagement efforts need to respond to the nature of disengagement in young offenders which was found to be characterised by heightened and exacerbated emotions and shaped by their relationships with staff and peers. The chapter begins by providing a background and context of the education of young offenders before outlining the research. A discussion of the conditions needed to be met for successful re-engagement, with a particular focus on the facilitators and barriers, is presented. This is followed by implications for practice, emphasising the need for flexibility in the structures of the secure setting which can result in considerable benefits for effective re-engagement.

Background and context

Between 86% and 90% of young offenders have been excluded from school (Little, 2015) at some point and many (36% boys and 41% girls) have not been to school since they were 14 years old (Murray, 2012). Young offenders are also likely to have higher levels of learning disabilities (Chitsabesan and Hughes, 2016) with a prevalence of 23–32% compared to 2–4% in the general population (Hughes, 2012). Additional emotional problems (Heinzen, Koehler, Smeets, Hoffer, and Huchzermeier, 2011; González, Gudjonsson, Wells, and Young, 2016) behavioural problems (Young, Moss, Sedgwick, Fridman, and Hodgkins, 2015), and language and communication difficulties (Snow, Woodward, Mathis, and Powell, 2016) are also more prevalent in young offenders with comorbidity not unusual. Poor educational experiences coupled with these difficulties can make engagement with education challenging, particularly in a secure context which brings with it additional trials, not least the restriction of movement and loss of autonomy. However, engagement is a necessary pre-requisite for any 'intervention' (including educational interventions) to have a chance of success (Case and Haines, 2015a, 2015b; Prior and Mason, 2010).

Research in the UK and Europe on the education of young offenders in custodial settings is limited (Hart, 2015). The extant literature is predominantly from the US and tends to be based on a 'correctional' approach focused on evaluating specific interventions which look to improve, for example, reading or writing skills (Wexler, Pyle, Flower, Williams, and Cole, 2014). The assumption is that in correcting the 'deficit' the 'problem' is solved in an unproblematic way. However, such approaches represent a unidimensional view with little acknowledgement of the background or contextual challenges and how these can impact on the young offenders' ability or willingness to engage in educational opportunities.

The secure context itself is significant in this regard. By its very nature, it is designed to restrict and limit movement. The findings from this research have indicated it to be a defining feature in how young offenders perceive education at the secure unit.

Why engagement?

Engagement is considered key to learning and academic success (Crick, 2012; Fredricks, Filsecker, and Lawson, 2016). It has protective benefits with regards to delinquent behaviours such as truanting, substance abuse, and offending (Hirschfield and Gasper, 2011; Wang and Fredricks, 2014). Importantly, engagement is a malleable construct responsive to teachers' or schools' efforts and thus an ideal point for interventions (Appleton, Christenson, and Furlong, 2008). However, teachers and practitioners report low engagement and disengagement as one of the biggest challenges of the Western classroom (Fredricks, 2011; Wang and Fredricks, 2014). Whilst it is difficult to draw direct causal inferences between engagement and offending, it is difficult to ignore when so many young offenders (over 90% in this research and that by Little, 2015) have dropped out of school due to disengagement.

Engagement with education and learning consists of three main components: behavioural, cognitive, and emotional (Fredricks, Blumenfeld, and Paris, 2004).

Behavioural engagement is shown through, for example, attendance, completing homework and other tasks as well as complying with school rules. Cognitive engagement is demonstrated through for example, asking questions, making connections, or going beyond the information provided. Emotional engagement refers to feeling a sense of belonging, being a part of a group, or having meaningful relationships within a learning context. Emotional engagement has been found to predict behavioural engagement (Skinner, Furrer, Marchand, and Kindermann, 2008; Lee, 2014). However, there is an argument that agentic engagement should be a fourth component (Reeve and Tseng, 2011) which is indicated by learner proactivity in shaping one's own learning. This appears necessary because the other components (cognitive, emotional, and behavioural) do not capture the individual learner's role in learning. A learner is not just reactive to a learning environment but proactive too. They bring to a learning context their own background experiences and knowledge which shape how they may decide to react. This is connected to autonomy, where a sense of autonomy is more likely to result in agentic engagement. This agentic aspect of component was critical in terms of learner empowerment within the three case studies explored in this chapter.

Engagement and motivation

Autonomy is one of the three key constructs in the psychological theory of motivation called self-determination theory (Deci and Ryan, 1985; 2008; 2010). Autonomy refers to the extent to which one can express who they are and be themselves – a sense of empowerment. When autonomy is respected one is more likely to engage and be motivated intrinsically. The other two constructs are relatedness and competence. Relatedness refers to the person's need to feel a belonging or part of a group, to feel supported. Relationships are of special significance to relatedness. Competence refers to how capable a learner believes they might be in a particular task. The secure context, by its very nature, impedes these basic psychological needs, restricting autonomy, relatedness and competence. Self-determination theory is useful in understanding and explaining the psychological process of engagement.

Goldspink and Kay (2009) distinguished between autonomy and agency because autonomy refers to a condition and the extent to which it is granted within a context. In this sense, autonomy is an environmental context that is 'given' or presented, whereas agency is about the extent to which the individual themselves acts on the environment. This is useful in understanding the secure context and the interplay between autonomy and agency.

Disengagement

Recent research is beginning to focus on disengagement as distinct to simply low engagement because the characteristics of the disengaged differ from those who have low engagement. Earl, Taylor, Meijen, and Passfield (2017) distinguished between active and passive forms of disengagement, describing animated and disruptive behaviours as active disengagement whereas passive disengagement is characterised by non-responsiveness to teachers and peers, refusing to be involved in learning activities. Earl et al. suggest that disengaged learners require different strategies for re-engagement. Given that young offenders are generally disengaged, this lends support to the idea of alternative strategies within a secure custodial setting.

The secure custodial setting for many is a final opportunity to re-engage young offenders with formal education (Little, 2015). Investing in the re-engagement of young offenders with education and learning whilst in custody could be transformative for them (Behan, 2014), especially as previous educational experiences have been negative (Ball and Connolly, 2000; Farrington and Welsh, 2007; Hirschfield and Gasper, 2011; Kirk and Sampson, 2013; Little 2015). In doing so, young offenders can be empowered to be more proactive (or agentic) in navigating their own educational pathways as they transition back in the community. Lanskey (2015) found that those who were engaged and determined whilst in custody found it easier to transition back into the community and continue with education.

The case studies

Research which explores the actual experiences of young offenders is not plentiful. Therefore, the case studies in this research offered a unique insight into the extent and process of engagement (or not). Five case studies generated data from 29 interviews, observations, and field notes and three of them are presented in this chapter.

Authentic inquiry

Authentic inquiry was the means through which the young people were re-engaged. This was a process of inquiry, action, and knowledge generation (Jaros and Deakin Crick, 2007). Authentic inquiry has been shown to appeal to disengaged learners because it is personal and authentic to them and they have the opportunity to achieve something tangible, such as a certificate or good mark for their work (Jaros and Deakin Crick, 2007). The aim is to connect the personal interest with an externally valued outcome and the creation of a poster, presentation, leaflet, or other artefact is a key feature of authentic inquiry. For example, it might start with something like a place that is of relevance or importance in the life of the learner. Through the learning journey this can develop into a geography project or a tourist brochure for the area which can be assessed. In this way the personal is connected to the public and a connection is made between the learner and outwardly assessed goals. In doing so it connects the participant's own interest to formal education. This is a vital part of authentic inquiry as for many young offenders, the curriculum is so distant from their own lives that they see no connection between what they are interested in and what is considered useful learning in school. Starting with the curriculum as it does in mainstream school has not been successful in engaging young offenders. Therefore, the opportunity to begin with an authentic starting point which is then connected to the educational outcomes has considerable value. In a sense, authentic inquiry reverses what tends to be the case in mainstream school, positioning the learner as the starting point rather than a curriculum. This is in line with the notion of disengagement being distinct where an alternative approach becomes necessary.

A further key element of the authentic inquiry is the role of a mentor. The mentor acts as a facilitator, enabling access to resources, posing questions, challenging when needed, and supportive when needed. This supports emotional component of engagement through relatedness with the learning context – of which the mentor is an important part. For young offenders who have been shown to have had complex lives with limited stable and supportive relationships, this becomes even more central. Furthermore, the authentic inquiries offered a space within which the young person could express some autonomy – one of the three constructs in self-determination theory. In doing so, there is an opportunity to empower which can manifest in feeling competent (also significant according to self-determination theory).

Using authentic inquiry, it was possible to re-engage all the young offenders in the case studies, albeit to varying degrees. This was dependent on a range of conditions which are discussed in the next section. The cases of Jack, William, and Andrea were selected for inclusion in this chapter because they represented a range of the complexities that many young offenders may experience.

Jack's authentic inquiry

Jack

Jack was 16 years old and of White British heritage. He was the only young offender at the secure unit who had come from a mainstream school and a relatively stable family life. Jack had achieved some GCSEs at school. Jack was on long term sentence of 12 months for a sexual offence though no previous known offence.

Jack was described by teachers as mild mannered and sociable, rarely raising his voice or being physically aggressive. Jack was however, constantly dissatisfied with the secure unit, its system, the staff, and lack of facilities. He was also dissatisfied with his weight gain which he attributed to the lack of healthy food available at the secure unit. Jack was very dependent on adult support and demanding of attention.

Jack agreed to participate in the authentic inquiry, initially attracted at the potential attention it might command from staff. Jack's topic was health and fitness – authentic because he was concerned about his recent weight gain and wanted to improve his fitness. He decided that he wanted to create a workbook on health and fitness and possibly present it to his fellow students to encourage them to increase their fitness and diet. There was a delay in Jack starting his authentic inquiry due to not being able to meet with his chosen mentor James, a member of the care staff. Jack remained committed to doing the authentic inquiry, despite initially engaging largely for utilitarian purposes, signifying sustained engagement. Jack also demonstrated agency and initiative in deciding his own topic.

Practitioners' perspectives

The science teacher had tried to mentor Jack, however, had to withdraw because Jack was not satisfied with her efforts. Jack did not feel that science connected to his chosen topic associating the science teacher with lessons and work – not related to his idea of developing his own fitness. Therefore, this mentoring relationship was not successful. Nevertheless, when Jack did eventually do his authentic inquiry with his chosen mentor, he was able to relate it to science in a way he had not done so in the earlier stages. A good relationship with the mentor emerged as an important facilitator.

Jack's mentor James, described him as enthusiastic and driven:

> Jack was really good and he had loads of ideas ... there was no 'Oh can you write it for me?' which you'd expect to find probably on a day to day basis in the schools but I think because he's interested in it he was straightaway writing it down.
>
> (James, Jack's mentor)

This was almost the exact opposite to Jack's teachers, who described him as lazy and demanding. Ironically, however, this was also how Jack described himself with regards to learning in his very first interview: 'The same thing over and over again. It just gets boring [...] Just like I said I haven't got the motivation, I'm too lazy' (Jack, first interview).

James indicated that the lack of time was a major barrier in the authentic inquiry. It resulted in limited access to resources such as the internet which led to frustration from both James and Jack. James reiterated what others had said: that due to being managed by the care staff team, it meant the Head of Education had little control over timetabling James and Jack together – other than an informal arrangement. This had been the source of Jack's earlier frustration and had it not been for Jack's enthusiasm for the topic, the authentic inquiry could easily have been abandoned

Analysis

Jack's re-engagement with education during and following the authentic inquiry demonstrated that re-engagement with education and learning was not beyond the reach of even the most disengaged (or laziest) of learners. Despite Jack's dissatisfaction, resentment and dependency, given the opportunity, he was able to re-engage himself with learning. Jack's learning was characterised by his own passion facilitated by the authentic inquiry opportunity. Through this, Jack was able to reclaim some autonomy restricted by the secure context. In so doing, Jack was able to apply his competencies to other areas beyond the authentic inquiry such as becoming a young person's representative, indicating a sense of belonging or relatedness. The constraints of the secure custodial setting through its structures of line management had been barriers to engaging in the early stages. However, as the authentic inquiry served to connect Jack to his own competences, he was able to emerge as a confident and engaged learner indicating a sense of empowerment. Whilst the authentic inquiry cannot claim all credit for this, it seems clear that the opportunity re-connected him to learning which permeated his entire presence at the secure unit. Jack was developing into a confident and energetic individual who was campaigning for better nutrition at the secure unit and had volunteered as a 'rep' for his fellow residents. This case demonstrated that engaging a young offender with education in a secure context is achievable and relatively quickly – once the conditions are right.

William's authentic inquiry

William

William was 16 years old and of African American heritage. Originally from the USA, his parents and family had come to settle in England just a few years ago. William's family had high expectations of him and William felt pressure to achieve the highest of grades. William was serving a sentence in excess of 12 months for aggravated burglary with no previous known offence.

William was described by teachers as a very able and a deep thinker. However, he had declined to take his GCSEs because he did not believe in them. William had dropped out of mainstream school and in lessons at the unit he was withdrawn, quiet, tired, sad. Whilst generally compliant, William did not engage with activities.

William's authentic inquiry also suffered a delayed start, primarily due to the lack of time available for him to identify a mentor. William's eventual mentor, Andrew, had volunteered himself. This self-selection shaped the authentic inquiry where Andrew led the entire process. It also meant that although William complied, he did not engage in the way that was transformative or meaningful as it had been for Jack. 'Andrew told me about it [the topic] but it's like okay because there's nothing else that's really like, as realistic so I just had to go for that one' (William, post authentic inquiry interview).

William's response to the best and worst things about the process was: 'The worst thing about it? How do I phrase this? Not being able to pick on one [topic] because of what other people think' (William, post authentic inquiry interview).

This demonstrated that not choosing the topic nor his own mentor meant that William did not experience the conditions that enabled him to engage in the authentic inquiry. William did not say anything about the 'best thing'.

Practitioners' perspectives

Andrew was an enthusiastic mentor who was passionate about getting the young people 'skilled up' (Andrew's words) ready for release. As a member of the care staff, with limited involvement in education, the authentic inquiry meant he could be more involved. However, in William's case, this had proved counter-productive because it meant that the opportunity for the inquiry to be authentic was hindered. It resulted in William continuing to be passively disengaged and just 'going through the motions'. Andrew was coming to the process with his own aims and goals, which although well-intended, did not serve the purpose for William. This was evident in the response William gave to a question on the 'product' he had created as a result of his authentic inquiry: 'I didn't really see the end result because it's like Andrew, he did most of it, but for me I just did like most of the maintenance, look up all the research so he did all the creative stuff' (William).

Andrew was unable to detect that William was simply complying, demonstrating only a behavioural level of engagement. In response to being asked if the topic was William's choice, Andrew responded: 'The topic was perfect really, because at the end of the project, he [William] kind of realised what he likes' (Andrew, William's mentor).

William was more suited to a mentor that stimulated and facilitated his thinking, like Jack's mentor had. Instruction was not suitable for William who needed greater stimulation for him to feel empowered enough to be agentic.

Although William rarely engaged in classes, a teacher identified one occasion when William had asked how the topic was going to help him:

> Because I do remember him saying to me 'How does this shit help me?' and I said to him 'Okay, let's look at it another way: how does it hurt you? That's perhaps what you need to think about'. And we did actually have quite a dialogue about that, because he kept saying 'But how does it help?' and I said 'Alright, let's stop and think about life in general and wind back to before you did your crime. If you had said to yourself 'How does this hurt me?' then you perhaps wouldn't have done it because if you knew that you were going to do that then consequences were going to be negative. If you pass your science GCSE nothing negative is going to come from it, potentially only positive and that's it. So, stop asking how is it going to help, start thinking about 'How is it going to damage me?''
>
> *(Teacher interview)*

This is an example of William attempting to engage. However, the conversation was taken in a different direction. Given William's beliefs about society and its institutions the conversation may not have encouraged engagement as he did not believe in exams. William had some strong political views, which may have been shaped because he had been exposed to different political systems in America and the UK. Taking the authentic inquiry approach, the teacher could have taken the opportunity of William's attempt at cognitive engagement to encourage him to search for the answers to his question himself. In so doing William could have explored the purpose of that particular lesson topic. It appeared that there were at least two known potential opportunities lost for engaging a learner like William: this incident in the lesson and the authentic inquiry itself.

Analysis

William had volunteered to take part, demonstrating a willingness to engage; however, William did not re-engage to the same extent as Jack. This was because William's mentor had emerged as a barrier rather than facilitator, resulting in William being disempowered further by the experience. The mentor had to be driven by the needs of the young person, highlighting the importance of relatedness and emotional engagement whereby a connection, even if it is just with one individual, becomes important. William's case demonstrated the importance of a mentor relationship which understands the young person. The authentic inquiry did not present conditions of autonomy for William and he was not able to express what he really thought or felt and so was unable to identify a topic of interest. It also showed how the structures of the secure custodial setting was not conducive in cultivating such a relationship. William had demonstrated that he was able and willing to engage when the opportunity arose, however the conditions of the secure context did not facilitate this.

Andrea's authentic inquiry

Andrea

Andrea was 17 years old, born in Britain though from a non-British background and multilingual in English, Czech, and Polish. Andrea had been a victim of abuse, had a chequered educational history, and, although undiagnosed, it was believed that she had a range of learning difficulties. Andrea was approaching the end of a six month sentence for robbery with no previous known offence.

Andrea was observed as challenging, aggressive, demanding, and generally uncooperative in lessons. Having been excluded from school without any GCSEs, Andrea had attended a pupil referral unit followed by time at a local college on a hair and beauty course. This was disrupted by her offence and subsequent sentence.

When Andrea agreed to participate in an authentic inquiry, she became quite excited, asking many questions – excitement is an indicator of emotional engagement and asking questions suggests cognitive engagement (Skinner et al., 2008). This was the direct opposite to teachers' reports who were convinced Andrea would not be willing to participate.

Andrea wanted to use the authentic inquiry to think about job and career prospects on her release. She wanted to produce a CV 'like the normal kids' (Andrea's words) as her 'end product'. Andrea produced pages and pages of writing in the notebook she was issued. Whilst much of the narrative lacked coherence and structure, reflecting teachers' reports of her communication and language difficulties, Andrea's work indicated a desire to use her multiple languages and experiences of trouble with the law to help other young people in her situation. This demonstrated behavioural, emotional, and cognitive engagement. However, Andrea regularly complained of how the staff never helped her. These complaints could have been interpreted as a request for help, but Andrea's challenging manner made supporting her especially difficult for the teachers.

Practitioners' perspectives

Andrea found identifying a mentor difficult as she believed nobody cared. When she did eventually think of a mentor, Emily, they never got to meet before the end of her sentence. Consequently, Andrea's authentic inquiry did not progress beyond her planning stage described above. The lack of a mentor was a serious blow to Andrea and her engagement was replaced with frustration, anger, despondency and a further sense of disempowerment. 'She [Emily] didn't help me with anything. Nobody even cares'. Andrea needed additional help in preparing her for release. She had seen the authentic inquiry as a chance to do this. The lack of help resulted in increased frustration and then a sense of despondency. Andrea attempted to conceal this disappointment by downplaying the work she had put in.

> It's only a notebook. It's only writing. It's not like I had a job interview and that. It's just that page I could write anything I wanted, but the thing is, like – there could have been something out of it rather than just doing like 13 pages of writing and then not doing nothing [...] the plan was to go and have a look on the computer and see what jobs there are that would interest me. Obviously, that hasn't happened, so I just thought it was a waste. I haven't been bothered doing it again because I thought, 'what's the point?'
>
> *(Andrea)*

For the remainder of this interview Andrea spoke about her anxiety at being released and of being fearful of being back in the community, when as soon as she turned 18 all the support would be withdrawn. Andrea was feeling vulnerable and frightened. Engaging her with learning after this point was difficult.

> How would you feel if you were in a secure unit, you were leaving in 2–3 days, you've got nothing in place, no house? You don't properly know exactly where you're going to live. You've got no money, you've got no National Insurance number, no birth certificate, nothing to sort myself out. I've never been 18 to know how shit runs when you're an adult, so how should I know? It's obviously going to be stressing. But they just don't give a shit.
>
> *(Andrea)*

Teachers reported that Andrea would abandon tasks without explanation and accuse them of not helping. Their assessment was that she had a short attention span, needy and with a desire to control:

> Andrea will appear keen on something, she will demand we do some particular task and then after ... it could be ten minutes, or it could be two days [...], she will just say 'I am not doing it', abandon it, not interested. I think it is a mechanism of control for her.
>
> *(Teacher)*

However, Andrea showed that she tried to engage with lessons. Although teachers recognised Andrea had additional needs, they did not appear to connect these as a possible reason for abandonment of tasks. A second teacher reported having a good relationship with Andrea, due to giving her one-to-one attention and reflected how Andrea was responsive to the social environment.

When asked if the teacher had free rein on what she could to help Andrea's education, the teacher responded with.

> If I had free rein with her I'd wrap her up in cotton wool and take her home and protect her from all the bad people out there. I think I would take advantage of the fact that she was bilingual and try and get her to do something that ... with her translating. I mean I say bilingual; I think she spoke more than two languages.
>
> *(Teacher)*

Teachers perceived Andrea's troubled childhood as having affected her ability to engage. However, interestingly, teachers did not attribute Andrea's lack of sustained engagement to the pedagogical features of the classroom of the secure setting nor their own teaching styles. In some ways it reflected the 'deficit in the learner' approach. The secure setting had exacerbated Andrea's emotions and her subsequent reactions. This had impacted on her ability to maintain engagement and the support she needed was not there.

Analysis

Andrea demonstrated when given the opportunity to engage, with the right support, she could have overcome challenges. However, the conditions within the secure context meant capitalising on this was not possible. Andrea was aware of what she needed to do on release and wanted to plan for it, demonstrating her agency in being able to assess the usefulness of the authentic inquiry to her. It offered her an opportunity to be autonomous, be herself, and use her skills to her benefit. However, she was continually frustrated at the perceived lack of support indicating the importance of relatedness. This contributed further to her frustration, disappointment, and fear because in some ways her competence or ability to do something for herself was compromised. The secure context had been a barrier to continued engagement in the authentic inquiry despite Andrea showing initial engagement.

The conditions

The case studies demonstrated the range of ways in which each young person had approached and engaged with their authentic inquiries. The overall finding was that authentic inquiry had the potential to re-engage even the most troubled and disengaged of young persons, though not all were successful to the same extent. Engagement was subject to a number of facilitators and barriers within the secure context and it became clear that certain conditions needed to be met for successful re-engagement. A range of facilitators and barriers were identified (Figure 16.1).

A clear distinction between these was not always possible for two reasons: firstly, because a facilitator could also become a barrier, depending on the conditions. Secondly, because the conditions were all inter-connected and inter-dependent. The discussions below illustrate these.

A context of autonomy

A context which enabled the young person to feel they could express themselves in terms of their own interests and choices featured as important for re-engagement in all the case studies. The secure custodial setting is designed to restrict individual autonomy, in terms of its physical structures and freedom of movement. The authentic inquiry provided a space within this context through which the individual could be autonomous. A context which enabled autonomy acted as a facilitator to re-engagement, empowering the learner to explore a task or topic that had value. Together, these acted as facilitators, enabling barriers to be navigated and overcome. Having some autonomy in an otherwise restrictive space was vital in re-engagement with education and learning as was illustrated in the case of Jack. Jack felt empowered through a sense of autonomy and was therefore motivated enough to be able to pursue the task and deal with the barriers even within secure context. However, a key to this was the relationship with the mentor (discussed in the section below).

The case study of William illustrates how a lack of autonomy can be a barrier to engagement. William did not feel he was able to express or be himself within the authentic inquiry which was led by his mentor. Consequently, William was not able to find the task to be of value or be agentic. Because he did not experience these things he was unable to negotiate the barriers of the secure context.

Autonomy seemed a necessary condition to enable agentic engagement as put forward by Reeve and Tseng (2012). Jack, when empowered by the conditions of autonomy, was agentic in his authentic inquiry. He was able to navigate the challenges and maintained his engagement to permeate through to other aspects of his life at the secure unit, such as becoming a 'rep' and campaigning for better quality

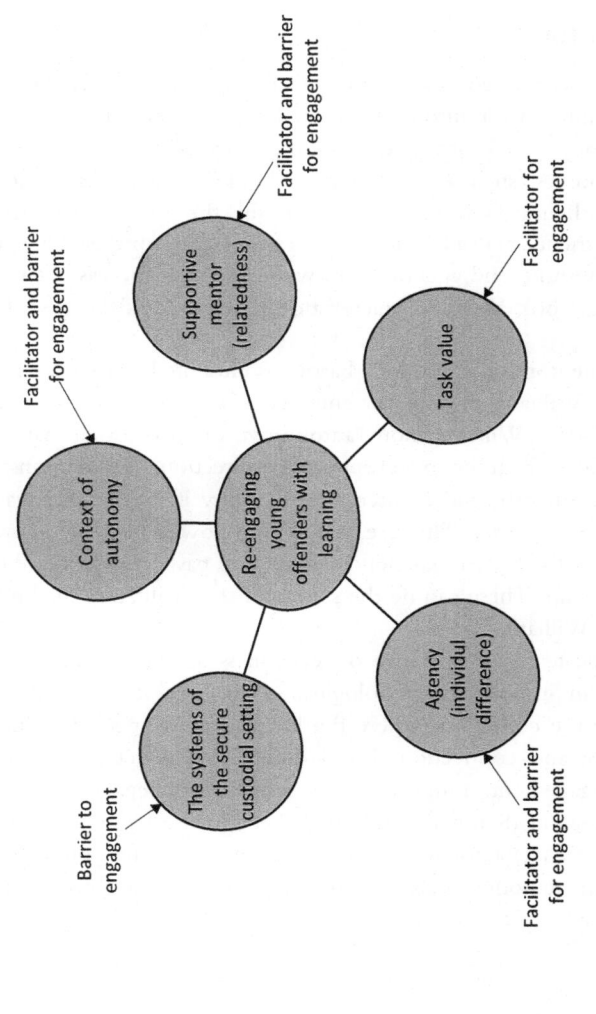

FIGURE 16.1 Facilitators and barriers to re-engagement with education in a secure custodial setting

food. William, however, did not experience this autonomy and consequently demonstrated little agency, other than what he had shown when he was introduced to the idea of the authentic inquiry. The opportunity had appealed to him, but in practice it emerged as more of the same prescriptive approach that he had disengaged him from education and learning. In this way, autonomy presented as a barrier and a facilitator and this was linked to the mentor.

Supportive mentor

A supportive mentor emerged as an essential facilitator. Mentors were instrumental in creating the conditions of autonomy through their support in encouraging the young person through questions or discussions. They were also vital in enabling the access to resources, such as the internet, books or stationery, and time to engage in their authentic inquiry. When successful, the mentor acted as a guide, facilitator, critical friend, and advocate whilst at the same time enabling the individual to be autonomous and agentic. This was evident in the case of Jack whose mentor James undertook all the characteristics of what could be described as an effective mentor.

However, the mentor could also be a barrier as illustrated in the case of William and Andrea. With William, the mentor emerged as a barrier because he needed a mentor who provided William more autonomy. On the other hand, Andrea would have benefitted from the extra support and direction. This demonstrates that a good fit between mentor and mentee was necessary if the mentor was to be a facilitator rather than a barrier. The case studies also showed how the mentor too is an active agent with their own experiences, aims, and passions which are expressed within the relationship. These can be the source of the facilitating or the barrier as was the case with William.

These cases indicate the importance of relatedness in self-determination theory and how this is an important psychological need. In a learning situation, the mentor can create the conditions where the learner feels respected, valued with a sense of belonging and connection. In so doing, it connects to the emotional component of engagement. Emotional engagement has been shown to predict behavioural engagement (Skinner et al., 2008, Lee, 2014). Therefore, a supportive mentor can be a key facilitator (or barrier) to re-engaging the young offender in learning, stimulating emotional and behavioural engagement through autonomy and relatedness.

Task value

This is a term associated with the expectancy-value theory (Eccles, 1983). It is based on the degree to which one expects to succeed (expectancy) and the value one places on the task itself (value). In the case studies task value was an important element of the authentic inquiry, represented by the topic selected and the 'end product' produced. Both of these had to have value for the individual to engage.

However, task value alone was insufficient. For example, Andrea had task value for her topic; however, the lack of a supportive mentor meant that the resources and support she needed for continued engagement were absent. Consequently, the engagement was not sustained. On the other hand, task value was a key driver for Jack, who persisted with insisting on time with his mentor in order to complete his task. However, this also showed how task value needed to be coupled with at least one other facilitator in order for it continue. In Jack's case this was his own agency.

When a task has value, there is greater chance of cognitive engagement. Within the case studies, the starting point was authentic to the learner and therefore had some intrinsic value. But the task also needed to have an expectancy of success. If this was diminished, then the task value would be reduced. This is connected to the competency need in self-determination theory because if one does not feel they can succeed in a task, then it does not meet this need. For example, Andrea abandoned her interest in the authentic inquiry topic and other lessons because her expectations of success tended to diminish. In doing so, this impacted on her competency needs. Thus, task value has an important role to play as an initial 'buy-in' to engagement but can lose its effect if the other conditions are not met which is why it can also present as a barrier.

Agency

All participants demonstrated agency by agreeing to participate. However, agency was demonstrated to varying degrees. For example, William engaged with the authentic inquiry at the compliance/behavioural level only whereas Jack demonstrated agency to the degree that he was in the driving seat of his authentic inquiry using his learning to benefit not only himself but other young people at the secure unit. This showed how agency was influenced by an individual's temperament and shaped how the individual negotiated the barriers. Jack's persistent (and demanding) manner had acted as a facilitator. However, for Andrea, her temperament had been a barrier in accessing the support she needed, and William's laid-back manner had meant that his mentor was able to drive the authentic inquiry in a direction that was not William's.

It is also noteworthy, however, that when conditions of autonomy were not present, there was greater opportunity agency, as in Jack's case, suggesting an interactive relationship between an environment which fostered autonomy and consequently agency. This is relevant in the secure context in which autonomy is restricted. In restricting autonomy, agency is also restricted. For young offenders who are described as disengaged with learning, fostering conditions of autonomy to facilitate agency could be an important endeavour. This reflects the point of Goldspink and Kay (2009) who distinguished agency and autonomy.

These case studies demonstrate that autonomy relates to creating conditions of empowerment (e.g. through the mentor relationship). However, agency refers to the extent to which the individual will use those conditions to self-direct their energy to their own defined goal. Jack demonstrated harmony between autonomy and agency and was able to navigate the challenges including those imposed on him by the secure context. However, William and Andrea did not experience the conditions of autonomy which could have facilitated agency.

Barriers due to the secure context

The secure context had considerable impacts on the young people. These manifested in generating and exacerbating emotional reactions which had an impact on behaviour. Given that emotional engagement predicts behavioural engagement (Li and Lerner, 2014; Lee 2014), the secure context presented significant barriers for engaging in the authentic inquiry. In addition to the impact on emotions, the nature of the secure context also impacted on practical aspects in terms of time with their mentor and access to resources to conduct their inquiry. In all cases mentors were selected from the care rather than education staff. Therefore, the biggest barrier here came from difficulty in being timetabled to be with their mentor and for their mentor to be able to arrange access to resources. In the case of Andrea, this barrier had resulted in the authentic inquiry not even getting off the ground. For William, not being able to identify a mentor resulted in the mentor self-selecting themselves which then led to an authentic inquiry with limited authenticity. Both these cases and others within the research demonstrated how the organisational features of the secure context, compounded by the locked and secure nature of this environment, presented as a barrier to re-engaging young offenders with education and learning.

Implications for practice

The opportunity

The opportunity for autonomy that the authentic inquiry presented is an exciting space through which to re-engage young offenders with learning. It offers an alternative approach to the model that has already failed for them in mainstream and other alternative school settings. The secure setting is also less wedded to the attainment culture found in mainstream schools and thus has a unique opportunity to be innovative in their approaches. For many young offenders it is very possible the final time in statutory education and is thereby a vital window in which to re-engage them.

Described as disengaged with learning and education where the nature of their disengagement is distinct, characterised by heightened emotions with relationships being of significance, they are less likely to respond to 'more of the same' type of approaches as those used in mainstream settings. Thus, alternative ways of re-engaging young offenders are vital, and this research shows that when alternative methods are used, re-engaging them can be relatively easy and within a short space of time, providing the conditions are met. This research has shown that embedding authentic inquiry as an integral and essential part of, for example, the induction process to the secure context, could be an important move in re-engaging young offenders with education and learning on arrival at the setting.

The realities

The locked environment of a custodial setting presented significant challenges for education. Education within the secure context was organised in classrooms, core subjects, a formal school day, and dedicated Head of Education (like mainstream school). Although the class size was based on a ratio of 1:4 in recognition of the additional needs of students, this was where the similarity with mainstream school ends.

This is because young people who enter the secure estate are disengaged with education and learning; classrooms are comprised of mixed age and mixed ability resulting in considerable pedagogical challenges for teachers, especially when they must deliver lessons to learners with little knowledge of previous attainment or ability. Further, there was no stability in the classroom composition as young offenders arrived and left at different times with different lengths of stay, compounded by the nature of some offences which prevented learning with particular resources. Added to this is the need to organise the class according to who was getting along with who. This catalogue of issues heightens the challenges for teachers who may have no specific training to meet the needs of such learners, made yet more difficult with the high staff turnover at secure units (Jeanes, McDonald, and Simonot, 2009).

The management structure, divided along the lines of care and education, with their own set of agendas and outcome measures also increased inherent problems of the secure setting. This added to the complexities and impacted on the authentic inquiries which required collaboration between care and education. The authentic inquiries were located within education but needed the co-operation of the care staff and flexibility in the structure of the secure unit to cultivate the conditions to facilitate engagement. In all cases, the structures of the secure context presented challenges. Although some of the young people were able to use their agency to navigate these structures, most yielded to them. For William and Andrea, the structures 'stifled' the initial glimpses of agency they had shown. Only Jack had been able to successfully navigate these, possibly because he had a longer sentence and therefore had time to persist, but also because of his own individual agency. The management structures of the secure unit also structured relationships. Being line managed by different departments had meant that coordination had proved difficult – the impact of which had been felt in all cases.

For the authentic inquiries to facilitate re-engagement with education and learning, a more systemic, co-ordinated approach within the entire secure unit to interconnect the teachers, mentors, and the young person would be required. This would enable staff and young people to form those much-needed relationships necessary for empowering young people for re-engagement with education and learning.

The irony

The greatest irony is that despite knowing the circumstances and situations of the young offenders, the aim is still to continue to try and fit them into a (mainstream) model that has simply not worked for them. Indeed, the situation is exacerbated because this time they are locked up. The distinct nature of disengagement in young offenders requires a different approach which recognises this and the context they are in.

Teachers did demonstrate acute awareness of the needs of the young people and recognised the need for different approaches. However, even at an individual level they did not feel able to respond to them, citing the constraints of the secure setting as the problem. In many ways, this research presented moments of frustration where to an observer, it seemed obvious what the young person needed; however none of the professionals seemed to be responding in a way that appropriately addressed the situation and, in some cases, actually worsened a situation. For example, teachers recognised that Andrea needed lots of help and support, but still attributed her behaviour to misconduct as opposed to a reaction to the continued mismatch of her needs with the support offered.

Teachers and practitioners usually enter such a profession in their desire to 'make a difference'. However, somewhere along the journey, the original passion perhaps wore down, perhaps because of the challenges of the secure setting, the young people themselves, or maybe a sense of disempowerment at not being able to 'make the difference' in the way envisioned. Whatever, the reason, the outcome was that staff were not as responsive to the needs of these young people – instead trying to fit them into the structures of the secure context, thereby exacerbating some of the issues.

It was notable that no participant in this research selected education staff as their mentors. It suggests that teachers were not viewed as being interested in what the young person might want to learn about. It further demonstrated the disconnect and disengagement between young offenders and formal learning.

Teachers need to reassess their crucial and valuable role in re-engaging young offenders, perhaps acting more as mentors as a practical application of their 'teacher identity'.

The lost opportunities

These issues were also apparent in the case studies. For example, with William there were several lost opportunities to engage him. Neither the teacher nor the mentor took the time to understand William as an individual, who he was, why he thought the way he did. Had they done this, they would have found that given the opportunity to explore what he wanted to, William could have excelled. This potential was clearly demonstrated in William's first interview, the teacher interviews, observations, and field notes. Instead, William was further exposed to the same hegemonic thinking that he was challenging in his mind. Therefore, in many ways, his lack of re-engagement was not entirely surprising. William's case illustrates the need to develop relationships comprised of trust rather than relationships defined entirely by the roles imposed by the secure custodial structures. Introducing William to the idea of being able to explore his own thinking through the authentic inquiry ultimately felt unethical because the promise was unfulfilled – ultimately serving to reinforce his negative views of society.

Potential was also evident in Andrea who was described by staff as difficult and hard to manage. When given the opportunity, Andrea demonstrated that she could be re-engaged and relatively easily. However, again, it was evident that the time taken to understand Andrea and her goals, fears, and aspirations was absent. This resulted in frustration and anger on the part of Andrea, expressed in her difficult behaviour. Even when a teacher recognised this, opportunities to try and develop a relationship were not taken, but instead difficulties were accepted as an inevitable feature of the secure context. The authentic inquiry offered hope, but which was also unfulfilled, representing another time when Andrea felt let down. This was one of the many ethical challenge posed in researching within this environment and with this participant group. Jack was similarly described as lazy; however as he seized the opportunity to take on the authentic inquiry, it was immediately evident that he was energetic and motivated. It could be that as Jack had been the only young person who had come from a mainstream school and situated within his family, he perhaps had not yet become as disillusioned with people letting him down.

The potential

This research has highlighted the importance of relationships for young people who are incarcerated, removed from their homes, family, and familiarity. Adding this to the difficulties and challenges described earlier in this chapter, makes for grim reading. This work, however, demonstrated that young people in custody can be re-engaged with education and learning when given an opportunity and with the right conditions. It demonstrates that young people continue to have hope despite the circumstances and will respond to opportunities if they are perceived as genuine.

Whilst authentic inquiry is not a silver bullet, it does offer several gains in addition to re-engagement with education and learning: for example, ascertaining educational levels earlier through the authentic inquiry, rather than a battery of tests as is currently the practice. In so doing, by the time the young offender enters the 'school' at the secure setting, they are in a better position to engage, have formed a relationship with their mentor and teachers. In turn, they will have greater knowledge of their educational level in order to maintain a measure of continuity in their education. These early relationships could also play key roles in managing the emotions which were shown to be heightened within the secure context. Emotions and relationships characterised the nature of disengagement in young offenders. The relationships at the secure unit had the potential to either exacerbate or manage heightened emotions. Thus, understanding and responding to these are an important aspect of successfully re-engaging young offenders with education and learning.

Conclusions

There is considerable evidence that young offenders' experiences of school and learning is disruptive and unfulfilling. It suggests that education in secure settings must do more than simply their minimum legal obligations of education. Time in custody is an ideal space to provide an engaging high quality, relevant, and meaningful education provision before transitioning back into the community. Young offenders recognise that education carries the prospect for change and demonstrate willingness to engage when given the opportunity.

The insight from these individual case studies of young offenders in a secure custodial setting is a breakthrough in new knowledge. Findings showed that re-engaging even the most disengaged learner within a relatively short space of time was possible, thereby representing a vital opportunity within the secure context. However, there are conditions that need to be met to foster this and include the need for a task to have value, to provide space for autonomy, to enable agency, for there to a supportive mentor, and for the secure context to be facilitative in terms of its institutional structure. However, changes to the systems within the secure unit and staffing arrangements are needed to enable the authentic inquiries to really benefit those who undertake them. These changes could be implemented within existing structures of individual secure units without the need for mass financial investment in resources. In so doing, relationships between staff (care and education) are brought into sharp focus in terms of the importance they have in supporting the management of emotions. Emotions and relationships emerged as crucial elements disengagement in young offenders. Attending to these creates the conditions which foster re-engagement with education and learning.

Note

This chapter describes the findings from all Phases of the research using three of the five case studies from Phase II as illustrations. For further information on the research contact the author on ashafi@glos.ac.uk

References

Appleton, J.J., Christenson, S.L., and Furlong, M. J. (2008) Student engagement with school: Critical conceptual and methodological issues of the construct. *Psychology in the Schools*, 45, 5, 369–386.

Ball, C., and Connolly, J. (2000) Educationally disaffected young offenders. *British Journal of Criminology*, 40, 4, 594–616.

Behan, C. (2014) Learning to escape: prison education, rehabilitation and the potential for transformation. *Journal of Prison Education and Reentry*, 1, 1, 20–31.

Case, S., and Haines, K. (2015a) Children first, offenders second positive promotion: reframing the prevention debate. *Youth Justice*, 15, 3, 226–239.
Case, S., and Haines, K. (2015b) Children first, offenders second: the centrality of engagement in positive youth justice. *The Howard Journal of Crime and Justice*, 54, 2, 157–175.
Chitsabesan, P., and Hughes, N. (2016) Mental health needs and neurodevelopmental disorders amongst young offenders: implications for policy and practice. In J. Winstone, *Mental health, crime and criminal justice*. Dordrecht: Springer, pp. 109–130.
Crick, R.D. (2012) Deep engagement as a complex system: identity, learning power and authentic enquiry. In S.L. Christenson, A.L. Reschly, and C. Wylie (Eds), *Handbook of research on student engagement*. Dordrecht: Springer, pp. 675–694.
Deci, E.L. and Ryan, R.M. (1985) The general causality orientations scale: self-determination in personality. *Journal of Research in Personality*, 19, 2, 109–134.
Deci, E.L. and Ryan, R.M. (2008) Self-determination theory: a macrotheory of human motivation, development, and health. *Canadian Psychology/Psychologie Canadienne*, 49, 3, 182.
Deci, E.L. and Ryan, R.M. (2010) *Self-determination*. Wiley Online Library.
Earl, S.R., Taylor, I.M., Meijen, C., and Passfield, L. (2017) Autonomy and competence frustration in young adolescent classrooms: different associations with active and passive disengagement. *Learning and Instruction*, 49, 32–40.
Eccles, J.S. (1983) *Expectancies, values, and academic behaviors*. San Francisco: Freeman.
Farrington, D.P. and Welsh, B. (2007) *Saving children from a life of crime: early risk factors and effective interventions*. Oxford: Oxford University Press.
Fredricks, J.A. (2011) Engagement in school and out-of-school contexts: a multidimensional view of engagement. *Theory into Practice*, 50, 4, 327–335.
Fredricks, J.A., Blumenfeld, P.C., and Paris, A.H. (2004) School engagement: potential of the concept, state of the evidence. *Review of Educational Research*, 74, 1, 59–109.
Fredricks, J.A., Filsecker, M., and Lawson, M.A. (2016) Student engagement, context, and adjustment: addressing definitional, measurement, and methodological issues. *Learning and Instruction*, 43, 1–4.
Goldspink, C., and Kay, R. (2009) Agent cognitive capabilities and orders of social emergence. In G. Trajkovski and S.G. Collins (Eds), *Handbook of research on agent-based societies: social and cultural interactions*. Hershey, PA: IGI Global.
González, R.A., Gudjonsson, G.H., Wells, J., and Young, S. (2016) The role of emotional distress and ADHD on institutional behavioral disturbance and recidivism among offenders. *Journal of Attention Disorders*, 20, 4, 368–378.
Hart, D. (2015) *Correction or care? The use of custody for children in trouble*. London: Churchill Memorial Trust.
Heinzen, H., Koehler, D., Smeets, T., Hoffer, T., and Huchzermeier, C. (2011) Emotion regulation in incarcerated young offenders with psychopathic traits. *Journal of Forensic Psychiatry and Psychology*, 22, 6, 809–833.
Hirschfield, P.J., and Gasper, J. (2011) The relationship between school engagement and delinquency in late childhood and early adolescence. *Journal of Youth and Adolescence*, 40, 1, 3–22.
Hughes, N. (2012) *Nobody made the connection: the prevalence of neurodisability in young people who offend*. London: The Office of the Children's Commissioner. Retrieved from: http://dera.ioe.ac.uk/16045/1/Neurodisability_Report_FINAL_UPDATED__01_11_12.pdf
Jaros, M., and Deakin-Crick, R. (2007) Personalized learning for the post-mechanical age. *Journal of Curriculum Studies*, 39, 4, 423–440.
Jeanes, J., McDonald, J., and Simonot, M. (2009) Conflicting demands in prison education and the need for context-specific, specialist training for prison educators: an account of the work of the Initial Teacher Training project for teachers and instructors in London

prisons and offender learning. *Teaching in Lifelong Learning: A Journal to Inform and Improve Practice*. University of Huddersfield. Retrieved from: https://doi.org/10.5920/till.2009.1128

Kirk, D.S., and Sampson, R.J. (2013) Juvenile arrest and collateral educational damage in the transition to adulthood. *Sociology of Education*, 86, 1, 36–62.

Lanskey, C. (2015) Up or down and out? A systemic analysis of young people's educational pathways in the youth justice system in England and Wales. *International Journal of Inclusive Education*, 19, 6, 568–582.

Lee, J.S. (2014) The relationship between student engagement and academic performance: Is it a myth or reality? *The Journal of Educational Research*, 107, 3, 177–185.

Li, Y., and Lerner, R.M. (2013) Interrelations of behavioral, emotional, and cognitive school engagement in high school students. *Journal of Youth and Adolescence*, 42, 1, 20–32.

Little, R. (2015) Putting education at the heart of custody? The views of children on education in a young offender institution. *British Journal of Community Justice*, 13, 2, 27.

Murray, R., Britain, G., Britain, G., and Board, Y.J. (2012) *Children and young people in custody 2011–12: an analysis of the experiences of 15–18 year olds in prison*. London: The Stationery Office.

Prior, D., and Mason, P. (2010) A different kind of evidence? Looking for 'what works' in engaging young offenders. *Youth Justice*, 10, 3, 211–226.

Reeve, J., and Tseng, C.-M. (2011) Agency as a fourth aspect of students' engagement during learning activities. *Contemporary Educational Psychology*, 36, 4, 257–267.

Skinner, E., Furrer, C., Marchand, G., and Kindermann, T. (2008) Engagement and disaffection in the classroom: part of a larger motivational dynamic? *Journal of Educational Psychology*, 100, 4, 765–781.

Skinner, E.A., Kindermann, T.A., and Furrer, C.J. (2008) A motivational perspective on engagement and disaffection: conceptualization and assessment of children's behavioral and emotional participation in academic activities in the classroom. *Educational and Psychological Measurement*, 69, 3, 493–525.

Snow, P.C., Woodward, M., Mathis, M., and Powell, M.B. (2016) Language functioning, mental health and alexithymia in incarcerated young offenders. *International Journal of Speech-Language Pathology*, 18, 1, 20–31.

Wang, M.-T., and Fredricks, J.A. (2014) The reciprocal links between school engagement, youth problem behaviors, and school dropout during adolescence. *Child Development*, 85, 2, 722–737.

Wexler, J., Pyle, N., Flower, A., Williams, J.L., and Cole, H. (2014) A synthesis of academic interventions for incarcerated adolescents. *Review of Educational Research*, 84, 1, 3–46.

Young, S., Moss, D., Sedgwick, O., Fridman, M., and Hodgkins, P. (2015) A meta-analysis of the prevalence of attention deficit hyperactivity disorder in incarcerated populations. *Psychological Medicine*, 45, 2, 247–258.

17

'THE BANTER LEVELS ARE GOOD'

Developing social and human capital through education

Anita Mehay and Nina Champion

'He helps me, he is funny and the banter[1] levels are good,' reads one letter. 'He lights up young people's days when they are down,' says another. Every summer the Prisoners' Education Trust's (PET) office is flooded with powerful letters such as these, nominating teachers, officers, peer mentors, and others for the annual Prisoner Learning Alliance (PLA) awards. At a time when report after report highlights the disgraceful lack of safety and purposeful activity in our custodial establishments holding young people (Her Majesty's Inspectorate of Prisons, 2008; HM Chief Inspector of Prisons, 2017; HM Inspectorate of Prisons, 2016; HM Chief Inspector of Prisons, 2006), these awards shine a light on the staff and peers who are transforming lives through education. This chapter will reflect on some of these examples of good practice to inspire researchers, policy makers, and educators to consider what education in prison could look like, especially for young people in custody,[2] who are recognised as a highly vulnerable, complex, and challenging group (Harris Review Panel, 2015; Bradley, 2009; HM Inspector of Prisons, 2016). Although the treatment of all people in custody is a concern, imprisonment of young people is particularly concerning in light of their developmental needs and transitioning into healthy adulthood which occurs up to age 25 years (Blakemore and Choudhury, 2006; Royal College of Psychiatrists, 2015). Choosing an appropriate intervention and approach can mean younger people are more likely to stop offending and less likely to prolong the time spent in the criminal justice system, as highlighted in a recent review: 'Dealing effectively with young adults while the brain is still developing is crucial for them in making successful transitions to a crime-free adulthood' (House of Commons Justice Committee, 2016: 13).

In contrast, interventions which do not recognise and support young adults' maturity can slow desistance and extend the period of involvement in the criminal justice system. This chapter, therefore, outlines learnings from a three-year programme, funded by the Paul Hamlyn Foundation, which specifically explores education for young people up to age 25 in custody through a number of objectives, including:

- Bringing distance learning into YOIs: pilot of a distance-learning programme for under 18s in custody (conducted in 2016–2017)
- Expanding access into university: pilot of a prison-university partnership for young adults (conducted in 2017)
- Strengthening relationships within YOIs: development and delivery of a symposium bringing together academics, practitioners, policy makers, and learners to discuss education in youth custody (held in January 2016) with a resulting report of these activities with recommendations (Taylor, 2016). In addition, the inclusion of a young people's estate category to the annual PLA awards (in 2016–2017).

Figure 17.1 illustrates the three objectives.

Before outlining each of the learnings from these activities, this chapter will first examine the role of education in custody and the theory of change underpinning the objectives of this programme.

What is education in custody for?

Education is one of the seven pathways to resettlement back in society identified by the National Offender Management System (NOMS)[3] in England and Wales

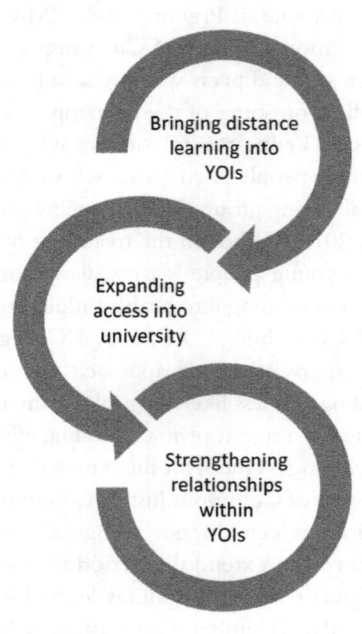

FIGURE 17.1 The three objectives.

and is proven to have a statistically significant impact on reducing re-offending (Hopkins, 2012; Clark, 2016; Davis et al., 2013). However, the challenge is now to tease out what works, for whom, and in what contexts requiring an in-depth analysis of whether prison education should be focused on producing effective workers or focused on personal growth (Armstrong and Ludlow, 2016). Dr Di Hart, speaking at PET's youth custody focused academic symposium, set this challenge to the sector to define what education for young people in custody was for and to articulate a clear theoretical framework:

> it's about going back to basics, asking the big questions about what custody is for and what will work to transform their lives. In comparison to the approaches taken in Spain, Finland and parts of the US, our use of custody in England and Wales looks very process driven and lacking in vision.

Indeed, similar calls for reflection and focus were highlighted in the Taylor Review, which suggested that education needed to:

> to help [young people in custody] to overcome their difficulties, address the causes of their offending and prepare them for successful reintegration into society when they are released.
>
> *(Taylor, 2016)*

The PLA worked with New Philanthropy Capital to examine this further and develop a theoretical framework with which to examine prison education. Using a 'collage as inquiry' approach, former prisoners who had undertaken education in prison or YOIs, and after release, were asked to make a collage and to take part in interviews to explore what education meant to them (Champion and Noble, 2016). Findings were used to develop an overarching 'theory of change', consisting of four individual outcomes: social capital, human capital, wellbeing, and employability, as well as an institutional outcome relating to the development of a learning culture (Figure 17.2).

This theory of change aims to stimulate debate and conversation about the purpose and value of prison education: how we can more strategically evaluate the benefits and how we can improve provision.

This chapter draws particularly on the relevance of social capital and human capital. Human capital refers to 'people's skills, learning, talents and attributes' (Keeley, 2007) where the Ministry of Justice describe developing human capital as 'being an asset' and 'unlocking potential'.[4] Indeed, the development of skills opens up different avenues and alternatives to crime (Lochner, 2004); however, human capital refers to more than just acquisition of skills but a greater personal process of change. A former prison teacher articulated[5] the personal processes prisoners undergo, stating:

> prisoners are asked to undergo the most difficult of all human processes, the process of change [...] 'Who am I? Where am I going?' [...] This is not to

FIGURE 17.2 Theory of change for prison education (Champion and Noble, 2016)

devalue literacy or numeracy, but to elevate self-discovery as the over-arching goal in education.

Social capital is the links, shared values, and understanding in society that enable individuals and groups to trust each other and so work together (Keeley, 2007). It enables a person to achieve more than would be possible if acting independently (Lafferty et al., 2016; Bourdieu, 1986). Social capital is a valuable social resource that encompasses a variety of dimensions, including:

1. Bonds: links to people based on a sense of common identity
2. Bridges: links that stretch beyond a shared sense of identity
3. Linkages: connections to people further up or down the social ladder.

Indeed, research exploring social capital in prison highlights the positive outcomes for young people in custody. A rapid evidence assessment conducted by the Ministry of Justice highlighted that young people value a relationship that is 'warm, open and non-judgemental' and that this factor is crucial to them engaging with 'interventions' and working towards change (Adler et al., 2016). A report into desistance and young people also highlighted that a 'trusting, open and collaborative relationship with their YOT worker or other professional, was the biggest factor in their achievement' (Her Majesty's Inspectorate of Probation, 2016: 17). Similarly, Dr Di Hart also found that good relations helped young people feel safe and learn new ways of thinking and feeling about their lives (Hart, 2016). In attempting to understand the development of human and social capital in prison further, the PLA have identified a variety of 'change processes' through which learning may contribute to human and social capital (Figures 17.3 and 17.4).

Although both human and social capital can be valuable resources, the usual avenues for building and accessing both are often not available to prisoners (Lafferty et al., 2016) where efforts should focus on opportunities for development. This is particularly relevant to children where contracts impose a 30-hour education target on young people with little regards to the approach, type, and quality of this education. However, in England and Wales, the Ministry of Justice have adopted a new outcome-focused definition of prison education which echoes the PLA Theory of Change, stating:

> Activities that give individuals the skills they need to unlock their potential, gain employment and become assets to their communities. It should also build social capital and improve the wellbeing of prisoners during their sentences.

This definition of education heralds a commitment to a more holistic understanding of prison education which draws parallels with the recent developments from the PLA and Coates Review (2016) to support human and social capital. When current contracts expire in the young people's estate they too may move towards a model of governor-led commissioning, as is happening in the adult estate. As such, PET embarked upon this programme to develop and examine examples of good practice based on the theory of change, as applied to young people in custody. The chapter continues to outline these activities and learning further.

Motivation to change
- Opportunity for reflection. Psychological sense of new beginning, having a goal, hope
- Feelings of progression and moving forward
- Gradual introduction to learning tailored to needs, strengths and interests
- Exposure to new possibilities, ideas and role models
- Encouraging imagination and a different world view
- Taking ownership and responsibility for learning: making choices, self direction, feeling of control

Moving forward
- Learning to appreciate own strengths and resources. Greater self awareness
- Experience of meeting challenges, achievement, making progress and pride
- Engagement in and practice new activities, roles and experiences
- Opportunity to express oneself, be creative in a positive way
- Learning and reflecting on personal history and gaining new perspectives on oneself
- Experience of concentration, patience, applying oneself, self discipline, focus

FIGURE 17.3 Human capital (Champion and Noble, 2016)

> **Belonging and community**
> - Teachers showing an interest and treating them with respect and kindness
> - Learning to trust teachers and changing attitudes towards education/authority
> - Shared education experience as point of commonality and collaboration
> - Exposure to different people, cultures and ideas
> - Practising new behaviours such as working together
> - Experience of helping others and seeing the benefits

> **Active engagement**
> - Development of functional and life skills
> - Knowledge and confidence to access services and support in prison and after release
> - Building resilience and confidence to challenge appropriately and persuasively
> - Developing a thirst for learning and interests
> - Increased understanding of family, relationships and parenting roles and impact of behaviours and attitudes on family
> - Experience of participation in prison civic life developing knowledge, skills and confidence.

FIGURE 17.4 Social capital (Champion and Noble, 2016)

Bringing distance learning into YOIs

Only a small number of young people leave custody with Level 2 qualifications or above (Rogers et al., 2014) and in his government review of youth justice, Charlie Taylor found that: 'There is also not sufficient provision for high-ability children who are capable of getting the top grades in their GCSEs and to go on to take A-levels and prepare for university'. He added that 'perhaps the most worrying finding is that in youth custodial establishments I have rarely encountered the culture of aspiration and discipline which is evident in the best alternative provision schools' (Taylor, 2016).

Over the last 18 months PET has funded over 20 children to do distance learning courses. One young applicant seeking funding for a Sociology A-level said:

> I'm an intelligent young man and I feel like my talents are being wasted [...] I have 9 A-C GCSEs under my belt but I am capable of more. I want to have a life other than getting into trouble.

Another young man applying for A-Level English wrote:

> Before coming to prison I had prospects and plans [...] Yes I did wrong and I let stupid decisions foil those plans. I came to prison thinking the only option I had left was a life of crime, that I would only be known and seen as a criminal. I was wrong. My goal is to study game technology at university.

The children have applied for a wide range of subjects, from book-keeping to business, plumbing theory to personal training. Having a wide distance learning curriculum has enabled them to make choices which reflect their individual interests and skills. In their mainstream education, due to 'keep apart lists', young people can often be put into classes they did not choose because they need to be kept separate from other individuals, often due to risks linked to gang violence. Having 30 hours of compulsory education in a young people's establishment means that the element of choice is restricted and the ability to 'take ownership' of learning is more difficult. Distance learning is education the young people are volunteering to apply for, above and beyond their regular 30-hour curriculum. Whether they complete the assignments and do the work is completely their own choice. There are no penalties for not completing, so self-direction and self-motivation are vital skills required to make a success of a distance-learning course. Both are key elements of human capital.

In a focus group PET held with young distance learners at one establishment, it was clear that they were grappling with self-directed learning, as it was something they had little experience of through their education either in school or in the YOI. 'You've got to be determined and have willpower' said one learner. 'You need self-motivation, to say to yourself, I'm going to do it today' said another. Even the motivation to get going when the package of resources arrives could be hard when they feel overwhelmed; 'When it arrived I thought s★★t, what am I supposed to do with this? That's a lot of work. How am I going to be able to do that?' One young man who has dyslexia said: 'Distance learning was a big change for me, I'm used to being in a class and having quite a lot of teacher support'.

Distance learning in prison also comes with a number of practical challenges, highlighted by the young men in the focus group. Barriers range from no access to the internet to needing notebooks, pens, and for one learner a scientific calculator. Fortunately, they had built positive relationships with the staff and felt able to ask for help. For example, during the focus group a teacher came in to lend one of the distance learners studying maths a pencil sharpener to use in front of her, as he was not allowed to take it back to his cell. Despite the obstacles in their way, the young men had clearly begun to find ways of overcoming these practical and personal challenges, thereby building their resilience and human capital.

Some learners had been able to call on family for support and motivation. For example, one learner, who is studying a course in electrical technologies theory, had support from an uncle who is willing to offer him practical training and possibly employment in this area after release. Another student explained that doing the course had brought him closer to his mum, from whom he had been estranged from prior to custody, as he was studying a subject she was knowledgeable in. One young man described how his mum had motivated him when he had been disappointed in failing his tenth assignment, having passed the first nine:

> My Engagement and Resettlement Worker and my mum encouraged me to keep going and re-do it. In October there was a celebration event at the prison. My mum and dad came as I had passed the first two assignments by

then. My mum asks me how my studying is going when I speak to her. You know what it's like, mums make you do stuff!

The students also encourage and help each other: 'I saw [another student] doing a bookkeeping distance learning course. He showed me the books and it's coz of him I applied'. When the two boys are in class together they can share challenges and experiences. The focus group students voiced that they would like a specific distance learning class to enable them to study together, preferably with access to word processing for essays, which were currently mostly being done by hand. Where learners had been able to come together on an informal basis, they had found it beneficial. One learner, studying psychology, described being able to carry out a memory test that was part of his first assignment on a fellow distance learner which had 'brought the learning to life' for him. Unfortunately, given the restrictions of 30-hour education contracts, the learners' suggestion of having a distance learning class as part of the core day would be a challenge for staff to implement; however they agreed to look into the possibility of an evening study group.

The process of expressing views and needs, for example through focus groups or a student council, is part of developing human capital. However, learners need to feel their voices are being heard by having their solutions and ideas tested where possible. Structural barriers, such as education contracts, regime issues, and lack of access to technology, can act as obstacles to enabling young distance learners to get the most from the opportunity. It is particularly important for this age group to have a social aspect to the learning experience and to access to technology to engage them and prepare them effectively for work and study in the community.

Some of the young people articulated an idea for sessions to help them with study skills, such as time management. There are various examples of international prison university partnerships supporting the development of study skills. For example, in California students from Cal Poly Pomona University go to a juvenile establishment 'Boys Republic' to provide weekly evening classes in study skills, working in small groups to discuss practical tactics.[6] In San Quentin prison in California, university lecturers run study skills classes in subjects such as comprehension to support learners to know how to structure and write academic essays.[7] PET has been working in partnership with Cardiff Metropolitan University in Wales to develop a study skills handbook which has been co-produced with prisoner learners, as well as delivering study skills support and training peer mentors to help distance learners of all ages. PET hopes to roll out this approach across England and Wales. PET has also set up a network called PUPiL[8] (Prison University Partnerships in Learning) to share good practice and support universities and custodial establishments to work together.

Despite the practical and personal obstacles identified during the pilot, most of the students are succeeding in their courses. Several of the learners began courses in YOIs and have now been transferred to the young adult or adult estate, where, due to the nature of distance learning, they can take the course materials with them and continue in their new establishment. A few have been released, including one who applied for a resettlement award and was successful in securing funds for an advanced course in the community. He said,

> I have come a long way from where I was getting in trouble a lot to being a role model and mentor to others [...] This course has allowed me to change my view on education and I would use this award to further my studies within sports (leisure management) [...] and pursue it as a career.

Distance learning can provide aspirational education opportunities for young people in custody. If establishments could develop social capital through peer support, in addition to developing human capital through independent learning, this could enhance the impact for this age group by providing positive opportunities for peer influence and role modelling.

Promoting prison-university partnerships

In addition to bringing education into prison through increasing provisions of distance learning, this programme sought to increase aspiration and access into university for young adults. Prison–university partnerships have begun to flourish in England and Wales where one of the aims of these initiatives is to raise aspirations amongst prisoner learners to attend university. A recent report by the Social Mobility Advisory Group (2016) reflects the potential impact of increasing access into university where 'Universities transform lives. Going to university leads to new ways of seeing the world, to new horizons and networks, and to significantly enhanced job opportunities' (Social Mobility Advisory Group, 2016: 1).

Learning Together prison–university partnerships seek to bring people in prison and university students together to co-learn at a higher education level. Students not only study together but they also learn with and from each other through discussions and the sharing of experiences and knowledge (Armstrong and Ludlow, 2016). Here, social and human capital is strengthened where everyone in the classroom is valued as a student which includes the facilitators, lecturers, and prison-based staff; all are learners with something to share and learn from, where no-one is excluded.

Learning Together presents an opportunity to meet some of the distinct and complex needs associated with young adults in prison and their transition to adulthood. Since the initial conception, Learning Together partnerships have flourished across the UK; however, there are few examples within a younger prison population, despite the potential relevancy to this group. Therefore, in 2017 PET developed a Learning Together partnership pilot project, involving the delivery of a ten-week social science research methods course. Young adults (mainly aged 18–25 years) were supported in learning research skills and the application of these skills through conducting a project to inform improvements to prison education. A total of 20 learners enrolled on the course (ten from the prison and ten from a university). An external evaluation of the partnership was conducted by Dr Anita Mehay, commissioned by PET, to explore some of the strengths and challenges in supporting human and social capital in this learning environment.

Learners spoke of developing human capital through the shaping and exploration of a multifaceted learner identity, with person-centred support, and the potential of through-the-gate support from the university, building confidence in what could be possible for their future selves. They described the course as 'opening their eyes' and raising their awareness about the world around them. As one student described his progress, stating, 'Social science for me opened my eyes to things that I didn't think about when making decisions that got me in here in the first place'. This had a transformative effect in developing their critical thinking skills, where they were less impulsive and judgmental towards others in light of this awareness of other people's lives and circumstances.

Learning Together was also described as an opportunity to build social capital through bringing groups of individuals together who may not ordinarily have met, and to challenge and be challenged about the judgements they held about each other. Trust was able to form between the learners, where the gender-mix and similarities in age fused the group into a unity where respectful 'banter' and social norms were part of a positive learning environment. Learning was inextricably fused by this connectedness to people and society where one student from the prison stated:

> I feel like this course was a real good bonding session for everyone and if that's what it's like in uni, I would love to go to university ... It taught me stuff that I never knew before, it opened my eyes to perceive the world as a much bigger and broader spectrum.

Learners reflected that week on week, there were never any incidences, trouble, or violence between the young men as they respected each other as learners. This was described by the prison learners as highly unusual within the prison environment which was marred by mistrust and volatility. More so, although learners all had differing levels of educational attainment, knowledge, and literacy (as selection had been based on motivation not academic credentials) they were keen to support each other to progress as a group, not just individually. There was a strong ethos that they had started the course together and wanted to successfully complete this as a group. Banter between all students was a way to bond and build rapport and friendships between them. As one prison learner noted, 'Everyone was having fun, having some banter. [But] no-one really pushed certain things too far'. This banter with learning was an important part of the process to feeling connected with each other, which created a relaxed and comfortable atmosphere for learning.

Social interactions and the influence of positive peers are important aspects of young adulthood which can be utilised in learning. Here, 'young adulthood' is an asset which can be utilised and supported for learning. However, there were specific complexities relating to the use of peer and social-based models of learning and in maintaining boundaries for risk management. Although learners in this evaluation were aware of the need for such rules and boundaries, some saw these as rigid and requiring further conceptualisation and fluidity within this context. For example, young people felt disappointed that social connections could not continue after the course. The findings suggest that there are complexities involved in building prison–university partnerships, but the benefits are worthwhile.

Strengthening relationships within YOIs

Learning experiences can provide an ideal opportunity to facilitate positive and pro-social relationships between and within staff and peer groups, thus building social capital and contributing to the desistance process. This can be seen in the nominations for the PLA annual awards from young people for outstanding teacher, officer, peer mentor, and individual. This section draws on the learning from these awards and efforts to embed this into policy and practice through workforce development.

In 2017 the winning teacher taught young people at HMYOI Werrington Barista skills, but it is clear that it wasn't just coffee making skills the young people gained: 'Great teacher-makes lessons fun, makes us work hard but we still enjoy it. He's very supportive,' said one nominee. Another said, 'He helps me, he is funny and the banter levels are good'. This is an example of how positive teaching experiences can build trust and develop positive attitudes towards learning and 'working hard'.

In 2016 the winning teacher at HMYOI Feltham was described by one young person as having,

> motivated me to do work when usually I wouldn't bother and she's made me think of other ways to deal with my anger. Even when I refuse to see her in the morning she comes back in the afternoon and doesn't give up on me.

This shows the importance of teachers showing a genuine interest and demonstrating kindness as this can change attitudes in the young people they work with. However, it is not just teaching staff who can help build social capital through learning. This year's winning prison officer in the young people's estate was described by the nominee as 'lighting up young peoples' days when they are down' and 'being a rock in all young people's lives'. In an interview with PET after collecting his award, the officer who is in his twenties described how he left the military at 22 years old and was looking for a job which would challenge him. 'The young people's estate does that and more' he described, 'but sometimes you go home after your shift and know you've made a change', citing an example of a young man he mentored who then gained qualifications and became the top of his class.

The award nominations also gave examples of the 'active engagement' element of social capital. The winner of the outstanding individual category was a senior youth co-ordinator for the charity Kinetic Youth. One nominee wrote 'he helps the young people for us to be heard'. In his interview the winner explained that due to 'growing up in an environment where many of my friends have ended up in prison or dead, I feel the least I can do is to educate youth and practitioners alike'. He described that, in preparing for a Youth Justice Board conference workshop about the experience of young black males in the criminal justice system, he spoke to young people 'so I could speak on their behalf. Some of their words were so powerful and alarming ... I don't believe their voices are heard often enough when measuring whether we are impacting on the realities they live in'. Active engagement was also a golden thread running through the nominations for the winner of the outstanding peer mentor category. His engagement and resettlement manager said, 'he has dedicated himself to helping others, using his position on the youth council to air other young people's views and help bring change on the wing. He is described by his peers as a role model'.

Having listened to young people about what they value in the professionals and peers they work with and seeing from their examples how these positive relationships can help promote education and build social capital, it is vital to embed this into policy and practice. The PLA has been working with new charity Unlocked Graduates in delivering a session for trainee prison officers as part of their full time Masters degree programme. The session included an overview of prison education, evidence about the value of prison education, and what makes an outstanding officer (based on a content analysis of PLA award nominations). As a result, many of the new recruits have been active in initiating educational opportunities on their wings, for example one set up a series of Black History Month activities. The PLA has also been involved in a review of the mainstream prison officer training programme (POELT). The review is considering how the current 12-week PowerPoint and security-focused training can be refreshed with more of a focus on developing interpersonal and relationship skills, which are particularly vital in engaging young people.

Conclusion

This chapter reflects on the learnings from a programme of work exploring education for children and young adults in custody. For many prisoners, education in prison is an adjunct to the overall apparatus of surveillance, control, and punishment which serves the interests of the institution rather than the individual needs of the prisoner. Prisoners often feel the 'pains of imprisonment' where the increasing number of assessments of their risks strips them of their identity where they are subjected to constant surveillance and judgement towards their behaviours, actions, and attitudes. Prison education is similarly often conceptualised through a risk and deficit framework where poor educational attainment needs to be 'treated' through interventions, rather than through a long-term strategy for personal development and transformation.

Indeed, prison education contracts and funding mechanisms based on 'output based' key performance indicators have led to the prioritisation of low level basic skills courses, which are easily audited and evidenced, over less tangible personal and social development. The 30-hour contracts for young people have, in some cases, meant that the quantity of education has taken priority over the quality of education. However, current policy developments giving governors the ability to commission education and the new outcome-focused definition of prison education heralds a move towards understanding prison education through a more holistic lens.

Our insights seek to guide efforts to develop human and social capital, which is particularly relevant to younger learners where education can support the transitions to adulthood and where peer support, social contact, and 'banter' are arguably important aspects of youth. Our insights suggest that these should be viewed as assets to be developed and promoted within education to build human and social capital rather than adopting a risk approach to prison education which views young people as untrustworthy, unreliable, and risky. Giving young people choice and independent study opportunities can develop human capital, but this should ideally be combined with face-to-face support from staff, family, external organisations, and peers to develop social capital and to build and maintain motivation.

Giving younger prisoners opportunities to learn alongside university students can build human capital through new hopes and identities, as well as building social links between groups who otherwise might not have come into contact. However, this programme also points to the current problems of prisons as institutions which are designed to restrict and control through various values, rules, and rituals; these are at odds with the notion that prisoners can be encouraged to learn through participation and transformative learning. Therefore, it is not simply enough to have learning opportunities available; the culture must be supportive. Staff must help promote education through building trust and rapport, including through 'banter'. As governors take more control of commissioning over the next few years this is an exciting opportunity to provide learning which meets the need of specific groups, including young people, for whom learning should aim to build maturity through a combination of activities that develop both human and social capital.

Notes

1 The playful and friendly exchange of teasing remarks
2 Including children aged up to 18 years and young adults aged 18–25 years.
3 Replaced by Majesty's Prison and Probation Service (HMPPS) as of 1 April 2017.
4 As presented at a Ministry of Justice event on 'Education Framework Market Engagement'
5 An opinion piece in Inside Times, a prison newspaper. Article can be found at https://insidetime.org/thoughts-on-olass-4/

6 This is one example of an initiative run by the Prison Education Project. More information retrieved from: http://www.prisoneducationproject.org/
7 This is one example of an initiative run by the Prison University Project. More information retrieved from: https://prisonuniversityproject.org/
8 More information retrieved from: http://www.prisonerseducation.org.uk/pupil

References

Adler, J.R., Edwards, S.K., Scally, M., Gill, D., Puniskis, M.J., Gekoski, A., and Horvath, M.A.H. (2016) *What works in managing young people who offend? A summary of the international research*. London: Ministry of Justice.

Armstrong, R., and Ludlow, A. (2016) Educational partnerships between universities and prisons: how learning together can be individually, socially, and institutionally transformative. *Prison Service Journal*, 225, 9–17.

Blakemore, S.-J., and Choudhury, S. (2006) Development of the adolescent brain: implications for executive function and social cognition. *Journal of Child Psychology and Psychiatry, and Allied Disciplines*, 47, 3–4, 296–312.

Bourdieu, P. (1986). The forms of capital. In J. Richardson, *Handbook of theory and research for the sociology of education*. Westport, CT: Greenwood, pp. 241–258.

Bradley, K. (2009) *The Bradley Report. Lord Bradley's review of people with mental health problems or learning disabilities in the criminal justice system*. Retrieved from: www.rcpsych.ac.uk/pdf/Bradley%20Report11.pdf

Champion, N., and Noble, J. (2016) *What is prison education for? A theory of change exploring the value of learning in prison*. Retrieved from: www.prisonerseducation.org.uk/data/Theory%20of%20Change%20Report%20FINAL.pdf.

Clark, R. (2016) How education transforms: evidence from the experience of Prisoners' Education Trust on how education supports prisoner journeys. *Prison Service Journal*, 225, 3–8.

Coates, D.S. (2016) *Unlocking potential: a review of education in prison*. London: MoJ.

Davis, L.M., Bozick, R., Steele, J.L., Saunders, J., and Miles, J. N. V. (2013) *Evaluating the effectiveness of correctional education: a meta-analysis of programs that provide education to incarcerated adults*. Rand Corporation. Retrieved from: https://www.rand.org/pubs/research_reports/RR266.html

Harris Review Panel (2015) *The Harris Review – changing prisons, saving lives report of the independent review into self-inflicted deaths in custody of 18–24 year olds*. Retrieved from: www.gov.uk/government/uploads/system/uploads/attachment_data/file/439859/moj-harris-review-web-accessible.pdf

Hart, D. (2016) *Correction or care? The use of custody for children in trouble*. Retrieved from: www.wcmt.org.uk/sites/default/files/report-documents/Hart%20Diane%20Report%202015%20Final.pdf.

Her Majesty's Inspectorate of Prisons (2008) *Older prisoners in England and Wales: a follow-up to the 2004 thematic review by HM Chief Inspector of Prisons*, July 2008. Retrieved from: www.justice.gov.uk/downloads/publications/inspectorate-reports/hmipris/thematic-reports-and-research-publications/older_prisoners_thematic-rps.pdf

Her Majesty's Inspectorate of Probation (2016) *Desistance and young people: an inspection by HM Inspectorate of Probation*. Retrieved from: www.justiceinspectorates.gov.uk/hmiprobation/wp-content/uploads/sites/5/2016/05/Desistance_and_young_people.pdf

HM Chief Inspector of Prisons (2017) *HM Chief Inspector of Prisons for England and Wales annual report 2016–17*. London: HMCIP. Retrieved from: www.justiceinspectorates.gov.uk/hmiprisons/inspections/annual-report-2016-17/

HM Chief Inspector of Prisons (2006) *Young adult male prisoners: a short thematic report.* London: HMCIP.

HM Inspector of Prisons (2016) *Children in Custody 2015–16: an analysis of 12–18-year-olds' perceptions of their experiences in secure training centres and young offender institutions.* London: HMCIP. Retrieved from: www.justiceinspectorates.gov.uk/hmiprisons/wp-content/uploads/sites/4/2016/11/Children-in-Custody-2015-16_WEB.pdf

Hopkins, K. (2012) *The pre-custody employment, training and education status of newly sentenced prisoners: results from the Surveying Prisoner Crime Reduction (SPCR) longitudinal cohort study of prisoners.* London: MoJ. Retrieved from: www.gov.uk/government/uploads/system/uploads/attachment_data/file/278832/newly-sentenced-prisoners.pdf

House of Commons Justice Committee (2016) *The treatment of young adults in the criminal justice system. Seventh Report of Session 2016–17, together with formal minutes relating to the report.* London: HCJC. Retrieved from: www.publications.parliament.uk/pa/cm201617/cmselect/cmjust/169/169.pdf?utm_source=169andutm_campaign=modulereportsandutm_medium=module.

Keeley, B. (2007) *OECD Insights human capital: how what you know shapes your life.* Paris: OECD Publishing.

Lafferty, L., Treloar, C., Butler, T., Guthrie, J., and Chambers, G. M. (2016) Unlocking dimensions of social capital in the prison setting. *Health and Justice,* 4, 9 [Online]. Retrieved from: www.ncbi.nlm.nih.gov/pmc/articles/PMC4993805/

Lochner, L. (2004) Education, work, and crime: a human capital approach. *International Economic Review,* 45, 3, 811–843.

Rogers, L., Hurry, J., Simonot, M., and Wilson, A. (2014) Inside education: the aspirations and realities of prison education for under 25s in the London area. *London Review of Education,* 175–183.

Royal College of Psychiatrists (2015) *Written evidence submitted by the Royal College of Psychiatrists to the young adult offenders inquiry* [Online]. Retrieved from: www.rcpsych.ac.uk/pdf/RCPSych%20Evidence%20to%20HSC%20Inquiry%20-%20Mar%2014.pdf

Social Mobility Advisory Group (2016) *Working in partnership: enabling social mobility in higher education* [Online]. Retrieved from: www.universitiesuk.ac.uk/policy-and-analysis/reports/Documents/2016/working-in-partnership-final.pdf

Taylor, C. (2016) *Review of the Youth Justice System in England and Wales.* Williams Lee Group on behalf of the Controller of Her Majesty's Stationery Office. Retrieved from: www.gov.uk/government/uploads/system/uploads/attachment_data/file/576383/youth-justice-review-final-report.pdf

18

'WHERE ARE WE GOING?'

Context and directions for policy and practice in children's education and learning in secure accommodation

Ross Little

In recent years there has been a considerable amount of policy attention, rhetoric, and review focussed on the subject of education in secure settings, including children's education: for example, the Coates Review, undertaken by Dame Sally Coates and, more relevant to our focus on children, the Taylor Review by Charlie Taylor. Both were commissioned by the same Justice Secretary (Michael Gove) and published in 2016. Since then, high-level political attention has been turned elsewhere and the Justice Secretary has moved, but there remains some government focus on making changes and improvements, including via the reformed Youth Justice Board (YJB).

This chapter considers the contemporary context for children's education and learning in custodial environments, particularly the 'secure estate' comprising young offender institutions (YOIs), secure training centres (STCs), and secure children's homes (SCHs). Reference will also be made to proposals relating to 'secure schools'. As noted elsewhere in this book, the ways and means by which children can be subject to custodial detention in England and Wales are many and varied. This complexity is not well appreciated; even for those working within the sector, its diversity can make it difficult to appreciate the different forms of custody, and the routes into them, beyond the forms one is most familiar with. Here, the work of Hales and Warner (2017) is important in understanding the different ways that children can be locked up and detained under one of three main types of legislative mechanism: criminal legislation, mental health legislation, and the Children Act 1989 (Secure Welfare Placement). They identify a further four types of 'secure care' unit detaining children: high dependency unit (HDU), psychiatric intensive care unit, low secure hospital, and medium secure hospital. As noted above, this chapter refers to education in criminal justice settings (YOIs, STCs, and SCHs). As noted elsewhere in this book, SCHs can take both welfare and justice placements. This chapter does not focus on mental health and welfare placements but related themes can be found.

The continued policy attention on children's education in criminal justice secure settings over several years reflects the seriousness of the situation the state has got us into regarding the detention of children. Reconviction rates for children following a custodial sentence remain high at around 70% or more. In the 12 months following release from custody, 69% of the 2014/15 cohort were proven to have reoffended (Ministry of Justice, 2016). This was even higher for those who served a sentence length of six months or less (77%). The most common disposal given to those who were proven to reoffend within a year of release from custody was another custodial sentence. Of those who reoffended, 35% received another custodial sentence for their first re-offence (Ministry of Justice, 2016).

The high re-offending rates, together with evidence of poor safeguarding practice, led the YJB to report, in mid-2016, that the young people's secure estate was 'no longer fit for purpose'. This was followed, in mid-2017, by a statement from Chief Inspector of Prisons expressing the 'staggering decline' in standards and safety witnessed at YOIs and STCs: 'The current state of affairs is dangerous, counter-productive and will inevitably end in tragedy unless urgent corrective action is taken' (HM Chief Inspector of Prisons , 2017: 10).

Soon after, this was followed up with a response from the Chair of the Local Government Association's Children and Young People Board: 'There is no other situation in which children and young people would be placed into environments that are known to be unsafe, and youth custody should be no exception' (Local Government Association, 2017).

These concerns combine with those expressed by campaign groups in recent years, to produce a picture of a custodial system in which it is incredibly difficult to undertake meaningful work that contributes to children's educational improvement, future desistance, and move towards better outcomes on release from custody. The government's response to the Taylor review recognised the high levels of vulnerability amongst children incarcerated:

> those 900 in custody represent some of the most complex and damaged children within society. Broken homes, drug and alcohol misuse, generational joblessness, abusive relationships, childhoods spent in care, mental illness, gang membership and educational failure are common in the backgrounds of many offenders.
>
> *(Ministry of Justice, 2016: 3)*

One indicator of this vulnerability is that one-third of new admissions to youth custody between April 2014 and March 2016 were recorded as having mental health concerns (Ministry of Justice, 2017). Twenty-nine per cent of new admissions to YOIs in this timeframe were recorded as having mental health concerns, lower than both STCs (41%) and SCHs (44%). This supports the idea that more of the most vulnerable children are placed in SCHs, relative to STCs and YOIs.

Associated with the greater proportion of new admissions to custody recorded as demonstrating increased levels of vulnerability in recent years, there has also been an increase in challenging behaviour. For example, the rate of incidents relative to the youth custodial population has increased over the past six years. There have been increased in assaults, incidents of self-harm, and restrictive physical intervention (RPI) by staff (Ministry of Justice, 2017).

A distinct system for children

The children's secure estate is distinct from the adult system in that children are, by law, required to be provided with a certain number of educational tuition hours each week. This requirement does not exist in the adult estate. A development touted as significant was the introduction, in 2015, of the requirement for children to receive 30 hours of educational tuition each week (this issue is only applicable to YOIs). This type of development is to be welcomed for a range of reasons, not least that it demonstrates that this hidden area of our society can occasionally command policy attention. As the chief executive of the Prisoner's Education Trust stated at the time: 'Increasing education in custody to 30 hours per week is welcome recognition of the importance of learning in helping young people gain the skills and attitudes to work towards more positive futures' (Prisoners Education Trust, 2015).

However, the government statement that announced this increase employed a rather selective, short term approach to the matter of education hours required for children in custody. Putting to one side the somewhat anachronistic and unhelpful insistence on using the label 'offenders' to refer to children involved with the criminal justice system, its statement for press consumption was a little misleading. 'The government is tackling the root cause of youth crime with an unprecedented package of education and training for young offenders, Justice Minister Andrew Selous announced today' (Gov.uk, 2015).

The requirement for children to be provided with 30 hours of education per week was indeed an increase on the 15 hours that was being provided at the time. However, the government had previously decreased the educational requirement from 25 to 15 hours in 2009. Prior to 2015, children in YOIs were on average receiving 11.4 hours of their mandated 15 hours of education a week. In response the 'core day' in YOIs was increased to 30 hours per week, made up daily of three hours in the morning and three hours in the afternoon (Parliamentary Office for Science and Technology, 2016). In 2015, new guidance was given that 60% of the 'core day' should be protected for education with no avoidable absences; 40% is unprotected and permissible absences (medical appointments, court appearances, interventions) can take place. How the 60/40 time is distributed throughout the week varies across YOIs. Education time seems to have increased for a period – to an average of 17 hours per week (Taylor, 2016a). However, this masks a range of educational contact where some children receive minimal hours of education and others the full 30 hours. In 2015, children in STCs were on average receiving their mandated 25 hours (UK Parliament, 2016).

According to the Secure Accommodation Network (SAN), children in SCHs 'typically attend 25–30 hours of school every week with lessons delivered by qualified teachers' (Secure Accommodation Network, 2018). SAN points out that young people within SCHs 'already achieve rates of progress far in excess of national expectations of good progress in relation to education. In Ofsted terms this progress would be deemed Outstanding'. A key point here is that whatever the mandated number of education contact hours, some institutions (particularly YOIs) will not be delivering it in practice. The lived experience of that education provision will also be highly variable. Time spent engaging in educational activities is important, but just as important is the extent to which the educational activity is engaged in voluntarily and willingly, the quality of that provision and the extent to which it has meaning for the life of the individual. In the annual Children in Custody report for 2016–2017, the Chief Inspector of Prisons, Peter Clarke, stated that 'the broader objectives of delivering education, training and creating a rehabilitative environment will not be achieved' while broader safety issues remain insufficiently addressed. In the same report he noted that 'these poor outcomes in safety are directly related to correspondingly poor outcomes in education' (HMCIP, 2017: 6).

There is indeed a huge challenge in fulfilling educational objectives in contexts in which children's broader social and welfare needs are so clearly not being met. In the two most recent Children in Custody reports published by HMCIP, for 2014–2015 and 2015–2016, around four in ten boys surveyed said that they had felt unsafe at some point during their imprisonment (46% in 2014–2015, 39% in 2015–2016, HMCIP 2017). The issue of safety, or lack thereof, is important. Children surveyed by HMCIP who said that they had felt unsafe at some point in their centre were significantly less likely to report that they had been given advice about training or jobs they might like to do in the future (33% compared with 69%, HMCIP, 2017: 22).

In 2016–2017, at the time of the HMCIP inspections, 73% of boys in YOIs said that they were involved in some form of education. This rate of participation varied between different YOIs, from 62% at Parc to 80% at Cookham Wood. The proportion of boys reporting that they were engaged in education, work or vocational skills training was lower in 2016–2017 than in any other reporting year since 2010–2011 (HMCIP, 2017). This sense of there being fewer educational activities for children in custody to do now relative to previous years is a recurrent inspection theme. Being locked up during core educational hours is a common experience for children in custody, particularly those imprisoned in YOIs:

> At Wetherby, we found 48% of boys locked up during the core day when they should have been in education or training, and it was a similar picture at Feltham, where 40% of boys were locked up. The issues were less pronounced at STCs but there were children who spent long periods of time separated from others for a variety of reasons and were insufficiently occupied when not able, or willing, to attend education with their peers.
>
> *(HMCIP, 2017: 16)*

As noted, the problems tend to be particularly pronounced in YOIs. This is not surprising given what is known about the low staff: child ratios (National Association for Youth Justice, 2016; 2017) within this type of establishment. As HMCIP notes, when comparing STCs and YOIs directly, it should be borne in mind that each type of establishment:

- is commissioned separately
- is funded differently
- has different roles
- deals with a different cohort of young people
- delivers different activities. *(HMCIP, 2017: 49)*

Therefore, some difference in findings in relation to aspects of children's experiences should not be too surprising, for example, the proportion of children who reported having access to education in each type of establishment. Furthermore, education provision within one part of a custodial institution may be very different to that found in another part of the institution. For example, for children that find themselves segregated from the main custodial population (Little, see Chapter 13 in this book). These children tend to be amongst the most troubled and troubling children held in custodial institutions. This reflects the growing proportion of extremely vulnerable and challenging children being held in custody in recent years (Taylor, 2016a; YJB/MoJ, 2018). It perhaps also reflects a greater ability, willingness, or lack of skill amongst staff to segregate children in some institutions where more spaces have become available. The issue came to greater public prominence due to a legal case brought by the Howard League for Penal Reform on behalf of a child, AB. AB was found to have spent more than 100 days isolated from his peers and was deprived of adequate education. The failure to provide him with the required amount of education – in this case no education at all for the first 55 days – was, according to Mr Justice Ouseley, illegal:

> It has not been possible to provide [education] because not enough thought, effort and resources have been put into it. I understand how doing so removes resources from elsewhere for someone who may not be thought deserving of so much attention ... Those who are troublesome in the way AB is and for the reasons he is, cannot be left merely to drift in their education, as if they were responsible adults making adult choices. He is in his GCSE year and has special educational needs.
>
> *(The Howard League for Penal Reform, 2017)*

A report by the European Committee for the Prevention of Torture (CPT) has also stated how children in Cookham Wood prison, in Kent, were 'regularly held in conditions akin to solitary confinement for periods of 30 days and some for as long as 60 days or even, on occasion, up to 80 days for reasons of discipline and good order' (Council of Europe, 2016: 10). The Committee also considered that it amounted to *'inhuman and degrading treatment'* (Council of Europe, 2016: 9).

At Cookham Wood YOI, juveniles on a normal regime spent on average only five hours out of their cells each day. The situation was particularly austere for those juveniles who were placed on 'separation' lists (denoted by vivid pink stickers of 'do not unlock' on their cell doors), who could spend up to 23.5 hours a day locked up alone in their cells. In the CPT's view, holding juveniles in such conditions amounts to inhuman and degrading treatment and all juveniles should be provided with a purposeful regime and considerably more time out of cell than is currently the case.

The rate of single separation per 100 children and young people in Secure Children's Homes and Secure Training Centres has seen a large increase in the latest year, from 52.3 to 93.9. As expressed by the Chief Inspector of Prisons, the recent deterioration in conditions has impacted further on children's educational experiences. For example, within the education and activities area, children detained during 2016–2017 were 'significantly less likely to say that they had been able to learn skills for jobs that they might like to do in the future, 44% compared with 68%' (HMCIP, 2017: 26).

A complex context

The secure estate for children is complicated further in practice by several features that have emerged, or become further entrenched, in recent years. Firstly, the continuing decommissioning of custodial places in SCHs has led to some noteworthy geographical discrepancies that cannot be quickly or easily reversed. For example, there is now no SCH in the Greater London area. This is particularly problematic when one considers the regional differences for custodial rates. London has the highest rate of custodial sentences relative to the youth population, followed by the North West. In 2015/2016, London had the highest number of custodial sentences (509) and the highest rate of custodial sentences per 1,000 of the 10–17 population (0.68) (Youth Justice Board/Ministry of Justice, 2017). In the year ending March 2017, the largest proportion (30%) of young people in custody were those attached to a London YOT. There is one secure establishment in London (Feltham YOI) and it accommodated 14% of the total custodial population (Youth Justice Board/Ministry of Justice, 2018).

Secondly, the return of private STC contracts to the Ministry of Justice has introduced the potential for staff in these children's establishments to be drawn from the prison service. This phenomenon does not support the aspiration, outlined by Taylor in his review (Taylor, 2016a), to create a more 'child-friendly' workforce and culture. These features have implications for the educational offer available to children detained within custodial institutions. These relatively recent changes are also associated with a period in which children's perceptions of safety in YOIs and STCs have deteriorated markedly (HMCIP, 2017). The view of the YJB is that current recruitment within STCs and YOIs means that staff are underprepared to manage the needs of young people. The YJB identify a significant failure to attract the right people and a poor retention record. They state: 'The workforce in custody are challenged, both mentally and physically, as a consequence of lacking effective tools to communicate, to build relationships and to provide effective support' (YJB, cited by Youth Custody Improvement Board, 2017: 4)

Recognising the problem(s)

In recent years, successive governments have acknowledged that there are profound issues with our youth justice system, particularly in relation to custodial detention, and for the young people who find themselves subject to it. Young people in custody often have troubled backgrounds, including histories of local authority care, absent parents, mental health needs, disrupted education, and in some cases self-harm (Ministry of Justice, 2013: 8)

The consultation paper 'Transforming Youth Custody: Putting Education at the Heart of Custody' cited a range of evidence that suggested that the custodial system is one way that we punish disadvantage (e.g. see Jacobson et al., 2010). Prior negative experiences of formal schooling, and associated difficulties, are the norm amongst those children that find themselves in custody

- Half of 15–17 year olds entering public sector YOIs were assessed as having the literacy levels equivalent to that expected of a 7–11 year old.
- 18% of sentenced young people in custody had a statement of special educational needs, compared to 3% in the general population.
- Of 15–17 year olds in YOIs, 88% of young men and 74% of young women had been excluded from school at some point.
- Of 15–17 year olds in YOIs, 36% of young men and 41% of young women were aged under 14 when they last attended school.
- Research suggests generalised learning disability is more common in young people in custody, with a prevalence of 23–32% compared to 2–4% in the general population.

(Ministry of Justice, 2013: 10)

The consultation points out the issues associated with the inconsistency of the education provision between different establishments: 'Currently, education varies across the different types of establishments in the youth secure estate, and quality is patchy. Frequently, young people do not get the required hours of education' (Ministry of Justice, 2013: 13).

Furthermore, there are failures in one of the key measures of system 'success', the rate of recidivism: 'However, the system is failing when it comes to those young people who do break the law and end up in custody. 73% of young offenders who are released from custody reoffend within 12 months' (Ministry of Justice, 2013: 12).

Government publications under recent administrations have claimed that these issues offer a new opportunity to put 'education at the heart of custody'. The proposed solution in 'Transforming Youth Custody' was the secure college idea. Few details of the intended regime were ever made public, but the vision was: 'Secure colleges providing education in a period of detention, rather than detention with education as an afterthought'. One thing that was clear is that these institutions would have been large institutions (comparable to some of the larger YOIs), in order to try to achieve cost efficiencies by lowering the cost per place. However, the primary concern here is not really with educational attainment per se. The primary concern was with the amount that a troubled and failing system *costs* the public purse.

> What's worse, we are also spending large sums of money to achieve such poor outcomes. Places in the secure estate in some cases cost more than £200,000 a year – five times the cost of sending a child to a top private boarding school. When we see many of the same young faces back at the gate within a matter of months, this level of spending cannot continue. We believe that with innovation and imagination, it is possible both to reduce the costs and improve the outcomes for society and for young offenders themselves.
>
> (Ministry of Justice, 2013: 4)

This line of thinking from government happened to coincide with attention grabbing headlines in the national and local tabloid press, such as 'Caging yobs costs six times more than Eton' (The Sun, 2012). A key element of the proposed 'transformation' was to reduce the level of expenditure on the youth justice system during a period of austerity within central government.

> For such disappointing results, the costs of youth custody are far too high. In 2012/13 the Ministry of Justice and YJB have budgeted that £245m will be spent on commissioning the youth secure estate. This equates to an average cost of almost £100,000 a place per annum – far higher than the average cost of a place across the whole National Offender Management Service (NOMS) estate at £38,000 per annum – and in some circumstances we are paying more than £200,000 per annum. At a time of significant financial challenge, and faced with such poor outcomes, things have to change.
>
> (Ministry of Justice, 2013: 14)

This rationale is, in some ways, difficult to argue against. It is indeed true that there are ways of improving the youth justice system, whilst also lightening the burden on the public purse. These savings are most likely to be realised if we instead reduce significantly our dependence on custodial 'solutions' for children in conflict with the law. Unless government is able to address the reasons for failure, rather than simply focussing on pressuring others to reduce costs, in turn further reducing the quality and capacity of educational provision, then it is difficult to envisage a much brighter future for the educational prospects of children experiencing custody. The Taylor Review of Youth Justice explained that: 'There needs to be a shift in the way society, including central and local government, thinks about youth justice so that we see the child first and the offender second. Offending should not mean forfeiting the right to childhood' (Taylor, 2016a: 3).

This review of the youth justice system was broadly well received by the sector, despite its limitations in not encompassing the minimum age of criminal responsibility within its remit, nor (initially, at least) the role of the courts. In one of its key recommendations, one that featured in the government's response, the review proposed a new network of secure schools. There were also a range of other recommendations relating to improving existing YOIs and STCs. These included a number of measures, such as a new pre-apprenticeship pathway, increasing numbers of frontline staff by 20%, developing additional support units for the most vulnerable, multi-disciplinary enhanced support teams of health and psychology staff, a new youth justice officer role, with specific training to work with young people, and assigning a dedicated officer to challenge them and support their reform. As noted by Hart, these latter changes to STCs and YOIs might generally be welcomed but they appear 'more cosmetic than significant' (Hart, 2017: 3). They will not lead to the 'transformation' required without a change of vision.

The key idea behind the creation of secure schools, in Taylor's words, was to re-imagine 'youth prisons as schools' (Taylor, 2016a: 40) to place education at the heart of youth custody, an ambition shared with the previous coalition government. These will be 'smaller custodial establishments of up to 60–70 places which are located in the regions that they serve'. The idea was that they should be set up within ('free') schools legislation, commissioned in England in a similar way to alternative provision free schools, and governed and inspected as schools.

The secure schools idea has some merit and is based on a solid review that clearly seeks to create a more 'child friendly' system that relies less heavily on custodial responses. There are, though, some potential issues with the approach and the attempt to implement it. These fall into three main areas. Firstly, the government's handling of the review did not inspire confidence. Publication of the Taylor review was delayed by around six months, partly caused by a change in the Secretary of State for Justice around the time of the EU Referendum. Relatively frequent changes in the person in the Justice Secretary role have undermined attempts at managing a variety of issues within the prison service and the secure estate for children. The government response was published almost at the same time as the review. The government response ignored large parts of the review, leading to a dilution of its holistic strength. One of the key areas chosen for further development was the secure schools idea, although very little further information was given. An 'urgent priority' to 'tackle the high levels of violence' (Ministry of Justice, 2016: 4) had been inserted, which skewed the more aspirational tone of the review itself. Secondly, there was a key question relating to the fact that we already have three different types of youth custody; why create a fourth? Introducing a fourth type of institution to the custodial mix for children was, according to campaign groups, unnecessary and unhelpful in the circumstances. In 'The State of Youth Custody' (Bateman, 2016), the National Association for Youth Justice argues that whilst the rapid replacement of YOIs and STCs is to be welcomed, secure schools are not necessarily the best way of doing this.

> 'Given the backgrounds of the children in detention, a model based on the premise of placement in a secure child care establishment offering high quality education (as opposed to a school in a locked setting) would better reflect the complex realities of the children's lives and would reinforce the importance of long term healthy development alongside education.
>
> *(Bateman, 2016: 8)*

The State of Youth Custody report argues that it would be wiser, and more effective, to invest further in the best existing type of secure custodial placements: SCHs. This is partly about the critical issue of the size of custodial institutions and their associated management. The proposed size of secure schools, at 60–80 places, makes them similar to the existing STCs. As Bateman (2016) argues:

> SCHs are already integrated into local authority provision in the required manner. Secure schools, which it appears would probably be developed on a 'free school' model, would by contrast be divorced from those local structures that facilitate easy alignment, potentially undermining high quality resettlement provision and inhibiting the movement of children from secure to non-secure provision at the earliest opportunity. The logical response, in light of these considerations, would be for the abolition of the YOIs and STCs to be achieved through an expansion in the SCH sector, rather than the creation of a new model of child imprisonment.
>
> *(Bateman, 2016: 9)*

Taylor acknowledges that the best SCH provision is the best available for children in the existing system. The main objection to investing further in SCHs is that they are perceived to be expensive. Just like the attempts to 'Transform Youth Custody' under Secretary of State for Justice Grayling in 2013, a primary governmental concern continues to be the cost per head of custodial provision.

As already mentioned, the average per annum cost of a placement in an SCH is approximately £200,000. Therefore,

> the entire existing custodial population could be accommodated in Secure Children's Homes for around £174 million. During 2015/16, the Youth Justice Board's expenditure on the provision of custodial placements was £136.9 million. The replacement of YOIs and STCs by SCHs could accordingly be achieved through a modest budgetary expansion of £37.1 million. Moreover, this increased figure is still 57% below the £316 million allocated for the provision of custodial accommodation in 2009/10
>
> *(Bateman, 2016: 9)*

Given the current state of youth custody, and the potential longer-term benefits, many, including the National Association for Youth Justice, consider this to be a price worth paying. Taylor himself said that the success of the secure schools relies on the quality of the staff: 'The quality of staff in Secure Schools will be critical to the success of these institutions' (Taylor, 2016a: 54). For these institutions to genuinely offer a transformative culture for staff and children would require considerable investment in staff pay, training, and resources made available for opportunities to continually develop professional practice. Commitments to these aspects have not been forthcoming over a year following the publication of the review. Research by Lanskey with young people in YOIs and STCs also highlighted the importance of these interactions, which form a crucial part of the learning experience in custody, beyond the formal classroom experience. For example:

> By far the most significant factor influencing the young people's perceptions of their treatment were the attitudes and behaviour of staff. It was often the small exchanges, the acts of kindness or unkindness that had the greatest impact on young people's perceptions of custody and the legitimacy of the custodial authority.
>
> *(Lanskey, 2016: 7)*

> young people through their experiences of custody receive a more general lesson about how they are valued by the society that placed them there. They will learn how they are regarded from the quality of the environment, the rules and daily regime set up for them, and their interactions with staff.
>
> *(Lanskey, 2016: 3)*

From a practical perspective, we cannot afford *not* to provide educational and learning opportunities to children in prison. These children reflect our society, are part of our society, and we need to help find more meaningful, and less harmful, ways to spend their time. In addition to moral and practical arguments, there are legal ones too. The legal frameworks that we have signed up to also contain principles that *require* us to provide this education. The introduction of the Children Act 1989 provided a comprehensive framework promoting the best interests of the child, a principle enshrined in the UN Convention on the Rights of the Child (UNCRC). The legal principles underpinning effective practice are helpfully laid out in a guide on the legal rights of children and young people in the criminal justice system in need of accommodation and support, published by The Howard League for Penal Reform (2012: 8). The overarching protection is the principle reflected in section 44(1) of the Children and Young Persons Act 1933 (the 'Welfare Principle'):

> (1) Every court in dealing with a child or young person who is brought before it, either as an offender or otherwise, shall have regard to the welfare of the

child or young person and shall in a proper case take steps for removing him from undesirable surroundings, and for securing that proper provision is made for his education and training.

(The Howard League for Penal Reform, 2012)

The guide also explains that the YJB's resettlement pathways and the National Standards both provide that resettlement planning should cover arrangements for, amongst other things, education.

The current situation

As things stand, the distribution of the child population in custody remains heavily weighted towards YOIs. In May 2016, for instance, 73% of all imprisoned children were held in such provision. By contrast, just over one in ten incarcerated children were accommodated in SCHs (Bateman, 2016). The welcome decreases over the preceding decade or so, in the number of children entering the criminal justice system for the first time, or being detained in custody (YJB/MoJ, 2018), have offered us an opportunity to alter our approach to more child-appropriate forms of secure provision. We have not taken that opportunity.

This is important as, in these conditions, it makes it even more difficult for children to progress with education, training, and employment opportunities. Some children are spending longer in these custodial environments than they would have done previously, particularly for indictable offences:

> For young people sentenced to custody, the average custodial sentence length varied significantly based on the type of offence they were sentenced for. While the average custodial sentence length remained broadly stable over the last 10 years for those sentenced for summary offences, it has increased for indictable offences in the same period, from 11.5 to 16.0 months, though there has been a small decrease in the most recent year.
>
> *(YJB/MoJ, 2018: 25)*

It is often not clear what is expected from these long sentences, beyond a longer period of individual incapacitation and a questionable hope that others will be deterred from future unlawful conduct. It was short sentences, though, that were criticised by Taylor as being particularly unhelpful. One of the many points raised by the review was that:

> government should remove or substantially restrict the availability of short custodial sentences. If a child is to be sentenced to custody, it is my view that the minimum amount of time they should spend in detention is six months (equivalent to the current 12-month DTO).
>
> *(Taylor, 2016a: 34)*

In 2015 there were around 1,000 children sentenced to spend between two and five months in custody as part of a DTO. These short custodial sentences often break vital links with family, education and support services, and provide little opportunity for secure establishments to tackle the child's problems.

(Taylor, 2016a: 29)

These points about sentencing lead us inevitably to questions about what a sentence is designed to *do*, what it is designed to help the child *achieve*. It brings us to a crucial point regarding what we think youth custody should be *for*. This is particularly important for children, who will typically be released back into the community for many years following a period in prison.

What is youth custody for?

The Taylor review, together with other respected commentators, has stated the importance of avoiding criminal justice disposals for children in conflict with the law as far as possible, noting the longer-term negative impact of involvement with the criminal justice system:

Evidence shows that contact with the criminal justice system can have a tainting effect on some children and can increase the likelihood of re-offending. Wherever possible crimes should be dealt with outside the formal youth justice system, and when a criminal justice response is required children should be dealt with at the lowest possible tier. The long-term implications of formal contact with the system must also be reduced so that these do not act as barriers to rehabilitation.

(Taylor, 2016a: 4)

Indeed, this is consistent with longitudinal research in Edinburgh, conducted over many years by McAra and McVie which demonstrated, amongst other things, that 'pathways out of offending are facilitated or impeded by critical moments in the early teenage years, in particular school exclusion; and diversionary strategies facilitate the desistance process' (2010: 179). For those small number of cases that do require custody, detention of a child should be for the shortest necessary period (Bateman, 2016; 2017).

The damage done by periods spent in custody to people, including, and particularly, children, is recognised more widely as time passes. Some of the harms perpetuated by the staff and system of governance in place at Medway STC were starkly presented in a BBC Panorama documentary (BBC, 2016). At the heart of these problems, and associated issues in our custodial system Hart argues, is a lack of imagination in our society about how to respond to childhood law breaking effectively. In her discussion paper, she draws on her own travels to explore different systems and philosophies. In contrast to our arrangements in England and Wales, establishments she visited in Spain, Finland, and the more progressive places in the United States of America all seemed to have a more clearly developed idea of what they wanted for their children.

> The common thread was a type of quasi-parenting: supporting healthy and positive development towards maturity. This was articulated in different ways: a policy-maker in Spain put it simply by saying that he wanted children to 'learn how to live' during their time in custody. The Diagrama establishments in Spain saw themselves as providing 'love and boundaries' until children learned to manage their behaviour and re-join the community. This process of re-integration was gradual, rather than the abrupt and rigid release arrangements to which children in England and Wales are exposed.
>
> *(Hart, 2017: 4)*

This concept of learning how to live during their time in custody resonates with Frierian educational philosophy. Part of Paulo Friere's philosophical approach is that education is essentially about how we learn to become 'more human' (Freire, 2001). Even in the more punitive US states, there is an increasing recognition that mass incarceration in 'correctional' facilities is expensive and ineffective. According to the Justice Center and Public Policy Research Institute (2015), a more therapeutic approach, the Missouri Model, is being adopted in several states (Hart, 2017). The model is based on a clear belief about the way children in secure care can be supported in a more positive way:

- Young people must be emotionally and physically safe before they can engage in a process of change.
- This safety is generated by stable and trusting relationships within a small group of young people and staff.
- Group treatment provides an opportunity for young people to practise new ways of communicating and develop healthy relationships.
- Staff must maintain constant 'eyes-on, ears-on supervision' to de-escalate tensions and other opportunities for young people to learn and mature.
- Facilities must provide a full range of daily activities, with minimal 'down' time.

This resonates with the content and tone of the Taylor review and the implementation of something similar in practice would represent a significant progress in our domestic context. In England and Wales, a report by the Youth Custody Improvement Board (YCIB) confirms that we are missing a requisite strong and clear vision about what we expect from our custodial institutions for children: 'a clear idea of what benefit is expected from imprisonment needs to be articulated' (YCIB, 2017: 4). The Taylor review confirmed that it is the deprivation of liberty that forms the punishment component of society's response to children's law breaking. Implicit here is the assumption that somehow an element of punishment is necessary, desirable or helpful.

> In custody children lose both their freedom and direct and immediate contact with their families and their friends. The aim then is to help them to overcome their difficulties, address the causes of their offending and prepare them for successful reintegration into society when they are released. Many of the children who offend come from complex and chaotic families, they are entrenched in established patterns of offending and need considerable help to change.
>
> *(Taylor, 2016a: 36)*

The YCIB found there was a lack of clarity around the purpose of STCs, and a culture within Medway that emphasised control and contract compliance rather than rehabilitation (HMCIP, 2017: 17). These cultural features most strongly associated with private providers run counter to the available evidence on the factors that most help children lead better lives. Taylor states that there is 'surprisingly little' (2016a: 4) robust evidence from the UK about which interventions are the most effective, but what is undoubtedly important is the quality of the worker who is involved with the child, and the relationship that they strike up. Prior and Mason explain that despite an apparent focus on 'what works', the question of how to secure young people's engagement was 'scarcely examined' in research on interventions. There was, for a period, a 'disjuncture' between the research and practice literatures, that,

> prevailing orthodoxies regarding what constitutes valid research evidence prevent certain questions about what works and how from being studied. It is suggested that both the practice literature and alternative research methodologies can provide rigorous evidence in response to these questions.
>
> *(Prior and Mason, 2010: 211)*

This has started to change in recent years as critiques have emerged of the narrow, limited focus of the centrally sponsored approach regarding 'what works' and understanding the limitations of risk factor research (e.g. Case and Haines, 2010).

Being 'education ready'

The evidence so far suggests that we can be aspirational about the role of education in custodial settings, but the system needs to radically change what it values and how it measures effectiveness and progress. While the system is so chaotic, these expectations unfortunately need to be adjusted. However, even in the best custodial institutions, there needs to be a recognition that many children who enter custodial environments will not be 'education ready'. As found by previous research (Cripps and Summerfield, 2012; Little, see Chapter 13 in this book), many children have had previous negative experiences of schooling, often combined with a host of other social disadvantages. Indeed, as Bateman explains:

Previous negative experiences of schooling, compounded by a broad gamut of other vulnerabilities, means that in order to engage children successfully in education it will first be necessary to ensure that they are 'education ready'. This points to the delivery of high quality care, emotional support and, where necessary, treatment as priorities.

(Bateman, 2016: 8)

Gilligan proposes a related approach, a useful starting place for work with young people in trouble:

helping is about drawing out the talent, the capacity and the resources that people may have and creating a space where good things may happen ... helping young people believe that they have something positive to offer society and that society has a positive place for them.

(Gilligan, 2006, cited in Byrne and Brooks, 2015: 10)

To some people this may sound like the practical implementation of youth work principles, and indeed there is a strong crossover. At its heart, youth work principles are about building strong, effective, professional relationships between trusted adults and young people. Engagement by the young person is voluntary and young people's voices are valued. As outlined by the National Youth Agency, youth work is underpinned by a set of values:

- Young people choosing to take part
- Utilising young people's view of the world
- Treating young people with respect
- Seeking to develop young people's skills and attitudes rather than remedy 'problem behaviours'
- Helping young people develop stronger relationships and collective identities
- Respecting and valuing differences
- Promoting the voice of young people. *(National Youth Agency, 2018b)*

Interestingly, there is perhaps a renewing recognition that youth work practice can play in custodial environments. The winner of the Youth Work Award at the sector press awards in 2017 was for a project working in a YOI (Children and Young People Now, 2017). This is not to suggest that there has been sudden resurgence in youth work against what is a backdrop of cuts to funding and services since 2010 (e.g. see National Youth Agency, 2018a). Or that it has taken hold in the custodial estate for children, it clearly has not. But, it is evidence of an interest for working with children in conflict with the law in different and creative ways, despite the fundamental issues with the system.

A summary of international evidence by Adler et al. (2016), published by the Ministry of Justice found that:

The importance of practitioner ways of working with young people, the 'therapeutic alliance', both in secure institutions and the community, is emphasised in qualitative research. Where young people are asked their views, they tend to value a relationship that is warm, open, and non-judgemental, indicating that this helps them to engage with the intervention and work towards change.

(Adler et al., 2016: 14)

This points towards what Warr (2016) has referred to as 'Re-privileging the informal' in education provided in custodial settings to support dialogue-based learning which is sensitive to the place and space in which it operates: 'These informal benefits or skills can include such diverse factors as the development of greater wellbeing as well as critical reasoning skills, self-confidence, self-esteem, empowerment, changed perspectives and, in specific circumstances, narrative change' (Warr, 2016: 18).

In the same article, Warr points to issues relating to how we problematise and individualise poor educational attendance and or/results: 'This is a problem in the modern penal context as poor educational attainment is perceived in the same positivistic light and therefore it becomes necessary for this to be treated or excised' (Warr, 2016: 21). Relatedly, he also points out that poor educational performance is as much to do with previous poor educational experiences, rather than an indicator of future potential attainment, particularly given that education may be perceived by many children as part of their punishment.

Our narrow conception of what learning is and how and where it takes place can be a problem here. In their exploration of the purpose of prison education, the Prisoner Learning Alliance explain that we cannot focus on education in the secure estate purely through an instrumental lens, with a primary aim of gaining employment. Instead, prison education is beginning to be seen a vehicle for continuous personal, social, and cultural development (Champion and Noble, 2016).

Central to hope and their sense of identity is an educational approach that starts where they are, listens to them, responds to needs, and does not necessarily seek to replicate formal teaching structures that many in custody associate with such negative experiences previously. Taylor warns against adjusting expectations of children due to their behaviour being very difficult: 'There is a great temptation to take the easy option and to place children only in the classes or the courses that they enjoy most' (2016a: 38–39). This is a reasonable point, but educational practice must also seek to engage individual children by starting with their interests, building a good rapport, and finding a hook that helps them to grow confidence in their ability as learners over a period of time.

Concluding comments

This chapter has set out a number of problems that beset education for children in the secure estate comprising YOIs, STCs, and SCHs. Many of these problems are relatively well known and certainly are known to the government, and inspectors of the different types of provision. As a result, the Youth Custody Improvement Board was moved to state unequivocally that:

> The one thing that is not needed is further analysis and diagnosis of what is going on in each of the eight establishments. The picture could not be clearer and improvement will not arise simply because a further report on a STC or YOI indicates things are getting worse there.
>
> *(YCIB, 2017: 2)*

Governments have focused a considerable amount of attention on this issue in recent years. Despite promising new types of institution (e.g. secure colleges and secure schools), these have been slow to appear. Taylor's commitment to achieving educational improvements within the secure estate cannot be sensibly doubted. The government response to his review, however, was considerably less ambitious. Their commitment to develop two secure schools was looking less clear within a year of its announcement.

More fundamentally, it is unclear how these changes are radically different from some of our current provision or how they would help to resolve the current chaotic and unstable situation. It is difficult to see how the outcomes for children in the near future will be any better than they are now, if a key governmental aim is to reduce the costs of custody for children. Recent opportunities have been missed to benefit from the welcome reductions in the number of children being sent to prison.

To date, there is no evidence that the situation has been 'transformed' in the way the government has stated that it wants. Indeed, 2017 saw the first substantive increase in the under 18 estate in the last ten years. While basic welfare needs go unaddressed, we should not expect particular improvements in the educational attainment of children in custody. This grim fact lends support to the argument in favour of abolishing prison for children. Indeed, Goldson (2005) has argued that custody for children should be abolished based on the harm perpetuated by the current system of incarceration, its failings in terms of crime prevention and community safety, and the burden it places on the public purse. Since this chapter was published, the number of children in YOIs, STCs, and SCHs has decreased markedly. However, as noted above, our government has not been able to capitalise on the reductions and invest further in the 'best' types of custodial provision.

While the current system of incarceration continues, our society needs to recognise that children in custody do need, and are *entitled* to, good quality educational opportunities. This benefits them as individuals, but just as importantly has collective benefits for us all. What we mean by this education is important though. A narrow focus on English and mathematics is unhelpful. The curriculum offered needs to be as broad as possible and engage children with negative experiences of education with learning opportunities that start from where they are.

Seeking to replicate formal education provision on the outside that they have typically been excluded from will not work for many children with such negative prior experiences. Investing the time, effort, and skills in ways that seek to unlock the potential inside each child is more likely to be an effective route forward.

References

Adler, J.R., Edwards, S., Scally, M., Gill, D., Puniskis, M.J., Gekoski, A., and Horvath, M. A. (2016). *What works in managing young people who offend? A summary of the international evidence*. London: MoJ. Retrieved from: http://eprints.mdx.ac.uk/18848/1/youth-justice-review.pdf

Bateman, T. (2016) *The state of youth custody*. The National Association for Youth Justice. Retrieved from: http://thenayj.org.uk/wp-content/uploads/2016/10/NAYJ-Briefing-State-of-Youth-Custody-2016.pdf

Bateman, T. (2017) *The state of youth justice*. London: The National Association for Youth Justice.

Bateman, T., Hazel, N., and Wright, S. (2013) *Resettlement of young people leaving custody: lessons from the literature*. London: Beyond Youth Custody.

BBC (2016) BBC Panorama: teenage prison abuse exposed. First aired on Wednesday 20 January 2016. Retrieved from: www.bbc.co.uk/programmes/b06ymzly

Byrne, B., and Brooks, K. (2015) *Post-YOT Youth Justice*. Howard League for Penal Reform. Retrieved from: https://howardleague.org/wp-content/uploads/2016/04/HLWP_19_2015.pdf

Case, K., and Haines, S. (2010) *Children first, offenders second*. Bristol: Policy Press.

Champion, N., and Noble, J. (2016) *What is prison education for? A theory of change exploring the value of learning in prison*. Prisoner Learning Alliance and New Philanthropy Capital. Retrieved from: www.prisonerseducation.org.uk/data/Theory%20of%20Change%20Report%20FINAL.pdf

Children and Young People Now (2017) *CYP Now award winners announced* [Online]. Retrieved from: www.cypnow.co.uk/cyp/news/2004529/cyp-now-2017-award-winners-revealed-on-night-of-celebration

Council of Europe (2017) *Report to the Government of the United Kingdom on the visit to the United Kingdom carried out by the European Committee for the Prevention of Torture and Inhuman or Degrading Treatment or Punishment (CPT), 30 March to 12 April 2016*. Council of Europe CPT/Inf. Retrieved from: https://rm.coe.int/168070a773

Cripps, H., and Summerfield, A. (2012) 'Resettlement provision for children and young people' and 'the care of looked after children in custody': findings from two HMIP thematic reviews. *Prison Service Journal*, 201, 31–38.

Freire, P. (2001) *Pedagogy of the oppressed*. London: Penguin Education.

Goldson, B. (2005) Child imprisonment: a case for abolition. *Youth Justice*, 5, 2, 77–90. Retrieved from: https://doi-org.proxy.library.dmu.ac.uk/10.1177/147322540500500202

Gov.uk (2015) 30 hours education a week for young offenders. Retrieved from: www.gov.uk/government/news/30-hours-education-a-week-for-young-offenders

Hales, H., and Warner, L. (2017) Do our secure institutions meet the needs of the young people detained within them?Royal College of Psychiatrists Faculty of Child and Adolescent Psychiatry Annual Scientific MeetingWednesday 13 and Thursday 14 September 2017East Midlands Conference Centre, Nottingham, UK.

Hart, D. (2017) The transformation of youth custody: a discussion paper. *The National Association for Youth Justice*. Retrieved from: http://thenayj.org.uk/wp-content/uploads/2017/05/NAYJ-Briefing-Transformation-of-Youth-Custody-May17.pdf

Her Majesty's Chief Inspector of Prisons for England and Wales (2017) *Annual report 2016–2017*. Retrieved from: www.gov.uk/government/uploads/system/uploads/attachment_data/file/629719/hmip-annual-report-2016-17.pdf

Jacobson, J., Bhardwa, B., Gyateng, T., Hunter, G., and Hough, M. (2010) *Punishing disadvantage: a profile of children in custody*. London: Prison Reform Trust.

Lanskey, C. (2016) Formal and informal learning in custodial settings for young people. *Prison Service Journal*, 226, 3–7. Retrieved from: www.crimeandjustice.org.uk/sites/crimeandjustice.org.uk/files/PSJ%20226%20July%202016.pdf

Local Government Association (2017) *Councils call for urgent action to improve safety in youth offending institutions* [Online]. Retrieved from: www.local.gov.uk/about/news/councils-call-urgent-action-improve-safety-youth-offending-institutions

McAra, L., and McVie, S. (2010) Youth crime and justice: key messages from the Edinburgh Study of Youth Transitions and Crime. *Criminology and Criminal Justice*, 10, 2, 179–209.

Ministry of Justice (2013) *Transforming youth custody – putting education at the heart of custody*. presented to parliament by the lord chancellor and secretary of state for justice by command of Her Majesty. Consultation Paper CP4/2013. Retrieved from: www.gov.uk/government/uploads/system/uploads/attachment_data/file/181588/transforming-youth-custody.pdf

Ministry of Justice (2016) *The government response to Charlie Taylor's Review of the Youth Justice System*. London: HMSO. Retrieved from: www.gov.uk/government/uploads/system/uploads/attachment_data/file/576553/youth-justice-review-government-response.pdf

Ministry of Justice (2017) *Key characteristics of admissions to youth custody April 2014 to March 2016*. YJB/MoJ Supplementary Analytical Paper. London: MoJ. Retrieved from: www.gov.uk/government/uploads/system/uploads/attachment_data/file/585991/key-characteristics-of-admissions-april-2014-to-march-2016.pdf

National Association for Youth Justice. (2016) *The State of youth custody*. London: NAYJ. Retrieved from: http://thenayj.org.uk/wp-content/uploads/2016/10/NAYJ-Briefing-State-of-Youth-Custody-2016.pdf

National Association for Youth Justice (2017) *The state of youth justice*. London: NAYJ. Retrieved from: http://thenayj.org.uk/wp-content/uploads/2017/09/State-of-Youth-Justice-report-for-web-Sep17.pdf

National Youth Agency. (2018a) *Cuts watch* [Online]. Retrieved from: www.nya.org.uk/supporting-youth-work/policy/cuts-watch/

National Youth Agency (2018b) *What is youth work?* [Online]. Retrieved from: www.nya.org.uk/careers-youth-work/what-is-youth-work/

Parliamentary Office for Science and Technology (2016) *Education in youth custody*. Houses of Parliament POSTNOTE. Retrieved from: http://researchbriefings.parliament.uk/ResearchBriefing/Summary/POST-PN-0524?utm_source=websiteandutm_medium=websiteandutm_campaign=pn524

Prior, D., and Mason, P. (2010) A different kind of evidence – Looking for 'What Works' in engaging young offenders. *Youth Justice*, 10, 3 [online]. Retrieved from: http://journals.sagepub.com/doi/abs/10.1177/1473225410381688

Prisoner's Education Trust (2015) *Education in youth custody increased to 30 hours per week* [Online]. Retrieved from: www.prisonerseducation.org.uk/media-press/education-in-youth-custody-increased-to-30-hours-per-week

Secure Accommodation Network (2018) *Services* [Online]. Retrieved from: http://www.securechildrenshomes.org.uk/services/

Taylor, C. (2016a). *Review of the Youth Justice System: an interim report of emerging findings.* London: MoJ.
Taylor, C. (2016b) *Review of the Youth Justice System by Charlie Taylor.* London: MoJ. Retrieved from: www.gov.uk/government/uploads/system/uploads/attachment_data/file/577103/youth-justice-review-final-report.pdf
The Howard League for Penal Reform (2012) *Resettlement: the legal rights of children and young people in the criminal justice system in need of accommodation and support.* London: The Howard League for Penal Reform. Retrieved from: https://howardleague.org/wp-content/uploads/2016/04/Resettlement-law-guide.pdf
The Howard League for Penal Reform (2017) High Court declares a child's isolation and lack of education at Feltham prison is unlawful [Online]. Retrieved from: https://howardleague.org/news/felthamsolitaryconfinementhighcourtjudgment/
The Sun (2012) Caging yobs costs six times more than Eton [Online]. Retrieved from: www.thesun.co.uk/archives/politics/1048923/caging-yobs-costs-six-times-more-than-eton/
UK Parliament (2016). *Prisoners: education: written question – 29845* [Online]. London: MoJ. Retrieved from: www.parliament.uk/business/publications/written-questions-answers-statements/written-question/Commons/2016-03-04/29845/
Warr, J. (2016) Transformative dialogues: (re)privileging the informal in prison education. *Prison Service Journal*, 225, 18–25. Retrieved from: www.crimeandjustice.org.uk/sites/crimeandjustice.org.uk/files/PSJ%20225%20May%202016.pdf
Youth Custody Improvement Board (2017) *Findings and recommendations of the Youth Custody Improvement Board.* London: MoJ. Retrieved from: www.gov.uk/government/publications/youth-custody-improvement-board-findings-and-recommendations
Youth Justice Board/Ministry of Justice (2017) *Youth Justice Statistics 2015/16, England and Wales* (Statistics Bulletin). London: YJB/MoJ. Retrieved from: www.gov.uk/government/uploads/system/uploads/attachment_data/file/585897/youth-justice-statistics-2015-2016.pdf
Youth Justice Board/Ministry of Justice (2018) *Youth justice statistics 2016/17, England and Wales (Statistics Bulletin).* London: YJB/MoJ. Retrieved from: www.gov.uk/government/statistics/youth-justice-annual-statistics-2016-to-2017.

INDEX

Page numbers in *italics* refer to figures.

A-levels 49, 52, 210, 304
ADHD (attention deficit hyperactivity disorder) 84–5, 89, 140
Adler, J. R. et al. 329–30
adult criminal system, U.S. 122–3
adult responsibilities 10
adulthood, transition to 182–3
adverse childhood experiences (ACE) 13–14; and behaviours (Hillside, Wales) 148–52; case studies (L, B, and X) 135–6, 139–40, 142–3; and diagnosis 84–5; rescuer role 81–2; Scotland 102–3, 104; U.S. 119; *see also* child sex exploitation (CSE); therapy
Advisory Council on the Misuse of Drugs (ACMD) 150
agency 279, 291–2
Aldine House 136–8
alignment role of therapist 173–4
animal-assisted therapies *see* birds of prey (Raptor project); nature-based residential treatment centre (Green Chimneys), U.S.
appearance/'personal front' of staff 64, 65, 67, 68, 69
approved schools 29–30, 31
ARC (attachment, regulation, and competence) framework 142
ASD (autistic spectrum disorder) 46, 50, 84–5

Atkinson Children's Home 138–41
attendance 77–8
authentic inquiry (case studies) 280–8; barriers in secure context 292; conditions 288–92; implications for practice 292–6
autonomy 279, 288–90, 291–2
Aycliffe 134–6

barriers to education 211–12, 237–8
barriers and facilitators of educational inclusion 248–9, 271–2; findings from quantitative data 269–71; individual factors 265–9; parenting and care related factors 254–7, 258, *259*; professional perspective 249–53, 254–7, 258–62, 265–7; school related factors 258–65; systemic factors 249–54; young people's perspective 253–4, 258, 262–5, 267–9
Bateman, T. 4, 6, 160, 238, 323, 325, 326, 328–9
Beck Youth Inventories (BYI) 88
behaviour management 54–5, 77, 136, 137–8, 140–1, 144–5; ARC framework 142; human-animal interactions 187–8, 189; minimising and managing physical restraint (MMPR) 235; Wales 154
behavioural engagement 279
birds of prey (Raptor project) 205–6, 214–15
black and ethnic minority (BME/BAME) children 4, 6, 234, 269, 310; case study 212

Index

borstals 25–7; problems 31; reforms 30–1
boundaries and flexibility in therapy 174
Bowlby, J. 4
British Association of Social Workers 132
British Medical Association 220, 222, 223, 224, 227–8, 231, 232
Bronfenbrenner, U. 248–9
Brown, S. et al. 132
Buckley, D. 26
Bullock, R. et al. 34
Byrne, B. and Brooks, K. 329

care and education staff roles and relationships 61, 72–3; education in secure children's homes (SCHs) 61–3; education staff 67–9; family staff 64–7; interactions and 'collective representation' 63–4; recommendations 73; tensions between education and 'family' staff 69–72
Carlile Inquiry 221, 233, 235
Carpenter, M. 21, 24
Case, S. P. and Haines, K. R. 10, 278
Centre for Youth and Criminal Justice (CYCJ), Scotland 96, 110
challenging behaviour *see* behaviour management
Champion, N. and Noble, J. 301, *302*, *303*, *304*, 330
change theory and processes 301–3, *304*
Child and Adolescent Mental Health Services (CAMHS) on-site provision 139; Surrey 15, 16; Transformation programmes 9; Wales 152
Child and Adolescent Mental Health Services (CAMHS) units 45, 59; case study (Frank) 85, 90; college environment 49–50; curriculum access 51–3; discharge transitions management 58–9; engaging learners 54; information gathering on admission 47–9; inspection and regulation 53–4; internet and social media safeguarding 50–1; learners on 46; learning preferences 51; managing challenging behaviour 54–5; multi-disciplinary approach (MDA) 49; parent/carer partnership 55–6; restricted patients and risk 46–7; rewards, use of 55; routine, importance of 50
child sex exploitation (CSE) 151; case study 52–3; Clare Lodge 141; formulation 80; risk assessment 132; *see also* sexual abuse, in custody
Children Act: (1908) 27; (1989) 4, 34–5, 61–2, 113, 155, 220; (2004) 219

Children (Scotland) Act (1995) 110
Children and Young Persons Act (1933) 324–5
Children's Commissioner 7, 8, 221, 222, 234–5, 239, 271; establishment of 36
Children's Hearings (Scotland) Act (2011) 102
Children's Hearings System 97–8, 101
children's rights: 2007–2016: renewed focus on education 35–7; and adult responsibilities 10; UNCRC 10, 36, 196, 229, 236
Children's Society 132, 262
choice in education 209–11
civic/social skills, valuing of 199–200
Clare Lodge 141–3
Clark, P. 317
client-centred approach 173
climate of secure setting 199
cognitive delays 180–1
cognitive engagement 279
collaborative working in therapy 173–5
'collective representation' 64
college education, CAMHS units 46, 47
college environment, CAMHS units 49–50
communication issues 139, 181, 197; case studies 88, 140; play language 166; Scotland 103, 107, 108; U.S. 119
community homes with education (CHEs) 32–4
Consulting Pupils Network 193–4, 201, 202
coping strategy work (case study) 88–9
correctional programmes, adult facilities, U.S. 123
corrections or commitment facilities, U.S. 121–2
Council of Europe 196, 318–19
counselling services, nature-based residential treatment centre U.S. 181
creative arts 166
cross border placements, Scotland 112–13
curriculum: CAMHS units 51–3; Clare Lodge 141–2; Lansdowne 144; Scotland 106, 109–10; and therapy 172–3

democratic citizenship 198
Department for Education (DfE) 132–3; and Department of Health (DOH) 45, 47–8; governance 56; HOPE services 15; and Ministry of Justice 236; National Curriculum 51–2; SEND code of practice 57–8; Social Care Innovation 9; Working Together to Safeguard Children 11

Department for Education and Skills 193–4
Department for Education, U.S. 117, 118, 122
Department of Health (DOH) 7, 45, 47–8; NHS England: Children and Young People's Mental Health Taskforce recommendations 8–9
detained youth, U.S. 119–21
developmental needs services 13–14
developmental trauma therapy 166–8
diagnoses 84–5, 179
disabilities 227, 234
discharge *see* transitions and transition management
disengagement and engagement with education 279–80
distance learning 304–7
diversion and systems management 11
dogs 185–6
domestic violence 150–1
Drama Triangle 82
dramatherapy 165–6, 167, 169–73
drug use 150
Dyadic Developmental Psychology 139

E-safe system 51
early intervention 11
Education Act (1996) 45
Education and Health Care Plan (EHCP) 47–8, 51, 58; and special educational needs 139–40, 142
education policy and social inequality, Scotland 99–102
Education Scotland and Care Inspectorate 107–8, 110, 111
Education Select Committee 133
education staff: emotional support of 82; nature-based residential treatment centre, U.S. 186–7; psychological training for 78–9; *see also* care and education staff roles and relationships
emotional abuse 220–2, 224–6
emotional engagement 279
emotional neglect 228–9
Emotional and Trauma Support (ETS) teams 163–4, 173–5
empowerment of education 105–6
engagement with education 277, 296; background and context 277–8; case studies and analyses *see* authentic inquiry; and disengagement 279–80; importance and components of 278–9; and motivation 279
engaging learners, CAMHS units 54
engaging parents in therapy 175

Every Child Matters (ECM) agenda 37, 155, 163
expectancy-value theory 290–1
expectation and hope, Scotland 109–10
experience of custody (case study) 87

facilitators *see* barriers and facilitators of educational inclusion
family: involvement, nature-based residential treatment centre, U.S. 183; staff roles and relationships 64–7, 69–72; systems, Surrey Family Services (SFS) 15–16; *see also* parents/carers
farm features: nature-based residential treatment centre U.S. 184–5
Fielding, M. 194–5, 198, 200, 201
Fischer Family Trust (FFT) 48, 54
flexibility and boundaries in therapy 174
food, clothing, and shelter provision 223–4
formal and informal learning 215–16
formulation 80–1
fun and meaningful learning 188
funding: and fundraising in CAMHS units 56–7; self-funding 155

gang lifestyle 257
GCSEs 52, 133, 159, 210, 236, 304
gender: girls (Clare Lodge) 141–3; women staff 66
Getting it Right for Every Child (GIRFEC) strategy, Scotland 97–8, 100–1, 112
Gill, O. 30
Goffman, E. 13, 63–4, 65, 67
Good Shepherd Centre, Scotland 107–8, 109, 111
Gove, M. (MP) 133
'grandparents' role of senior care staff 66–7
Green Chimneys *see* nature-based residential treatment centre, U.S.

Hagell, A. and Hazel, N. 22–4, 25, 28, 33
Hales, 4, 5
Halfon, R. (MP) 133
Hart, D. 301, 302, 322, 326–7
Hart, R. 194, 278
Higher Education Opportunity Act (2008) 123
Hillside *see* Wales
historical perspective 21–2, 37–8; 1850s–1910s: schooling in religion, industry, and discipline 22–8; 1920s–1940s: liberal vision of education and citizenship 28–31; 1950s–1980s: treatment vs punishment and minimalisation of education 31–4;

1990s–2000s: education and punitive control 34–5; 2007–2016: rights and rhetoric 35–7; Scotland 96–9
HM Government 219, 220, 222–3
HM Inspectorate/Chief Inspector of Prisons 6, 164, 219–22, 223–4, 225, 228, 229, 233, 234, 235, 238–9, 315, 317, 318, 319, 328
holistic approach 14
Home Office approved schools 29–30, 31
Hood, R. G. 30, 31
HOPE services, Surrey 15, 17
horses 185, 188, 189
horticultural therapy 186
Howard League for Penal Reform 206, 211, 214, 222, 226, 229, 230, 231, 232–3, 318, 324–5
human capital 301–3, 306, 308

immigrant children, U.S. 118–19, 120
index offence work (case study) 89
individual factors as barriers and facilitators 265–9
Individualised Education Programme (IEP), U.S. 181–2
industrial schools 22–6
informal, universal, and normalising approaches 11–12
informal and formal learning 215–16
information gathering on admission to CAMHS unit 47–8
Inreach mental health teams 75–6, 82–3
inspection and regulation: CAMHS units 53–4; see also Ofsted
integrated approach 8–9, 13
integrated care and support pathway, Surrey (case study) 15–17
'integrated inspection': Education Scotland and Care Inspectorate 107–8, 110, 111
internet and social media safeguarding, CAMHS units 50–1

Joint Justice and Education Unit 36
junior care staff role as 'parents' 64–6

Karpman, S. B. 82
Kilbrandon, Lord 97–8, 101, 114

labelling 151–2
language: play language 166; see also communication issues
Lansdowne 143–5
Lanskey, C. 36, 195, 197, 200, 237, 324; and Ruddick, J. 198
'Learn and Earn' programmes 186

learning preferences, CAMHS units 51
learning support assistants (LSAs)/teaching assistants 68–9, 159
Legislative Consent Memorandum, Scotland 113
Little, R. 205, 236, 237, 277–8, 280; et al. 8, 9
local authorities: cross-border placements, Scotland 113; education 45; funding 56–7; secure children's homes 35
Local Government Association 315

McAra, L. and McVie, S. 101, 103, 326
MacBeath, J. et al. 200, 201
McIntosh 110
'manner' of staff 64, 65, 67, 68, 69
meaningful learning 188
medical care and treatment 227–8
Medway Secure Training Centre (STC) 6, 224–6
mental health: assessment 151–2; diagnoses 84–5, 179; information gathering on admission to CAMHS unit 48; secure facilities 5, 7–8; see also Child and Adolescent Mental Health Services (CAMHS); psychological services and education; safeguarding
Mental Health Act (1983) 36; types of section 47
mental health nurse (RMHN) roles 79, 83
mentors 281, 290
metaphors in therapy 171–2
minimising and managing physical restraint (MMPR) 235
Ministry of Justice 36, 58, 206, 238, 316; and Department for Education (DfE) 236; Taylor review 8, 16, 21, 36, 155, 210, 215, 226, 236, 237, 238, 239, 301, 304, 315, 318, 319, 322, 324, 325–8; 'Transforming Youth Custody' 320, 321; Youth Justice Board and (YJB/MoJ) 220, 229, 230, 231, 234–5, 319, 325
Missouri Model 327
Moodie, K. and Gough, A. 103, 104
motivation 279
multidisciplinary approach (MDA): CAMHS units 49; integrated approach 8–9, 13; mental health professionals 75–6, 79–80; Secure Stairs strategy 92–4; and silo working 82–4, 159
Munby, Sir James 113

National Association for Youth Justice 160, 318, 323, 324
National Youth Agency 329

nature-based residential treatment centre (Green Chimneys), U.S. 178; animal-assisted therapies 186; discharge from 183–4; education staff, impact on 186–7; family involvement 183; farm features 184–5; implementation of human-animal interactions 187–8; inappropriate behaviour with animals 189; individualised treatment programmes 181–2; pathways to 179; relationship model and well-being of animals and environment 188–9; transition to adulthood 182–3; trauma-informed practice 179–81
neglect 222–9
Newbolt Report (Board of Education) 28
NHS England 5, 8–9
normalising approach 11–12
Not in Employment, Education, or Training (NEAT) 46, 52, 248

Ofsted 133, 134, 225, 236, 265–7; CAMHS units 53, 54, 56, 59; youth offender institutions (YOIs) 213, 214–15

parents/carers: engagement in therapy 175; factors in educational inclusion 254–7, 258, *259*; junior care staff role 64–6; partnership 55–6; *see also* family
participation 12; *see also* youth voice and participation
Paterson, A. 30, 31
Pates, R. M. and Hooper, K. 147, 150, 152
personal, social, health, and economic (PHSE) education 52–3
'personal front'/appearance of staff 64, 65, 67, 68, 69
personal stories and new beginnings 163–4
physical abuse 219–20, 224–6
physical restraint (MMPR) 235
play 167–8; language 166; projective 170–1
playful, accepting, curious, empathetic (PACE) technique 139
policy and practice context and directions 314–16; being 'education ready' 328–30; complex contexts 319–20; current situation 325–6; distinct system for children 316–19; purpose of youth custody 326–8; recognising problem(s) 320–5; summary 330–2
pre-custody education experiences 208–9
Prior, D. and Mason, P. 328
prison settings 299–300, 310–11; aims of education in custody 300–4; distance learning 304–7; prison-university partnerships 307–9; strengthening relationships in 309–10
prison-university partnerships 307–9
Prisoner Learning Alliance (PLA) 299, 301, 302–3; award winners 309–10
Prisoners' Education Trust (PET) 299, 301, 303, 304, 305, 306, 307–8, 309, 316
probation homes 27–8
Professional Association of Therapeutic Horsemanship (PATH) 185
professional perspectives on educational inclusion 249–53, 254–7, 258–62, 265–7
protection/prevention *see* safeguarding
psychological services and education 75, 94; attendance 77–8; basic assumptions underpinning joint working 75–6; behaviour management 77; case study (Frank) 85–91; diagnosis 84–5; emotional support of education staff 82; environment 76; external world connection 76–7; formulation 80–1; multidiscipinary approach: Secure Stairs 92–4; psychological training for education staff 78–9; psychologist role 79–80; rescuer role 81–2; restricted education provision 92; silo working 82–4; transition from SCH 91–2
psychological training for education staff 78–9
psychologist role 79–80; case study (Frank) 86–91; Inreach 82–3
psychometric assessments 88
punishment vs treatment 31–4
punitive control vs education 34–5
pupil referral units (PRUs) 91, 132–3

Radzinowicz, S. L. and Turner, J. C. 27
Raptor project 205–6, 214–15
re-engagement *see* engagement with education
reciprocity in secure setting 199
Reed, D. K. and Wexler, J. 120, 121, 123
reformatory schools 22–5
relationships 14, 272, 290, 294–6; in prisons 309–10; and well-being of animals and environment 188–9
remand homes 27–8
rescuer role 81–2
Resiliency Scales for Children and Adolescents 88
restorative approach 14–15
rewards in CAMHS units 55
risk assessment and management 46–7, 49–50, 153–4, 155–6; barrier to

education 211–12; child sex exploitation (CSE) 132; in therapy 165
Risk Factor Prevention Paradigm (RFPP) 249
routine in CAMHS units 50
Ruddick, J. 194, 195, 199; and Flutter, J. 193, 198, 199; Lanskey, C. and 198

safeguarding: enabling best life chances 235–9; formulation 80–1; HM Government definition 219; internet and social media 50–1; preventing impairment of health and development 231–3; protecting from maltreatment 219–31; providing safe and effective care 233–5; Wales 152–6
Safety, Stability and Structure model 154
school related factors as barriers and facilitators 258–65
Scotland 96; adversity, social inequality, and education policy 99–102; cross border placements 112–13; empowerment of education 105–6; experience of secure care 102–4; history of education and secure care 96–9; hope and expectation 109–10; recommendations 113–14; transition support and readiness 110–13; whole child and 'whole school' approach 106–9
Scottish Children's Reporter Administration (SCRA) 102
Secure Accommodation Network (SAN) 317
Secure Care National Project *see* Scotland
Secure Children's Homes (SCH) 4–5, 6–7; education in 61–3; perspectives and practices 131–45; youth voice and participation 195; *see also* care and education staff roles and relationships; policy and practice context and directions; psychological services and education
secure mental health facilities 5, 7–8
secure settings: placement 4–6; responses 6–8, 9–10
Secure Stairs strategy 92–4
secure training centres (STCs) 35, 195; *see also* policy and practice context and directions
self-determination theory 279, 281, 290
self-harm 149–50
senior care staff role as 'grandparents' 66–7
senior leadership team (SLT), CAMHS units 51, 56
service principles 12–15

sexual abuse: in custody 229–31; *see also* child sex exploitation (CSE)
shared principles in service responses 9–10
shelter dog interaction programme 185–6
sheltered youth, U.S. 118–19
silences, understanding 195–7
silo working 82–4, 159
Silva, E. 197
SIMS software 50
Skuse, T. and Matthews, J. 148, 154
social capital 301–3, *304*
Social and Emotional Development Level (SEDAL) assessment 148
social inequality and education policy, Scotland 99–102
social media safeguarding, CAMHS units 50–1
Social Research Unit 9
Social Work (Scotland) Act (1968) 97
social-emotional skills delays 180–1
social/civic skills, valuing of 199–200
solitary confinement 221–2
special educational needs (SEN) 248, 270–1; Education and Health Care Plan (EHCP) 139–40, 142; SEND code of practice (DfE) 57–8
substance use 150
Summary of Needs and Responses (SONAR) assessment 147
supervision 226–7
Surrey: integrated care and support pathway (case study) 15–17
Sutton Trust 51
systems approach 12–13; barriers and facilitators 249–54; in therapy 174–5
systems management 11
systems principles 10–12

task value: authentic inquiry (case studies) 290–1
Taylor, C. *see* Ministry of Justice, Taylor review
teachers 67–8
teaching assistants/learning support assistants (LSAs) 68–9, 159
Team–Teach principles 54–5
'therapeutic contracts' 165
therapy 162–3; beginning 164–5; case studies 167–8, 169–73; collaborative working 173–5; creative arts 166; developmental trauma 166–8; dramatherapy 165–6, 167, 169–73; handling dynamite 168–71; metaphors for real life 171–2; navigating stories 163–4;

outputs and outcomes 175–6; school curriculum 172–3; *see also* nature-based residential treatment centre
time considerations in therapy 175
transitions and transition management 91–2; CAMHS units 58–9; nature-based residential treatment centre, U.S. 182–4; Scotland 110–13
trauma: nature-based residential treatment centre, U.S. 179–81; *see also* adverse childhood experiences (ACEs); therapy
Trauma Recovery Model (TRM) 148, 154
Trauma Symptom Checklist for Children (TSCC) 88, 147–8

'U R Boss project': YOI research and summary of findings 206–8
United Nations: children's rights 10, 36, 196, 229, 236
United States (U.S.) 117, 124; corrections or commitment facilities 121–2; detained youth 119–21; recommendations 123–4; secure care placements and movement 117, *118*; sheltered youth 118–19; youth offenders in adult criminal system 122–3; *see also* nature-based residential treatment centre, U.S.
universal, informal, and normalising approaches 11–12
university-prison partnerships 307–9

voice *see* young offender institutions (YOIs); young people's perspectives on educational inclusion; youth voice and participation

Wales (Hillside) 146; care management 152–6; clinical perspective: issues and problems 147–52; education management 156–9; outcomes 159–60; referrals 147
Warr, J. 215–16, 330
Weschler Intelligence Scale for Children 88
Wexler, J. et al. 121–2, 278; Reed, D. K. and 120, 121, 123
whole child and 'whole school' approach, Scotland 106–9
wildlife rehabilitation and education 185
Willow, C. 224, 225–6, 230, 235
women staff 66

young offender institutions (YOIs) 35; children's views of education in 208–16; 'U R Boss project': research and summary of findings 206–8; *see also* policy and practice context and directions
young people's perspectives on educational inclusion 253–4, 258, 262–5, 267–9
Youth Custody Improvement Board (YCIB) 232, 233, 236–7, 327, 328, 331
Youth Justice Board (YJB) 319–20; and Ministry of Justice 220, 229, 230, 231, 234–5, 319, 325
Youth Justice Service (YJS) 164, 173–5
youth offenders in adult criminal system, U.S. 122–3
Youth Offending Service (YOS) data 249
youth voice and participation 193–5, 201–2; re-shaping and expanding acoustic 199–200; in secure settings 195; sounding out possibilities 197–9; understanding silences 195–7

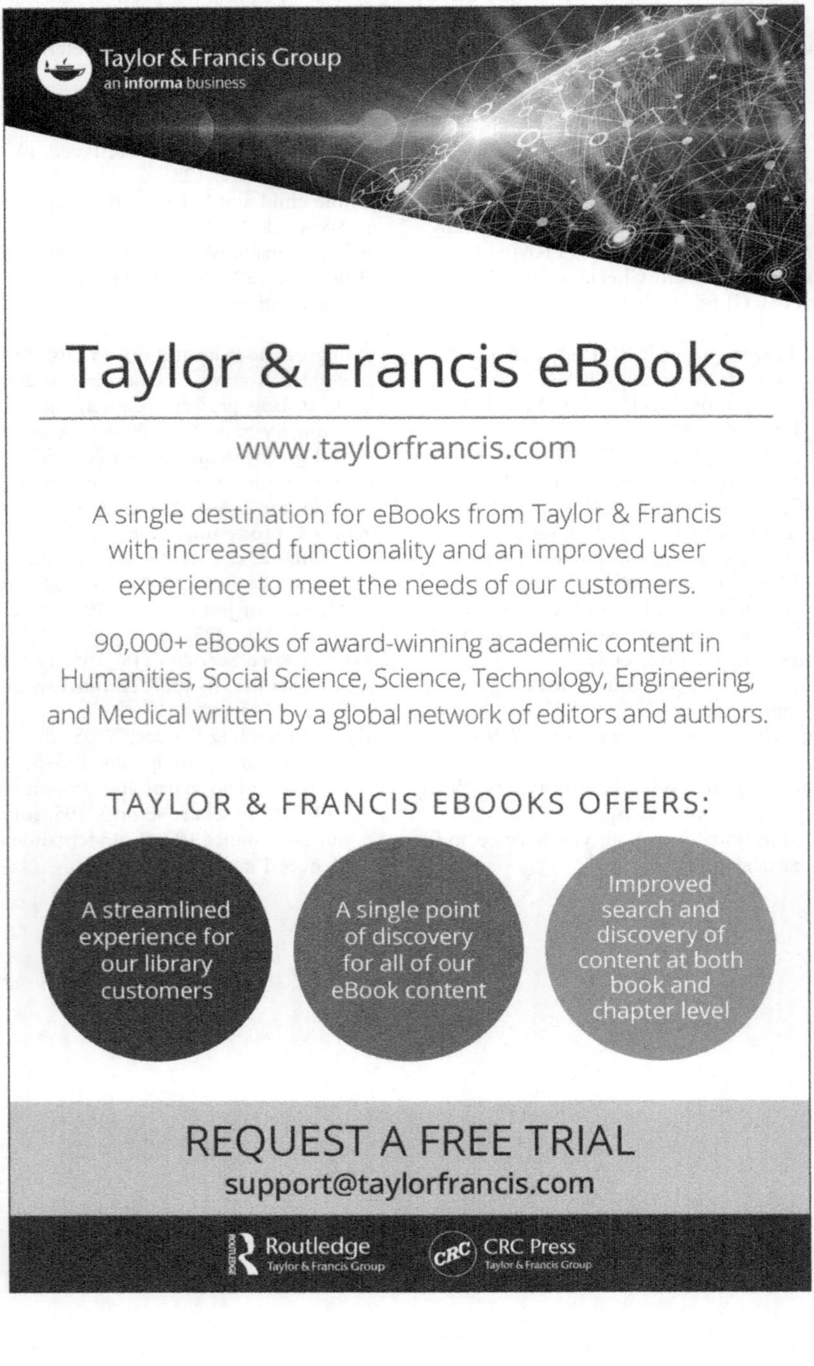
Taylor & Francis Group
an informa business
Taylor & Francis eBooks
www.taylorfrancis.com
A single destination for eBooks from Taylor & Francis with increased functionality and an improved user experience to meet the needs of our customers.
90,000+ eBooks of award-winning academic content in Humanities, Social Science, Science, Technology, Engineering, and Medical written by a global network of editors and authors.
TAYLOR & FRANCIS EBOOKS OFFERS:
A streamlined experience for our library customers
A single point of discovery for all of our eBook content
Improved search and discovery of content at both book and chapter level
REQUEST A FREE TRIAL
support@taylorfrancis.com
Routledge
Taylor & Francis Group
CRC Press
Taylor & Francis Group